The Legacy of John Austin's Jurisprudence

Law and Philosophy Library

VOLUME 103

For further volumes:
http://www.springer.com/series/6210

Michael Freeman • Patricia Mindus
Editors

The Legacy of John Austin's Jurisprudence

Springer

Editors
Michael Freeman
UCL Law School
London, UK

Patricia Mindus
Uppsala University
Uppsala, Sweden

ISSN 1572-4395
ISBN 978-94-007-4829-3 ISBN 978-94-007-4830-9 (eBook)
DOI 10.1007/978-94-007-4830-9
Springer Dordrecht Heidelberg New York London

Library of Congress Control Number: 2012948290

Printed on acid-free paper

Springer is part of Springer Science+Business Media (www.springer.com)

Preface

The role of John Austin (1790–1859) in the founding of analytical jurisprudence is unquestionable. Among his most remarkable contributions, mention should be made of his particular conception of jurisprudence ("general jurisprudence"), the command theory of law, the definition of positive law as the command of the sovereign, his peculiar idea of sovereignty, the sharp distinction between law and morality, the harsh criticism of the concept of natural law and rights, his particular conception of liberty, his strong commitment to codification or rule by law, and the various classifications of the law, most notably the distinction between the law of things and the law of persons, and primary and secondary rights and duties.

After a century and a half, time has come to assess his legacy. This book is intended to fill a void in the existing literature. Work on Austin is, in fact, surprisingly scant for one of the great names of both jurisprudence and utilitarian ethics. Even though Austin appears in most textbooks and in a great many articles, and his theory is still a crucial point of reference in the classroom, there are few books presenting Austin's legal and ethical thinking in relation to the different perspectives within legal theory.

This is the first-ever collected volume on Austin, assembling 15 papers presented at the 150th Anniversary Conference *John Austin and His Legacy*, organised by Michael Freeman at Austin's home institution, University College London, 16–17 December 2009. The chapters in this book correspond to papers given at the conference in the order they were originally presented. Only minor changes, such as titles, have been made so as to reflect the spirit of the meeting: "this 150th Anniversary Conference was the greatest assemblage of talent devoted to the jurisprudence of John Austin since John Stuart Mill attended his lectures" as James Murphy wrote to the editors. Scholars coming from different traditions of thought with diverse outlooks singled out, presented and discussed John Austin's legacy in jurisprudence. So this collection reflects the various currents within the broad set of post-positivistic, constitutionalist, and normativity-focused theories today dominating the scene in legal theory, as well as realist approaches to law. By harvesting the different sensibilities of those contributing to this collection, the aim is to offer a nuanced, vibrant and richly diverse picture of John Austin, on the backdrop of the major trends in jurisprudence – a difficult task for any single scholar to accomplish.

Besides giving interesting insights to the historical origins of jurisprudence, the idea is to survey the wider issue of theoretical disagreement as it persists within contemporary legal theory, as well as to assess Austin's problematic relation to legal reasoning and provide some topical comparative analyses with other major movements in legal theory, such as positivism (including normative positivism) and legal realism. The volume applies multiple perspectives, reflecting Austin's different interests – stretching from moral theory to theory of law and state, from Roman law to constitutional law – and offers a comparative approach focusing on Austin's legacy in the light of the contemporary debate. This approach makes his jurisprudence accessible to both students and scholars as it sheds new light on some of the central issues of practical reasoning: the relation between law and morals, the nature of legal systems, the function of effectiveness, the value-free character of legal theory, the connection between normative and factual inquiries in the law, the role of power, the character of obedience and the notion of duty.

A focal point is naturally the theory of sovereignty and power: Pavlos Eleftheriadis (Mansfield College, Oxford) develops an innovative interpretation of two rival theories of sovereignty in Austin, namely sovereignty for a single person and for a "determinate body." Detailed assessments of the key concept of sovereignty permit testing of Austin's conclusion according to which sovereignty lies, ultimately, with the electors and discussion of the public and intelligible character of sovereignty. David Dyzenhaus (University of Toronto) engages in a dialogue with Eleftheriadis on the Austinian conception of sovereignty as the unfettered discretion of the supreme political authority to make judgements about the general welfare. A series of parallels with great names of the positivist tradition are drawn here, where the stakes are high indeed: the issue calls on constitutionalist perspectives on power and ultimately on the nature of legitimate authority.

The positivist methodology is another focal point. Andrew Halpin (National University of Singapore) and Brian Bix (University of Minnesota) make significant contributions to the understanding of the method of general jurisprudence in the light of the current debates. By confronting the ability of some contemporary accounts of the nature of law, such as Joseph Raz's exclusive legal positivism and Ronald Dworkin's interpretivism, the issue is raised of when deviations from conventional understandings of legal practice constitute grounds for dismissing a theoretical account and to what extent Austin's theory of law might offer an account that better fits the facts than conventionally assumed. This is also the occasion for stressing that Austin was adamant about the fundamental importance of linking theoretical inquiry to practical concerns, and in times of global changes to law, moving contemporary legal theory ahead from a condition inherited from Austin might require us to pay greater attention to what Austin did leave us.

"The ties" between law as it is and law as it ought to be, at the societal and normative levels, is further explored by Isabel Turégano Mansilla (Universidad Castilla-La Mancha) who deals with the separation thesis and the problem of the connection between the ethical and the legal dimensions of Austin's work; and by

Michael Rodney (London South Bank University) who discusses the key notion of habit in Austin so as to capture the often overlooked point that the diachronic existence of any social structure, including a legal system, requires regularised social practices which are constituted by the repeated activities of those that go to make up such structures.

Moreover, Michael Lobban (Queen Mary, University of London) explores the lasting influence of German Pandectism on Austin's positivism and its complications for the command theory of law: none of the rights Austin discussed – neither the primary right protected nor the secondary right to have one's wrongs redressed by a court – derive from a command. This entails questions such as whether judges are best said to be creating or recognising rights and if there can be such a thing as customary law. Taking an even longer perspective into account, Andrew Lewis (UCL) accounts for the Austinian view on Roman law, regarded as the essence of developed legal thinking. Contrarily to the idea that reference to Roman law in Austin locates him in a bygone age – following the spirit in which the study of Austin's work is too often approached nowadays – Lewis shows how subtle Austin's understanding of Roman law actually is; firmly grounded on the distinction between the pristine purity of classical Roman law on one hand and on the other the Roman heritage in the civil law tradition prevailing in much European law.

Wilfrid Rumble (Vassar College) takes on the puzzling question of why, after 1832, Austin published nothing that focused on jurisprudence. Was it really, as some suggest, because he developed an entirely different legal theory? If this is so, it would dramatically modify our understanding of his jurisprudence: the alleged changes would require us to revise not only our understanding of Austin's legal philosophy, but our evaluation of it. The riddle of whether Austin remained an Austinian is addressed with the great accuracy that only the very knowledgeable scholar masters.

Yet, it is also important to remember that Austin was concerned with much more than jurisprudence: stability of social interaction does not depend exclusively on external regularities of behaviour but on a common attachment to normative authority. So the emphasis on ethics is topical because his meta-ethical insights as well as his rule-utilitarianism are likely to find renewed attention after the recent re-edition of Bentham's *On Laws in General* that has spurred interest in Austin's "master" and the early positivist movement in the English-speaking world, notably because of the latter's prominent place in the field today. One of the overarching claims of the present collection is that Austin's positivism is, as Schauer puts it, "entitled to at least co-equal claims on the positivist tradition as the work of H. L. A. Hart."

This is why the collection focuses on close-up comparative analyses of the most important trends in legal theory: Frederick Schauer (Virginia University) gives an historical and philosophical account of Austin's legacy within mainstream positivism; Lars Vinx (Bilkent University) examines his legacy in relation to normativism, especially in the version of Kelsen; Patricia Mindus (Uppsala) and Jes Bjarup (Stockholm) offer differing views of Austin's reception in Scandinavian Legal Realism, where his theories cemented a new path different from the positivists' main road, whereas James Bernard Murphy (Dartmouth College) offers a well-argued account of Austin's debt towards the natural law tradition, in particular in relation to the notion of divine law. To complete the picture, a comparative study of the great contemporaries that influenced Austin is included: Philip Schofield (UCL) examines the relation between Austin and Mill, and Bentham.

This range of interests shows why a collection on Austin is timely. As Dyzenhaus stresses, attention to Austin helps us to grasp significant continuities between his theory and that of many contemporary legal scholars. The historical perspective on philosophy of law enables us to appreciate the wealth of implications of the basic divide in legal theory, i.e. between those, on one hand, who focus on the distinction between the rule of law from the rule of men by stigmatising the arbitrary character that law may assume when it no longer is answerable to the ideal of legality and those, on the other hand, who perceive the rule of law in continuity with the reliance on the neutrality of legal science and its rule by law tradition where the nature of modern law raises questions of efficacious transposition into practice of choices made by policymakers and lawmakers.

Finally, the usefulness of gathering work on Austin, making arguments readily available and easier to overview, was made possible by the contribution and work of many. Some papers are reprinted here on authorisation of the prestigious journals that first published them: Chap. 2 by Andrew Halpin, entitled *Austin's Methodology? His Bequest to Jurisprudence*, first appeared on the *Cambridge Law Journal* in 2011 (vol. 70); we would like to thank Linda Nicol and the Cambridge University Press staff for allowing us to republish the paper. We would also like to thank Richard Bronaugh, at Law School, University of Western Ontario, Canada, for his permission to republish the papers that appeared in *Canadian Journal of Law and Jurisprudence*, volume XXIV, No. 2 in July 2011, that correspond to Chap. 8, entitled *Austin and the Electors* by Pavlos Eleftheriadis; Chap. 11, entitled *Austin, Hobbes, and Dicey* by David Dyzenhaus; and Chap. 14, entitled *Positivism before Hart* by Frederick Schauer. *The Canadian Journal of Law and Jurisprudence* also hosted different parts and earlier versions of Chaps. 1 and 4, respectively Brian Bix on *John Austin and Constructing Theories of Law* and Lars Vinx on *Austin, Kelsen, and the Model of Sovereignty: Notes on the History of Modern Legal Positivism*. This is also the occasion for thanking those who updated and revised their texts. We also thank Neil Olivier at Springer for his perseverance in getting this volume published.

Michael Freeman
Patricia Mindus

Contents

Chapter 1
John Austin and Constructing Theories of Law*

Brian H. Bix

1.1 Introduction

One of the standard criticisms of John Austin's work is that his portrayal of law, as essentially the command of a sovereign to its subjects,[1] does not fit well with the way law is practiced in many or most contemporary legal systems or the way that it is perceived by lawyers, judges, and citizens who are participants in those systems. The argument continues: that since the theory "fails to fit the facts," Austin's theory must be rejected in favour of later theories that have better fit.

This seems like a standard move in theory construction. Where the objective is to describe or explain some practice, any conflict between the theory and the practice being described counts strongly against the proposed theory, and we should search for an alternative theory that fits the practice better.

The importance to jurisprudential theory-construction of fidelity to participants' understanding has been reinforced by the move in English-language legal theory towards a hermeneutic approach to legal theory (as in the "internal point of view" introduced by Herbert L. A. Hart,[2] and accepted by theorists as far apart

* An earlier version of this paper was presented at the University College London Conference, "John Austin 150th Anniversary" and a different version of portions of the paper was published in (2011) 24 *The Canadian Journal of Law and Jurisprudence* 431–440. I am grateful for the comments of Andrew Halpin, the other participants at the University College London Conference, and Brian Tamanaha.

[1] John Austin, *The Province of Jurisprudence Determined* ed. by Wilfrid E. Rumble (Cambridge: Cambridge University Press, 1995) (first published, 1832); John Austin, *Lectures on Jurisprudence, or The Philosophy of Positive Law* ed. by Robert Campbell (4th edition, rev., London: John Murray, 1873) [Bristol: Thoemmes Press reprint, 2002], two vols.

[2] Herbert L. A. Hart, *The Concept of Law* (rev. ed., Oxford: Clarendon Press, 1994) at 56–57, 84–91.

B.H. Bix (✉)
School of Law, University of Minnesota, 229 19th Ave. S. Minneapolis, MN 55455-0400, USA
e-mail: bix@umn.edu

M. Freeman and P. Mindus (eds.), *The Legacy of John Austin's Jurisprudence*, Law and Philosophy Library 103, DOI 10.1007/978-94-007-4830-9_1,

methodologically as John Finnis and Joseph Raz[3]). In very rough terms, this approach argued (or, at times, merely assumed) that theories of law would be better to the extent that they accounted for the perspective of those citizens who viewed the law as giving them reasons for action. This approach to legal theory, in turn, reflects the general "hermeneutic" or "*Verstehen*" approach to the social sciences: a view that knowledge of social institutions is distinctly different from knowledge in the physical sciences, and that a primary focus of theorizing is and should be awareness of the motivations and purposes of participants, emphasizing participants' understanding, not merely their behaviour.

For many influential modern approaches to the nature of law, including Joseph Raz's exclusive legal positivism and Ronald Dworkin's interpretivism, while they criticize the lack of fit of theories like Austin's, those theories themselves unapologetically offer characterizations of legal practice that deviate in significant ways from the way most people practice or perceive law. Thus, at least at first glance, it appears that many contemporary legal theorists wish to have it both ways: they use the deviations from conventional understandings as grounds for dismissing some theories by other scholars, but forgive or overlook comparable deviations in their own theories.

This chapter will begin to explore what general principles can be learned, or developed, regarding when or to what extent deviation from the way law is practiced and perceived is appropriate in a theory of the nature of law. Additionally, the chapter will also consider whether, in light of the proper approach to fit and mistake in theory-construction, Austin's theory of law might be a more viable alternative than is conventionally assumed.

1.2 Deviations and Mistakes

Joseph Raz writes:

> John Austin thought that, necessarily, the legal institutions of every legal system are not subject to – that is, do not recognize – the jurisdiction of legal institutions outside their system over them. (…) Kelsen believed that necessarily constitutional continuity is both necessary and sufficient for the identity of a legal system. We know that both claims are false. The countries of the European Union recognize, and for a time the independent countries of the British Union recognize, the jurisdiction of outside legal institutions over them, thus refuting Austin's theory. And the law of most countries provides counterexamples to Kelsen's claim. I mention these examples not to illustrate that legal philosophers can make mistakes, but to point to the susceptibility of philosophy to the winds of time. So far as I know, Austin's and Kelsen's failures were not made good. That is, no successful alternative explanations were offered.[4]

[3] John Finnis, *Natural Law and Natural Rights* (Oxford: Clarendon Press, 1980) at 3–18; Joseph Raz, *Practical Reason and Norms* (Princeton: Princeton University Press, 1990) at 170–177.

[4] Joseph Raz, "Two Views of the Nature of the Theory of Law: A Partial Comparison" (1998) 4 *Legal Theory* 249 at 258 (footnotes omitted).

In a sense, this sort of criticism of Austin, and of Kelsen, is, within the jurisprudential literature,[5] perfectly common-place. Both theorists are presented as having interesting theories, but ultimately ones that are deeply flawed. In recent years, if scholars and students are familiar with Austin's work at all, it tends to be through H. L. A. Hart's use of Austin's work as a stepping stone to his own approach: the way Hart used purported weaknesses in Austin's command theory to justify Hart's own quite different form of legal positivism.[6]

Hart offered a series of criticisms of Austin's theory that are often now taken as proven accusations, with little attention given to potential defences of the theory. Hart's criticisms included: (1) that, contrary to Austin's theory, law contains much greater variety than is presented by a theory that equates law (only) with commands; (2) that Austin's theory cannot distinguish a legitimate legal system from the rule of gangsters or terrorists; (3) that theories that equate law with the command of a sovereign cannot account for the legal status of custom, and may also have trouble accounting for judicial legislation; and (4) that many communities do not have anything that would count as a "sovereign" in the sense used by Austin, a person or institution that has no limits or constraints. In fact, Austin noted many of these objections in his own works, and offered responses,[7] but these responses (some inevitably more substantial than others) have been largely forgotten in the rush to place Austin in his role as "the sincere but limited theorist whose faults were corrected by later and wiser writers."

This is not the place to give any final reckoning to the individual criticisms of Austin's work, but to consider the general sort of criticism raised. In particular, what I find intriguing about Raz's quoted criticism of Austin and Kelsen, is that the author of the criticism himself offers claims about law that other theorists and observers might similarly characterize as subject to "counter-examples," or as simply "mistaken" or "false."

Raz has famously argued for what others have labelled "exclusive legal positivism," a view that holds that moral evaluation can never play a role in determining what the law is (though it can play a role in determining what the law *should be*). When critics argue that there are clear contrary examples – moral standards in constitutional provisions or the use of moral reasoning in determining the content of common law legal norms – Raz denies that these are in fact refutations, or even counter-examples, to his theory. In the face of purported counter-examples, Raz notes that the judges'

---

[5] Here, as elsewhere in this paper, the reference is to the English-language jurisprudence literature. I am well aware that the traditions and discussions in other jurisprudential literatures are quite different (starting from the fact that, in many other countries, Austin, along with Hart and Raz, may be relatively unknown, while more emphasis is given to Kelsen's work).

[6] Herbert L. A. Hart, "Positivism and the Separation of Law and Morals" (1958) 71 *Harv. L. Rev.* 593 at 594–606; Hart, *The Concept of* Law, *supra* note 2 at 18–78; see also Scott J. Shapiro, *Legality* (Cambridge, MA: Harvard University Press, 2011) at 51–78.

[7] For example, Austin offers some detailed responses to possible objections to his claim that all societies have an unlimited sovereign, in Austin, *Province*, *supra* note 1 at Lecture VI, 190–242.

characterizations of what they are doing in opinions are often the result merely of conventions of presentation, or slightly mis-leading labels used so as not to provoke those naively attached to certain preconceptions (*e.g.*, that judges do not legislate).[8]

However, one would think that comparable arguments could be offered on behalf of Austin (and Kelsen, for that matter): arguing that whatever lack of fit there appears to be between their theories and current practices and perceptions would be removed or minimized by careful re-characterizations. Yet, for some reason, that move is rarely made by those commentators who are (too) quick to dismiss these theories.

1.3 Hart and Errors

And it is not just the rejected legal theorists of prior eras who must face accusations of lack of fit between theory and practice. Such claims reach even more established theorists.

The usual narrative of analytical jurisprudence, at least as given in most English and American university courses and in countless books and articles, is that John Austin has the merit of being the first, or one of the first, legal positivists, but that his theory was deeply flawed, flaws pointed out most clearly by H. L. A. Hart, whose own work set the standard for modern theories of law. However, though Hart's work is treated, in this narrative, as significantly superior to Austin's, and as the groundwork of all of merit in what has come since, there are occasional references to possible mistakes.

Some of the alleged errors are not relevant for our purposes, *e.g.,* because they relate to propositions that are tangential to Hart's theory of law; they can be abandoned without affecting the basic structure and basic claims of the theory (*e.g.*, regarding the tenability of Hart's practice theory of rules[9]). However, other claimed errors in Hart's work cannot be so easily shrugged off: *e.g.*, as to whether legal systems should be equated with the union of primary and secondary rules, whether every legal system has one (and only one) rule of recognition, and whether law is mostly a matter of rules.[10]

As regards the union of primary and secondary rules, Simon Roberts argued that this criterion for the designation "legal system" (or "*non-primitive* legal system") improperly excluded many communities with more informal dispute-resolution and

---

[8] See, *e.g.,* Joseph Raz, *Ethics in the Public Domain* (Oxford: Oxford University Press, 1994) at 210–21; Joseph Raz, *Between Authority and Interpretation* (Oxford: Oxford University Press, 2009) at 190–202.

[9] Of which both Dworkin and Raz have given effective rebuttals. See Raz, *Practical Reason and Norms*, *supra* note 3 at 50–58; Ronald Dworkin, *Taking Rights Seriously* (rev. ed., Cambridge, MA: Harvard University Press, 1978) at 48–58.

[10] See, *e.g.*, Joseph Raz, *The Authority of Law* (Oxford: Clarendon Press, 1979) at 95–96; Dworkin, *Taking Rights Seriously*, *supra* note 9 at 14–130.

norm-creation systems.[11] To which, one might answer, on Hart's behalf, that the mere fact that under some definition of law, or set of criteria for law, not all communities would be said to have law (or to have law in its fullest sense) is not, by itself, a reason to reject that definition or set of criteria.[12]

More central, perhaps, are two other criticisms. Under Hart's approach, all legal systems (at least all *sophisticated* legal systems) have a rule of recognition, which sets the criteria by which one determines which norms are part of that legal system. The rule of recognition is the highest (or, to change the metaphor, the most basic) norm in the chain of justification and authorization within the legal system. And, more implied than either asserted or argued for, each legal system has only one such rule of recognition. Raz has argued that there is no reason to assume that this will in fact be the case; that legal systems could well have two (or more) rules of recognition.[13] And Dworkin has argued forcefully that legal systems have principles as well as rules, legal standards that cannot be correlated with the sort of content-neutral "pedigree" criteria associated with a Hartian rule of recognition.[14] These claims of error cannot be brushed aside as easily as Roberts', and the arguments for and against have created a substantial literature, to which this article cannot do justice.[15]

1.4 Trade-Offs

One point I hoped to make by this too-quick tour of major legal theorists and their critics is that accusations that theories deviate from practices and perceptions are widespread, and by no means the end of the discussion. Perhaps, it would be better if a theory matched perfectly participants' perceptions of a practice, but it is acceptable if it does not, as long as there is some benefit one gets in return. More to the point, perhaps, a perfect match between theories on one side, and practices and perceptions on the other, is not to be expected.

[11] See Simon Roberts, *Order and Dispute* (Harmondsworth, England: Penguin, 1979) at 23–25.

[12] See Brian H. Bix, *Jurisprudence: Theory and Context* (5th ed., London: Sweet & Maxwell, 2009) at 23–24.

[13] Joseph Raz, *The Concept of a Legal System* (2nd ed., Oxford: Clarendon Press, 1980) at 197–200.

[14] Dworkin, *Taking Rights Seriously*, *supra* note 9 at 14–45.

[15] One might note in passing a couple of possible lines of response: first, that for Hart, as for Kelsen before him, the notion of a single rule of recognition (for Kelsen, the single *Grundnorm* or "Basic Norm" – *e.g.*, Hans Kelsen, *Introduction to the Problems of Legal Theory* trans. by Bonnie Litschewski Paulson and Stanley L. Paulson (Oxford: Oxford University Press, 1992) at 55–65 – is more of an assumption, by legal officials and citizens as much as by theorists, based on the systematic nature of legal systems rather than a description or observation; and, second, that Dworkin's legal principles are more moral reasons for changing the law than they are aspects of the law as it currently is. See Joseph Raz, "Legal Principles and the Limits of Law" in *Ronald Dworkin and Contemporary Jurisprudence* ed. by Marshall Cohen (Totowa, NJ: Rowman & Allanheld, 1984) at 73–87.

Theories are models: efforts to "boil down" complicated reality, and the variety of experience over time and across societies, to claims regarding what is "essential" amid the details and the differences. One could even argue that the problem is with theories of law that work *too* hard to account for nuance (*e.g.*, accounting for all the different kinds of legal rules, etc.,) that they lose the basic insight about law's nature. They are like maps that are large and detailed, almost as big as the area they purport to describe, creating realistic portraits of the area, but doing so at such a large size that they are no longer functional, and can no longer serve their intended function of helping us to find quickly the best route from one place to another.[16]

Theories and models involve, by their nature, trade-offs. The power or insight of the theory is to be weighed against the simplification, distortion, or mis-characterization involved in reducing the complexity of life to a simple picture. In economic modelling, it is sometimes argued that any distortions of human behaviour presented in the model are compensated for by the value of the model in predicting human behaviour. There is debate regarding whether in fact economic models *are* successful in predicting behaviour,[17] but that is, for our purposes, beside the point. What is relevant is that prediction of events is a (relatively) objective matter, a marker most of us can agree upon as a valuable counter-weight to the cost of any distortion within the model.

However, within jurisprudence there are additional problems. How can one discuss the meta-theoretical trade-offs in theories of law if there is no consensus regarding either intermediate or ultimate values? One must first know what one is aiming for and what would count as success before one can even think about costs and benefits in relation to theory construction. What is it that we are doing, or trying to do, when we theorize about (the nature of) law?

This is a basic question for legal philosophers – as Nigel Simmonds put it in discussing the challenge facing Herbert L. A. Hart and those who came after him: "once essentialism (…) was avoided as an option, it became hard to see how an investigation of law's nature could be anything other than an empirical matter."[18] Is there something *philosophical* to be said about law, that goes beyond mere historical and sociological investigations? But certainly Kelsen and Hart, and Finnis, Dworkin, and Raz – and likely Austin as well – thought of themselves as doing something different than empirical investigation.

What is the benefit we seek from a successful theory of law? Raz speaks of the ultimate objective of legal theory as explaining part of our community's self-understanding.[19] For Ronald Dworkin, it is an interpretive process that reworks

[16] For a discussion of "reductionism" in the theories of John Austin, Hans Kelsen, and James W. Harris, see Brian H. Bix, "Reductionism and Explanation in Legal Theory" in *Properties of Law: Essays in Honour of Jim Harris* ed. by Timothy Endicott, Joshua Getzler and Ed Peel (Oxford: Oxford University Press, 2006) at 43–51.

[17] See, *e.g.*, *Judgment Under Uncertainty: Heuristics and Biases* ed. by Daniel Kahneman and Paul Slovic Amos Tversky (Cambridge: Cambridge University Press, 1982).

[18] Nigel E. Simmonds, "Law as a Moral Idea" (2005) 55 *U. Toronto L.J.* 61 at 69–70.

[19] Raz, *Between Authority and Interpretation*, *supra* note 8 at 17–46.

existing practices in their best moral or political light.[20] For Liam Murphy, it is selecting or constructing the theory whose belief by society would have the best consequences.[21] For Sean Coyle, it is part of an exploration of the role of law in realizing the good.[22] For John Finnis, similarly, the objective of legal theory is, or should be, about asking the "why" question: "Why have law?" How does law fit within the moral requirement to seek the common good?[23] If we do not know what the objective of theorizing is, or if we cannot agree on what it should be, it will be difficult even to begin the discussion of when a theory's lack of fit is justified by its achievements.

Ronald Dworkin's concept of constructive interpretation gives an example of how trade-offs might be understood in theorizing. According to Dworkin, an interpretation (here of a social practice, though for Dworkin the claim is generalized to all interpretation) must meet some minimal level of fit with the practice being interpreted; otherwise it would not even qualify as an interpretation. Beyond that, one would either choose the best interpretation that also had the minimal level of fit (according to an early version of the theory[24]) or choose the theory that had the best combination of fit and value (according to later versions[25]).

A different question arises when it is not a straight trade-off, but rather a weighted choice. When Hart urges us to take into account the internal point of view, his argument is that this perspective is more central and (therefore) more important than the perspective of those who do *not* perceive the law as giving them reasons for action.[26] It is because this is a richer, better, fuller, or more central explanation that the theory should be built around it, rather than on a different basis, even if that other basis might have a better overall fit with perceptions and practices.[27]

It is in the nature of trade-offs, that the greater the insight one believes that the theorist (Austin or Raz or Kelsen or Dworkin) has offered, the greater the deviation from participant perception ("lack of fit" or "mistakes") that one will condone in the details of the theory. Even granting this much, the problem is that the existence and quality of an "insight" often seems to vary from one reader (observer) to another, and also over time. Thus, while in one era a theory's mistakes might seem trivial relative to the insight offered, in another era that same lack of fit might seem fatal. Thus, to many, and perhaps to most, Austin's theory looks untenable now, and, for these same observers, it may not be easy to understand how Austin's theory could

[20] Ronald Dworkin, *Law's Empire* (Cambridge, MA: Harvard University Press, 1986).

[21] Liam Murphy, "The Political Question of the Concept of Law" in *Hart's Postscript* ed. by Jules Coleman (Oxford: Oxford University Press, 2001) at 371.

[22] Sean Coyle, *From Positivism to Idealism* (London: Ashgate, 2007) at 10.

[23] John Finnis, "Law and What I Truly Should Decide" (2005) 48 *Amer. J. Juris.* 107.

[24] Dworkin, *Taking Rights Seriously*, *supra* note 9.

[25] *E.g.*, Dworkin, *Law's Empire*, *supra* note 20.

[26] See Hart, *The Concept of Law*, *supra* note 2 at 82–91; see also Finnis, *Natural Law and Natural Rights*, *supra* note 3 at 3–18.

[27] *Cf.* Finnis, *Natural Law and Natural Rights*, *supra* note 3 at 4–11 (criticizing Kelsen's theory for seeking "the lowest common denominator" of all legal systems: *ibid.* at 10).

ever have been as dominant as it was. While for many of these same contemporary commentators, any lack of fit exhibited by, say, Joseph Raz's exclusive legal positivism is worth carrying for the insights that theory offers about the connections between law, rules, reasons for action, and authority. How much deviation from practice one believes a theory can carry will inevitably be a matter of *judgement*.

1.5 Not (Quite) Trade-Offs

Perhaps we move too fast to be speaking of trade-offs for theories of law. Some theorists argue that there is no need to speak of trade-offs, because the theories in question in fact do not suffer from any lack of fit. Rather, the practices and perceptions that purport to differ from the theories are in fact untenable. For example, under a Razian analysis, judges may think that because they are applying moral-sounding constitutional provisions, they are declaring a pre-existing legal status, rather than making new law, when they invalidate a statute. However, Raz would say that this cannot be, for it is contrary to matters essential to the nature of law.[28] Similarly, under a Dworkinian analysis, a judge may think that she is declaring the legislators' intentions for some statute, intentions that are purely matters of fact, but Dworkin would insist that this simply misunderstands what legislative intentions are or could be.[29]

A final example, further afield, comes from the Scandinavian legal realists (*e.g.*, Alf Ross, Karl Olivecrona, and Vilhelm Lundstedt), who criticized the normative language (*e.g.*, "right" and "duty") used in law.[30] The Scandinavian realists believed that concepts like "legal right" and "legal duty" were phrases without a reference, and could be explained only in terms of subjective psychological feelings of power or bindingness, or the residue of ancient beliefs about magical powers. These theorists did not doubt that citizens and legal officials referred to "legal right" and "legal duty" as though they were objects that somehow existed in the world, but in that, the Scandinavian realists argued, the citizens and officials were simply deceiving themselves.

A different alternative to a "trade-off" analysis would be that theorizing should be understood in terms similar to Willard V. O. Quine's "web of beliefs." Under this analysis, we have inter-connected views, that hang or fall together, and facts that do not initially seem to fit into our beliefs may require adjustments in aspects of the interconnected propositions, but that almost any such fact can be accommodated, albeit at times with some uncomfortable stretching in those beliefs.[31]

---

[28] See, *e.g.*, Raz, *Ethics*, *supra* note 8 at 204–10.

[29] See Dworkin, *Law's Empire*, *supra* note 20 at 313–54.

[30] See, *e.g.*, Brian H. Bix, "Ross and Olivecrona on Rights" (2009) 34 *Australian J. Legal Phil.* 103.

[31] *E.g.*, Willard V.O. Quine, Joseph S. Ullian, *The Web of Belief* (New York: Random House, 1970). Quine was referring to the effect of sensory experiences on the periphery of our web of beliefs, but the notion also works, in broad analogy, with the topics discussed in the text.

Theorists who do not entirely deny that there are mistakes or deviations in comparing their theories to actual practices and perceptions may instead discount the importance of the deviations. These discounting arguments come in certain common forms. First, there is the argument that the way certain judges, lawyers or citizens speak about the law does not reflect their actual views about the law, but instead reflects only certain conventions of presentation. This argument is often used in response to the observation that judges frequently speak about "finding" or "discovering" existing law (rather than creating new law) even when the outcome seems far different than prior decisions and other settled law.[32] Second is the argument that judges and lawyers may characterize their actions in a certain way to respond to the political pressures and misunderstandings by naïve citizens (*e.g.*, who do not want to think of their unelected judges as making new law, or making "political" judgements in interpreting and applying the law); according to this argument, these judges and lawyers do not believe the characterizations they report. Third (though this is seen far less often than the other two) is the claim that the judges, lawyers, and some citizens as well, are simply deceiving themselves. When the great English common law judges and commentators of the medieval and renaissance periods claimed that judges merely discover existing law, is it possible that at some level even these sophisticated and worldly observers actually believed that? Perhaps some of them did, and perhaps they did because it helped them to avoid facing unpleasant political and legal issues.

1.6 Is Law Distinctive?

In discussing legal theories, past and present, in this work, I have spoken in abstract terms regarding the process of building theoretical models, and the trade-offs within a theory. One issue left unconsidered is whether law, and theorizing about law, might be different in important ways from other theorizing about social practices, distinctive in ways that affects our thinking about models and trade-offs.

One difference that might be worth noting that is law has a role (at least an arguable role) in our practical reasoning – reasoning about what we ought to do and how we ought to live – that most other social practices do not have or claim to have. This aspect of law has been particularly emphasized by natural law theorists, but is accepted, to different degrees and in various ways, by many other theorists as well. As John Finnis has argued, law has a "double life": it is simultaneously a social/historical fact and a normative system.[33] Law as a social-historical fact is constituted

[32] *Cf.* Scott Altman, "Judicial Candor" (1990) 89 *Mich. L. Rev*. 296; Paul Butler, "When Judges Lie (and When They Should)" (2007) 91 *Minn. L. Rev.* 1785.

[33] *E.g.* John Finnis, "The Fairy Tale's Moral" (1999) 115 *Law Quarterly Review* 170, 170; John Finnis, "On the Incoherence of Legal Positivism" (2000) 75 *Notre Dame Law Review* 1597, 1602–6.

by the actions of officials within a particular legal system from its beginning to the present. There are propositions about law which are primarily summaries of what decisions legislatures and judges, and perhaps also administrative agencies and executive/enforcement officials, have made over time. Such claims are made by social scientists and other academics, as well as by legal practitioners and judges.

Often, when claims are made about the law, there is some ambiguity regarding whether the claims are descriptive/historical, regarding what actions were actually taken by officials in the past, or whether there is some element of modifying, re-characterizing, or reforming the rules to make the current (or future) cases better. And when theories are offered of areas of law, the detailed case outcomes are built into generalizations in ways that reflect a conscious bias towards making the overall picture more just or at least more coherent. This is sometimes described as "rational reconstruction."[34]

The way that law has an aspect of social practice and an aspect of practical reasoning certainly complicates any effort to theorize about the nature of law. And it may make a difference on what counts as a cost or a trade-off in theorizing about law. However, it is not clear that law's distinctive nature changes the general meta-theoretical question about how one balances insight and distortion: the comparison of costs and benefits appears to remain comparable with what occurs with theories in other areas.

1.7 A Different View of Austin

I want here to take a brief break from general discussions of theorizing and lack of fit to return to Austin, and consider what arguments might be raised on his behalf.

The argument for Austin might go as follows (and no claim is being made that this argument can be found in Austin's own works, or even that he would have approved of it had it been brought to his attention). Austin's theory simplifies, and therefore distorts, but the simplification is a necessary cost for an important objective: uncovering a basic insight about law.

Regarding the problem of theoretical objectives, discussed earlier, one might note first that there are significant doubts regarding what Austin saw himself as offering in this theory. At one or two points in his lectures on jurisprudence – but (to my knowledge) not much more often, in the course of over 1,000 pages of text – Austin describes his work as offering a "science" of law.[35] This may parallel the continental European theorists he had read, and later continental theorists like Kelsen, who saw their conceptual analyses as part of a "science" of law. At the same

---

[34] Rational reconstruction is comparable to what Ronald Dworkin has called "constructive interpretation." Dworkin, *Law's Empire*, *supra* note 20 at 49–53.

[35] See Austin, *Lectures*, *supra* note 1 at vol. 2, 1107–08.

time, modern commentators find that Austin's discussions could be as easily interpreted as description (this is what is true of all known legal systems) as conceptual (this is what is necessarily true of any legal system).[36] A conceptual objective would make it easier to speak of "insights" that justify any lack of fit.

There are different (but related) ways of characterizing the insight(s) about law that can be drawn from Austin's command theory. First, that law is essentially about power.[37] Second, that law is best understood (and best practiced) as a top-down institution, with norms imposed by the government on its citizens, rather than as a bottom-up institution (as both the classical commentators on the English common law and the continental historical jurisprudence theorists would have it). Third, that every legal system has some entity whose power is effectively unconstrained.[38]

From the perspective of some of these perspectives, it is a benefit, not a drawback, that Austin's theory does not incorporate the perspective of citizens who view the law as creating reasons for action. From this Austinian approach, it is the Hartian legal positivist approach that is mistaken, in its apparent willingness to join certain strains of natural law theory in focusing too much on how law can or should create (moral) reasons for action.[39]

Of course, one response to a revised Austinian theory would be in much the same tune as prior criticisms: that this is a theory built on a poor fit with actual practices and perceptions (what might less delicately called "mistakes"), and thus cannot claim to have uncovered insights, only distortions. Under the Dworkinian analytical structure mentioned above, the argument is that the theory's fit with the practice is too poor to even qualify as an "interpretation." (Perhaps under a coherentist view, like Quine's web of beliefs or Thomas Kuhn's discussion of "paradigms,"[40] it is the claim that certain facts are so hard to incorporate into the existing analytical or conceptual structure that the whole structure must be rejected and replaced).

To some extent this is the argument that is still going on in legal theory, relating not only to Austin's work, but more generally regarding the role of coercion in the

[36] Roger Cotterrell, *The Politics of Jurisprudence* (2nd ed., London: LexisNexis, 2003) at 81–83. Here, contrast William L. Morison's view of Austin, William L. Morison, *John Austin* (London: Edward Arnold, 1982) at 2 (Austin's focus was to portray law "empirically") with Julius Stone's view, Julius Stone, *Legal System and Lawyer's Reasoning* (London: Stevens, 1964) at 68–69 (Austin as a conceptual theorist).

[37] *Cf.* Grant Lamond, "Coercion and the Nature of Law" (2001) 7 *Legal Theory* 35; Grant Lamond, "The Coerciveness of Law" (2000) 20 *Oxford J. Legal Stud.* 39; Danny Priel, "Sanction and Obligation in Hart's Theory of Law" (2008) 21 *Ratio Juris* 404; Frederick Schauer, "Was Austin Right After All?: On the Role of Sanctions in a Theory of Law" (2010) 23 *Ratio Juris* 1; Nicos Stavropoulos, "The Relevance of Coercion: Some Preliminaries" (2009) 22 *Ratio Juris* 339.

[38] Portions of the above paragraph derive from Cotterrell, *Politics of Jurisprudence*, *supra* note 36 at 49–77.

[39] See Frederick Schauer, "Positivism Through Thick and Thin" in *Analyzing Law* ed. by Brian H. Bix (Oxford: Oxford University Press, 1998) at 65–78.

[40] Thomas S. Kuhn, *The Structure of Scientific Revolutions* (2nd ed., Chicago: University of Chicago Press, 1970).

nature of law.[41] Those who believe that coercion is central to law's nature think that theories of law that omit or discount coercion are missing something basic. Theorists on the other side of the issue make comparable criticisms, asserting that it is the coercion-centred theories that are missing something essential.[42]

1.8 Conclusion

Of course, there are no bright-line rules for determining when a theory of some practice is tenable and when it is not, and when an existing way of understanding a practice needs to give way in the face of purportedly recalcitrant facts. (And this is not merely because we are dealing here with social practices rather than the physical sciences; a similar lack of bright lines applies also to when one Kuhnian paradigm within science must give way to another[43]).

To some extent, the success or failure of a theory becomes a matter of perception and a matter of judgement among the consumers of theory. Legal theories – like all other ideas – arise in response to the intellectual questions and practical concerns of the time in which they arise.[44] They may yet adapt or be re-characterized in ways that make them seem responsive to the questions and concerns of another period, but inevitably there will come a time when a theory that once seemed powerful and important begins to seem instead quaint and without use to a new generation of thinkers. And such changes in perception likely occur also at the level of components of theory, and components of theory-construction. For one generation, the insights of Austin's (or Kelsen's or Raz's) theory might seem central, and the deviations trivial, while for a later generation, the insights might seem small or hard to accept, while the deviations seem fatal.

Theories of the nature of law are relatively "unmoored," lacking, on one hand, the constraint of prediction of events; and, on the other hand, any agreed purpose. It should thus not be surprising that there is significant disagreement among theorists. There is disagreement about how to characterize certain of the facts on the ground, but even where agreement can be found on that, disagreement remains, as reasonable people can choose differently when faced with theories that make different choices about what is important, what counts as "insight," and how much of participants' perceptions or "common sense views" one can or should throw overboard in the name of theory-building.

---

[41] See publications listed *supra* note 37.

[42] And, a similar debate goes on around economic theories of law, where the question is whether the rational actor model is a great insight around which to build a predictive model, or is instead a politically biased and empirically disproven misreading of human nature.

[43] See Kuhn, *Structure of Scientific Revolutions*, *supra* note 40.

[44] A point made by Joseph Raz, among others. See, *e.g.*, Raz, *Between Authority and Interpretation supra* note 8 at 3.

The theorist has resources available when faced with apparent deviations between a theory and people's practices and perceptions. It can be argued that apparent deviations just reflect conventions of presentation, deceptions, or self-deceptions. Alternatively, it can be argued that any characterization of the relevant practices other than the one offered by the theory is unsupportable. Beyond that, a theorist's claim in the face of recalcitrant data will be some variation of the trade-off metaphor: that the cost involved in deviating from the practices and perceptions is worth accepting in light of the insights discovered and displayed by the theory.

Theory construction, especially where the theory is not anchored by falsifiable predictions, is often more a matter of persuasiveness, rather than a matter of truth. And if John Austin's theory seems less sustainable than it once did, that may say as much about us, and what concerns us, as it does about his theory.

Chapter 2
Austin's Methodology? His Bequest to Jurisprudence

Andrew Halpin

2.1 Introduction

Contemporary Anglophone legal theory[1] attracts some of the brightest minds in the legal academy. Their output is intellectually sophisticated, vibrant, occasionally flamboyant, and richly diverse. To engage with this material as a student can be rewarding in terms of broadening and deepening the academic study of law in ways that other subjects do not even aspire to. If some students fail to engage, this can still be regarded as a sign of the elevated status of legal theory, or jurisprudence, as a subject: only those with real aptitude and application can scale its heights. Yet there are other cases of disengagement which are less easy to dismiss.

One cause for concern is the disengagement of the professions with legal theory. Although this could be regarded as part of a blanket attitude on their behalf towards academic law,[2] an inability by legal theorists in this wider setting to communicate anything of use to practitioners would still raise fundamental questions about the purpose and value of jurisprudence. The concern becomes more marked when

---

[1] Recognition of a different relationship between academic law and legal practice within Continental Europe, and the implications of that for the development of legal theory, provide reasons for constraining the present essay to a consideration of legal theory in the English-speaking world. Despite acknowledging the influence of Continental legal theorists (see *infra* note 12), the emergence of a modern subject of Anglophone jurisprudence is treated here as a distinct event. Although historically something of an artificial construction (that also overlooks pre-Austinian Scots legal theory), it exerts a dominant influence on the shape and subject matter of Anglo-American jurisprudence today.

[2] Influential examples of such attitudes are provided by Harry Edwards, "The Growing Disjunction between Legal Education and the Legal Profession" (1992) 91 *Michigan Law Review* 34, and Robert Goff, "The Search for Principle" (1983) 69 *Proceedings of the British Academy* 169.

A. Halpin (✉)
Faculty of Law, National University of Singapore, Singapore, Singapore
e-mail: halpin@nus.edu.sg

M. Freeman and P. Mindus (eds.), *The Legacy of John Austin's Jurisprudence*, Law and Philosophy Library 103, DOI 10.1007/978-94-007-4830-9_2,

the disengagement takes place among other legal academics, of a more doctrinal or practical persuasion, who see no value added from legal theory to their own academic interests. Such an attitude is less prevalent now than it was 30 or 40 years ago, but it is far from extinguished. For one thing, theoretical intrusions into subjects such as Torts, Contract, and Criminal Law, tend to be limited to the particular concerns of the subject in question rather than engaging with the general questions of jurisprudence. More significantly, there remain leading figures in these other fields who are openly dismissive of legal theory, either modestly claiming that it is beyond their reach, or confidently asserting it is of no use – "Theorists can spend their time theorising the subject; my job is to get on with actually doing the subject."[3]

Although the disengagement of students, practitioners, and other legal academics might ground genuine concerns, it is not my purpose to address them here, except to suggest tangentially that any such concerns may be related to the root concern I shall investigate. These other concerns can properly be expressed in questions about the purpose and value of jurisprudence. However, we do not need to look so far for the insinuation that jurisprudence is of no earthly use at all, and that the work of legal theorists has acquired the self-indulgence of medieval scholasticism. This is a charge that has been made from within legal theory itself.[4] For all the intellectual energy that has been poured into the subject, legal theory today as a discipline is fragmentary and schismatic. Its debates are often ferocious, and more often inconclusive. The root concern to be addressed here is that legal theorists are disengaged from each other.

This may be regarded as a root concern in two senses. In the instrumental sense already given, it may lie at the root of the disengagement and disenchantment with legal theory found among other potential stakeholders in the subject. That sense, I have already indicated, will not be developed here beyond the scope of the suggestive. The primary sense to be investigated in detail is intimately bound up with the subject itself and deeply historical. The concern is that at its roots jurisprudence in the English-speaking world emerged as a subject already disengaged with itself, or, less cryptically, in a state that made the mutual disengagement between legal theorists inevitable.

In order to trace and explain this state of affairs, we shall need to excavate the historical origins of jurisprudence, and survey the wider issue of theoretical disagreement as it persists within contemporary jurisprudence. If the concern is substantiated, two tantalising lines of inquiry open up. What could have happened differently at the founding of jurisprudence as a subject? What might be different in the state of legal theory today? The radical opportunity then presents itself. If the current disengaged state of legal theory is traceable to a particular historical moment in

---

[3] Evidence for this class of the disengaged is best kept anecdotal and anonymised, but is readily available.

[4] Initially brought against legal positivism by Ronald Dworkin, it has also been turned against Dworkin himself. See Andrew Halpin, "The Methodology of Jurisprudence: Thirty Years Off the Point" (2006) 19 *Canadian Journal of Law and Jurisprudence* 67 at 77, 97 (V)(j); 86–87.

establishing its foundations, could an adjustment to that process produce (across all aspects) a more engaged theory of law?

These issues are explored within the following five sections of this essay. In the next Sect. 2.2, the controversy over establishing a "province of jurisprudence" is introduced. This controversy is linked to the attempt to establish an exclusive determination of the subject matter of jurisprudence against a backdrop of contestability. Section 2.3 then broadens the discussion of theoretical contestability and disagreement, and identifies three particular strategies by which a favoured theoretical viewpoint can take command of a subject as against opposing viewpoints: axiomatic disengagement, ambitious insight, and a split field of inquiry. Austin's approach is suggested here as taking the form of ambitious insight, a suggestion that is fully examined in Sect. 2.4, focusing on Austin's key distinction between what law is and what law ought to be. The details of Austin's approach, as examined in this section, are considered incompatible with his having established a common methodology for analytical jurisprudence. Section 2.5 uses Austin's own doubts about the success of his project as a platform for a critical challenge to his simple is/ought divide. The challenge arises from recognising a hybrid category of what the law ought to be regarded as being, associated with the activity of legal reasoning once the insufficiency of existing legal materials is acknowledged. The final Sect. 2.6, discusses a common aversion to legal reasoning when expounding a general theory of law shared by leading legal positivists. The combination of this characteristic with a tendency towards exclusivity in shaping the subject matter of jurisprudence is regarded as the greater part of Austin's bequest to jurisprudence, and as the basis for attributing responsibility to him for the current disengaged state of legal theory. However, the section concludes with the neglected part of Austin's legacy, found in his doubts, and his insistence that legal theory should be engaged with practice. It is this part of his legacy that is regarded as an overlooked inspiration for a fundamentally different direction for legal theory.

2.2 The Controversy

When John Austin's introductory lectures were published in 1832 under the title, *The Province of Jurisprudence Determined*,[5] that title was sufficient to signal the intention of Austin to capture as the subject matter of jurisprudence what had previously been obscure or contestable, or both. Subsequent allusions to the title have indicated that Austin's efforts, for all their significance in promoting jurisprudence as a distinct subject, have not succeeded in resolving the controversy over its subject matter.

[5] John Austin, *The Province of Jurisprudence Determined* (first published, 1832) ed. by Herbert L. A. Hart (London: Weidenfeld & Nicolson, 1954); ed. by Wilfrid E. Rumble (Cambridge: Cambridge University Press, 1995). Citations below are from the Hart edition, with page references to the Rumble edition provided in square brackets.

Halfway through the last century, Julius Stone in *The Province and Function of Law*,[6] argued against an exclusively analytical aspect to the Province, insisting that room should be made for questions of justice, and the social meaning of law. More recently, Allan Hutchinson's choice of title for his book in 2009, *The Province of Jurisprudence Democratized*, leaves no doubt that the subject matter remains contestable. Hutchinson adopts a more radical approach to Stone, seeking to dismiss analytical jurisprudence entirely in favour of a jurisprudence that is politically committed to local concerns and informed by a notion of strong democracy.[7]

The precise nature of this contest is not altogether clear. What is clear is that it is not simply a dispute with Austin's jurisprudence, with the particular details of his theory of law or with the positions adopted by Austin in addressing specific jurisprudential topics. Whatever evaluation, or re-evaluation, may be made of Austin on those points,[8] there remains something less personal and more far reaching in Austin's legacy to jurisprudence. One way of capturing this is to treat Austin as the progenitor of an analytical tradition in jurisprudence.[9] Those following in his line may no longer exhibit the detailed characteristics of their forebear, but they are undeniably indebted to him for their present position and standing. Although a more rigorous account would explore other distinct influences on the tradition, notably from Kelsen, and consider the details of significant variations within analytical approaches to jurisprudence,[10] the historical role of Austin in the founding of analytical jurisprudence is unquestionable.[11] As for the intellectual role, that is a broader issue, encompassing Austin's intellectual debt to Bentham, and the German and

[6] Julius Stone, *The Province and Function of Law: Law as Logic Justice and Social Control, A Study in Jurisprudence*, second printing with corrections (Sydney: Maitland Publications, 1950). The title of the first chapter, which previously appeared in two parts in (1944) 7 *M.L.R.* 97 and 177, makes Stone's relation to Austin unmistakeable: "The Province of Jurisprudence Redetermined."

[7] Allan Hutchinson, *The Province of Jurisprudence Democratized* (Oxford 2009). I consider Hutchinson's position in detail in a conjoined study, sharing much of the scene-setting material with the present article, "The Province of Jurisprudence Contested" (2010) 23 *Canadian Journal of Law and Jurisprudence* 515.

[8] For discussion, see William L. Morison, *John Austin* (London: Edward Arnold, 1982); Wilfrid E. Rumble, *The Thought of John Austin: Jurisprudence, Colonial Reform, and the British Constitution* (London: The Athlone Press, 1985); Robert Moles, *Definition and Rule in Legal Theory: A Reassessment of H. L. A. Hart and the Positivist Tradition* (Oxford: Basil Blackwell, 1987); Wilfrid E. Rumble, *Doing Austin Justice: The Reception of John Austin's Philosophy of Law in Nineteenth-Century England* (London: Continuum, 2004); Neil Duxbury, *Frederick Pollock and the English Juristic Tradition* (Oxford: Oxford University Press, 2004) at 97–106.

[9] Hutchinson, *The Province of Jurisprudence Democratized*, *supra* note 7 at 1–7, 21–24, 29. See also, Stone, *The Province and Function of Law*, *supra* note 6 at 11, in equating the "hegemony of Austinianism" with "the monopoly held by analytical jurisprudence."

[10] On both the influence of Kelsen and different approaches to analytical jurisprudence, see, *e.g.*, Joseph Raz, *The Authority of Law* (2nd ed., Oxford: Oxford University Press, 2009) at 293, 335. The need to differentiate both influences and outputs, becomes particularly acute when Brian Leiter and Ronald Dworkin are brought into an Austinian tradition (as Hutchinson, *The Province of Jurisprudence Democratized*, *supra* note 7, suggests).

[11] Stone, *The Province and Function of Law*, *supra* note 6 at 3, refers to "The Austinian Revelation."

Romanist influences, among others, on Austin. Austin himself, at the start of his "Outline of the Course of Lectures" which was appended to the original publication of *The Province*, admits to borrowing terminology from Hugo and to a lack of originality in the "subject and scope" of his enterprise, which he considered had been recognised by Hobbes, Plato, Aristotle, Cicero and others.[12]

This still leaves open the questions of what exactly it is that Austin bequeathed to analytical jurisprudence, and how that affects the contestability of its subject matter. A simple observation to make is that it is the exclusivity of an analytical approach, traceable to Austin, that lies at the heart of the controversy. Both Stone and Hutchinson take issue with this but differ in their responses. Where Stone adopted a more expansive approach open to "gaining what insights we can from all the approaches to legal theory,"[13] Hutchinson replaces one exclusivity with another: the resources of jurisprudence are to be diverted wholly to "advancing the democratic project."[14] Stone's generosity in welcoming all insights made him less concerned to dwell on what transmitted an exclusivity to analytical jurisprudence. He overlooked the intriguing question of why exactly it was that theories of justice, which Stone was prepared to admit as a branch of his scheme of jurisprudence, were left outside Austin's province of jurisprudence, despite, as Stone acknowledged, Austin's recognition of their significance.[15] Stone contented himself in drawing attention to the lack of fit between a restrictive analytical approach and the actual practice of law,[16] and in suggesting, by way of explanation, that it was the product of its age[17] (an explanation that grows dimmer with the persistence of exclusive analytical jurisprudence through different ages). Hutchinson, in more combative mood, explains and rejects the exclusivity of an analytical approach to jurisprudence in terms of a flawed methodology.

The flawed methodology attributed by Hutchinson to Austin, and to the tradition of analytical jurisprudence that Hutchinson considers has followed Austin's false lead, is "philosophical," focusing on the universal and general rather than the local and particular, employing conceptual analysis in order to provide an account of the essential nature of law.[18] Yet as Hutchinson himself concedes, a conscious interest in

---

[12] John Austin, *Lectures on Jurisprudence, or the Philosophy of Positive Law*, rev. and ed. by Robert Campbell (5th ed., London: John Murray, 1885) at 32. See further, Stanley Paulson, "The Theory of Public Law in Germany 1914–1945" (2005) 25 *O.J.L.S.* 525 at 525–526.

[13] Stone, *The Province and Function of Law*, *supra* note 6 at 42–43.

[14] Hutchinson, *The Province of Jurisprudence Democratized*, *supra* note 7 at 11.

[15] Stone, *The Province and Function of Law*, *supra* note 6 at 32 and n. 122, 10, accepts the alternative appellation of censorial jurisprudence for theories of justice; acknowledges this was recognised as "censorial jurisprudence" (in Bentham's terminology) or "the science of legislation" (in Austin's terminology); and, was regarded as important by both Bentham and Austin.

[16] *Ibid.* at 42, 71–73. For illuminating discussion on a general tendency towards lack of fit between theory and practice and its possible benefits, related to Austin, see Brian H. Bix, "John Austin and Constructing Theories of Law" (2011) 24 *Canadian Journal of Law and Jurisprudence* 431–440.

[17] Stone, *The Province and Function of Law*, *supra* note 6 at 4–5, 42.

[18] Hutchinson, *The Province of Jurisprudence Democratized*, *supra* note 7 at 3, 15, 23; 11, 18, 60; 22–23, 30–31, 40–41.

methodology has come relatively recently to analytical jurisprudence.[19] When it has emerged, methodology has not proven a unifying force for exponents of analytical jurisprudence but rather an arena for hostilities between them, particularly if Dworkin is admitted among their number,[20] as Hutchinson considers he should be.[21] Although we shall return to the issue of Austin's methodology in some detail below, these preliminary comments on methodology suggest that the factor linking together Austin's bequest to jurisprudence, the exclusivity of analytical jurisprudence, and the contestability of the subject matter of jurisprudence may be found elsewhere. An alternative place to commence the search is the competitive manner in which Austin sought to establish the province of jurisprudence. This competition is sharpest among Austin and Hutchinson with their exclusive claims over the Province. Stone, with his pacific inclinations, can for this stage of the investigation be stood down.

2.3 Theoretical Contestability and Theoretical Disagreement

Any theoretical endeavour is likely to encounter obscurity. Why call on theory if everything is already perfectly clear? And within a particular field of theoretical inquiry we can expect competing theoretical accounts of the subject matter to arise, which aim to offer in their respective ways some sort of illumination on that obscurity. So, in a trivial sense, obscurity of subject matter is easily linked to contestability of theoretical viewpoint.

But this trivial link between obscurity of subject matter and theoretical contestability is insufficient to convey the competition on which Austin embarked and which Hutchinson has more recently joined. Each in his own way has sought to radically alter our perception of the subject matter of jurisprudence so as to reveal a very different field of inquiry. Within the appropriate field of inquiry, the appropriate "province of jurisprudence," obscurities can be illuminated by competing theoretical viewpoints, *but outside of the appropriate field of inquiry no useful theoretical work can be undertaken*. Theoretical work attempted outside will be positively harmful in its effects, yielding illusion rather than illumination.

We need to pause in order to appreciate the magnitude of Austin's (and Hutchinson's) claim. The comprehensive illusion suffered by working in an inappropriate field of inquiry is not equivalent to the failing of a particular theoretical viewpoint, which in the ordinary course of the theoretical enterprise loses a contest with other competing

[19] *Ibid.* at 33. For general discussion, see Andrew Halpin, "Methodology" in ed. by Dennis Patterson, *A Companion to Philosophy of Law and Legal Theory* (2nd ed., Hoboken, NJ: Wiley-Blackwell, 2010).

[20] Dworkin has used methodology to mount a fierce attack against his positivist rivals, but even elsewhere within contemporary analytical jurisprudence, methodological differences tend to map theoretical disagreements. For discussion, see Halpin, "Methodology" *supra* note 19.

[21] Hutchinson, *The Province of Jurisprudence Democratized*, *supra* note 7 at 5, 43–44.

viewpoints, no matter how spurious and unhelpful that particular theoretical viewpoint is then considered to be. Such a failed theoretical viewpoint has still engaged within a common field of inquiry alongside other competing viewpoints, in which its merits or otherwise can be tested, and so may contribute fruitfully to the general theoretical enterprise. In contrast to that, what Austin or Hutchinson is claiming is that a theoretical viewpoint falling outside the appropriate understanding of the field of inquiry, just because it is allied to the alternative, inappropriate, understanding of the field of inquiry, will entrench that false understanding in its competition with any other viewpoints it is prepared to compete with. The outcome of that competition can then only yield illusory results.

Perhaps an analogy may prove helpful. Suppose our concern is with the science of the wind. More particularly, we wish to understand how to obtain a fair wind to carry our ships to their preferred destination. One understanding of the appropriate field of inquiry treats the subject matter as essentially involving discernment of the mood of a deity in control of the wind and what is required to appease that deity. So, for Agamemnon, illumination eventually arrives when the seer Calchas reveals that the anger of the goddess Artemis will only be appeased by the sacrifice of Agamemnon's daughter, Iphigenia, in order to release the wind that will carry the Greek ships to Troy. An alternative understanding of the appropriate field of inquiry treats the subject matter as essentially involving discernment of the relationships between different atmospheric phenomena so as to predict their outcome as manifested in a particular form of weather. So, for NASA, illumination is sought from experienced meteorologists as to when a fair wind can be expected to assist the passage of Endeavour on its voyage to the international space station.[22] Granted that Calchas was the best seer available to Agamemnon, and that NASA employs the best meteorologists to be found, neither party can produce anything but illusion from the viewpoint of the other's understanding of the field of inquiry (though both purport to be dealing with predicting the wind).

Having taken the trouble to emphasise the magnitude of the claims made by Austin and Hutchinson, we should now express some caution over the readiness to overstate such claims. It can sometimes be too easy to cut off theoretical debate by proclaiming from one side that the opposition is so steeped in unacceptable axioms regarding the nature of the subject matter that no fruitful engagement with them is possible. Ronald Dworkin has advanced this type of argument in recent years.[23] The practice borrows some credibility from an approach to scientific understanding epitomised in Thomas Kuhn's "paradigm shift."[24] Yet even here it is possible to

---

[22] In July 2009 NASA delayed the launch of the space shuttle Endeavour for three evenings in a row due to bad weather.

[23] Technically, Dworkin has primarily employed the argument to scatter his enemies by the device of placing them in an impossible position with each other. For discussion, see Halpin, "The Methodology of Jurisprudence: Thirty Years Off the Point" *supra* note 4 at 79–81.

[24] Thomas S. Kuhn, *The Structure of Scientific Revolutions* (2nd ed., Chicago: University of Chicago Press, 1970).

break out of the apparently self-contained and mutually insulated paradigms, to find some common ground over which engagement between them becomes possible. Kuhn himself acknowledged the additional ground of human experience over which rivalry between paradigms might be contested.[25]

So it is not inconceivable that even Agamemnon and NASA might find their opposing views on the nature of the wind brought into resolvable conflict through the acknowledgement of some common experience which has to be admitted on both sides and favours the one viewpoint rather than the other. After all, they can both agree on identifying the same occurrence as the wind – it is in understanding its nature that they move so far apart.

This brings us to the crux of the matter. If a number of theoretical viewpoints have *identified* in common a particular subject matter, how precisely does one theoretical viewpoint, with its distinctive understanding on the nature of that subject matter, engage with other theoretical viewpoints which *understand* the nature of that subject matter in quite different ways?

Finding a case of axiomatic disengagement, where it is concluded that there is no possibility of meaningful discourse between the opposing viewpoints, should be a last resort. While there is still common acceptance of the identity of the subject matter, there remains the prospect of finding an argument drawing on some facet of the experience of that subject matter which will weaken the understanding of one viewpoint in favour of the other.[26] Nevertheless, where the axiomatic base of a particular viewpoint extends beyond an understanding of the subject matter in question so as to embrace a comprehensive worldview (such as one based on belief in the Greek Pantheon, or on scientism), then it may have to be conceded for all practical purposes that no engagement is possible. If so, we should at least record the basis of the disengagement, so as to clarify where the real opposition between the theoretical viewpoints lies.

Avoiding axiomatic disengagement, how is it possible for one theoretical viewpoint to make a claim of the magnitude we have attributed to Austin and Hutchinson? The claim is extensive, we may recall, because it purports to establish not the detail of a particular viewpoint on the understanding of the subject matter, but the general approach to be adopted to understanding the nature of that subject matter – tantamount to establishing a distinct field of inquiry (a "province") for the subject. Frankly, it would be easier to regard this as a case of axiomatic disengagement such that the claim's force would lie in adopting an axiom strong enough to be irreconcilable with all rival theoretical viewpoints and so dispossess them of explanatory power at the very threshold of engaging in argument. However, the evidence is that Austin and Hutchinson are keen to engage with their opponents, and we should seek an alternative explanation if we can find one.

[25] *Ibid.* at 72, 77.

[26] For an illustration of this employing Dworkin's engagement with Hart, see Halpin, "The Methodology of Jurisprudence: Thirty Years Off the Point" *supra* note 4 at 81.

An alternative might be found in the form of their providing an insight on the subject matter that relates to one or more of the key tenets held by opposing viewpoints but is powerful enough to knock out all of those viewpoints for failing to follow through the clear implication of that insight, which leads ineluctably into the favoured field of inquiry as opposed to that previously followed by the opponents. Cast in this form, Austin's engagement with his opponents can be rendered in a simplified manner along the following lines. We commence with the insight delivered on the back of the accepted tenet: you accept that law can be made by the legislature, but on occasion it can be observed that the law so made proves to be far less than justice requires. The clear implication: in order to understand law, we need to be able to understand the law that is unjust. The ineluctable conclusion: we shall not succeed in understanding law by treating the field of inquiry as involving the study of the pursuit of justice, but rather as the study of what processes are capable of producing law.[27]

The magnitude of Austin's claim that any theoretical viewpoint capable of bringing illumination must operate within his field of inquiry now lies not in the strength of an irreconcilable axiom which disengages all opposing viewpoints before debate can commence. Rather, it lies in the ambition of his insight which engages his opponents on common ground before dismissing them fundamentally and comprehensively for failing to attach to that insight the clear implication that he has grasped. The size of the ambition is measured by a dual confidence, that the insight will first be accepted as an insight, and secondly that it leads to the particular implication which broadens out into a recognition of the appropriate field of inquiry for the subject.

Axiomatic disengagement and ambitious insight can be recognised as two distinct routes to reaching the kind of claim made by Austin and Hutchinson over the province of jurisprudence. Before considering in detail what motivated Austin[28] to establish an exclusive field of inquiry for jurisprudence, and the arguments he puts forward to vindicate his claim, there is an ancillary matter that needs to be briefly mentioned.

Another strategy can be adopted to set apart a particular theoretical viewpoint within its own field of inquiry so as to disengage opposing viewpoints. This is to employ the device of splitting the subject matter. The preferred viewpoint is then permitted to reign within a field of inquiry that is limited to one side of the divided subject matter, immune from debate with theoretical viewpoints operating across the divide within the excluded side. The strategy is illustrated by Herbert Hart's suggestion in his Postscript that he and Dworkin had been engaged in separate inquiries (relating, respectively, to a general understanding of law applicable to all municipal legal systems, and an understanding of law within a particular municipal legal system) and hence had not been engaged in the same debate.[29] Putting to one side

[27] Compare Austin, *The Province*, *supra* note 5 at 184–185 [157–158].

[28] For a detailed consideration of Hutchinson's position, see Halpin, "The Province of Jurisprudence Contested" *supra* note 7.

[29] Herbert L. A. Hart, Postscript, *The Concept of Law* (2nd ed.) ed. by Penelope A. Bulloch and Joseph Raz (Oxford: Oxford University Press, 1994) at 240–241.

the plausibility of Hart's suggestion,[30] his motive seems conciliatory rather than hostile, in that both inquiries in such a division can coexist with complementary roles.

Nevertheless, hostilities may break out here. An attempt to impose a split field of inquiry can be resisted by theorists working the other side of the divide who do not accept that their work is as limited as has been suggested, or even feel marginalised by the division. They may consider that their theories do have something pertinent to contribute to the issues on the other side, as is surely the case with Dworkin in relation to Hart, and would appear to be likely for any theorist working on a particular legal system in relation to issues thrown up by a general theory of law – unless we are prepared to countenance a general theory that need not relate to particular instances.[31] The feeling of marginalisation may arise from a sense that the division does not merely represent a practicable division of labour, but introduces a hierarchical ordering of significance: making the work on the other excluded side to be of primary importance. This sentiment has appeared among those who criticise Hart for setting the limits of his field of inquiry to official state law, and deriving a general concept of law exclusive to that limited field of inquiry, thus denigrating other legal phenomena with a lesser status.[32]

Although arranging the boundaries of a field of inquiry, either by actively splitting a recognised field, or by omitting to move beyond the restrictions settled by a recognised field, concerns more the identification of the subject matter than an understanding of the nature of that subject matter, it would be a mistake to deny the connection between the two. Setting the boundaries for what is identified as the subject matter for theoretical investigation will obviously impinge upon how we can view the nature of that subject matter. Put simply, the more expansive the identification of subject matter, the more demanding and competitive it will become to propose a common nature to that subject matter favoured by a particular theoretical viewpoint. Conversely, the narrower the area of field of inquiry that is split off, the easier it is to maintain a particular theoretical viewpoint favouring an understanding of the nature of that subject matter and to isolate it from competing viewpoints.

[30] For discussion, see Halpin, "The Methodology of Jurisprudence: Thirty Years Off the Point" *supra* note 4 at 87, 103 (XI)(a).

[31] Insisting on some commerce between general theory and particular instances becomes problematical for a strict reading of the "philosophical" methodology dealing with law's essential nature or necessary characteristics, attributed to analytical jurisprudence in general by Hutchinson (see *The Province of Jurisprudence Democratized*, *supra* note 18), but certainly found in the work of Joseph Raz. For discussion, see Brian H. Bix, "Raz on Necessity" (2003) 22 *Law and Philosophy* 537, and "Raz, Authority, and Conceptual Analysis" (2006) 50 *American Journal of Jurisprudence* 311; Halpin, "Methodology" *supra* note 19 at 612–614.

[32] See works cited in Halpin, "The Methodology of Jurisprudence: Thirty Years Off the Point" *supra* note 4 at 100 (VII)(k).

2.4 Austin's Ambitious Insight and Methodology

The rendering of Austin's engagement with his opponents in the previous section as a matter of "ambitious insight" can now be examined more closely. It will be recalled that the ambition of the insight was broken down into, first, a confidence that the insight would be accepted, and secondly, a confidence that its acceptance would lead to a recognition of the appropriate field of inquiry, namely, Austin's determination of the province of jurisprudence.

Austin expresses his confidence in no uncertain terms:

> The existence of law is one thing; its merit or demerit is another. Whether it be or be not is one enquiry; whether it be or be not conformable to an assumed standard, is a different enquiry. A law, which actually exists, is a law, though we happen to dislike it, or though it vary from the text, by which we regulate our approbation and disapprobation. This truth, when formally announced as an abstract proposition, is so simple and glaring that it seems idle to insist upon it.[33]

The insight is "so simple and glaring," but as Austin's following pages illustrate, there are numerous cases where it "has been forgotten." However, Austin remains confident that from the illumination gained from his recalling of the insight, such lapses can readily be written off as "stark nonsense," "to talk absurdly," "abuse of language," "confusion of ideas" and "contemptible imbecility."[34]

Allow then that Austin's confidence in his insight is justified. Once jolted from any forgetfulness we are prone to by his forceful presentation of the facts, we all accept it is possible to have a law that exists but which lacks merit, or fails some standard we would apply to it. The existence of the law is one thing, its failing another. Austin's confidence then naturally flows over into the second stage: acceptance of the clear implication and the ineluctable conclusion. We have to accept that our study of law will have to take in law with and law without merit, law that passes and law that fails a standard of approval; and, in turn, that our study of what law is will differ from our study of whether laws meet some standard or are regarded as having merit. Within that conclusion, already expressed in the passage quoted above, we have all the argument necessary to win us over to Austin's exclusive province of jurisprudence, the study of positive law.

The opening words of Lecture 1 of *The Province* proclaim, "The matter of jurisprudence is positive law."[35] At this point, the title of Austin's book might simply have been, *Jurisprudence: The Study of Positive Law*. The need to determine a province

---

[33] John Austin, *The Province*, *supra* note 5 at 184 [157].

[34] *Ibid.* at 184–188 [157–161].

[35] *Ibid.* at 9 [18]. Words echoed at the commencement of *The Uses of the Study of Jurisprudence*, *ibid.* at 365 [not contained in the Rumble edition]: "The appropriate subject of Jurisprudence, in any of its different departments, is positive law."

of jurisprudence follows a few lines further down, once Austin has pointed out a problem: the subject of his chosen study can be, and is, easily confused with other subjects. The task of *determining* the province of jurisprudence is the same as the task of *distinguishing* the subject of jurisprudence from those other subjects: "I begin my projected Course with determining the province of jurisprudence, or with distinguishing the matter of jurisprudence from those various related objects."[36]

Since Austin can show that the subject of law that exists differs from the subject of law that we approve of or has merit (the obvious insight), the province of jurisprudence is determined to include the one and to exclude the other. The other subject of study is entitled by Austin, "the science of legislation: which affects to determine the test or standard (…) by which positive law ought to be made, or to which positive law ought to be adjusted."[37] There is no startling methodological technique in establishing the exclusivity of Austin's Province, no distinctive methodology of analytical jurisprudence that arises at this point. Accept the insight, and all else follows, aided only by the familiar method of *per genus et differentiam*, a method Austin adopted without innovation, and tirelessly. In this respect, Austin's approach can be distinguished from the analytical approaches of Bentham and later theorists.

Hart contrasts Bentham's innovations in the exposition of fictitious legal entities with a straightforward application of *per genus et differentiam*, referring to Bentham's techniques of phraseoplerosis, paraphrasis and archetypation.[38] The problem as Bentham saw it, reported by Hart, was the absence of a meaningful superior genus to which fictitious entities belonged. Yet at the very point Bentham is denying the genus, he provides some clue as to its possible construction: "being of the number of (…) fictitious [legal] entities"; and at a prior point in his lengthy note, he has acknowledged that they "are all of them (…) the results of some manifestation or other of the legislator's will."[39] Moreover, the three innovative techniques mentioned above do not in themselves preclude the application of *per genus et differentiam*: one simply has a greater store of material by which to recognise membership of a genus or species.

An alternative explanation for Bentham giving up on the process, was that it was simpler and far less work to stop at exposition by reference to the distinctive use of these fictitious legal entities (which is what the first two innovative techniques amount to) or their distinctive connotations (covered by the third), rather than then proceeding to go through all the possible distinctions generated by a rigorous process of *per genus et differentiam*. This explanation is supported by Bentham himself claiming in the same note to have actually undertaken the "uninviting" labour with

---

[36] *Ibid.* at 9 [18]. The alternative representations of Austin's task as determining or distinguishing are repeated subsequently: *ibid.* at 131, 192–193 [116, 164–165].

[37] *Ibid.* at 366 – from *The Uses of the Study of Jurisprudence*. See also, *supra* note 15.

[38] Herbert L. A. Hart, *Essays on Bentham: Studies in Jurisprudence and Political Theory* (Oxford: Clarendon, 1982) at 129–131.

[39] Jeremy Bentham, *An Introduction to the Principles of Morals and Legislation* ed. by James H. Burns and Herbert L. A. Hart (Oxford: Oxford University Press, 1996) ch. XVI para. XXV n. 1.

"voluminous" results as regards only a part of these fictitious legal entities, the rights and powers of property. Further support for the tendency of Bentham to avoid such painfully extensive labour is perhaps provided by John Stuart Mill's contrast between Austin's untying of intellectual knots with Bentham's cutting of them, the latter finding more use for the battering ram than the builder's trowel.[40]

Hart also suggests that Austin followed Bentham in departing from *per genus et differentiam*,[41] relying on Austin's reference to terms that "will not admit of definition in the formal or regular manner."[42] However, Austin makes it clear that these merely form a case of complexity, soluble by "long, intricate and coherent" work. His illustration of this work is sufficient to demonstrate his continuing adherence to *per genus et differentiam*: distinguishing the "various classes" of "Laws or Rules," detaching law from morals, and allowing the student to attend to "the distinctions and divisions which relate to law exclusively."[43]

It is also clear that Austin displays no peculiar affinity to philosophy such as to lead to a special "philosophical" methodology for analytical jurisprudence, contrary to what Hutchinson has suggested.[44] In contrast to Hart, whose primary academic discipline was philosophy, and whose targeted peers to judge his initial academic efforts were Oxford philosophers,[45] Austin's frustration was not to have had his academic output assessed as "a schoolman of the twelfth century – or a [nineteenth century] German [law] professor."[46]

Although it is notoriously difficult to tie Hart down to a specific methodology (philosophical or otherwise),[47] it is undeniable that contemporary exponents of analytical jurisprudence under the influence of Hart have openly embraced a philosophical approach, the most overtly philosophical in methodology being Joseph Raz.[48] However, where Austin makes reference to "essential" or "essentials," the "essence"

---

[40] In Mill's review of Austin's *Lectures on Jurisprudence* in the Edinburgh Review of October 1863, collected under the title, "Austin on Jurisprudence" in Mill's *Dissertations and Discussions* III (1867) and republished in *The Collected Works of John Stuart Mill* XXI ed. by John M. Robson (Toronto: University of Toronto Press, 1984). I am grateful to Philip Schofield for suggesting the significance of Mill's comment.

[41] Hart, *Essays on Bentham*, *supra* note 38 at 130.

[42] Austin, *The Province*, *supra* note 5 at 370–371 – from *The Uses of the Study of Jurisprudence*.

[43] *Ibid.* at 371. See also, Morison, *John Austin*, *supra* note 8 at 60, where Austin's remark on terms not admitting of definition is attributed to "probably just retailing recollected Bentham." Morison points out that Austin "then (…) proceeds to his work on the opposite basis."

[44] Hutchinson, *The Province of Jurisprudence Democratized*, *supra* note 18.

[45] See Nicola Lacey, *A Life of H. L. A. Hart: The Nightmare and the Noble Dream* (Oxford: Oxford University Press, 2004).

[46] As reported by his widow, Sarah, in her Preface to Austin, *Lectures*, *supra* note 12 at 12. Sarah Austin refers specifically to Hugo and Savigny as German professors whose position Austin envied.

[47] See Halpin, "Methodology" *supra* note 19 at 615.

[48] See *supra* note 31, and *infra* note 56.

or "nature," "essential difference," and "essential or necessary property,"[49] his purpose is to identify those characteristics of various objects or notions (such as law, positive law, independent political society, sovereignty) by which they can be distinguished from others, in order to get on with his standard method of *per genus et differentiam*. There is no quest by Austin for an elevated philosophical grasp of "essential nature" or "necessary characteristic." He simply seeks to extrapolate from empirical observation[50] the character or marks[51] of one thing which set it apart from another.

Austin's use of character and mark clearly demonstrates a directly empirical and philosophically unsophisticated approach. His liberality in employing these terms synonymously, and as synonyms for his variety of other terms already mentioned for conveying essential or necessary properties, distances his vocabulary and approach yet further from the later philosophically elevated pursuit of essential nature or necessary characteristics.[52]

William L. Morison sought to argue for a "naïve empiricism" on the part of Austin as making his approach quite distinct from Hart's approach to analytical jurisprudence.[53] Although Morison's amplification of naïve empiricism has not been well received,[54] his underlying insight that the methodological and philosophical approach of Austin differs fundamentally from that of Hart, and in a way that takes a less sophisticated and more direct approach to empirical observation, is undoubtedly sound. One particular manifestation of the empirical grounding of Austin's theoretical approach is seen when he laments the imperfections of his analysis at the point where empirical evidence throws up contrary examples.[55] Austin never thinks to use Raz's demurrer: that his conceptual analysis is not contingent but "philosophically necessary," and so not refutable by empirical evidence.[56]

---

[49] John Austin, *The Province*, *supra* note 5 at 3, 213–16, 372; 3, 214; 8–9, 193; 211 [12, 181–3, –; 12, 182; 16–17, 165; 179–80].

[50] *Ibid.* at 366 [–], "principles abstracted from positive systems are the subject of general jurisprudence"; 373 [–], "a description of such subjects and ends of Law as are common to all systems."

[51] *Ibid.* at 131–2, 192, 213, 356 [116–17, 164, 181, 289–90] for examples of "character"; and at 131–2, 192, 195, 356 [116–17, 164–65, 167, 289–90] for examples of "mark."

[52] *Ibid.*, *e.g.*, at 213 [181], "a character or essential property"; and, "the two distinguishing marks" of sovereignty at 195 [167] become "two essentials" at 214 [181].

[53] Morison, *John Austin*, *supra* note 8 at 178 ff.

[54] For critical reviews of Morison, see David Lyons, "Founders and Foundations of Legal Positivism" (1984) 82 *Michigan Law Review* 722; Jerome Bickenbach, "Empiricism and Law" (1985) 35 *University of Toronto Law Journal* 94.

[55] Notably in his discussion of "anomalous cases" which render his definition of positive law "defective or inadequate" – Austin, *The Province*, *supra* note 5 at 354 [288].

[56] The starkest presentation of the demurrer is to be found in Joseph Raz, *Between Authority and Interpretation* (Oxford: Oxford University Press, 2009) at 25; see also, *ibid.* at 91–92.

Nevertheless, commentators on Austin have persistently posed a problem in working out whether Austin's work should be regarded as *either* descriptive-empirical *or* conceptual.[57] This dilemma was raised, even prior to Hart, by Stone,[58] drawing on a couple of sentences from "The Uses of the Study of Jurisprudence" in which Austin refers to the "necessary" subjects of general jurisprudence.[59] Stone considers this establishes Austin's ambition for a "universalist analytical jurisprudence" as distinct from the descriptivist "'comparative' jurisprudence" Stone detects elsewhere. Although Austin does also refer here to a criterion of "logical coherence" for these necessary elements, there is nothing to suggest Austin is departing at this point from what can be empirically discovered and described. A stronger suggestion to the contrary arises from the fact that both the necessary elements, and what Austin later distinguishes as being the elements that are "not necessary,"[60] are "to be found" or "in fact occur."[61]

Wilfrid Rumble seeks to perpetuate the descriptive-empirical/formal-conceptual tension by suggesting Austin's work is ambiguous, but then has to implicate John Stuart Mill for failing to appreciate the ambiguity.[62] Michael Lobban rightly finds the suggestion unconvincing and calls for a fuller explanation.[63] The explanation offered here is that to see conceptual analysis as opposed to empirical work through a philosophically specialist perspective on "necessary characteristic" or "essential nature" is to move beyond Austin's (and Mill's) frame of reference where no such tension existed; any detected ambiguity is anachronistically imposed by the observer.[64]

Moreover, it is not as though the move to a more sophisticated, contemporary grasp of philosophical necessity in itself solves the problems of relating theoretical work to the empirical, as can be seen from examining Raz's work.[65] The complexity of his arguments cannot be fully treated here, but two points can be briefly made on the apparent opposition between philosophical necessity and empirical contingency. In the passages previously cited,[66] Raz does allow for the contingency of political and

[57] Discussed by Brian H. Bix, "John Austin and Constructing Theories of Law" *supra* note 16 at 13, and in his entry on Austin in *The Stanford Encyclopaedia of Philosophy*, available at http://plato.stanford.edu/entries/austin-john/.

[58] Julius Stone, *The Province and Function of Law*, *supra* note 6 at 67–69.

[59] John Austin, *The Province*, *supra* note 5 at 365–367 [–].

[60] *Ibid.* at 368–369.

[61] *Ibid.* at 366, 369. See also the passages cited in *supra* note 50.

[62] Wilfrid E. Rumble, *Doing Austin Justice*, *supra* note 8 at 96.

[63] Michael Lobban, Review of Rumble's *Doing Austin Justice* (2006) 45 *Journal of British Studies* 221 at 222.

[64] Despite acknowledging the trap of temporal dislocation, Bickenbach, "Empiricism and Law" *supra* note 54 at 106, comes close to falling into it.

[65] Raz, *Between Authority and Interpretation*, *supra* note 56. The chapters of Raz's book have been published previously, and as such have met with the engagement of Bix (see "Raz on Necessity" *supra* note 31). For a critical review of the book, covering the issues discussed here, see Allan Hutchinson, "Razzle-Dazzle" (2010) 1 *Jurisprudence* 39 at 45–49.

[66] See Raz, *Between Authority and Interpretation*, *supra* note 56.

social institutions and practices, in contrast to the philosophically necessary (legal) characteristics of law. He fails to explore the possibility of necessary political and social connections for law, or the possibility of contingent features of legal institutions. Yet in both cases of the political and the legal aspects of legal institutions it is possible for universal abstract characteristics to meet contingent particular instantiations – suggesting that what is deemed to be a "necessary" characteristic will depend upon a judgement as to what level of abstraction is regarded as theoretically significant. Secondly, the very contingencies, which Raz has contrived to ignore, of those legal institutions which he places at the heart of his concept of law,[67] raise questions that Raz has suppressed in asserting that his (what he refers to as "our") concept of law applies to Jewish religious law or contemporary Iranian law.[68]

Whatever might be made of the philosophical influences that entered analytical jurisprudence through Hart, it is not possible to transpose their impact back through time on Austin. As Frederick Schauer has pointedly observed, Austin lived before "the largely analytic, nonspeculative, nonempirical, and language-focused style of philosophy that characterized much of Anglo-American philosophy from Bertrand Russell through the time that Hart did his most important work."[69]

2.5 The Detection of Doubt

Towards the end of Lecture VI, the final lecture contained in *The Province of Jurisprudence Determined*, Austin announces that his determination of the Province is imperfect: "is not a perfectly complete and perfectly exact determination."[70] Part of his concern clearly expressed here is the inadequate definition of the elements of the subject matter that gave a distinctiveness to the Province. If he has not produced an adequate definition of positive law, then the Province cannot be adequately determined by reference to that as an exclusive subject of study.

For this part of his concern, Austin offers himself some relief. The inadequacy of the definition of positive law is seen in certain "anomalous cases" which do not quite fit the definition he has proposed, such as where laws bind those who are not members of the independent political society. Austin suggests that these anomalous cases can be worked out through further refinement (or "supplement") to his definition within the details of his further lectures on the science of jurisprudence.[71] Austin similarly disposes of a related problem he detects, how precisely to determine who is and who is not a member of a particular independent political society.

---

[67] Raz, *Between Authority and Interpretation*, *supra* note 56 at 27–31, 40.

[68] *Ibid*. at 40–41.

[69] Frederick Schauer, "(Re)Taking Hart" (2006) 119 *Harvard Law Review* 852 at 857.

[70] As heralded in the marginal note, and then expressed in the main text, Austin, *The Province*, *supra* note 5 at 350–51, 354 [285, 288].

[71] *Ibid*. at 354–55 [288–89]. (The further lectures being found, together with Lectures I-VI, in Austin, *Lectures*, *supra* note 12).

Empirically, it is obvious to him that there is not a single uniform test that applies across all communities.[72] This problem is also reserved for the "detail of jurisprudence."[73]

It is the other part of his concern, which goes without relief, or indeed, any hint of further discussion from Austin in the *The Province*, that has greater importance for our present interests. This is the problem of "the ties" between positive law and the other subjects from which it has been distinguished by Austin:

> To determine the province of jurisprudence is to distinguish positive law (the appropriate matter of jurisprudence) from the various objects (noted in the foregoing lectures) to which it is allied or related in the way of resemblance or analogy. But so numerous are the ties by which it is connected with those objects, or so numerous are the points at which it touches those objects, that a perfect determination of the province of jurisprudence were a perfect exposition of the science in all its manifold parts.[74]

Although this problem too is reserved to work that extends beyond the scope of the introductory lectures in *The Province*, Austin is less specific here as to where and how it might be carried out – unlike the definitional "supplement" to deal with the anomalous cases, that could be expected in his remaining lectures. One conjecture is that Austin had further work entirely in mind, beyond his course of lectures, where he might have brought about the "perfect exposition of the science in all its manifold parts." Robert Moles has suggested that Austin's planned but never executed book, *The Principles and Relations of Jurisprudence and Ethics*, is an indication not simply of how *The Province* might have been completed, but also of how it should be understood.[75] It is not possible to do justice to the richness of Moles's argument here, but fundamental problems arise, not least in Moles treating his own confidence, in extracting from certain texts or unpublished fragments of Austin a coherent scheme, as being capable of retrospectively annulling the doubts felt by Austin himself in *The Province*.

Certainly in the *Analysis of Lectures* with which Austin prefaces *The Province*, it is clearly stated that the problem of the ties concerns the relationship between positive law and divine law, and more specifically, between positive law as it is and positive law as it ought to be (the latter being part of divine law in Austin's worldview).[76] And it is here that Austin refers to their respective branches of study, the science of jurisprudence and the science of legislation, as "kindred," and "connected by

---

[72] *Ibid.* at 356–58 [290–91].

[73] *Ibid.* at 357 [291]. Austin is perhaps sensing (though not fully addressing) here the problem of contingent variation in the instantiation of a general definitional element, raised in relation to Raz, *Between Authority and Interpretation*, *supra* note 56. In Austin's terms, how can we be sure that these differences are not significant in upsetting the common classification of the laws of different societies employing *per genus et differentiam*?

[74] *Ibid.* at 354 [288].

[75] Moles, *Definition and Rule in Legal Theory*, *supra* note 8, particularly at 12–16.

[76] Austin, *The Province*, *supra* note 5 at 6–7 [14].

numerous and indissoluble ties."[77] Indeed, in his Analysis Austin makes a defence of spending such a considerable portion of *The Province* in dealing with what, according to its principal thesis, should not fall within the province of jurisprudence at all: the nature of the way in which man ascertains divine law.[78] The only submission in his defence is that this subject matter is required in order to deal with "the *rationale* of jurisprudence" or "the *rationale* of positive law."[79]

Despite these prefatory remarks on the connection between positive law as it is and positive law as it ought to be, within the body of *The Province* Austin reinforces his obvious insight, that the existence of a law differs from an assessment of its merit,[80] with a strong invocation of the is/ought divide. This acts in general as a kind of running title on the lengthy note at the end of Lecture V (which amounts to a manifesto for Austin's campaign for jurisprudence), and in particular as a setting for the ambitious insight, quoted above, which appears in the paragraph immediately following these words:

> *Note* – on the prevailing tendency to confound what is with what ought to be law or morality, that is, 1st , to confound positive law with the science of legislation.[81]

The admonition continues, disposing of a number of other is/ought confusions and serving as a comprehensive endorsement of the is/ought divide. There appears to be no opportunity here for raising the problem of the ties as in some way qualifying the possibility of separately determining the province of jurisprudence.

What then are we to make of Austin's doubts on this particular matter? A simple answer to the quandary would be to suggest that Austin was stressing the value of complementing a science of jurisprudence with a science of legislation, in the same way that Bentham sought to promote both an expository jurisprudence and a censorial jurisprudence.[82] There is clear evidence elsewhere that Austin upheld this view. However, this response does not do justice to the unequivocal link Austin makes at the end of Lecture VI between the problem of the ties and the incomplete and imperfect determination of the Province. The ties between positive law as it is and positive law as it ought to be are not to be unravelled in order to establish the external relations of jurisprudence, but to fully determine the internal nature of jurisprudence itself.

It would be fruitless to speculate on where these doubts might have led Austin, and whether they would have been dispelled in his projected work, *The Principles and Relations of Jurisprudence and Ethics*. An air of unfulfilment lingers over the

---

[77] *Ibid.* These ties are not to be confused with the "ties of resemblance and analogy" mentioned earlier in the "Analysis of Lectures" (*ibid.* at 2 [11]), which Austin announces will be dealt with in "the six ensuing lectures."

[78] *Ibid.* at 3–4 [12–13]. The subject extends across two whole lectures and a greater part of a third, out of six. For Austin's principal thesis, *The matter of jurisprudence is positive law*, see *supra* note 35 and accompanying text.

[79] *Ibid.* at 4, 3 [13, 12]. Italics in original.

[80] See John Austin, *The Province*, *supra* note 5.

[81] *Ibid.* at 184 [157].

[82] See *supra* note 15.

life and work of John Austin.[83] However, it would be equally wrong to ignore these doubts. A sensitivity to subtlety and a capacity for astute observation can be discerned in his work beyond that which is often credited to him.[84] If Austin had doubts, there were probably good reasons for them, even if those reasons remained obscure to Austin himself. So let us return to Austin's obvious insight, buttressed by the is/ought divide, and consider whether anything will give.

Austin insists on recognising the two distinct categories: (1) what the law is; and, (2) what the law ought to be. To assail this distinction is to invite the ridicule that Austin readily employed against those who failed to heed it, ranging from the accusation of nonsense to the diagnosis of imbecility. This we shall avoid. Nevertheless, it is possible, without denying the distinctness of the two categories, to add a third.

The third category arises as soon as it is accepted that the present state of (1) is inadequate to provide a clear answer in every case requiring legal judgement. What the law is comprises legal materials that do have a bearing upon the case in question, but they leave it open to further argument as to whether the case should be disposed of in favour of the one party or the other, and what precise consequences should follow. Such argument, what is commonly referred to as legal reasoning, does not, however, amount to category (2). For that category covers the *open field* of reasoning from whatever grounds are thought appropriate, whatever standards meet with the approval of the reasoner, whatever is considered to be the outworking of "the index to the tacit command of the Deity" (*i.e.* utilitarianism) in Austin's view,[85] in order to suggest a way of dealing with the case. It is perfectly plausible for a number of people to engage in (2); for each to come up with a different conclusion,[86] all of them respected as valid instances of (2); *and* for each of them to accept that his or her own conclusion differs from what the law might be in disposing of the case at hand. Not so with legal reasoning.

Legal reasoning involves, first of all, *some constraint* on the modes and the possible outcomes of the reasoning used to dispose of the case at hand.[87] Secondly, the person

---

[83] In general, see Lotte and Joseph Hamburger, *Troubled Lives: John and Sarah Austin* (Toronto 1985). See also, Rumble, *Doing Austin Justice*, *supra* note 8.

[84] See the positive review of Rumble's *Doing Austin Justice*, *supra* note 8, on this theme by Matthew Kramer (2008) 20 *Utilitas* 252.

[85] Austin, *The Province*, *supra* note 5 at 6 [14]. Austin, *ibid.* at 186 [159], concedes that due to the insufficiency of utilitarianism as an index to the divine will, different people may come to different conclusions in applying it.

[86] Not simply dealing with the binary issue, favour party *A* or favour party *B*, but also determining ways in which the unfavoured party should be made to answer to the favoured party; suggesting that a different party should be held responsible; suggesting radical reforms whereby legal liability should be avoided altogether in favour of compulsory insurance; etc.

[87] A point made pithily by Frederick Schauer, *Thinking Like a Lawyer: A New Introduction to Legal Reasoning* (Cambridge, MA 2009) at 11: "In a society governed by the wise and the good, legal reasoning is likely simply to get in the way." The precise nature of the constraint is highly contestable, and is probably better viewed as a tension between doctrinal certainty and social critique, which eases in different locations at different times – see *The Use of Legal Materials*, ch. 1 of my *Definition in the Criminal Law* (Oxford: Hart, 2004).

engaged in legal reasoning advances an argument as to what the law ought to be regarded as being in order to dispose of the case at hand. This cannot be expressed as being incompatible with what the law is,[88] nor can it be tolerant of opposing views. The purpose is to exclusively reach what the law is, but through argument rather than incontrovertible deduction.

We have here then a third category differing both from what the law is and from what the law ought to be, a hybrid ought-is: (3) what the law ought to be regarded as being. This third category challenges the sufficiency of Austin's obvious insight which restricts us to the distinction between (1) and (2). And if that restriction lies at the heart of Austin's exclusive determination of the province of jurisprudence, then this too is challenged.

Category (3) may act as a bridge between (2) and (1), in that some of what would fall under (2), as a view of what the law ought to be, can make its way across through what the law ought to be regarded as being, into what the law is regarded as being, which amounts to (1), what the law is. That is to say, legal reasoning may operate as a bridge between morality and positive law.[89]

How does this affect the Province? It provides one way of settling Austin's anxiety, considered above, of how to deal with the problem of the ties. Legal reasoning provides the venue in which it is possible to maintain a dynamic relationship between positive law as it is and positive law as it ought to be; some sort of relationship between what Austin referred to as the science of jurisprudence and the science of legislation. However, this is only possible if legal reasoning is allowed into the province of jurisprudence. In order to achieve this the exclusivity of Austin's Province would need to be breached: acknowledging that the law by which the subjects in a political community are governed is not limited to that which has been "set by political superiors"[90] but extends to the outcome of reasoning with those settled materials. This is something Austin himself did not contemplate in *The Province*, restricting himself there to fleeting endorsements of judicial legislation, and some acknowledgement of the need to deal with vague terms, without detracting from his understanding of law as the command (or rule) established by a political superior.[91]

---

[88] For the case at hand. It is possible to argue that law previously established for dealing with previous cases should be overturned, but again there are constraints on the legal reasoning that may be effectively employed to this end.

[89] Taking positive law in the sense used by Austin, *The Province*, *supra* note 5 at 9, 202 [18, 172]: "law, simply and strictly so called: or law set by political superiors to political inferiors"; "every positive law, or every law simply and strictly so called, is set directly or circuitously by a monarch or sovereign number to a person or persons in a state of subjection to its author." For Austin, that covers both legislation and judge-made law.

[90] See *supra* note 89.

[91] Austin, *The Province*, *supra* note 5 at 32 [36], endorsing judge-made laws as tacit commands of the sovereign; at 190–91 [162–63], endorsing Lord Mansfield in "assuming the office of a legislator" (while objecting to his enforcement of morality); at 207 [176], recognising vague terms in positive law without affecting its status. Both topics are held over for his later lectures. See *infra* note 93.

Nevertheless, at the end of *The Province*, Austin expressed his own doubts over the exclusive province of jurisprudence that he had constructed. Here, I have expressed more specific doubts over the sufficiency of Austin's obvious insight which undergirds his construction. By challenging the restriction imposed by the is/ought divide, I have opened up the possibility of including legal reasoning within the Province. This would provide a bridge between law and morality, or allow some exploration of "the ties" between positive law as it is and positive law as it ought to be. Whether or not this is regarded as a satisfactory explanation for Austin's doubts, we do know that the exclusion of legal reasoning from a general theory of law has been cause for doubt elsewhere. Hart, in his own final reflections on his major work, admitted to an oversight in that he had "said far too little (…) about the topic of adjudication and legal reasoning."[92] He might reasonably have blamed this omission on the influence of Austin.

2.6 Reassessing Austin's Legacy

If, as was suggested in Sect. 2.5, we should reject a particular methodology for analytical jurisprudence attributable to Austin, how then are we to understand his legacy? Is his influence on the exclusion of legal reasoning from a general theory of law, mentioned at the close of the previous section, really so significant? At first sight, it would hardly seem so. It is not as though Austin had nothing to say on topics related to legal reasoning. In his remaining lectures, Austin tackles judge-made law ("judiciary law" as he preferred to label it), legal interpretation, and the use of analogy with a keen eye for the details of the processes involved.[93] However, the significance of excluding legal reasoning from the Province cannot be appreciated without bearing in mind that its absence supports a grander ambition, to take exclusive control of the subject matter of jurisprudence in a fiercely fought contest.

The problem portrayed above with legal reasoning is that it occupies a hybrid ought-is form and operates as a bridge between law as it is and law as it ought to be, even between law and morality. This is an unwelcome presence at the point the battle is being waged to preserve the identity of what law is against the threat of alien forces that would submerge it into some moral or other conception of what law ought to be. The threat is not simply a risk of contamination from the alien influences the other

---

[92] Hart, *Postscript*, *supra* note 29 at 259. In the remaining pages of the Postscript, as edited, Hart accepts the significance of legal principles (as well as rules), but in effect only so far as they are introduced through a rule of recognition (*ibid.* at 267); and reverts (*ibid.* at 272–276) to his former position on judicial discretion – relying on a restrictive analysis exhausted by settled law or judicial legislation ("judicial law-making"), which is pure Austin. This hardly amounts to saying *more* on the topic of legal reasoning, but it is impossible to speculate how much more Hart might have said, and what its significance might have been.

[93] Austin, *Lectures*, *supra* note 12, Lectures XXVIII-XXXI, and the appended incomplete *Essays on Interpretation and Analogy*. Further consideration of vague terms is also found here, *e.g.*, at 998–999.

side of the bridge. The threat spreads in the admission that the material collected within the fortified conception of law as it is (law as commands – or rules, or norms) is not in itself adequate to deliver the operations law must perform (disposing of every case requiring legal judgement). The admission exposes that material to a broader sweep of its attributes beyond those constituting its narrow legal status or pedigree (as a command, rule or norm). This may adopt an aetiological approach which regards the material as formed by a previous view of what law ought to be, or may attribute to the material some present view of what law ought to be, in order to work out the full effect of that material within the process of legal reasoning.[94]

In this light, it should come as no surprise to learn that Austin's aversion to legal reasoning within his general theory of law is shared by other leading positivist exponents of analytical jurisprudence. Austin's own position on judge-made law differs from Bentham's. As David Dyzenhaus explains it, Austin shared with Bentham an antipathy towards the common law, but not towards judicial legislation, due to Austin's greater faith in an elite judiciary than a popular legislature to decide matters for the benefit of society.[95] However, he takes up a common position with Bentham in excluding legal reasoning from an understanding of law.[96] Hart's position has already been mentioned. The position of Raz is more extreme than Hart's. Far from being susceptible to doubt over not having said enough about legal reasoning, Raz has contributed much on the subject but in doing so has always rigidly demarcated his theory of legal reasoning from his theory of law.[97] As for Kelsen, Stanley Paulson has observed, "The editor of *The Collected Works of Hans Kelsen* reported to me that his published writings – books, articles, and reviews – come to some 17,500 pages. In all that I have read thus far, I have yet to encounter a single page on legal reasoning."[98]

---

[94] Again, Austin is not unaware of these issues. Consider the fleeting reference to the "rationale" of positive law (*supra* note 79) in *The Province*, or the extensive discussion of the causes of judge-made law in his *Lectures*, *supra* note 12 at 634–635, 644–647. Nevertheless, Austin rigidly avoids setting these topics within a discussion of legal reasoning – the judicial function is exhaustively determined by either applying a rule or creating a rule (*e.g.*, *ibid.* at 998–1000), and it is the rules (or commands) that form the subject matter of *The Province*. See further, Rumble, *The Thought of John Austin*, *supra* note 8 at 116–118.

[95] David Dyzenhaus, "The Genealogy of Legal Positivism" (2004) 24 *O.J.L.S.* 39; Austin, *The Province*, *supra* note 5 at 191 [163].

[96] Gerald Postema, *Bentham and the Common Law Tradition* (Oxford: Clarendon Press, 1986) at 463, concludes his assessment of Bentham's hostility to any judicial legislation with a criticism of Bentham's narrow "identification of law with the execution of *already achieved* agreement or consensus," and his failure to allow into a general theory of law the recognition of "the capacity of (…) legal practice to provide both a *matrix of* and *forum for* the continual forging and reforging of consensus."

[97] See Raz, *Between Authority and Interpretation*, *supra* note 56 particularly chs. 3, 8 and 14. For criticism, see Hutchinson, *The Province of Jurisprudence Democratized*, *supra* note 7 at 77–78, on the lack of "analytical credibility for a concept of law that tells most judges and lawyers (…) that, whatever they are doing, they are not doing law when they go about the prosaic routines of their lawyering or judicial lives."

[98] Personal communication to author.

It may be easy to account for the motivation of these authors in excluding legal reasoning from a theory of law, which they seek to construct so as to avoid contamination or confusion with a view of what law ought to be according to some moral or other non-legal standpoint. This does not provide justification for the exclusion. The justification provided by Austin's obvious insight goes as far as upholding the distinction between what law is and what law ought to be.[99] It does not extend to the more complex phenomenon of the hybrid-form legal reasoning, which deals with arguing for how the law ought to be regarded as being in order to dispose of a particular case.

The unjustified exclusion of legal reasoning from a theory of law produces a flaw in the foundations of the theoretical enterprise. If as a matter of descriptive fact, the state of the law (as it is) comprises legal materials that are insufficient to dispose of cases requiring legal judgement, and yet a theory of law sets itself up to account for the nature of law as that social phenomenon which has a principal function of disposing of such cases, there is still something left over to be described. By restricting their analysis to those legal materials alone, positivist theories of law ironically sabotage their own positivistic ambitions. Ideally, perhaps, a system of municipal law would contain sufficient materials in an appropriate condition so as to provide by a process of incontrovertible deduction the resolution of all disputes and the regulation of all transactions between its citizens – and *then* an exclusive analysis of those materials would provide an adequate theory of positive law as it is. But, at best, this is a theory of an ideal system of law, or, positive law as it ought to be, not positive law as it is.

More than destabilising the foundations of legal positivism, the approach left to us by Austin is responsible for the disengagement between legal theorists I referred to in the introductory section. This, in two ways. First, and more obviously, the "something left over to be described" by the legal positivists produces a clear opportunity for competing theorists to seize upon the unused part of the analysandum and make of it what they will. But whatever they might make of it, there is no possibility of engagement with the positivists for the simple reason that they have excluded that very part from what they are prepared to deal with in a theory of law.

If this first aspect of the disengagement is made out, we should expect to see some of the most intractable disputes within legal theory revolve around the nature and status of legal reasoning. This is not the place to attempt a rigorous proof of the hypothesis, but as grounds for allowing its credibility consider the following. The Hart-Dworkin debate, which still has not run out of steam, has been presented in terms of disputes over rules versus principles, descriptive versus normative, the separation versus the connection of law and morality; in terms of issues of methodological differences and theoretical disagreement. Each of these dividing lines can be viewed as separating positions which respectively do not and do admit legal reasoning as part of the subject matter that a theory of law has to deal with. Once we recognise the significance of the attitude towards legal reasoning in sustaining division here, it is not difficult to detect it elsewhere: for example, in wider

[99] This is the common justification relied upon by all the positivist authors mentioned.

disagreements over the normative/descriptive divide, including the antagonism between hard and soft positivism.

The second aspect of the disengagement that can be regarded as part of Austin's legacy is less obvious but possibly has had a deeper impact. It has to do with the very attempt to establish a province of jurisprudence. All theory building is territorial in the sense introduced in Sect. 2.3 when discussing the contestability of theoretical viewpoints. Theorists seek to capture an area of ignorance or confusion through dispelling the obscurity with their own theoretical illumination. The distinction with establishing "a province" or "an exclusive field of inquiry" lies in the theorist in that case seeking to exclude certain ways of understanding the subject matter of the inquiry. The promotion of an exclusive field of inquiry necessarily favours certain theoretical viewpoints over others, which would operate with a different understanding of the nature of the subject matter, requiring an alternative field of inquiry.

Nevertheless, Austin's technique for establishing the Province by means of ambitious insight was regarded more highly than the use of axiomatic disengagement, in that there was at the point of constructing the Province an engagement with rival theorists on the common ground held by the insight. There was also more than a hint in Sect. 2.3 that deploying ambitious insight was a more honest strategy than relying on a split field of inquiry which could surreptitiously demote competing viewpoints by artificially excluding or marginalising them. However, the virtue of open engagement with opposing viewpoints, which lifts ambitious insight over axiomatic disengagement or splitting a field of inquiry as a theoretical technique, is found only at the creation of the Province. Once the Province is established as an exclusive field of inquiry, engagement with opposing viewpoints which might challenge the distinctiveness of that field is precluded.

What this may mean, as we discovered in the case of Austin, is that the strength of the obvious insight can dazzle the theorist into a more far-reaching confidence when establishing the exclusivity of a field of inquiry than the ambitious insight can actually bear. Despite initially engaging with viewpoints that Austin discerned could beneficially learn from his insight, by insisting on an exclusive field of inquiry – a province of jurisprudence *fully determined* – he foreclosed engagement outside of the Province with viewpoints providing insights Austin was as yet not ready to assess.

It is this proclivity to exclusivity that constitutes the second aspect of the disengagement between legal theorists, that can be traced to Austin. Mention has already been made in Sect. 2.2 of the general exclusivity of analytical jurisprudence. This has reached positions in terms of philosophical elevation (encountered in Sect. 2.4) and positions involving a narrowing of the general jurisprudential agenda away from matters of practical and political concern, which would have been quite alien to Austin and Bentham,[100] but are wholly understandable as an extension of the exclusivity in determining the subject matter of jurisprudence that Austin bequeathed to his successors.

[100] For arguments that the nature of the earlier positivists' work has been narrowly interpreted, so impoverishing legal positivism, see Oren Ben-Dor, *Constitutional Limits and the Public Sphere: A Critical Study of Bentham's Constitutionalism* (Oxford: Hart, 2000); David Dyzenhaus, "Positivism's Stagnant Research Programme" (2000) 20 *O.J.L.S.* 703; William Twining, *Globalisation and Legal Theory* (London: Butterworths, 2000) at 16–20, 94–98.

So deep set is this problem within jurisprudence that attempts to alleviate it, such as Stone's effort to add sociological and normative branches to the analytical branch of jurisprudence, considered in Sect. 2.2, only serve to sustain the underlying exclusivity. The idea that there should somehow be a link between analytical and sociological jurisprudence is a matter for contemporary puzzlement rather than resolution,[101] and the analytical-normative relationship is almost invariably hostile.[102] Unsurprisingly so, if the separation into exclusive approaches was from the start wholly artificial.

The exclusivity and disengagement does not bite only at the level of general approaches to jurisprudence. Individual theorists appear burdened with taking exclusive control of the subject matter of jurisprudence by redetermining the province of jurisprudence, by analysing *the* concept of law, by providing the definitive statement of what law *is*, instead of offering theoretical insights that are open to engaging with further insights to contribute to a fuller understanding of law.

Often the frailty of the endeavour which rests a restrictive understanding of law on a single insight is obvious to everyone except the theorist and loyal supporters. The multiplication of this scenario, sadly, does not undermine the credibility of the endeavour. Instead, each faction persists in the atavistic quest for complete control of the subject matter of jurisprudence. They heap scorn on their rivals to the point of ignoring what value their rival's insights might possess. They shore up their own preferred model with abstruse refinements to protect it from attack, but by so doing distort the very insight they seek to preserve and render it incapable of the illumination it originally shed. Few legal theorists will fail to recognise the process described. A number have committed a similar analysis to print. The tendency, however, is to acknowledge it only so far as it affects one's rivals.

The resultant picture of mutual academic disengagement, from both aspects of Austin's legacy, spills over easily into disengagement from other potential stakeholders in legal theory. Fierce hostility over the basis on which legal reasoning can even be admitted as part of the subject matter of jurisprudence, coupled with abstruse and distorted theoretical insights turned in against each other rather than outwards towards issues of practical concern, does not present a friendly interface to stimulate the engagement of those whose priorities are less theoretical.

Yet if this is Austin's legacy, it certainly was not his will. The two aspects of disengagement in his bequest, that have been charted here, ignore the doubts that Austin also left to us. These doubts unquestionably spoke to a more integrated view of legal theory, embracing "the ties" between law as it is and law as it ought to be,

---

[101] The puzzle has been raised in particular over Hart's purported affiliations with both descriptive sociology and analytical philosophy, see Lacey, *A Life of H. L. A. Hart*, *supra* note 45, and also her "Analytical Jurisprudence Versus Descriptive Sociology Revisited" (2006) 84 *Texas Law Review* 945; William Twining, *General Jurisprudence: Understanding Law from a Global Perspective* (Cambridge: Cambridge University Press, 2009) ch. 2.

[102] A notable exception is John Finnis' insistence that some sort of synthesis between the analytical and normative is required in any adequate theory of law in his *Natural Law and Natural Rights* (Oxford: Clarendon Press, 1980). However, his remarks remain allusive and undeveloped.

within "a perfect exposition of the science [of jurisprudence] in all its manifold parts." Austin was also adamant about the fundamental importance of linking theoretical inquiry to practical concerns:

> This is the main, though not the only use of *theory*: which ignorant and weak people are in a habit of *opposing* to practice, but which is essential to practice guided by experience and observation. (…) Unless the terms of a theory can be resolved into particular truths, the theory is mere jargon: a coil of those senseless abstractions which often ensnare the *instructed*; and in which the wits of the ignorant are certainly caught and entangled.[103]

Moving contemporary legal theory from a condition I have argued is inherited from Austin, requires us to pay greater attention to what Austin did leave us. Although it may be impossible to imagine how the founding of jurisprudence would have differed had Austin himself resolved his doubts and had the opportunity to respond to his wider vision for the science of jurisprudence, his further prompts still have the potential to assist in reshaping legal theory today, 150 years after his death. There is, furthermore, at the present time an impetus from the changing practical condition of law. The questioning of established insight is unavoidable in the face of novel forms of legal phenomena in the global context; and the complexity found there will test even more severely efforts to narrow the field of inquiry in pursuit of a solitary insight. Likewise, the insufficiency of legal materials to dispose of all cases requiring legal intervention in the global context renders legal reasoning an indispensable part of the subject matter.[104] The historical moment for a fully engaged legal theory is upon us.

Acknowledgements I am grateful to Michael Freeman and the participants at the John Austin 150th Anniversary Conference, *John Austin and his Legacy*, UCL, December 2009, for much stimulating discussion and helpful comments on an earlier draft of this essay presented as a paper at that conference. I am particularly grateful to Stanley Paulson for further helpful discussion thereafter. This chapter was previously published in (2011) 70 *Cambridge Law Journal* 175 and is reproduced by the kind permission of Cambridge University Press.

---

[103] Austin, *The Province*, *supra* note 5 at 49–50 [50–51]. To avoid the risk of the following words of Austin being transformed into another "ambitious insight," it should be stressed that such insight that they contain needs to engage with further insights, notably relating to the matters that are importantly raised in Bix, "John Austin and Constructing Theories of Law" *supra* note 16. The critical issue to explore is how a lack of fit between theory and practice is used to shed light on practice as it is, on practice as it might be, or on other concerns related to but not affecting that practice as it is currently experienced or conceived (very loosely: descriptive theory, normative theory, and blue sky theory). Raising and answering the question would indicate some advance. Evaluating the answers might alleviate Austin's anxiety, or exacerbate it.

[104] See *Theorising the Global Legal Order* ed. by Andrew Halpin and Volker Roeben (Oxford: Hart, 2009), chs. 1 and 14; and, more widely, Twining, *General Jurisprudence*, *supra* note 101; Jack Goldsmith and Daryl Levinson, "Law for States: International Law, Constitutional Law, Public Law" (2009) 122 *Harvard Law Review* 1791.

Chapter 3
"Darkening the Fair Face of Roman Law": Austin and Roman Law

Andrew Lewis

3.1 Introduction

Anyone – and perhaps in this context that should be everyone – who has taken the trouble to read past the *Province of Jurisprudence Determined* into the *Lectures on Jurisprudence* will have been struck by the prominence of Roman law in Austin's material. In effect, Common law and Roman law are together regarded by him as constituting the essence of developed legal thinking. In the eyes of a modern reader, conversant perhaps with the former but not the latter, the appearance of Roman law in Austin will be seen as one further feature which firmly locates Austin in a bygone age and such is the spirit in which the study of John Austin's work is generally approached nowadays I do not doubt but that my title raises expectations that I am to show the extent to which our author has yet again failed to attain the standard expected of a competent jurist and has managed to disfigure Roman law as he is taken to have misunderstood and mangled Bentham.

But my title is actually a quotation from Austin himself. Austin's approach to Roman law, as we shall see, is both unusual and subtle. In particular he firmly and clearly distinguishes between the civil law tradition of much European law and the Roman law original which influenced it. The phrase "darkening the fair face of Roman law" is one he uses to take to task one of the prominent later civilian jurists, Heineccius, from whose works Austin himself seems to have first learned the subject, for his failure to preserve the prestign purity of classical Roman law.

To be sure any reader of Austin's *On the Uses of Jurisprudence* will have encountered his spirited defence of the value of Roman law and his comparison of it to the endeavours of later ages: *e.g.* "Its merits are appropriate and in perfect taste. It bears the same relation to that of Blackstone and Gravina, which a Grecian statue bears to a milliner's doll in the finery of the season."

A. Lewis (✉)
University College London, Law School, Endsleigh Gardens, Bentham House, WC1 OEG, London, UK
e-mail: a.d.e.lewis@ucl.ac.uk

M. Freeman and P. Mindus (eds.), *The Legacy of John Austin's Jurisprudence*, Law and Philosophy Library 103, DOI 10.1007/978-94-007-4830-9_3,

As an example from the *Lectures* of what appears to a romanist Austin's own perfect taste one might pick almost at random the following passage on the topic of Judicial legislation in Lecture XXIX. Having considered and rejected what he calls Mr Bentham's "pithy and homely" phrase "judge-made law" Austin goes on: "judges legislating avowedly in the manner of the Roman Praetors might do the business better than any of the sovereign Legislatures which have yet existed in the world."[1]

3.2 Austin's Knowledge of Roman Law

When the Council, the then governing body of UCL as the self-proclaimed University of London, announced that they intended to fulfil the original intentions of the founders and advertise a chair in Roman law, Austin wrote to Coates, the College Secretary, to intimate that he had always understood that his chair of Jurisprudence encompassed the study of Roman law and that he supposed that he might continue to teach it. As we have noted this comes as no surprise to the reader of the *Lectures*. A significant part of Austin's material is devoted to an exposition of the basic structure and features of the Roman system. Austin neither presumes that his audience will have much prior knowledge of the Roman system nor leaves a great deal to be accomplished towards gaining a fundamental understanding of it. Had Thomas Jefferson Hogg, by his own account the leading candidate for the chair of Roman law, been appointed, there would have been a struggle. As it was no appointment was in the end made and the frustrated Hogg was left to publish his already prepared but undeliverable inaugural lecture.

Austin seems also to have regarded International law as falling within his remit. In large measure this probably arose from the fact that the College's original intention had been to found four law chairs in English Law, Roman law, International law and Jurisprudence but in the end only proceeded initially to fill the first and last of these. Rightly judging that his colleague in the chair of English law, Andrew Amos, would not be covering either of the other two topics Austin seems simply to have arrogated them within his own sphere of responsibility. Whatever the proper sphere of his teaching responsibilities the evidence from the published text of the *Lectures* is that Austin possessed and utilised a deep acquaintance with Roman law.

Where had Austin learned his Roman law? There was a formal curriculum in Roman law at both Oxford and Cambridge which was followed by those intending to qualify at Doctors' Commons for practice in the civil law and ecclesiastical courts. But Austin had not attended university either before entering the army in 1807 or after his discharge in 1812. From 1814 to 1818 he was preparing himself for

[1] John Austin, *Lectures on Jurisprudence, or The Philosophy of Positive Law* ed. by Robert Campbell (4th edition, rev., London: John Murray, 1873) [Bristol: Thoemmes Press reprint, 2002, two vols.], Lecture XXIX, 533.

practice at the bar. Before the introduction of the Bar examinations after 1846 there was no formal requirement for a bar student to learn Roman law: pupil barristers merely read what their pupil master required. Roman learning was sufficiently displayed in the reported decisions of the courts for an acquaintance with its principles to be considered a useful accomplishment. It is true that Austin was a close associate of Bentham's in the period when he was attempting to start a practice at the bar but Bentham's knowledge of Roman law was rather rudimentary and essentially historical in nature. Austin's own Roman law was, however, as we shall see, substantial and analytical.

During his 6 month period of study in Germany in the winter of 1827–1828 prior to taking up his chair Austin studied with a pupil of Savigny and the list of books he brought back with him and annotated includes several standard German civil law volumes, references to which are to be found in the printed *Lectures*. Despite the carping comment of Crabbe Robinson to the effect that Austin (unlike his wife Sarah) knew no German, he contrived to make good use of his time there. He seems to have attended lectures but also to have studied privately with a pupil of Savigny: this was of course the standard mode of study in German universities at the time but it was peculiarly appropriate to one of some maturity and perhaps limited ability in the German language. (Sarah Austin, whose competence in German extended to the publication of translations of several works including notoriously the travelogue of Prince Pückler-Musgau, never comments on her husband's familiarity with German except to state in the preface to the *Lectures* that in the spring of 1828 he left Germany a "master of the German language" which might or might not substantiate Crabbe Robinson's remark.)

Nevertheless it must be doubted whether this period of study abroad would alone have been sufficient to enable him to display the knowledge of both ancient Roman and German civil law demonstrated in the written *Lectures*. Although the matter has yet to be thoroughly elucidated it appears that Austin made few changes to the text of the lectures from his first writing of them. The printed *Lectures*, albeit supplemented with students' notes, principally those taken by John Stuart Mill at their first delivery, do display small corrections and modifications of earlier matter the author made on subsequent occasions. This is of course a familiar phenomenon to those who have ever reused their lecture notes. It is now difficult to tell what Austin did on the occasion of subsequent delivery, in those places where the text explicitly corrects errors in earlier lectures, as for example in Lecture XXII: "I said in a former lecture, that an obligation to *will* is impossible. Why I said so, I am somewhat at a loss to see."[2]

Moreover we have unimpeachable evidence that Austin was sufficiently acquainted with Roman law in 1821–1822 to teach it, alongside Blackstone, to the 17-year-old John Stuart Mill. This was at a time when Austin's career as a barrister seems to have failed before it had properly begun. The Austins and the Mills were both close neighbours of Bentham in Queen Square Place. James Mill had taught his

[2] Austin, *Lecture XXII*, *supra* note 1 at 404, fn 51. Oddly the objectionable sentence is not itself preserved except in John Stuart Mill's notes: *cf.* at 461, fn 90.

formidably precocious son at home but himself lacked those legal elements which he, probably under Bentham's influence, regarded as prerequisite. Quite probably it was Bentham who suggested Austin as a tutor.

We know what Mill and Austin read together from Mill's account of the episode in his *Autobiography*: "with Mr Austin I read Heineccius on the Institutes, his Roman Antiquities and part of his exposition of the Pandects, to which was added a considerable portion of Blackstone."[3] This was by no means an unusual undertaking at the time: Sir Walter Scott recalled in his memoirs how with a fellow student "in the course of two summers, we went, by way of question and answer, through the whole of Heineccius' Analysis of the Institutes and Pandects."[4] Scott and his friend probably used the translation of the Heineccius published in Edinburgh in 1780.[5] But Austin and Mill almost certainly read from the original Latin which Austin himself occasionally quotes extensively in the *Lectures*.[6]

Austin's library was bequeathed by his widow to the Inner Temple where it was largely destroyed during the Second World War but the catalogue published by Robert Campbell in his *Advertisement* to his editions of the *Lectures* reveals that it contained a copy of Heineccius' *Recitationes in elementa Juris civilis secundum ordinem Institutionum*[7] and the 1822 edition by Haubold of Heineccius *Antiquitatum Romanarum Jurisprudentiam illustrantium syntagma.*[8] The latter is undoubtedly the text referred to by Mill as *Roman Antiquities*, and which, it is worth noting, was frequently cited by Bentham. "Heineccius on the Institutes" is the *Recitationes* also known as the *Elementa Iuris Civilis* which is a section by section discussion of Justinian's Institutes. Mill's surviving library, now at Somerville College, Oxford, contains his copy of Heineccius' *Elements of the Institutes*. Mill's "exposition of the Pandects" is almost certainly the less well known *Elementa Iuris civilis secundum ordinem Pandectarum* first published in 1740, of which, however, neither Austin's nor Mill's library preserved a copy.

A considerable surprise is that Austin also possessed an 1823 copy of Goeschen's edition of the *Institutes of Gaius*. To appreciate the significance of this we must make a short excursus into our sources of knowledge of Roman law. Roman law was a living system from the middle of the fifth century BC until the middle of the fifth century of our era. In the 500's AD it underwent a process of codification

---

[3] John Stuart Mill, *Autobiography*, in *Collected Works* ed. by John M. Robson and Jack Stillinger (London: Routledge and Kegan Paul, 1981) Vol. 1, 69, *cf.* 77, 79.

[4] John Gibson Lockhart, *Memoirs of the Life of Sir Walter Scott*, Volume I (Edinburgh: Cadell, 1837) at 83.

[5] See P. Stein, "Actio de effusis vel dejectis and the concept of quasi-delict in Scots Law" 4 *International and Comparative Law Quarterly* (1955) at 374.

[6] *E.g.* Austin, *Lecture XIV*, *supra* note 1 at 386.

[7] Johann Gottlieb Heineccius, *Recitationes in elementa juris civilis secundum ordinem institutionum* (Vratislaviae: Impensis Io. Friderici Kornii, 1789).

[8] Johann Gottlieb Heineccius, *Antiquitatum Romanarum Jurisprudentiam illustrantium syntagma* ed. by Christ. Gottl. Haubold (Frankfurt a.M.: Sumptibus H.L. Broenneri, 1822).

which in effect brought 1,000 years of legal development to an end (though this was not the intention of its codifiers). Our major sources of earlier Roman law come in the form of these codified and edited texts of earlier legislation and legal writings published by the emperor Justinian around 530 AD, together with a contemporary introductory text attributed to the emperor himself, Justinian's *Institutes*. For 1,500 years, Justinian's *Institutes* and commentaries upon them, like Heineccius's, have been the starting point of a student's learning in Roman law.

Romanists have always been drawn between the competing needs of scholarship and practice, between understanding the true meaning of their ancient sources and providing a contemporary significance for this understanding. The texts preserved by Justinian's codification were the basis of legal practice in early modern Europe. But from the sixteenth century onwards they were also the means for recovering the historical roots of the Roman system in the period of the late Republic and early Empire which, it was generally agreed, was the most interesting dynamic and classical period of Roman law. Although legal writings from this period were transmitted as part of Justinian's legacy, they were preserved in a bowdlerised and edited form.

In 1819 the world of Roman legal history was transformed by the publication of a text, the *Institutes of Gaius*, more or less complete and in its original form as it was written in the second century AD. It had been found in the cathedral library at Verona by Neibuhr, a pupil of Savigny. Goeschen published an edition in 1820. Austin acquired a copy of the 1823 reprint, and according to Campbell's list of his books it was "full of analytical notes." The bulk of Austin's Roman law, as his German law library was obtained during his stay in Bonn in 1827, but it seems possible that, stimulated by his reading with John Stuart Mill, he began a deeper study during the period before his appointment to the UCL chair. It is perhaps relevant that in 1824 a much improved edition of Gaius' text was issued by Goeschen incorporating Bluhme's readings. Had Austin acquired his Gaius in 1827 it would likely have been the 1824 edition. As it is his library contains the earlier one and probably from an earlier time.

3.3 Austin's Use of Roman Law

In his lectures Austin was not teaching Roman law. Had he done so he would undoubtedly have followed the text of Gaius and Justinian's *Institutes* which move from a brief exposition of the sources of law through the law of persons to the law of property, including both inheritance and obligations, before finishing with the law of procedure or actions.

Austin's scheme is naturally more analytic. He starts in Lecture XII with an analysis of pervading notions dealing successively with Right, Person, Thing, and Acts and Forbearances. He then proceeds from Lecture XVIII onwards to an examination of Will, Motive, Intention and Negligence before concluding with Sanction.

In all this Austin's starting point is not Roman law, neither is it, of course, Common law but rather the positive scheme of express or tacit commands of a sovereign to which he occasionally refers. His Roman law references therefore are in the form of secondary illustrations rather than primary proofs. He would no more have found a demonstration of positivism in the writings of the Roman jurists than in the judgements of English judges. The first appearance of Roman learning occurs in lecture XII where Austin is considering the meaning of the term Person. Modern civilians, he says, use the term "person" to refer to someone with legal rights, from which it is a simple step to construct fictitious persons out of entities which have such rights. But the classical Roman jurists used "person" principally to mean physical or natural persons and included within the compass of the term those, like slaves, who expressly had no rights. The jurists also used person in a secondary sense to mean status, as when they characterised an individual person as having several *personae*: as a human might be a citizen, a son and a father. Austin shows that the modern use, limiting person to the second of these meanings, arises from a confusion between the notion of *status* and *caput*, the use of which is distinct in the Roman sources but confused in modern analysis. In particular he shows that the proper translation of *jus personarum* is not *law of persons* as in Hale and Blackstone but *law of status*; *personarum* here being used in its secondary meaning. In demonstration of this he points to the sixth century Greek paraphrase of Justinian's *Institutes* by Theophilus which translates the phrase as "division of statuses." Austin claims in Lecture XIII with some plausibility that this confusion has further led to the mistaken idea that *ius in rem* has something to do with things as opposed to persons: whereas it really means rights applying generally.[9] Austin uses the authority of the Roman jurists as a basis for his own broad use of the term person.

Austin's exposition of Roman law frequently makes use of the *Institutes of Gaius* which preserve details of the earlier classical law which were removed from the texts transmitted in Justinian's codification and which had, therefore, had only very recently come to notice following Niehbur's discovery. For example in dealing with rights *in rem* in Lecture XV, Austin refers to the form of conveyance known as *mancipatio*, details of which are contained exclusively in Gaius as the institution had dropped out of use by Justinian's time and references to it were accordingly deleted from the sources he uses.

Beyond the characteristic definition of terms which occupies Lectures XII-XXVIII Austin proceeds to give his main discussion three main divisions: Law in relation to its Sources; The Law of Things; and the Law of Persons. This threefold division is directly taken from the Roman Institutional model – that is, the pattern of exposition taken by Gaius in his Institutes and followed by Justinian in what is in effect a revised version of Gaius' text. In the Roman model the matter of sources is disposed of in a few opening sentences in the nature of an introduction. The main Roman divisions are the Law of Things, the Law of Persons and the Law of Procedure. Already in Justinian's Institutes, the law of procedure is very truncated, reflecting a major change consequent upon the development of state-sponsored adjudication. (Adjudication in early Roman law is more akin to arbitration than our court system.) There is no great

[9] Austin, *Lectures XIII, supra* note 1 at 374.

surprise that Austin found no room for a discussion of Roman procedure save in the form of an extended analysis of the nature of judicial legislation which forms part of the law of sources.

However, although Austin follows the remaining Roman divisions into the Law of Persons and the Law of Things he inverts the Roman order. For Gaius the law of status precedes the law of things because it is a means of clearing out of the way all those natural persons who lack full capacity, those Roman citizens of full age and capacity for whom the law of things exists. It is a striking feature of the Roman scheme that the nature of full capacity is expounded negatively by determining all those who lack it and positively only by an expositions of the rights themselves in the Law of Things. Austin rightly complains that the Gaian scheme poses difficulties of exposition. To comprehend the nature of the divisions of status it is necessary to refer to some aspects of the law of things. A striking example, which continues to present difficulties to this day to Roman law students following the Gaian scheme, is the inclusion within the analysis of the law of family status of the mode of conveyance known as *mancipatio*. A detailed knowledge of this feature of the Roman law of property is critical to an understanding both of how Romans freed the subordinate members of their family from the burden of *patria potestas* (so that they might become independent citizens in their own right) and, more importantly in practice, how subordinates of one family might be adopted into another. I am not the only modern Romanist to sometimes treat the law of things, including modes of conveyance, before the law of persons in my undergraduate class, precisely to overcome this difficulty.

There is a further consideration which, I suspect weighed with Austin who was not after all primarily expounding the Roman law but giving a general analysis of principles which he considered universal, at least for developed European legal systems. As we have noted, one of the justifications for the Roman order is the need to clear out of the way the considerable number of individuals whose status excludes them from the benefits of the law of things. Chief among these were slaves, but the list includes also all children (of whatever age) whose fathers are still alive, women married in traditional form (*in manu*) and also all women whose fathers were dead but who had not by various means escaped the requirement of having a perpetual legal guardian. The list also included, in some respects, freedmen (*i.e.* former slaves manumitted by their masters). This is a considerable number of individuals and emphasises the extent to which full Roman legal status was restricted to a limited class of (mainly) elderly men. By contrast in most modern systems, even in Austin's day, the numbers of those with full civic status were considerably greater and the arguments for dealing with the central case of those with full rights first and the exceptions thereafter, shifts accordingly.

The state in which Austin's lectures have come down to us has, however, mutilated his conception of the relationship between Status and Property, Persons and Things. It is clear from the scheme set out in the *Outline of the Course of Lectures* that Austin intended to conclude his Lectures with the Law of Persons. It is worth remarking that although Austin set out to deliver his course on five separate occasions (aside from his lectures at the Inns of Court) he seems never to have completed them as he intended. Certainly the remaining published matter breaks off, at lecture LVII, in the early stages of the exposition of the Law of Things which begins in lecture XLV.

The unfinished nature of the project is unfortunate as it leaves as Austin's only treatment of the law of persons or status the material in lectures XL-XLIII, which he regarded as merely preliminary matter. To the casual observer it might seem, therefore, that Austin had simply followed the Roman pattern of putting Persons before Property, whereas he very firmly intended the opposite. I regard this as important not as indicating any fundamental criticism by Austin of the Roman institutional scheme derived from Gaius but rather as indicating the extent to which he had so immersed himself in the Roman material as to feel confident to present it in a new pattern, one which was more in keeping with its continued relevance to modern legal analysis.

Austin held a robust view of the respective merits of the classical Roman lawyers who had formed the material of Roman law and their successors who had attempted to collect, collate and interpret their remains. His most supportive remarks are reserved for the lawyers of the first age of rediscovery of Roman law in Europe, the Glossators and Commentators. In this he was but following Savigny though it was far from the contemporary wisdom. In Europe for the most part the effect of the Humanist revolution in scholarship, not to speak of the Enlightenment, was to consign the glossator Accursius and his followers to the dungeon of the middle ages. In England they were scarcely known at all. For Austin they represented a purity of grasp and understanding of the Roman texts which few of their successors could match. Indeed few of the early modern exponents of Roman civil law escape Austin's censure. His greatest scorn, following Savigny, is reserved for the compilers of the French *Code civil* (and we see here perhaps an echo of that anti-French sentiment perhaps to be expected of one who was under arms against Napoleon). He attributes to them: "ignorance of, combined with servile respect for, Roman law."[10] But even Grotius is damned with faint praise as when his definitions of *jura in rem* and *in personam* are quoted: "this definition also, like the former, was, I believe devised by Grotius: in neither of them is there any great merit."[11] Heineccius, to whom as we have seen Austin was indebted for some of his earliest reading in the subject, was nevertheless taken to task for "darkening the fair face of Roman law"[12] by conflating the right to acquire something with the property right in something – in Latin confusing the *jus ad rem* with *jus in rem*, or in more modern terms conflating the contractual right to acquire with the property right when acquired.

Austin is not afraid to extend his criticism to the Romans themselves. In the fragmentary material on obligations which follows lecture LVII (and which the editor Robert Campbell seems at one stage to have referred to as "Lecture LVIII"

[10] Austin, *Lectures, supra* note 1 at 1071.

[11] Austin, *Lecture XIV*, *supra* note 1 at 381.

[12] Austin, *Lecture LVII*, *supra* note 1 at 995.

in footnote 7 at page 52) there is a section on quasi-contracts and quasi-delicts. These categories, we now see clearly, were invented by Justinian and form no part of Gaius' institutional discussion. Austin saw this much: "Gaius makes no distinction between delicts and quasi-delicts, though he adverts to quasi-contracts." In fact Austin is mistaken in this criticism. Gaius does use the phrase "quasi ex contractu" in a discussion of the liability of one who has been handed a payment mistakenly to reimburse the donor. Unlike a genuine loan there is no contract, but Gaius says he should repay as though there were a contract. But it is Justinian's compilers who seek to make this a substantial category of obligation, quasi-contract, and then invent quasi-delict to keep it company. But Austin is fiercely critical: "the distinction between quasi-contract and quasi-delict seems to be useless."[13]

3.4 Conclusion

I have shown that Austin's grasp and interest in Roman law was considerable, going beyond what might have been found elsewhere in England at the time. His ideas about law are illustrated as much by Roman as English example. He is not afraid to engage with his authorities, whether modern or ancient and demonstrates a clear appreciation of the merits of the traditional Roman analysis whilst remaining free to advance beyond it. It is the greatest of pities that he never concluded his mature work.

[13] *Ibid.* at 945.

Chapter 4
Austin, Kelsen, and the Model of Sovereignty: Notes on the History of Modern Legal Positivism*

Lars Vinx

4.1 Introduction

The relationship between Hans Kelsen and John Austin may, at first glance, appear to be of limited interest. Kelsen's Pure Theory of Law did not develop under the influence of Austin's work, and there is no evidence of a serious interest in Austin in the German works Kelsen published before his emigration to the US. Kelsen only began to discuss Austin's views in his later English works.[1] He had evidently come to realize that Austin's project was in some respects comparable to his own, and that the attempt to introduce the Pure Theory of Law to an English-speaking audience would benefit from an analysis of the relation between the Pure Theory and Austinian legal theory.

Kelsen's rather critical discussion of Austin, I would like to suggest, casts an interesting light on the development of modern legal positivism. Herbert L. A. Hart's *The Concept of Law* is in many respects a response to Kelsen's attack on Austin. This is obscured by a tendency on Hart's part to assimilate key elements of Kelsen's legal theory to Austin's.[2] In fact, Kelsen anticipates most of Hart's criticisms of Austin. It therefore seems reasonable to assume that Hart was influenced

---

* This paper is a slightly revised version of a paper that was published in the *Canadian Journal of Law and Jurisprudence* in vol. XXIV, no. 2. The author would like to thank the editor of the CJLJ, Prof. Richard Bronaugh, for his permission to republish the paper.

[1] See Hans Kelsen, "The Pure Theory of Law and Analytical Jurisprudence" in Hans Kelsen, *What is Justice? Justice, Law, and Politics in the Mirror of Science. Collected Essays by Hans Kelsen* (Berkeley, CA: University of California Press, 1957) at 266; Hans Kelsen, *General Theory of Law and State*, trans. by Anders Wedberg (Cambridge, MA: Harvard University Press, 1945) at 30–37, 62–64, 71–74, 77–83.

[2] See Herbert L. A. Hart, *The Concept of Law* (2nd ed.) ed. by Penelope A. Bulloch and Joseph Raz (Oxford: Oxford University Press, 1994) at 35–42.

L. Vinx (✉)
Department of Philosophy, Bilkent University, Ankara, Turkey
e-mail: vinx@bilkeut.edu.tr

M. Freeman and P. Mindus (eds.), *The Legacy of John Austin's Jurisprudence*, Law and Philosophy Library 103, DOI 10.1007/978-94-007-4830-9_4,

by Kelsen's discussion of Austin. But despite the fact that Hart endorses most of Kelsen's criticisms of Austin, his overall conception of positivist legal theory is closer to Austin's than to Kelsen's. Hart's theory of law is an attempt to defend the view that the existence of law is a kind of social fact in light of the vulnerabilities of the Austinian conception of law exposed by Kelsen.

This Hartian response to Kelsen's criticism of Austin, and this will be my second (albeit wholly unoriginal)[3] suggestion, points to a problem in Kelsen's argument for the Pure Theory of Law. Kelsen held that the Pure Theory of Law is the only positivist legal theory that can avoid the problems he diagnosed in Austin's view. That this latter claim is false has been established beyond doubt by Hart. And this would appear to leave a choice for the Pure Theory of Law (over other positivist theories not afflicted by the peculiar weaknesses of Austin's view) unmotivated. I will therefore suggest, finally, that Kelsen's Pure Theory of Law may have greater contemporary relevance if read as a normative theory concerned with the value of the rule of law than if read as a purely descriptive legal science.

4.2 Austin, Kelsen, and the Aims of Legal Theory

Kelsen's most extended discussion of Austinian jurisprudence culminates in the following assessment:

> Since the Pure Theory of Law limits itself to cognition of positive law, and excludes from this cognition the philosophy of justice as well as the sociology of law, its orientation is much the same as that of so-called analytical jurisprudence, which found its classical Anglo-American presentation in the work of John Austin. Each seeks to attain its results exclusively by analysis of positive law. While the Pure Theory of Law arose independently of Austin's famous *Lectures on General Jurisprudence*, it corresponds in important points with Austin's doctrine. It is submitted that where they differ the Pure Theory of Law has carried out the method of analytical jurisprudence more consistently than Austin and his followers have succeeded in doing.[4]

The first part of this assessment alludes to Kelsen's well-known demand that a theory of law ought to meet a double requirement of purity: legal theory must be separated sharply from the theory of justice, which is concerned with what the content of the law ought to be from a moral point of view, as well as from legal sociology, which is concerned with inquiry into the causal effects of legal norms on people's behaviour as well as with inquiry into the causal origins of legal decisions. Only if legal theory submits to this double requirement of purity will it come to offer a

[3] See Stanley Paulson, "Introduction" in Hans Kelsen, *Introduction to the Problems of Legal Theory. A translation of the First Edition of the Reine Rechtslehre or Pure Theory of Law* ed. by and trans. by Bonnie Litschewski Paulson and Stanley L. Paulson (Oxford: Clarendon Press, 1992) xvii at xlii.

[4] Kelsen, "The Pure Theory" *supra* note 1 at 271.

theory of the law itself, and not merely of moral or social phenomena somehow related to law.[5] Elsewhere in his discussion of Austin, Kelsen adds a third requirement: an adequate theory of law must be "a general theory of law, not a presentation or interpretation of a special legal order." The Pure Theory of Law aims to "discover the nature of law itself" from a comparison of "all phenomena which go under the name of law."[6]

Kelsen plausibly assumes that Austin's jurisprudence is committed to the same conception of the aims of legal theory. According to Austin, the purpose of jurisprudence is to "distinguish positive law (…) from the various objects to which it is related by resemblance, and to which it is related, nearly or remotely, by a strong or slender analogy."[7] This project, for Austin, requires a separation of legal theory from the philosophy of justice[8] and it is clearly committed to meeting the requirement of generality put forward by Kelsen. It would seem, moreover, that Austin, though he explains the existence of a legal system as a kind of social fact, is not engaged in the project of offering a legal sociology. Kelsen, then, has good reason to claim that Austinian jurisprudence is committed to the methodological requirements that guide the Pure Theory of Law.

Kelsen argues, however, that Austin violated these methodological requirements in the execution of his jurisprudential project and that he consequently failed to offer a truly positivist legal theory. To see whether Kelsen can substantiate this radical challenge we need to turn to the details of his attack on Austin.

4.3 Kelsen's Rejection of the Command Theory

Kelsen's fundamental attack on Austin takes issue with the view that laws are a species of commands. Kelsen presents three general objections that clearly anticipate Hart's criticism of the command theory.[9]

The first of these objections[10] is based on the claim that if laws are commands, they must be binding or obligatory commands, since law is binding or obligatory. Kelsen observes that Austin appears to agree, as he tries to explain what it means to be obliged or bound by a legal norm. According to Austin, what makes a command binding is the fact that the person to whom it is addressed is liable to be subjected

[5] See Kelsen, *Introduction to the Problems of Legal Theory, supra* note 3 at 7–19.

[6] Kelsen, "The Pure Theory" *supra* note 1 at 266.

[7] John Austin, *The Province of Jurisprudence Determined* ed. by Wilfrid E. Rumble (Cambridge: Cambridge University Press, 1995) at 38.

[8] See *ibid.* at 157–63.

[9] See Hart, *The Concept of Law*, *supra* note 2 at 26–78.

[10] See Kelsen, "The Pure Theory" *supra* note 1 at 272–4; Kelsen, *General Theory*, *supra* note 1 at 30–2.

to a sanction in the case of non-compliance.[11] But this analysis of what it means for a command to be binding, so Kelsen, wrongly identifies the concept of "command" with the concept of "binding command." The mere fact that I threaten to inflict an evil upon you in case you refuse to comply with my wish does not make it the case that you have an obligation to behave as I say. Law, as Hart would later put it, is not the "gunman situation writ large."[12]

A command is binding, according to Kelsen, if and only if the person who issues it is authorized to do so by a normative order that we assume to be binding:

> A command is binding, not because the individual commanding has an actual superiority in power, but because he is "authorized" or "empowered" to issue commands of a binding nature. And he is "authorized" or "empowered" only if a normative order, which is presupposed to be binding, confers on him this capacity, the competence to issue binding commands.[13]

Of course, Hart's theory of the rule of recognition offers an interpretation of what it means for a legal order to be presupposed to be binding that differs radically from Kelsen's theory of the basic norm.[14] Nevertheless, Hart concurs with Kelsen's view that a mandatory directive issued by a public authority will be legally binding only if it can be shown to have been enacted through the exercise of a normative power directly or indirectly conferred by a fundamental rule of legal system that is not itself a command.

Kelsen offers a second criticism of Austin's conception of law as command which resembles Hart's claim that a habit of obedience to a sovereign person must fail to explain the permanence of legal systems.[15] Kelsen argues that a command can exist only for as long as two necessary conditions are met: there must be "an act of will, having somebody else's behaviour as its object, and the expression thereof, by means of words or gestures or other signs."[16] The first of these two conditions is understood by Kelsen as the continuous psychological presence of a wish on the part of the person who issues the command that the addressee behave in a certain way. The fact that someone expressed a wish that I act in a certain way does not ensure the present existence of a command that I act in that way. It must be the case that the person who expressed the wish still wishes me to act in that way. If some person were to give me a command to act in a certain way, and if I came to know, at a later point, that she no longer wishes me to act in that way, I would no longer stand under a command to act in that way.[17]

---

[11] See Austin, *Province*, *supra* note 7 at 22.

[12] Hart, *The Concept of Law*, *supra* note 2 at 80–83.

[13] Kelsen, *General Theory*, *supra* note 1 at 32.

[14] See Hart, *The Concept of Law*, *supra* note 2 at 100–110.

[15] See *ibid*. at 50–66.

[16] Kelsen, *General Theory*, *supra* note 1 at 32.

[17] See *ibid*. at 32.

By contrast, the existence of a legal obligation is not tied to a persistent will on the part of the person or persons who enacted the norm. A statute, unless repealed, will remain binding even after all members of the parliament that enacted it have passed away. It is not even necessary, for the law to come into existence, that there is a shared wish on the part of the members of the legislature that the addressees of the law behave in a certain way at the point of enactment. Most laws, as Kelsen observes, are enacted by legislators who are not even vaguely familiar with their content. What explains the persistence of legal norms is the continuing existence of a system of norms of which the enacted norm has come to form a part.[18] This of course entails that, in Kelsen's view, no law is a command, since no law's persistence is grounded in a continuing psychological wish on the part of some person or group of persons that someone else behave in a certain way.

Once again anticipating themes in Hart's critique of Austin, Kelsen admits, finally, that some laws may indeed bear a certain resemblance to commands, in the sense that they are, at least at the point of initial enactment, based on a wish of a superior in power that inferiors in power behave in a certain way. However, such resemblance does not hold true of all legal norms. A particular legal norm created through contract, for example, is as binding and authoritative on the parties as a general statutory norm. But it makes no sense to say that the parties to a contract have given themselves a command to act in a certain way. Such disanalogies between laws and commands are not limited to the sphere of contractual norms. Customary norms or democratically enacted laws cannot reasonably be interpreted as commands given by superiors to inferiors.[19] The command theory, Kelsen therefore argues, provides a thoroughly misleading picture of the structure and functions of the legal order.

4.4 Austin and Kelsen on Legal Duties and the Structure of Legal Norms

According to Kelsen, Austin's mistaken view that laws are a species of commands, apart from being wrong in itself, leads to an inadequate treatment of a number of central jurisprudential problems. Kelsen focuses on two major issues: first, Austin's conception of law, Kelsen argues, entails a misrepresentation of the notion of a legal duty. Second, Austin's conception makes it impossible, so Kelsen, to develop an adequate conception of the state and of its relation to law, including its relation to international law. In this section, I will discuss the first of these two points.

[18] See *ibid.* at 32–34.

[19] See *ibid.* at 34–37.

To understand Kelsen's criticism of Austin's conception of legal duty, we must take a brief look at Kelsen's analysis of legal duty, which is tied to his understanding of the structure of legal norms. According to Kelsen, a legal norm makes certain behaviour (the "delict") into the normative condition of the application of a sanction. A jurisprudential statement describing a legal norm states that if a person engages in behaviour the law has qualified as a delict, then a sanction ought to be applied in the way provided for by the law. So understood, legal norms do not, like commands, directly address themselves to those whose behaviour is to be guided by the law. Rather, legal norms are addressed to those who are to execute the sanction that the law determines ought to follow the delict. They authorize the application of a sanction on the condition that a delict has been committed.[20]

This conception of the structure of legal norms and of legal duty needs to be understood in the context of Kelsen's account of the function of legal order. Especially during the 1940s, while he was engaging with Austin, Kelsen vigorously defended the view that any legal system must necessarily claim a monopoly of the legitimate use of force in the society it purports to govern.[21] Wherever there is a legal system, the use of violence is permissible, from the legal point of view, only if it is legally authorized, as a sanction that responds to a prior delict. Any legally unauthorized use of violence is itself a delict that ought to be followed by a sanction. In this way, every legal system, Kelsen claims, provides a comprehensive regulation of the use of force among its subjects, thus securing social peace.

Though legal norms are not directly addressed to the subjects of the law, they entail legal duties that typically fall on potential delinquents (and not on those who apply the law): subjects of the law are under a legal duty to avoid the commission of the delict that a law has made into the normative condition of the application of a sanction. What it means to say that I have a legal duty to do x or to forbear from x is that the law determines that if I do not do x or do not forbear from x a sanction ought to be applied. Given the claim that every legal system provides a comprehensive regulation of the use of force, we arrive at the implication that wherever there is a legal system, all human beings who are subject to that system have a legal duty to abstain from all uses of force that have not been legally authorized.

Kelsen's view of the structure of legal norms implies that, strictly speaking, there are no laws that mandate performance of legal duty. If we wanted to say that the law mandates performance of legal duty, Kelsen claims, we would have to picture the structure of legal norms in a different way. We would have to separate the Kelsenian norm into two separate norms, one of which mandates performance of duty, while the other imposes a sanction in the case of non-performance of duty. Kelsen admits

[20] See Kelsen, *Introduction to the Problems of Legal Theory*, *supra* note 3 at 26–32; Kelsen, *General Theory*, *supra* note 1 at 30–58.

[21] See for example Kelsen, *General Theory*, *supra* note 1 at 21–23; Hans Kelsen, *Peace Through Law* (Chapel Hill, NC: University of North Carolina Press, 1944) at 3; Hans Kelsen, *Principles of International Law* (New York: Rinehart & Company, 1952) at 13–5, 17–8.

that such separation may be practically useful since the "the representation is of law is greatly facilitated."[22] But he holds that it is nothing more than a pragmatic device. From the point of view of legal science, Kelsen claims, "law is the primary norm, which stipulates the sanction" (*ibid.*) and it is "only the sanction [that] ought to be executed."[23]

Let us now turn to Kelsen's criticism of Austin's conception of legal duty. At first glance, Austin's conception would appear to be rather similar to Kelsen's. After all, Austin claims that "being liable to evil from you if I comply not with a wish which you signify, I am bound or obliged by your command, or I lie under a duty to obey it."[24] But the appearance of similarity is misleading. Austin's view that laws are commands clearly understands laws as commands addressed to the subjects of the law, that is, as laws that mandate performance of legal duty. Hence, Austin is committed to the view, according to Kelsen, that the norm that mandates performance of legal duty is really the primary or fundamental form of a law. A law is a command issued by a superior to an inferior to behave or not to behave in a certain way. But this view, Kelsen argues, is inconsistent with the idea that to have a legal duty is to be liable to sanction:

> If, as Austin presumes, the legal duty is a consequence of the sanction, then the behaviour which it is our legal duty to observe cannot be identical with the behaviour which the legal norm commands. What is commanded can only be the sanction. The legal norm does not stipulate the behaviour which forms the legal duty. (…) It is because the legal norm attaches a certain sanction to a certain behaviour that the opposite behaviour becomes a legal duty. Austin, however, presents the matter as if the legal norm, by him called "command," prescribed the behaviour which forms the legal duty. Thereby, he contradicts his own definition of legal duty. In Austin's command there is no room for the sanction. And yet it is only by means of the sanction that the command is obligating.[25]

Kelsen's argument here seems to rely on the assumption that if what it means to have a legal duty is to be liable to a sanction then the law that gives rise to the duty must be a norm that determines the conditions under which the sanction ought to be applied. But in this case, the law must take the form of the Kelsenian legal norm, and this implies that it cannot take the form of a command addressed to the subject of the law to perform the legal duty. Hence, the theory that legal norms are commands addressed to the subjects of the law is incompatible with the view that to violate a duty is to fulfil the conditions under which a sanction ought to be applied. If one wants to hold on to the latter view, Kelsen concludes, one must reject the command theory and individuate laws his way.

An Austinian might well ask why it should be impossible for a sovereign command to be phrased as a conditional of the form "Do x, or I will sanction you," *i.e.* as a threat to subjects that they will be punished in case they fail to exhibit the

[22] Kelsen, *General Theory*, *supra* note 1 at 61.

[23] *Ibid.* at 60.

[24] Austin, *Province*, *supra* note 7 at 22.

[25] Kelsen, *General Theory*, *supra* note 1 at 62.

behaviour desired by the sovereign. What is commanded, in that case, is the performance of legal duty, not the application of the sanction. But there clearly is room for a sanction in Austin's command, so understood.[26] A reconstruction that conceives of the legal norm as a threat of punishment directed to subjects seems to be needed, in any case, to explain why legal duty is a consequence of the sanction. If the threat that one will be sanctioned if one does not do x is credible and the potential sanction sufficiently severe, one has a conclusive reason to do x, which would account for the motivating force of legal duty. And why would one want to claim that to have a duty is to be obnoxious to a sanction unless one were interested in accounting for the bindingness of legal duty in this way?

Though the claim that Austin's theory of legal duty is incoherent since Austinian commands cannot make reference to a sanction would appear to fail, it is not too difficult to see how Kelsen's view of legal norm and legal duty differs from Austin's. For Kelsen, the reason why I have a legal duty to do x is that the law determines that a sanction *ought* to be applied if I do not do x. In other words, that I have a legal duty to do x means that the application of a sanction will be legally justified if I do not do x. Strictly speaking, the Kelsenian norm that determines that a sanction ought to be applied if I do not do x is not a command. It is an authorization to officials to apply a sanction in reaction to a delict.[27] And this authorization is not valid because it was issued by a person or group of persons with the *de facto* power to compel the obedience of those who are to execute it. Rather, it is valid because it was in enacted in accordance with legislative procedures themselves validated by a basic norm. For Austin, by contrast, the reason I have a duty to do x is that I can expect that I *will be* harmed by the sovereign if I do not do x. In an Austinian framework, the question whether the sovereign or his representatives are permitted or authorized to harm me by applying a sanction simply does not arise.

The real problem with Austin's conception of legal duty, from a Kelsenian perspective, then, is not that it is incompatible with any coherent version of the view that legal norms must include sanctions. The real problem for Kelsen is that Austin's conception is incompatible with the idea that wherever there is law *all* legitimate uses of force must be legally authorized. Kelsen's claim that legal norms, in their primary form, determine the conditions under which sanctions ought to be applied is rooted in the view that what the law does, first and foremost, is to authorize the use of force in a society, in the form of sanctions that react to prior delicts, and to criminalize all use of force not so authorized. This conception of legal order is the polar opposite of the Austinian view that the law is the expression of a *de facto* power that is not itself authorized by the law to produce law and that, one presumes, may consequently exercise force with impunity even where it is not yet legally

[26] Austin, *Province*, *supra* note 7 at 21 defines command as follows: "If you express or intimate a wish that I shall do or forbear from some act, and if you will visit me with an evil in case I comply not with your wish, the expression or intimation of your wish is a command."

[27] See Kelsen, "The Pure Theory" *supra* note 1 at 275–76.

authorized to do so. According to Kelsen, by contrast, prior legal authorization is required to turn any use of force into an exercise of public power in the first place.[28]

This fundamental difference between Austin and Kelsen seems to have been lost on Hart. Hart discusses Kelsen's claim that "law is the primary norm, which stipulates the sanction" and that it is "only the sanction [that] ought to be executed"[29] as though it were an attempt to salvage the Austinian view that all laws are orders to subjects backed by threats. Hart agrees with Kelsen that it is possible to present a legal system as a system of norms that determine the conditions for the application of a sanction. But he denies that there could be any reason so to present the law once one comes to acknowledge the inadequacy of the view that all laws are coercive orders to the subjects of the law. Kelsen's conception of the structure of legal norms, Hart concludes, lacks an adequate jurisprudential motivation: it expresses a misguided urge for the greatest possible degree of theoretical uniformity and simplicity, an urge that distorts and unduly simplifies our perception of legal phenomena.[30]

At the very least, this assessment is uncharitable. It overlooks that Kelsen's adherence to the view that all legal norms, in their primary form, are conditionals authorizing the application of force is a way of making Hart's point that one cannot assimilate legal governance to the gunman situation writ large. To be sure, Kelsen's conception of the structure of legal norms, in contrast to Hart's, attempts to reduce all legal norms to one and the same form, by interpreting power-conferring secondary norms as parts of norms that provide authorization for the application of sanctions. But this move is not tied to the questionable assumption that law must be backed up by an un-commanded commander superior in *de facto* power to the subjects of the law, it is tied to its rejection.

What is more, Kelsen's conception of the structure of legal norms clearly has room to accommodate Hart's emphasis on the fact that law empowers individuals to shape their normative situation, instead of merely subjecting them to the will of a political superior. There is no reason, from Kelsen's point of view, why the law should not empower its individual subjects to participate, either as democratic citizens or as private contractors, in determining the conditions under which sanctions ought to be applied.

Finally, though Kelsen argues that legal norms are conditionals that authorize the application of sanctions, and that legal duties are duties not to perform acts that, according to the law, ought to trigger a sanction, he rejects the idea that the fear of being sanctioned is the typical motive for compliance with a legal duty. According to Kelsen, people conform to the law for all kinds of reasons, including moral

[28] Kelsen, *General Theory, supra* note 1 at 36: "That is the authority of the law, above the individual persons who are commanded and who command. This idea that the binding force of the law emanates, not from any commanding human being, but from the impersonal anonymous 'command' as such, is expressed in the famous words *non sub homine, sed sub lege*."

[29] Kelsen, *General Theory, supra* note 1 at 60.

[30] See Hart, *The Concept of Law*, *supra* note 2 at 35–42, and more recently Scott Shapiro, *Legality* (Cambridge, MA: Harvard University Press, 2011) at 66–68.

beliefs, patriotic attitudes, or theological convictions. While a legal system can only exist if it passes a threshold of efficacy, the fear of sanction usually only plays a minor role in motivating compliance with law. Kelsen's interest in sanctions, then, is not based on the assumption that the psychological fear of punishment is needed to explain the bindingness of law.[31] It is based, rather, on the view that the fundamental point of legal order is to comprehensively determine the conditions of the legitimacy of the use of force in a society.

The seeming equivalence in Austin's and Kelsen's conceptions of the structure of legal norms and of legal duty thus dissolves on closer inspection. The Pure Theory should not be dismissed on the ground, implied by Hart, that the weaknesses that afflict the command theory likewise afflict Kelsen's conception of the structure of legal norms.

It should be admitted, however, that the defence of the Pure Theory's conception of the structure of legal norms just offered does not suffice to put Hartian worries about Kelsen's conception of the structure of legal norms fully to rest. Even if it is acknowledged that the picture of legal order given by Kelsen differs as radically from the idea that law is the gunman situation writ large as Hart's, one might still argue that Kelsen's claim that all complete legal norms provide conditions for the application of sanctions lacks adequate motivation. The pluralist approach to the individuation of legal norms we find in Hart, after all, equally avoids the obvious shortcomings of the command theory, and it is arguably capable of greater descriptive nuance.

As we have seen, Kelsen's conception of the structure of legal norms is based on the view that any legal system must necessarily claim to provide a comprehensive regulation of the legitimate use of force in some society, in order to be able to help to realize the value of social peace. The key question in the dispute between Kelsen and Hart, then, is whether we should accept Kelsen's view of the essential purpose of legal order. If we do, we ought to acknowledge, as Kelsen himself did not, that the Pure Theory of Law is driven by a normative ambition, and that it cannot be defended on purely descriptive grounds.

4.5 Austin, Kelsen, and the Illimitability of Sovereign Power

The second major strand of Kelsen's criticism of the implications of the command theory takes issue with Austin's view that a legally illimitable sovereign is essential to the existence of a legal system as well as with the denial of international law. In both cases, the command theory turns out to be too constraining, Kelsen argues, to allow for a descriptively adequate account of legal phenomena. While this is undoubtedly true, Kelsen's development of the point betrays a normative agenda implicit in the Pure Theory of Law.

[31] See Kelsen, "The Pure Theory" *supra* note 1 at 274–76.

Austin's claim that sovereign power is legally illimitable is a straightforward implication of the command theory.[32] If what it means to be subject to law is to pay habitual obedience to the sanction-backed command of a sovereign who does not pay obedience to anyone else, a sovereign cannot possibly be subject to legal limitation. Since there must be a sovereign power wherever there is law, every legal order necessarily presupposes a legally illimitable sovereign. Kelsen, in response, rather brusquely observes:

> This concept of the sovereign is sociological or political, but not juristic (…). This is difficult to reconcile with the theoretic method of analytical jurisprudence, which derives its concepts only from an analysis of positive law. In the norms of positive law no such thing as a "sovereign," a person or group "incapable of legal limitation," can be found. The central difficulty is that the jurisprudence of Austin, while it deals with the concept of the sovereign which is not the state but only an organ of the state, does not concern itself at all with the problem of the state itself.[33]

Kelsen gives little further explanation, in his discussion of Austin, of what it means for a concept of sovereignty to be sociological or political and not juristic.[34] It seems clear, however, that he would accept the following as at least a partial description of his claim: the existence, in a society, of a person or group of persons who are habitually obeyed but who do not pay habitual obedience to anyone else is nothing more than a social fact. And the social fact that some person or group of persons is habitually obeyed without paying obedience to anyone else simply does not entail that that person or group of persons is authorized to enact legal norms. Austin's concept of sovereignty is therefore jurisprudentially irrelevant, as it misrepresents the nature and sources of legal authority.

This much would presumably find the support of other positivist critics of the command theory. However, Kelsen does not just claim that we cannot identify someone's having legal authority with his receiving *de facto* obedience. This mistaken identification, Kelsen suggests, is the result of a general methodological error, namely of the tendency to confuse legal and sociological categories. Kelsen holds that legal norms exist in the mode of validity. They do not determine that something will happen given such and such conditions, but rather that something ought to be done, given such and such conditions.[35] Since it is impossible to derive an "ought" from an "is," the validity of a legal norm, Kelsen argues, can only be grounded in another legal norm that authorized its creation. Ultimately, all norms must draw

[32] See Austin, *Province*, *supra* note 7 at 212.

[33] Kelsen, "The Pure Theory" *supra* note 1 at 281.

[34] See *ibid.* at 269–71. Kelsen offers an exhaustive discussion of the relation of the Pure Theory to the sociology of law and state in Hans Kelsen, *Der soziologische und der juristische Staatsbegriff. Kritische Untersuchung des Verhältnisses von Staat und Recht* (Tübingen, FRG: J.C.B. Mohr/ Paul Siebeck, 1928).

[35] See Kelsen, "The Pure Theory" *supra* note 1 at 267–78; Kelsen, *General Theory, supra* note 1 at 30.

their validity from a basic norm that directly or indirectly authorizes the creation of all other legal norms and that must be presupposed to be valid.[36] Kelsen elsewhere concludes from this line of argument that any attempt to ground the existence of law in any kind of social fact must fail.[37]

I do not intend to offer a discussion of the merits of Kelsen's theory of the basic norm in this paper. But I think we can make the following observation: the failure of the view that to have legal authority is to receive *de facto* obedience does not suffice to show that any legal theory that attempts to ground the existence of law in social fact must fail, at least not if it is possible to develop a theory of law that grounds the existence of law in social fact and that is at the same time free of the obvious descriptive deficiencies of the command theory. If it is possible to develop such a theory, as Hart has clearly shown, then Kelsen has not established that the fact that Austin tried to ground the existence of law in social fact is the cause of the apparent descriptive inadequacy of his view. And if this has not been established, the failure of Austin's view provides no warrant for summarily rejecting all theories that try to explain the existence of law in terms of social fact.

Similar problems afflict Kelsen's claim that Austin's conception of sovereignty violates the "theoretical method of analytical jurisprudence," which Kelsen takes to consist in deriving legal-theoretical concepts from an analysis of the positive law, and the positive law only. That Austin violates this methodological prescription, Kelsen thinks, follows from the fact that we find no such thing as a sovereign with legally illimitable powers "in the norms of the positive law."[38] An office or institution will be in the norms of positive law, presumably, on the condition that the norms of positive law explicitly provide for that office or institution, by endowing it with a certain legislative authority. Needless to say, that an illimitable sovereignty is not in the norms of positive law would not have surprised or embarrassed Austin. Austin's claim that there must be a sovereign wherever there is law is surely not to be understood as a claim about the content of the positive law. It is a claim about the essential features of law as a social institution.[39] To go on to argue, as Kelsen does, that we must, for methodological reasons, reject any theory of the nature of law that makes reference to something which is not in the content of the norms of the positive law takes us back to the impasse we already encountered. We have not been shown that Austin's theory fails for the methodological reason that it makes reference to a social fact that is not in the content of the law.

---

[36] See Kelsen, *General Theory*, *supra* note 1 at 110–11; Kelsen, *Introduction to the Problems of Legal Theory*, *supra* note 3 at 59–62.

[37] See the discussion of Max Weber's legal theory in Kelsen, *Der soziologische und der juristische Staatsbegriff*, *supra* note 34, at 156–70. For a (qualified) defence of Kelsen's rejection of sociological jurisprudence see Joseph Raz, "The Purity of the Pure Theory" in Joseph Raz, *The Authority of Law. Essays on Law and Morality* (2nd ed., Oxford: Oxford University Press, 2009) at 293.

[38] Kelsen, "The Pure Theory" *supra* note 1 at 281.

[39] See Austin, *Province*, *supra* note 7 at 164–83, 211–23.

Can Kelsen's argument be strengthened if we focus on the substantive claim that Austin's legal theory "does not concern itself at all with the problem of the state?"[40] Kelsen's development of this claim is rather brief and somewhat difficult to follow.[41] But his line of thought seems to be this: a sovereign can at best be an organ of the state. A sovereign, after all, acts in the name of the state or as a representative of the state. An organ of state, however, can wield authority in the name of the state only on the basis of some legal authorization. The idea of authorization, in turn, implies limitation, or at least limitability, since it entails that the organ that stands under authorization lacks the legal power to do what it has not been legally authorized to do. Since the state, as a legal person, can act only through its organs, the state's authority is identical to the legal authority of its organs. Neither the powers of the state itself nor those of any of its representatives can be essentially illimitable.[42]

Austin's jurisprudence, according to Kelsen, lacks the resources to arrive at this insight since it did not develop a legal concept of the state. To be sure, Austin uses the concept of an "independent political society,"[43] but this concept is itself analyzed in terms of the brute fact of habitual obedience to sovereign power. Austin cannot, therefore, conceive of the sovereign as an organ of state or of the state as a legal person that must act through its authorized representatives.[44]

Our assessment of this criticism will have to depend on what exactly Kelsen takes himself to have shown here. One way to read Kelsen's argument is to take it to focus on the role of the sovereign in the constitution of a legal system. On this reading, Kelsen simply argues that a sovereign's decisions can only have legislative effects if there already is a legal rule that empowers the sovereign to legislate. This principle denies that a legal norm could be the product of a legally unauthorized and legally illimitable sovereign and thus suffices to reject Austin's conception of the role of sovereignty in the constitution of law. The problem with this interpretation, it seems, is that it can be endorsed by the Hartian theorist who wants to base the validity of laws on the existence of a rule of recognition (that is a matter of social fact).[45] Kelsen, then, still has not shown that the failure of Austin's theory of sovereignty establishes that the Pure Theory is its only feasible alternative.

However, Kelsen is clearly after something more than just the claim that Austin's theory of sovereignty fails as a theory of legal system when he says that the central difficulty of Austin's jurisprudence is that the latter does not concern itself with the problem of the state. Kelsen does not just argue that an act of state must have legal authorization in order to have legislative effects. He makes the far stronger claim

---

[40] Kelsen, "The Pure Theory" *supra* note 1 at 281.

[41] See *ibid.* at 278–83.

[42] For a more detailed development of these themes see Kelsen, *General Theory, supra* note 1 at 181–207; Kelsen, *Der soziologische und der juristische Staatsbegriff*, *supra* note 34 at 114–204.

[43] See Austin, *Province*, *supra* note 7 at 165–83.

[44] See Kelsen, "The Pure Theory" *supra* note 1 at 280–1.

[45] But see Hart, *The Concept of Law*, *supra* note 2 at 144–50.

that it is inconceivable for the state to act in legally unauthorized ways since the state and its legal order are identical.[46] In Kelsen's view, no purported act of state qualifies as a genuine act of state if the organ in question, in performing that act, exceeds the bounds of its legally determined authority. And if a purported act of state that lacks proper authorization involves a use of force or coercion it will inevitably constitute a criminal act that is itself subject to a legally determined sanction, for the reason that any legal order, in Kelsen's view, must outlaw all unauthorized use of force.[47]

This conception of the relation of law and state has consequences that seem to set it apart from the Hartian rejection of the theory of sovereignty. One way to bring out the difference is to consider Locke's conception of powers of prerogative. Locke defines the power of prerogative as the power "to act according to discretion, for the publick good, without the prescription of the Law, and sometimes even against it."[48] In Locke's view, a state (or its executive) can legitimately claim this power regardless of whether the positive law makes reference to it or not. Since the state is an association formed to pursue and protect the public good, the state must have the power to pursue and protect the public good without legal authorization and in violation of existing legal norms, should this turn out be necessary.[49]

It would appear that one can support the Hartian rejection of Austin's theory of sovereignty as a theory of legal system while acknowledging the existence and perhaps the legitimacy of a state's power of prerogative. A power of prerogative, in the Lockean view, is not a legislative power, a power to enact legal duties or to confer legal rights. Rather, it is a power to engage in the *de facto* action that is judged necessary to avert some imminent threat to the public good. Such action may involve the use of coercive force on the part of the state against certain individual persons, but not as legal punishment or sanction. It should therefore be possible for a Lockean to agree with the claim that the state's decisions can never have legislative effect unless they are legally authorized (and thus to reject the idea that the legal system is constituted by a legally unauthorized sovereign power) and yet to refuse to restrict the state's legitimate power to the making and the execution of law.

---

[46] Kelsen, "The Pure Theory" *supra* note 1 at 281: "One of the distinctive results of the Pure Theory of Law is its recognition that the coercive order which constitutes the political community we call 'state' is a legal order. What is usually called 'the legal order of the state,' or 'the legal order set up by the state' is the state itself." See also Kelsen, *Introduction to the Problems of Legal Theory, supra* note 3 at 97–106. For critical discussion of Kelsen's thesis of the identity of law and state see Joseph Raz, "The Identity of Legal Systems" in Raz, *The Authority of Law*, *supra* note 37 at 97–102 and François Tanguay-Renaud, "The Intelligibility of Extralegal State Action: A General Lesson for Debates on Public Emergencies and Legality" (2010) 16 *Legal Theory* 161. A recent defence in Alexander Somek, "Stateless Law: Kelsen's Conception and its Limits" (2006) 26 *Oxford Journal of Legal Studies* 753.

[47] See *supra* note 21.

[48] John Locke, *Two Treatises of Government* ed. by Peter Laslett (Cambridge: Cambridge University Press, 1988) at 375.

[49] See *ibid.* at 374–80.

Kelsen, by contrast, is committed to denying that there can be such a thing as a power of prerogative (though he will admit, of course, that it is possible to make legal provision for situations of emergency or for the preventative use of force). According to the theorist of prerogative, an exercise of the power of prerogative is an official use of force that does not take the form of a sanction in reaction to a prior delict authorized by an already existing legal norm. But Kelsen insists, as we have seen, that wherever there is a legal order, all uses of force must either fall into the category of legally authorized sanction or into the category of sanctionable delict. The view that this alternative applies only to the acts of individual subjects of the law but not (or not necessarily) to acts of state is precisely the kind of authoritarian fiction to which Kelsen – arguing against the likes of Carl Schmitt[50] – wanted to provide the jurisprudential antidote.[51]

Kelsen's willingness to concern himself with the problem of the state, then, sets his view apart from Hart's. Kelsen is as anxious to show that we cannot coherently conceive of the state in terms of social fact as he is to show that we cannot coherently conceive of law in terms of social fact. If it were possible to conceive of the state in terms of social fact, we would, presumably, have to let go of the view that legally unauthorized uses of force can never be attributed to the state and must always be regarded as punishable delicts. Kelsen's claim that the state is identical to its legal order and that public officials cannot use force without legal authorization would fail. Hence Kelsen's refusal to limit his criticism of Austin to the claim that Austin invoked the wrong kind of social fact to explain the existence of law.

The Hartian positivist is likely to object that it is unclear why a positivist and purely descriptive theory of legal system must at the same time be or directly imply a full theory of the state, or why a theory of the state must be committed to a normative, as opposed to a descriptive, sociological perspective. Surely, Kelsen's theory of the state and its relation to law is not forced upon us as a result of the failure of Austin's theory of sovereignty as an account of legal system. One might suspect that Kelsen's conception of the relationship between the state and the law results from a moral valuation of the rule of law that puts further pressure on the claim that the Pure Theory is a purely descriptive legal science.

[50] Schmitt identified the view that all public authority must rest on legal authorization as the core tenet of liberal constitutionalism and emphatically rejected it. See Carl Schmitt, *Constitutional Theory* ed. by and trans. by Jeffrey Seitzer (Durham, NC: Duke University Press, 2008) at 62–66, 169–80.

[51] It may be objected that the contrast I am trying to draw here is undermined by Kelsen's view that the law formally authorizes even acts of state that constitute material violations of the law. See Stanley L. Paulson, "Material and Formal Authorization in Kelsen's Pure Theory" (1980) 39 *Cambridge Law Journal* 172. For a reply see Lars Vinx, *Hans Kelsen's Pure Theory of Law. Legality and Legitimacy* (Oxford: Oxford University Press, 2007) at 78–100.

4.6 Austin, Kelsen, and the Status of International Law

Austin's model of sovereignty carries the implication that international law is not proper law. If all laws are commands issued by sovereigns to subjects, and if it is essential to sovereignty that a sovereign does not himself stand under someone else's command, there can be no "proper" law that regulates relationships between sovereigns.[52] Kelsen argues that this view of the nature of international law is plainly inadequate. No jurisprudence that aims for descriptive adequacy should deny legal quality to international law on purely definitional grounds.[53]

The Pure Theory holds that the existence of genuine international law is not ruled out by the nature of law. The rules of international law exhibit the standard structure of legal norms in that they provide the conditions under which sanctions (war, reprisal) ought to be applied against a delinquent state. There is no reason to think that the norms of international law could not form a genuine legal system. For that to happen, Kelsen argues, the norms of international law must come to provide a comprehensive regulation of the legitimate use of force among states. All use of force among states must come to fall either into the category of international delict or the category of international sanction. If such a development is possible, and possible without the establishment of a highly centralized global political authority that does away with the independence of states, there is no reason to think that there could never be true international law.[54]

Kelsen admits that it is questionable whether international law can be said to have reached this stage of development. Some states still claim the right to use force at their own discretion, and not just in reaction to a prior delict, to protect what they see as their vital interests. If one does not recognize international law as providing a comprehensive regulation of the use of force between states, Kelsen argues, one must conceive of international legal norms as having validity only within national legal systems that have chosen to adopt them. Under such a view, international law cannot be said to exist as a legal order in its own right. Both approaches are, for the time being, jurisprudentially feasible. International law is presently in a transitional stage of development. It has clearly already developed into something more than mere international morality, but it arguably has not yet unambiguously taken on all the characteristic features of a fully developed legal order. The legal theorist thus has to choose whether to adopt the national or the international perspective in describing international law.[55]

---

[52] See Austin, *Province*, *supra* note 7 at 123–5, 171.

[53] See Kelsen, "The Pure Theory" *supra* note 1 at 283–87.

[54] Kelsen, *Principles of International Law, supra* note 21 at 18: "International law is law in the same sense as national law, provided that it is, in principle, possible to interpret the employment of force directed by one state against another either as sanction or as delict." See also Kelsen, *General Theory, supra* note 1 at 328–41.

[55] See Kelsen, *General Theory*, *supra* note 1 at 376–88; Kelsen, *Introduction to the Problems of Legal Theory, supra* note 3 at 111–25.

Kelsen does not deny that a jurist's choice of perspective is likely to be conditioned by judgements of value, and in particular by his sympathy, or lack thereof, for the ideal of a cosmopolitan legal order that has supremacy over national legal orders. He certainly does not hide his own sympathies for the cosmopolitan option.[56] However, the Pure Theory as a legal science, Kelsen argues, cannot make judgements of value, and it therefore cannot claim that only one of the two perspectives, but not the other, is scientifically legitimate.[57] Nevertheless, Kelsen is anxious to deny scientific respectability to the view that an international lawyer, in describing international law, can avoid to choose between the cosmopolitan and the national perspective. Some legal theorists, Kelsen observes, while they want to hold that international law is genuine law, also want to hold that international law does not have to possess or to claim supremacy over national law. They argue instead "that national law and international law are two completely distinct and mutually independent systems of norms, like positive law and morality."[58]

Kelsen is opposed to this legal-pluralist view in part because he sympathizes with legal cosmopolitanism and thinks that it would be detrimental to the cause of cosmopolitanism if international lawyers were to convince themselves that the choice between national or international supremacy can somehow be avoided.[59] To hold that we need not answer the question of supremacy, Kelsen thinks, is a way of denying international law's claim to be the only legitimate basis for the international use of force, and thus of denying its status as proper law, while avoiding the argumentative burdens that would attach to an explicit denial of international law. Of course, this criticism of legal pluralism presupposes that the question of supremacy is indeed jurisprudentially unavoidable. To defend this assumption, Kelsen argues that any form of legal pluralism is logically incoherent:

> The Pure Theory of Law shows that such a dualistic concept of the relation between national and international law is logically impossible (…). If one assumes that two systems of norms are considered as valid simultaneously from the same point of view, one must also assume a normative relation between them; one must assume the existence of a norm or order that regulates their mutual relations. Otherwise insoluble contradictions between the norms of each system are unavoidable, and the logical principle that excludes contradictions holds for the cognition of norms as much as for the cognition of natural reality. (…) But once it is conceded that national and international law are both positive law, it is obvious that both must be considered as valid simultaneously from the same juristic point of view. For this reason, they must belong to the same system of norms, they must in some way supplement each other.[60]

[56] See for a general account of Kelsen's theory of international law that rightly stresses Kelsen's sympathies for cosmopolitanism Jochen von Bernstorff, *The Public International Law Theory of Hans Kelsen: Believing in Universal Law* (Cambridge: Cambridge University Press, 2010).

[57] See Kelsen, *General Theory, supra* note 1 at 388.

[58] Kelsen, "The Pure Theory" *supra* note 1 at 284.

[59] See Hans Kelsen, *Das Problem der Souveränität und die Theorie des Völkerrechts. Beitrag zu einer Reinen Rechtslehre* (Tübingen, FRG: J.C.B. Mohr/ Paul Siebeck, 1920) at 314–20.

[60] Kelsen, "The Pure Theory" *supra* note 1 at 284.

The supplementation that Kelsen talks about in the last sentence of this quote can only take two forms: either national legal systems must form subordinate parts of one global legal system which determines their competence and provides their ground of validity, or international law must be conceived as part of the national legal system whose perspective the legal theorist has chosen to adopt. This is Kelsen's famous legal monism. Regardless of which point of view we adopt, all valid law must turn out to belong to one and the same legal system.[61]

It should not occasion surprise that this radical claim has not found universal favour with later legal theorists.[62] Kelsen's argument for legal monism appears to rest on two independent claims. The first is that it is impossible for a legal system to contain norms that make contradictory demands on the behaviour of the subjects of the law. The second is that all valid (or, what amounts to the same thing, all existing) law must be described from the same point of view and thus form part of the same legal system.

The first of these two claims would appear to be less intuitively implausible than the second. While it may not be clear why it should be logically impossible for a system of positive law to contain legal norms that make contradictory demands, a legal system containing such contradictory norms clearly is a bad legal system, even from a positivist point of view, insofar as it fails to provide behavioural guidance. And it is therefore unsurprising that actually existing legal systems invariably tend to contain rules of precedence for the solution of such conflicts.

Be this as it may, Kelsen's second claim appears to be so problematic as to make his argument indefensible. It may be true that legal norms that are considered as valid simultaneously and from the same point of view must have some normative relationship to each other; if not as a matter of logic, then in order to allow the law to provide effective guidance. But it is much harder to understand how it follows from the fact that national and international law are both positive law that they must both be considered as valid from the same point of view (or put more generally, how it follows from the fact that two norms a and b are norms of positive law that they must belong to the same legal system).

Kelsen's own explanations of the point are based on the view that legal norms exist in the mode of validity. What it means for a legal norm to exist is for it to be the case that a sanction ought to be applied to certain behaviour the norm specifies as a delict.[63] But it cannot be true that, according to the law, a sanction ought to be applied to some behaviour and that a sanction ought not to be applied to that behaviour. Hence, if there are two legal norms that make conflicting demands, the law

---

[61] See *ibid.* at 284–85.

[62] See for important criticisms: Herbert L. A. Hart, "Kelsen's Doctrine of the Unity of Law" in H. L. A. Hart, *Essays in Jurisprudence and Philosophy* (Oxford: Clarendon Press, 1983) at 309; Joseph Raz, *The Concept of Legal System. An Introduction to the Theory of Legal System* (Oxford: Oxford University Press, 1970) at 95–109. A qualified defence of Kelsen's monism is offered in Vinx, *Hans Kelsen's Pure Theory of Law, supra* note 51.

[63] See Kelsen, "The Pure Theory" *supra* note 1 at 267–68.

must contain provisions to solve the conflict, and these will ensure that both norms are normatively related and thus form part of the same system.[64] This reasoning, it would appear, already assumes what is to be shown, namely that both norms are part of the same legal system. That there must be a normative relation between two norms if they are valid from the same point of view does not show that all legal norms must be valid from the same point of view.

A Kelsenian might reply that positive legal theory is concerned to provide a description of what people ought to do, according to the law, and not to record the social facts that underpin the existence of legal systems. To perform this task, the legal theorist must inevitably choose to take the perspective of a particular legal system and tell us what ought to be done according to that perspective. But from any such perspective there will only ever be one legal system, since all the laws that bear on what one ought to do, from the chosen perspective, must stand in some normative relation.

Even if we grant this point it is unclear why the legal theorist should not also adopt an external perspective of social fact, to observe that there seem to be several legal systems or different normative points of view which appear to contain differing sets of legal norms. The counter that positivist legal theory ought to refrain from adopting such a perspective to preserve its scientific purity is open to the objection that it will then be unable to speak about a number of important features of law: it will not be able to make sense of the apparent plurality of legal systems, and it will fail to explain to us what distinguishes one from the other. These would surely be grave deficiencies in a theory of law that aims for descriptive adequacy and generality.

As in the case of the identity of law and state, however, Kelsen's assumptions about the essential normative purpose of legal order seem to provide an alternative motivation for the monist approach. If it is true, as Kelsen argues, that any legal system must claim a monopoly of force, since the essential purpose of law is to preserve social peace, then international law must claim a global monopoly of force. And this claim clearly would conflict with any claim on the part of a national legal order to provide a supreme and self-sufficient regulation of the conditions under which its organs are authorized to apply coercive force. What is more, this conflict would not be a mere theoretical conflict. It would be a conflict that must be resolved on a practical level. Since a legal system, according to Kelsen, can only exist if it meets a threshold of effectiveness,[65] the existence of international law will require a sufficiently successful factual suppression of uses of force that challenge international law's monopoly of force. Hence, the question of supremacy of national or international law is indeed unavoidable. Not for logical reasons, but for the reason that two competing claims to a monopoly of force in the same territory cannot both be successful.

[64] See Kelsen, *Introduction to the Problems of Legal Theory, supra* note 3 at 111–12.

[65] See *ibid.* at 59–63.

The Hartian positivist is likely to respond that the question of supremacy becomes unavoidable, then, only because Kelsen's conception of legal system is laden with excess baggage that has no place in a purely descriptive theory of law. Kelsen's argument, while being critical of Austin's conception of sovereignty, imports some traditional attributes of the sovereign state, such as the claim to a monopoly of coercive force in a specific territory or the essential function of securing peace, into the concept of law.[66] The resulting legal monism supports the hope for a supreme global legal order whose absence Kelsen perceives both as a political tragedy and as a defect of legality. The law, for Kelsen, necessarily aims to overcome anarchy, or legally uncontrolled violence, and the complete attainment of that goal requires a supreme global legal order. Clearly, the conception of the purpose and of the value of legality that is in play here cannot be defended on logical or methodological grounds alone. It must be based on the view that the legal control of coercive force is of overriding moral importance.

4.7 Conclusion

The problematic nature of legal monism is well-encapsulated in Kelsen's final verdict on Austinian jurisprudence:

> As it is the task of natural science to describe its object – reality – in one system of laws of nature, so it is the task of jurisprudence to comprehend all human law in one system of rules of law. This task Austin's jurisprudence did not see; the Pure Theory of Law, imperfect and inaccurate though it may be in detail, has gone a measurable distance toward this accomplishment.[67]

We are confronted here with a description of the task of legal theory that appears to go well beyond any uncontroversial reading of the methodological demands – double purity and generality – that Kelsen initially put forward. The requirement of descriptive generality, or the aim to give a general theory of the nature of law, applicable to all legal phenomena, has now turned into the demand to interpret all law as part of one legal system.

Austin was certainly not the only positivist who, while being interested in developing a general theory of law, did not consider it a necessary task of legal theory to comprehend all human law in one legal system. And some of those who have sided with Austin have clearly been able to develop legal theories that avoid the obvious descriptive shortcomings of the view that laws are sanction-backed commands issued by a legally illimitable sovereign. The Pure Theory, I conclude, will appear to be the only possible theory of positive law only if the methodological requirements of positivism are interpreted in ways that non-Kelsenian positivists can reasonably reject.

---

[66] This point is made explicit in Kelsen, *Das Problem der Souveränität*, *supra* note 59 at 85–101.

[67] Kelsen, "The Pure Theory" *supra* note 1 at 287.

Kelsen's encounter with Austin is nevertheless an important episode in the development of positivism. Hart's attack on Austin in *The Concept of Law* adopts Kelsen's criticisms of Austin's command theory. At the same time, Hart manages to integrate Kelsen's criticisms of Austin into a theory that, like Austin's, treats the existence of a legal system as a social fact. The result of this Hartian reconstitution of the Austinian approach is a legal theory more strongly separated from normative political-theoretical concerns than Kelsen's Pure Theory. Those who aim to develop a purely descriptive account of the nature of law should welcome this result.

This is not to say, however, that Kelsen's work is irrelevant today. As political theorists, we need a theory of the state that concerns itself with the relationship of law and state, and with the role that legality plays in the constitution of legitimate political power. Hartian legal theory tends to assume that the question whether the power of the state is exercised under constraints of legality or not is only of limited importance, since what primarily counts, from a moral point of view, is the moral quality of the purposes for which political power is employed.[68] Those who find this deflationary account of the value of the rule of law unconvincing have good reason to take another look at Kelsen's theory of law and state. An interest in the political-theoretical content of Kelsen's jurisprudential work is long overdue, especially if Kelsen's claim that the Pure Theory of Law offers the only viable descriptive account of the nature of law is unsupportable.[69]

---

[68] See for example Joseph Raz, "The Rule of Law and Its Virtue" in Raz, *The Authority of Law, supra* note 37, 210; Hart, *The Concept of Law*, *supra* note 2 at 203–07.

[69] See Hersh Lauterpacht, "Kelsen's Pure Science of Law" in *Modern Theories of Law* ed. by W. Ivor Jennings (London: Oxford University Press, 1933) at 105; Vinx, *Hans Kelsen's Pure Theory of Law*, *supra* note 51.

Chapter 5
Austin and Scandinavian Realism

Patricia Mindus

5.1 Introduction

In this paper I argue that John Austin was an important steppingstone in the development of Scandinavian legal realism (SLR). There are of course several differences between the outlooks of SLR and Austin. First, in order to show why a comparison is worth doing, we need to go beyond the silence of some realists (Lundstedt, Ross) and focus on what others (Hägerström, Olivecrona) had to say about analytical jurisprudence.

Then – in Sect. 5.2 – we look at some strong resemblances, such as (1) the respect for Hume's principle, (2) the common methodological *afflatus*, *i.e.* conceptual analysis as the key to unlock the doors of general jurisprudence, and (3) the pivotal role of legal theory for enhancing systematisation of law.

Section 5.3 explores the Scandinavian readings of Austin's theory, chiefly by reconstructing (1) the main arguments of Axel Hägerström's criticism of the will-theory and (2) Olivecrona's proposal of independent imperatives.

In Sect. 5.4, emphasis is laid on the core differences that denote the final dividing line between the two perspectives: (1) the view on morals and (2) the view on coercion. On the basis of a suggestion by the Italian legal theorist Norberto Bobbio (1909–2004), I would like to draw attention to an often-overlooked divergence between the Austinian and the Scandinavian theorising of the relationship between law and force.[1]

[1] All translations from Swedish, German, Italian and Spanish are mine, where nothing else is indicated.

P. Mindus (✉)
Philosophy Department, Uppsala University, Uppsala, Sweden
e-mail: patricia.mindus@filosofi.uu.se

M. Freeman and P. Mindus (eds.), *The Legacy of John Austin's Jurisprudence*,
Law and Philosophy Library 103, DOI 10.1007/978-94-007-4830-9_5,

5.2 Comparing Apples and Oranges, and Why Bother

Prima facie, there seems to be some good reasons for *not* comparing all too closely the founder of analytical jurisprudence, John Austin, with the movement of SLR,[2] mainly represented by Axel Hägerström (1868–1939), Vilhelm Lundstedt (1882–1955), Karl Olivecrona (1897–1980) and Alf Ross (1899–1979).

First of all, from the scientific perspective, several differences can be stressed. Lest ensnaring ourselves into the *vexata questio* of whether the theorists of SLR were "positivists" and then in what sense,[3] let us start by mentioning two aspects that appear in most textbooks descriptions:

(a) Austin made the imperative theory (or command theory) famous, the Scandinavians declared it infamous;
(b) the first elaborated a theory with much accent on the *State*'s legislative function in an ode to codification, while in the second group Hägerström, in particular, repeatedly distanced himself in various ways from State-focused theories of law, disgusted by the idea of turning the State into God.

Secondly – in relation to ethics – there is something lying, so to say, in-between Austin and the Scandinavians that cannot be easily overlooked: moral and religious matters. While Austin had a high opinion of both, the Scandinavians would go to the books as desecrating atheists and moral revolutionaries. Hägerström, in particular, was universally recognised as the father of the so-called *axiological nihilism*, celebrated by some, hated by others, but clearly irreducible to any traditional Lutheran conservatism. I shall come back to this point further on. Here it is enough to recall Austin's interest for *divine law* as law "properly so-called" – an aspect present to the

[2] The so-called Uppsala school of philosophy, unified by the method of conceptual analysis (in Hägerström's sense, or as Phalén's "denunciation of dialectics") is a separate group from that of Scandinavian legal realism, even though Hägerström surely counts as inspirational source for both. Folke Schmidt's *The Uppsala School of Legal Thinking* from 1978 (one of the few accounts in English from the 1970s) made the two groups overlap, creating some confusing ideas in non-Scandinavian scholars. See Folke Schmidt, *The Uppsala School of Legal Thinking*, Scandinavian Studies in Law, vol. 22 (Stockholm: Almqvist & Wiksell International, 1978) and Patricia Mindus, *A Real Mind. The Life and Work of Axel Hägerström* (Dordrecht: Springer, 2009) at 70.

[3] We shall not engage here in the long-seller on the various forms of positivism and the arranging of authors into subgroups of different colouring. It is enough to stress that the main representatives of Scandinavian legal realism have been classified both inside and outside positivism: For instance, Claes Peterson ["Uppsalaskolan och politiseringen av rättsvetenskapen" (2003) 3 *Juridisk Tidskrift* 580–585] considered Hägerström to represent a quite undramatic expression of the tradition of legal positivism, whereas Enrico Pattaro proposed a reading of Scandinavian legal realism as alternative to positivism. See Enrico Pattaro, "Il realismo giuridico come alternativa al positivismo giuridico" (1971) 1 *Rivista Internazionale di Filosofia del Diritto* 61–126; Enrico Pattaro, *A Treatise of Legal Philosophy and General Jurisprudence – The Law and the Right* (vol. I) (Dordrecht: Springer, 2005).

modern scholar even though it was omitted by W.J. Brown in his editorial work[4] –; an interest his junior Northern colleagues did definitely not share.

Thirdly, political preferences also divide the two outlooks: SLR is associated, as well as American realism, with political progressivism, while John Austin was a renowned conservator (unsurprisingly, we may add, for a friend of François Guizot's). Generally speaking, the Scandinavian so-called "value nihilistic theory was closely associated with a progressive political movement."[5] In fact, social-democracy counted on some very influential names, including Ingmar Hedenius, Herbert Tingsten, Alva and Gunnar Myrdal, all allegedly inspired by Hägerström. Alf Ross was also a prominent name in the Danish debate on democracy and advocated broadly for the social-democratic program;[6] Vilhelm Lundstedt was an active left-wing politician and was elected MP. Clearly, we are poles apart from Austin, whose "political outlook veered pointedly to the right in the latter stages of his life."[7] We need not assess whether there is any link between the latter's political ideas and legal thought,[8] it is sufficient here to recall Austin's *A Plea for the Constitution*, published the year he died; a justification of the British Constitution that has been described as "a defence of aristocratic power that would have aroused either Jeremy Bentham or James Mill from the slumbers of death."[9]

Considering the distance separating the Scandinavians from Austin on these three major points, the silence on Austin in the Scandinavian literature fits the facts: according to the index in Alf Ross' major work *On Law and Justice* from 1958, John Austin is mentioned just once, which is less than Léon Duguit, Rudolph von Jhering, Wesley Newcomb Hohfeld, Jerome Frank or John Chipman Gray. Vilhelm Lundstedt was no overwhelmingly eloquent interpreter either: Austin is virtually absent from some of his major works, such as *Die Unwissenschaftlichkeit der Rechtswissenschaft* from the 1930s and his later *Legal Thinking Revised* from the 1950s.[10] I added to this general lack of communication when recently writing on the

[4] John V. Orth, "Casting the Priests Out of the Temple: John Austin and the Relation between Law and Religion" in *The Weightier Matters of Law: Essays in Law and Religion. A Tribute to Harold J. Berman* ed. by John Witte and Frank S. Alexander (Atlanta: Scholars Press, 1988) 230–249.

[5] Johan Strang, "Why Nordic Democracy?" in *Rhetorics of Nordic Democracy* [Studia Fennica Historica 17] ed. by Johan Strang and Jussi Kurunmaki (Helsinki: Suomen Kirjallisuuden Seura, 2010) 83–113.

[6] Alf Ross, *Hvorfor Demokrati?* (København: Munksgaard, 1946) [Eng. trans. in *Scandinavian Democracy* ed. by Jospeh Albert Lauwerys (Copenhagen: Danish Institute/Norwegian Office of Cultural Relations/The Swedish Institute, 1958)].

[7] Wilfrid E. Rumble, *The Thought of John Austin. Jurisprudence, Colonial Reform and the British Constitution* (London: The Athlone Press, 1985) at 6.

[8] Wilfred Löwenhaupt, *Politisches Utilitarismus und bürgerliches Rechtdenken. John Austin (1790–1859) und die "Philosophie des positiven Rechts"* (Berlin: Dunker & Humblot, 1972).

[9] Rumble, *The Thought of John Austin, supra* note 7 at 193.

[10] To be accurate, in the first volume of *Die Unwissenschaftlichkeit der Rechtswissenschaft*, Austin's theory is briefly discussed at 191–198 but mainly in its relation to Bergbohm and Holland; and in the second volume I should mention a quick reference on page 231 to Austin's *Lecture XXV* and the idea of *unlawful intention.* In *Legal Thinking Revised* I only counted six references (at 24, 92, 142–43, 337 and 397), which is far less then Thon or Jhering, and Austin only appears here in relation to Bentham.

founder of the Scandinavian movement, Axel Hägerström: I am afraid that mention of Austin was rather scarce.[11] If I were to name the authors of reference in the literature of SLR – in the sense of the scholars that left a hallmark, that became sources of inspiration, that were quoted with deference, etc. – John Austin would probably not figure. His name, in this context, has a critical ring to it. When it is made, it is generally to substantiate a criticism. Lundstedt is, in this respect, exemplary. He bluntly comments on Austin and his "English school" that "no criticism of legal ideology seems to exist,"[12] that the notion of sovereignty is "reine Phantasie"[13] and that Austin merely advanced a "hidden law of nature."[14]

The reluctant behaviour of the Scandinavians is nothing new when we deal with Austin. Rumble correctly remarked that "the reason for Austin's significance is *not* universal support for his ideas."[15] Indeed, many scholars have adopted the view expressed by Henry Sumner Maine, according to which there is not the smallest necessity for accepting all the conclusions of Bentham and Austin "but there is the strongest necessity for knowing what these conclusions are."[16] Therefore, we shall add another piece to the puzzle of the already existing literature of Austin-comparisons,[17] without searching so much for common conclusions as looking for the reasons *why* (at least some of) the Scandinavians found *the strongest necessity for knowing* what Austin's conclusions had been in order to develop their own views.

To pave the way for such a reading, and show why a comparison is worth doing, some facts needs to be stressed: under the assumption that frequency of reference is (at least) sign of a perceived need to confront the reference intellectually, it is worth noticing that in Karl Olivecrona's 1971-edition of *Law as Fact*, I counted references

---

[11] Mindus, *A Real Mind, supra* note 2.

[12] Vilhelm Lundstedt, *Legal Thinking Revised: My Views on Law* (Stockholm: Almqvist & Wiksell, 1956) at 337.

[13] Vilhelm Lundstedt, *Die Unwissenschaftlichkeit der Rechtswissenschaft (*Berlin: Rothschild 1932–36, vol. 1) at 197.

[14] Vilhelm Lundstedt, *Law and Justice* [1950] (Stockholm/Uppsala: Almqvist & Wiksell, 1952) at 43; *cf.* Lundstedt, *Legal Thinking Revised, supra* note 12 at 142–43.

[15] Rumble, *The Thought of John Austin, supra* note 7 at 1.

[16] Henry James Sumner Maine, *Lectures on the Early History of Institutions* [reprint fac. sim. 7th ed. 1914] (London: Dawsons of Pall Mall, 1966) at 343.

[17] A lengthy list could be drafted, especially in relation to Hart, but I shall limit my references to the following (not always very well-known but not less worthy of praise) comparisons: with Hobbes and Bentham, Mario A. Cattaneo, *Il positivismo giuridico inglese* (Milano: Giuffré, 1962); José Juan Moreso, "Cinco diferencias entre Bentham y Austin" (1989) 6 *Anuario de Filosofía del Derecho* 351–357; with American realism, see Wilfrid E. Rumble, "The Legal Positivism of John Austin and the Realist Movement in American Jurisprudence" (1981) 66 *Cornell Law Review* 986–1031; with Hermann Heller, see Ernesto Garzón Valdéz, "Hermann Heller y John Austin. Un intento de comparación" (1983) 57 *Sistema* 31–50; with Joseph Story, see Michael H. Hoeflich "John Austin and Joseph Story: Two Nineteenth Century Perspectives on the Utility of the Civil Law for the Common Lawyer" (1985) 29 *The American Journal of Legal History* 36–77. No comparison, as far as I have been able to establish, has ever been attempted between Austin and Scandinavian legal realism.

to Austin some 53 times,[18] which means that Austin is quoted more often than, for instance, Bentham (to whom, nevertheless, Olivecrona dedicated quite some work); more than Bergbohm, one of the leading German scholars of law with whom Olivecrona regularly maintained a conceptual dialogue; more than Grotius, Hart, Savigny, Lundstedt, Pufendorf, and Ross. Basically, only Hägerström and Kelsen beat Austin in the ranking of quotations. These are, undisputedly, telling figures.

Add to this that Alf Ross, in his early work on the sources of law from 1929, dedicated chapter IV on the *Englische Doktrin* to "der Begründer der englischen *wissenschaftlichen* Jurisprudenz"[19] and offered a reconstruction of Austin's theory by focusing on both the concept of law and his notion of sovereignty, the latter being, in his view, the *Kernpunkt* of the theory.[20]

Moreover, Axel Hägerström – the "spiritual father" of Scandinavian realism[21] – made Austin the steppingstone in formulating his own thought.[22] Although Hägerström found several ways of attacking him, he gave Austin *l'honneur des armes*. Among Hägerström's works, the 1921-essay entitled *Idén om staten som ett härskarförhållande* [On the Idea of the State as a Power Relation] was dedicated to a discussion of Austin's concept of sovereignty. He credited the founder of analytical jurisprudence with being, together with Jellinek, "the most important political scientist" for his "ideas on the nature of the state."[23]

---

[18] References can be found at 26, 31–33, 39, 45, 51, 57, 59 ff., 70, 73, 79, 82 ff., 120–125, 154–56, 186.

[19] Alf Ross, *Theorie der Rechtsquellen. Ein Beitrag zur Theorie des positiven Rechts auf Grundlage dogmenhistorischer Untersuchung* (Leipzig/Wien: Deuticke, 1929) at 79.

[20] The "English doctrine" is presented on the background of, and in relation to, the German tradition: See Ross, *Theorie der Rechtsquellen, supra* note 19 at 90 "Die englische Schule dagegen entstand in Kontinuation der positiven, analytischen Schule," even though "auf der anderen Seite übte die englische, analytiche Schule (…) so gut wie gar keinen Einfluß auf den Kontinent aus. Austins Name blieb unbekannt" (*Ibid.* at 77). A criticism of Austin's account of the sources of law can be found in *ibid.* at 91.

[21] Dennis Lloyd, *Introduction to Jurisprudence* (London: Stevens & Sons, 1965) at 292.

[22] Hägerström dedicated quite some work to discussing Austin's theses: Without attempting to offer any exhaustive list of references to Austin in Hägerström (which would require significant effort in going through the archive of unpublished manuscripts), it is sufficient here to recall the essay *Representationsidéens djupare grundvalar* now in Axel Hägerström, *Rätten och staten. Tre föreläsningar om rätts- och statsfilosofi*, ed. Martin Fries (Stockholm: Natur & Kultur, 1963) esp. at 171 ff.; part of the second section in the essay collection from 1963 on *The State and Its Forms* (*ibid.* at 120–153); see also Axel Hägerström, *Rätten och viljan. Två uppsatser av Axel Hägerström* ed. by Karl Olivecrona (Lund: Gleerup, 1961) at 63 ff. and at 78–82 and 95. For the English reader, in *Inquiries*, apart from the essay *Is Positive Law an Expression of Will?*, we should mention the critique of Austin's doctrine according to which tacit consent grounds custom: see Axel Hägerström, *Inquiries into the Nature of Law and Morals* (Uppsala: Almqvist & Wiksell, 1953) at 60 ff.; the attack on the imperative theory (*ibid.* at 201–209) where he never actually quotes Austin but his presence is nonetheless felt. In parallel with some of Austin's themes, Hägerström suggested an analysis of the notion of command (*ibid.* at 106–143) and discussed the conative power of habit (*ibid.* at 155 ff.). Generally, Hägerström's account of the experience of duty may be read on the background of Austin's theory (*ibid.* at 105–141).

[23] Hägerström, *Rätten och staten, supra* note 22 at 120; *cf.* Hägerström, *Inquiries, supra* note 22 at 257.

We may conclude that neither Hägerström, nor Olivecrona disliked Austin. In *Rätten och viljan*, a collection of essays by Hägerström that Olivecrona edited in 1961 – while discussing Hägerström's classifying of Austin into "sociological positivism" – Olivecrona claimed that "of the four sociological theories of positivism [Austin's theory] *is indubitably the closest to reality*."[24] In the second edition of *Law as Fact* he repeated this after extolling Austin as having laid "the scientific foundation for the study of law by *fitting law into the world given to us in experience*."[25] He evidently appreciated this effort since his own scientific program intended to "reduce our picture of the law in order to make it tally with existing objective reality."[26] Also Alf Ross recognised his debt, on the methodological level, towards the founder of the "analytical school" for dealing with the law "regarded as a system of positive, that is, actually effective norms"[27] and not merely law as it should be.

However, the founder of the realist movement, Hägerström himself, was hardly persuaded by any Austinian theory of law. In *Is Positive Law an Expression of Will?* from 1916, and in *Till frågan om den objektiva rättens begrepp* from 1917, partly translated by C.D. Broad with the title *On the Question of the Notion of Law*, Austin's core notions of command, sovereignty and will are targeted. It is here that the imperative theory of law exemplified in the work *of* Austin becomes the object of the pioneering criticism that sparkled off SLR. In these two essays, Hägerström established his main thesis on the deliberate voluntary features in legal science, better known as the *criticism of will-theory*.[28] My plea is that this criticism cannot be adequately assessed if we do not look first at the affinities that to a large extent justify the nearing of Austin and the Scandinavians.

5.3 Affinities

5.3.1 A Family Resemblance with Hume's Principle

Ever since John Stuart Mill first declared that "Mr Austin's subject was Jurisprudence, Bentham's was legislation,"[29] it has become commonplace to recall that Austin was

---

[24] Karl Olivecrona, *Introduction* in Hägerström, *Rätten och viljan, supra* note 22 at 15.

[25] Karl Olivecrona, *Law as Fact* 2nd ed. (London: Stevens & Sons, 1971) at 32 and 67.

[26] Karl Olivecrona, *Law as Fact* 1st ed. (Copenhagen/London: Munksgaard/Milford, 1939) at 27; see also Olivecrona, *Law as Fact* 2nd ed., *supra* note 25 at vii.

[27] Alf Ross, *On Law and Justice* (London: Stevens & Sons, 1958) at 1.

[28] See *infra* section 5.4.

[29] John Stuart Mill, "Austin on Jurisprudence" in Id. *Dissertations and discussions*, Vol. III (London: Longmans, 1867) at 209.

concerned with law as it *is* and not as it *ought* to be. The standard formulation of this basic idea can be found in a note to Austin's fifth Lecture:

> The existence of law is one thing; its merit or demerit is another. Whether it be or be not is one enquiry; whether it be or be not conformable to an assumed standard, is a different enquiry. A law, which actually exists, is a law, though we happen to dislike it, or though it varies from the text, by which we regulate our approbation and disapprobation.[30]

This air of distinction, reminiscent of Hume's principle, is to be found, albeit in different terms, in a text that might well be described as the starting point for the Scandinavians: The canonical reference is to Axel Hägerström's inaugural lecture from the 18th of March 1911, *On the Truth of Moral Propositions*:

> Even if it is absolute, a reality can never include within itself a supreme value. The existence of a divine will or an inner demand can never imply, in and of itself, that we ought to follow it, that to follow it is of supreme value. Existence and value signify something entirely different.[31]

Hägerström thus emerged as a true adversary of all regressive confusion between *is* and *ought*. His purpose was primarily to defend a "positivistic" and "scientific" as well as "value-free" method, as opposed to the idealistic dogmatism then prevailing in the academic world. It was part of the Scandinavian project to abandon scientific programs reducing social complexity and human emotion to the traditional frame of a metaphysical principle upholding a system of morals, aesthetics and so forth. This is why Hägerström was often classified among the strong advocates for the distinction between *is* and *ought* – a position he ultimately adopted pursuant to his refutation of ontological dualism.[32]

This feature of Scandinavian realism should be put in relation to Austin's famous thesis on the separation of law from morals.[33] What appealed to the Scandinavians was that Austin pointed out "that there is much that is law that is not moral, and what makes something law does nothing to guarantee its moral value."[34] In this sense, Austin, like the Scandinavians, reacted towards the wishful thinking characterising

[30] John Austin, *The Province of Jurisprudence Determined* [1832] ed. by Wilfrid E. Rumble (Cambridge: Cambridge University Press, 1995) at 157.

[31] Axel Hägerström, *Philosophy and Religion* (London: Allen & Unwin, 1964) at 87.

[32] Mindus, *A Real Mind*, *supra* note 2 chapter 2; and my "À l'origine du non-cognitivisme moderne: Axel Hägerström" (2008) *Analisi & Diritto* 159–176. For a discussion of the connection between this outlook and forms of naturalism especially in Ross and Olivecrona, see Torben Spaak, "Naturalism in American and Scandinavian Realism: Similarities and Differences" in *De Lege. Uppsala-Minnesota Colloquium: Law, Culture and Values* ed. by Mattias Dahlberg (Uppsala: Iustus förlag, 2009) 33–83.

[33] Samuel Enoch Stumpf, "Austin's Theory of the Separation of Law and Morals" (1961) 14 *Vanderbilt Law Review* 117–149; from the historical perspective, see also Richard Cosgrove, "The Reception of Analytic Jurisprudence: The Victorian Debate on Separation of Law and Morality" (1981) 74 *Durham University Journal* 47–56.

[34] Brian H. Bix, "John Austin" in *Stanford Encyclopaedia of Philosophy*, available at: http://plato.stanford.edu/entries/austin-john/#2 (last accessed 22/04/2012) at 6.

a lot of natural law theories and idealistic metaphysics. Legal scholars cannot disregard that "the most pernicious laws, and therefore those which are most opposed to the will of God" – for Austin – have been and are "continually enforced as laws by judicial tribunals."[35] Austin's example was slavery – an "utmost abhorrence" – but nonetheless a legal institution.

It has been suggested that this "separation thesis" should be viewed foremost in terms of "distinction":

> The word "separation" to describe Austin's conception of the relationship between law and morals is misleading. The term that much more accurately describes his views is "distinction" between law and morals. Despite the many links between them, they have different natures (…). This distinction is imperative, Austin insisted, because the *existence* of positive laws is not logically *dependent* upon their moral or ethical goodness.[36]

This way of understanding the relationship between law and morals seems to capture the specific facets of the separation argument that appealed to Austin on one hand and to the Scandinavians on the other. The separation thesis enabled Austin to advocate an unbiased study of law at the same time as he developed a "theory of resistance" against unjust legal systems. To the Scandinavians it permitted the refutation of axiological knowledge, including the kind of knowledge that would ground Austin's theory of resistance.

However, it is not only the general respect for what later came to be known under the label of Hume's principle that makes it possible to assimilate Austin and the Scandinavians. At least in the case of Hägerström, there is explicit and clear similitude in the choice of vocabulary as well. In perfect concord with the later Swede, Austin denounced natural law as based on unreal fictions. Among the "senseless fictions" Austin deplored we find many examples of the "jargon" criticised by Hägerström, such as the appeal to the rights of man, inalienable liberties, immutable justice, original or social contract: it was thus clear to both that the formulas making up the contemporary political rhetoric would probably lead to increasing conflict and political violence. Austin warned that these "fustian phrases (…) must (…) take to their weapons, and fight their difference out,"[37] just like Hägerström pressed forward the admonition that all sorts of sinister interest will "cloak themselves in a shroud of righteousness"[38] and therefore peaceful compromise will become impossible.

This ultimately reverberates on their negative view of natural law. In Austin's phrasing, the notions of natural law are "merely convenient cloaks for ignorance or sinister interest" insofar, according to Austin – they mean either that "I hate the law to which I object and cannot tell why, or that the law, and that the cause of my hatred

---

[35] Austin, *The Province, supra* note 30 at 158.

[36] Rumble, *The Thought of John Austin, supra* note 7 at 81.

[37] Austin, *The Province, supra* note 30 at 55; Cattaneo, *Il positivismo giuridico inglese, supra* note 17 at 255.

[38] Axel Hägerström, *Socialfilosofiska uppsatser* (Stockholm: Bonnier, 1939) at 215.

is one which I find it incommodious to avow."[39] Both Austin and Hägerström believed that the first benefit of observing Hume's principle is the elimination of unnecessary conflicts, whether scientific or social.

It should yet be observed that, similarly to the Scandinavian legal realist movement, Austin insisted on the separation of law and morals although he gave a different interpretation thereof. Whereas both Austin and legal theorists such as Hägerström and Olivecrona maintained Hume's law in strict terms, Austin was a moral philosopher to an extent and in a sense that the Scandinavians were not. Olivecrona noted this by emphasising that most often the characteristic feature of legal positivism is said to be that it *separates law and morals*. This refers, in Olivecrona's view, in the first instance, to Austin's theory. In fact, he claimed that "the same separation of law and other systems of rules is found in the present leader of legal positivism, Hans Kelsen."[40] However, the separation thesis is not what defines this positivistic view on the nature of law. The separation of law and morals is "not bound up with either Austin's or Kelsen's view on the nature of law."[41] The reason why Olivecrona felt unsatisfied with the identification between positivism and the doctrine of separation of law and morals is because "the criterion of legal positivism then amounts to its being based on a non-cognitive theory of value"[42] and, indeed, there is no need to embrace non-cognitivism in order to sustain the separation thesis. This misperception ultimately leads, as we shall see further on, to quite some classificatory problems as far as Austin's relationship to positivism is concerned.[43] For the moment being, let us look at another affinity: methodology.

5.3.2 The Common Methodological Afflatus

The accent on conceptual analysis is a characteristic feature both in Bentham and Austin. This methodological *afflatus* is close to the one we find in Hägerström, Olivecrona and other realists. In harmony with the Benthamite idea that jurisprudence needs to limit itself to the analysis of the terms that define legal concepts, common to all civilized nations – "power", "obligation", "liberty" and so forth –,[44]

[39] Austin, *The Province, supra* note 30 at 159.

[40] Olivecrona, *Law as Fact* 2nd ed. *supra* note 25 at 57.

[41] *Ibid.*

[42] *Ibid.* at 58.

[43] See §1 in section 5.5. on the core differences.

[44] This is Austin's view of legal concepts but it was challenged already by Binding, Zitelmann, Jellinek and many more because it focuses on what we would today label comparative law, *i.e.* the study of the permanence of a specific institution, say marriage, across the spectrum of national legal systems rather than across the spectrum of legal disciplines; a distinction, it has been stressed, that sets the methodological difference between *allgemeine Rechtslehre* and philosophy of law. For this distinction see Åke Frändberg, "Den allmänna rättsläran – tidlös och ständigt aktuell" in his *Rättsordningens idé* (Uppsala: Iustus, 2005) 9–20, at 10–12.

Austin insisted that the elucidation of legal language was an essential prerequisite of an exposition of law's fundamental principles. The call for clarification derived from such considerations as "the purely verbal puzzles" generated by "mysterious jargon" that jurisprudence recurrently uses, and "the numerous ambiguities" afflicting the basic building blocks of law, such as "right", "duty" etc. Austin was indeed persuaded that most of the definitions we find in legal science "instead of shedding light upon the things defined (…) involve it in thicker obscurity."[45] Therefore, his professional effort consisted in "labouring to rectify misconceptions."[46]

This way of understanding the role of legal philosophy is very close to the one embraced by the legal realists in the North. The Scandinavian also focused on conceptual analysis. The very motto in Uppsala was *Let us determine the concepts!*[47] In the 1935 essay, *The Conception of a Declaration of Intention in the Sphere of Private Law*, Hägerström underlined that:

> Jurisprudence has become one of the special sciences (…). The representatives of the special sciences long ago issued to philosophers the command "Hands off!" But what induces a certain boldness in the philosophers, notwithstanding this command, is the fact that the notions which are used for describing what is actual may very well be delusive.[48]

As early as 1910, he had made clear that much would be gained if empirical questions were dealt with empirically, and the preconditions of experience, and "generally the concepts with no empirical significance that we continuously use, were subjected to conceptual analysis."[49]

As Henry Sumner Maine claimed, the post-Austinian jurisprudence came to be called *analytical* not because it was grounded on analysis of language as later analytical philosophy, but because it was opposed to the historical and comparative form of *jurisprudence*.[50] This is, to a large extent, true also *vis-à-vis* the Scandinavians: conceptual analysis was first and foremost a way of emphasising the internal contradictions of concepts following a *dialectical* scheme.[51] This was also the kind of conceptual analysis used by the co-founder of the philosophical school of Uppsala, Adolf Phalén (1884–1931).

While there was in Austin and the *English doctrine* – as Ross referred to it – a strong interest for language, this interest was much feebler in the first generation of realists.

---

[45] Quote from Rumble, *The Thought of John Austin, supra* note 7 at 73–74.

[46] Austin, *The Province, supra* note 30 at 15.

[47] Konrad Marc-Wogau, *Studier till Axel Hägerströms filosofi* (Falköping: Prisma, 1968) at 7.

[48] Axel Hägerström, "Begreppet viljeförklaring på privaträttens område" (1935) *Theoria* 1: 32–57 and 2: 121–138, at 99.

[49] Axel Hägerström, "Kritiska punkter i värdepsykologien i värdepsykologien" in *Festskrift tillägnad Erik Olof Burman* (Uppsala: Appelgrens boktr., 1910) at 16.

[50] Maine, *Lectures, supra* note 16 at 7.

[51] Gunnar Oxenstierna, *Vad är Uppsalafilosofien?* (Stockholm: Bonnier, 1938); Harry Meurling, "Om begreppsanalys" in *Festskrift tillägnad Axel Hägerström den 6 September 1928 av filosofiska och juridiska föreningarna i Uppsala* ed. by Efraim Liljeqvist (Uppsala: Almqvist & Wiksell, 1928) 330–336.

Truth is that Bentham had not only determined the *object* of jurisprudence (the basic legal concepts). In *An Introduction to the Principles of Morals and Legislation* (1789) he also outlined the *way* to conduct analysis of language; a methodological option later adopted by twentieth century analytical philosophy.[52]

In continuity with such a reading, it seems undisputed that Austin was an ardent believer in the necessity of conceptual and linguistic analysis.[53] What happened in Scandinavia was slightly different. It took a long time before the analytical philosophy emerging from the linguistic turn broke through in the legal realm. We need to wait for the so-called "second generation" of realists and, in particular, for Olivecrona's discovery of the "other" Austin – John Langshaw (1911–1960) – and his analysis of the *performative function* of language.[54] The older generation, among which Hägerström, had a more "classical conception of philosophical analysis, according to which such an analysis aims to establish an analytically true equivalence between the *analysandum* (…) and the *analysans*,"[55] where what is analysed does not always correspond to an object of the real world (this was, *e.g.*, the case of "values" for Hägerström). Despite these differences, conceptual analysis should be inventoried among the affinities between the two perspectives that induced both Austin and his Nordic counterparts to attribute great importance to the systematisation of "general jurisprudence" or "theory of law."

5.3.3 The Interest for General Jurisprudence

The scope of Austin's course was *general jurisprudence*, or *abstract jurisprudence* as he also labelled it in *The Province of Jurisprudence Determined*, in opposition to the particular jurisprudence characterising any given legal system. Here we are at the very core of the *Philosophie des positiven Rechts*.[56] To Austin, the purpose of general jurisprudence appeared as follows:

> General jurisprudence, or the philosophy of positive law (…) is concerned directly with principles and distinctions which are common to various systems of particular and positive

[52] Alan R. White "Austin as a Philosophical Analyst" (1978) 64:3 *ARSP* 379–399; Gerard Maher, "Analytical Philosophy and Austin's Philosophy of Law" (1978) 64:3 *ARSP* 401–415; Moreso, "Cinco diferencias entre Bentham y Austin" *supra* note 17.

[53] Mohamed El Shakankiri, "Analyse du langage et droit chez quelques juristes anglo-américains de Bentham à Hart" (1970) 15 *Archives de Philosophie du Droit* 113–149.

[54] Silvana Castignone, *Diritto, linguaggio, realtà. Saggi sul realismo giuridico* (Torino: Giappichelli, 1995), esp. at 151–216 and 293–318; Johan Strang, "Two Generations of Scandinavian Legal Realists" (2009) *Retfaerd* 12:1.

[55] Torben Spaak, "Karl Olivecrona's Legal Philosophy: A Critical Appraisal" (2010) 24 *Ratio Juris* 155–92.

[56] Gustav Hugo, *Lehrbuch des Naturrecht als einer Philosophie des positiven Rechts* (Berlin: Mylius, 1798).

> law; and which each of those various systems inevitably involves, let it be worthy of praise or blame, or let it accord or not with an assumed measure or test.[57]

It is noteworthy that Hägerström agreed with Austin on this crucial point concerning the role of general jurisprudence: "legal theory must play an important part, since it offers a fundamental systematization."[58] Austin's tendency to *generalise* concepts, as well as his identification of the principles and concepts *common* to all "maturer systems of refined communities" set off a debate on the allegedly more "rationalistic" (and "essentialist") or more "empiricist" features of his thought.[59] What matters here is to stress that the Scandinavians registered chiefly this second character of general jurisprudence.

Following Morison who advanced that Austin's conceptualization was of interest insofar as it aimed to describe the basic concepts of law in purely factual terms leading them back to the causative "social processes,"[60] it is clear that this part of Austin fascinated the realists. For instance, Olivecrona insisted on his "empirical approach"[61] at the heart of his own distinction between the two different types of legal positivism:

> The kind represented by Bentham and Austin may be called *naturalistic* legal positivism because it purports to give a purely factual, naturalistic explanation of the nature of the law. In contrast, the predominant German type may be called *idealistic* legal positivism. It contains an idealistic element in that the obligatory force is supposed to be a property of the law.[62]

Unsurprisingly, Olivecrona scorned the "rationalist" reading of Austin offered by Julius Stone in *Legal System and Lawyer's Reasoning* where the latter had claimed that Austin's main purpose and contribution would have been to suggest a framework for viewing "the propositions of a legal order as a logically self-consistent system, not to provide a theory of how power was or ought to be distributed in society."[63] To Olivecrona, "it might occur to an author of our day (…) to attempt viewing the propositions of a legal order as a logically self-consistent system" – *i.e.* to jurisprudents in the wake of Kelsen's Pure Theory – but, claims Olivecrona, "this way of thinking – which is highly artificial – was undoubtedly alien to Austin's positivism."[64] To the Scandinavians, who showed an overall sensibility for historical

---

[57] John Austin, *Lectures on Jurisprudence, or The Philosophy of Positive Law* ed. by Robert Campbell (4th edition, rev., London: John Murray, 1873) [Bristol: Thoemmes Press reprint, 1996, two vols.] at 33.

[58] Hägerström, *Inquiries*, *supra* note 22 at 84.

[59] Isabel Turégano Mansilla, *Derecho y moral en John Austin* (Madrid: Centro de estudios politicos y constitutionales, 2001), esp. 127–216.

[60] William Loutit Morison, "Some Myth about Positivism" (1958) 68 *The Yale Law Journal* 294–304, esp. at 221; and Morison, *John Austin* (London: Edward Arnold, 1982).

[61] Olivecrona, *Law as Fact* 2nd ed. *supra* note 25 at 32.

[62] *Ibid.* at 40.

[63] Julius Stone, *Legal System and Lawyer's Reasoning* (Stanford: Stanford Univ. Press, 1964) at 74.

[64] Olivecrona, *Law as Fact* 2nd ed. *supra* note 25 at 32.

matters, it seems that the Austin they read was the Austin of the utilitarian school about which Leslie Stephen once claimed that its strong point was "reverence for facts."[65]

Apart from the empiricist imprinting, there is something else in Austin's general jurisprudence that attracted the Scandinavians. He took a step away from traditional "philosophy of law" as the reflection over what justice is and what justifies our obedience towards the State; with Austin, we enter the distinct territory of (the theory of) positive law, where the search for the qualifications of the *optima res publica* no longer offers a scientific venue. More precisely, with Austin, legal theory is not only held to answer the question "what is law?" but also to approach the issue of "what is a norm?"

On one hand, the problem of determining law's nature, *i.e.* the specific difference that discriminates law from morals, religion, custom, etc. became the central question for the nineteenth century philosophy of law and a crucial aspect of Austin's work. On the other hand, Austin also offered a thorough reflection over what a norm or rule is, a question that would raise the attention of theorists much later, with the passing of the nineteenth century onto the twentieth century. In this sense, the Scandinavians recognised that Austin was ahead of his time. In Ross' phrase, Austin's merit is to have painted the broad brushstrokes of "Rechtswissenschaft als eine Normwissenschaft."[66] By distinguishing the positive, legal norm from other "extrajudicial" kinds of norms: "Austin's lebte in 19., er schrieb aber für das 20. Jahrhundert."[67]

Austin famously defined the "essentials of a law or a rule" in that:

> Every *law* or *rule* (…) is a *command.* Or rather, laws or rules, properly so called, are a *species* of commands (…). A command is distinguished from other significations of desire, not by the style in which the desire is signified, but by the power and the purpose of the party commanding to inflict evil or pain in case the desire be disregarded (…). A command, then, is a signification of desire. But a command is distinguished from other significations of desire by this peculiarity: that the party to whom it is directed is liable to evil from the other. Being liable to evil from you, if I comply not with a wish which you signify, I am *bound* or *obliged* by your command, or I lie under a *duty* to obey it (…). Command and duty are therefore correlative terms: the meaning denoted by each being implied or supposed by the other.[68]

It is foremost the development of this *norm-theory* as a form of *imperativism* that stimulated the realist movement. As known, Austin understood the simple element of general jurisprudence – *law* – to be a general and abstract form of command issued, explicitly or tacitly, by the sovereign.

> Of the laws and rules set by men to men, some are established by *political* superiors, sovereign and subject: by persons exercising supreme and subordinate *government*, in independent nations, or *independent political societies*.[69]

Precisely here, the paths of Austin and that of the Scandinavians do part.

---

[65] Quote from K. J. M. Smith, *James Fitzjames Stephen: Portrait of a Victorian Rationalist* (Cambridge: Cambridge Univ. Press, 1988) at 44.

[66] Ross, *Theorie der Rechtsquellen, supra* note 19 at 83.

[67] *Ibid.* at 85.

[68] Austin, *The Province, supra* note 30 at 25.

[69] *Ibid.* at 18.

5.4 Criticising the Will Theory

What the Scandinavian realists started to question was the very basis of what was then held to be the only viable scientific study of law, namely what Morris R. Cohen in 1933 put so neatly: "in nearly all jural and political discussion that styles itself scientific, law is defined as the will of the sovereign."[70] To Hägerström, "the idea of a command or a declaration of intention appears as a mere juridical fiction;"[71] his plea is that no will is at work in law and, therefore, he considered Austin's theory of sovereignty to be misleading.[72] More precisely, Hägerström had two different strains of criticism against voluntarism: the very idea of the will of the state as *volonté générale* as it appears in public law and the idea that private law amounts to declarations of intentions. Olivecrona later restricted the scope of Hägerström's criticism by claiming that Austin had correctly understood that there is an *imperative dimension* in law but that the underlying imperative cannot be properly comprehended as the will of the sovereign. For Olivecrona, we are dealing with "independent imperatives."

5.4.1 Hägerström Reads Austin

Hägerström's criticism of the will-theory – held by Olivecrona to be one of the deepest of its kind – was presented in a mature form in his 1916 essay on valid law (some ideas were present earlier but shall not be addressed here). Hägerström used several different arguments to refute the so-called "will-theory" – being "the prevailing theory as to the nature of positive law"[73] – all of which are not directly linked to Austin's version of the imperative theory.[74] Here we shall briefly recollect the main arguments, the overall point being that law cannot be reduced to any idea of will.

---

[70] Morris R. Cohen, *Law and the Social Order* (New York: Harcourt, Brace & Co., 1933) at 249.

[71] Hägerström, *Inquiries, supra* note 22 at 34.

[72] Hägerström also held command and duty not to be correlative terms. This line of argument was developed in a lengthy phenomenological assessment of command and duty from 1917 that I will not touch upon here. For more information, C.D. Broad, "Hägerström's Account of Sense of Duty and Certain Allied Experiences" (1951) 26 *Philosophy* 99–113; Bo Petersson, *Axel Hägerströms värdeteori* (Uppsala: Filosofiska föreningen vid Uppsala universitet, 1973); Enrico Pattaro, *Il realismo giuridico scandinavo,* vol. I: *Axel Hägerström* (Bologna: Cooperativa libraria universitaria editrice, 1974) esp. chapter 3; Dieter Lang, *Wertung und Erkenntnis. Untersuchungen zu Axel Hägerströms Moraltheologie* (Amsterdam: Rodopi, 1981); Castignone, *Diritto, linguaggio, realtà, supra* note 54 at 223–240.

[73] Hägerström, *Inquiries, supra* note 22 at 56.

[74] A complete reconstruction in Mindus, *A Real Mind, supra* note 2 in chapter 4.

According to the first line of argument, if the state is conceived as *persona iuridica* it has no will: "we can reject as circular the theory which regards will, whose content expressed in a certain way is to constitute law, as *itself determined by the law.*"[75] Basically, one cannot have one's cake and eat it: if law is the will of the state, but the state is only a creation of law, the answer just begs the question. To talk of the will of the state as the will of the legal order "is quite obviously a council of desperation."[76]

Hägerström's second line of reasoning holds that law is neither what we all want, nor what the majority desires.

Above all – he argued – law in force or valid law cannot be scientifically described as some form of common will (*Gesammtwille* or *Gemeinwille* in the German wording). Law has nothing to do with the "will of all (members of society)."[77] Who would ever believe that a criminal really wants the law enforced on himself? "Do criminals as a rule feel such a burning desire that the judges shall apply the criminal law to them?"[78] The connection Hägerström saw between will and consciousness led him to use Austin's same argument – our incapacity of grasping all the details of an existing legal system – *against* imperativism. There is no such thing as a general will that equals to what everybody wants, because the individual has no adequate knowledge of the rules of law which hold in his society, and therefore cannot demand that they shall be observed: "no particular rule of law can be a demand of the general will, on this view, since its special content is not demanded by that will but is a matter of indifference to it."[79]

This also implies that law cannot be understood as a form of "general will" in the tradition of organicism: society is no "psycho-physical organism."[80] Such beliefs originate in an "universal anthropomorphizing tendency"[81] that suggests that "the organism (…) carries out its decisions in law-making through individuals as its organs."[82] Hägerström showed the absurdity of the organic perspective by using one of his key examples: the case of a monarch angrily sanctioning anarchism. "If one is angry as a private individual, without any legal consequences, the feeling can be explained in the ordinary, natural way"[83] but for the monarch, whose feelings

---

[75] Hägerström, *Inquiries, supra* note 22 at 18; *cf.* Axel Hägerström, *Är gällande rätt uttryck av vilja?* in *Festskrift tillägnad prof. Vitalis Norström på 60-årsdagen den 29 januari 1916* (Göteborg: Elanders Boktryckeri, 1916) 171–210, at 172.

[76] Hägerström, *Inquiries, supra* note 22 at 101.

[77] *Ibid.* at 20; *cf. Är gällande rätt, supra* note 75 at 62.

[78] Hägerström, *Inquiries, supra* note 22 at 21; *cf. Är gällande rätt, supra* note 75 at 175; *Rätten och staten, supra* note 22 at 126 and 132.

[79] Hägerström, *Inquiries, supra* note 22 at 21; *cf.* Hägerström, *Är gällande rätt, supra* note 75 at 175.

[80] *Ibid.* at 25; *cf.* Hägerström, *Är gällande rätt, supra* note 75 at 179.

[81] *Ibid.* at 41.

[82] *Ibid.* at 25; Hägerström, *Är gällande rätt, supra* note 75 at 180.

[83] Hägerström, *Conception of a Declaration of Intention, supra* note 48 at 25.

seem to engender legal consequences, no explanation is at hand. At the end of the day, holistic arguments on *bonum commune* only amount to a return to the doctrine of natural law.[84]

Furthermore – if the state is not the *magnus homo* where a "common will" can be detected since our political association is no "community of destiny" – perhaps another way of claiming that law is a command would be to assert that it is the command of the *democratic* sovereign. Accordingly, the "common will" might be conceived as the sum of fragmented singular wills; the various individual (neuro-physiologic) desires could then be composed into unity through the so-called will of the majority. But Hägerström refused this conjecture for two reasons:

1. People have incompatible aims and interests: the so-called "will of the majority" is only a meaningless term. "In reality the separate wills here are not thought of in the least as being unified through a common aim;"[85] The will of the representative assembly is "merely legal fiction. Thus it cannot be defined as a real will directed towards the law."[86] Rather, "law is, at any rate to a large extent, an expression of interests (…). The real state of affairs (…) is that, in the conflict of interests within a society, certain interests come to express themselves in the form of laws."[87]
2. There can be no self-obligation, because it is not possible "for any person to be bound to himself; because he that can bind, can release" as Hobbes affirmed in *Leviathan*.[88] Hobbes' classical argument against limited sovereignty was used by Austin who held that supreme power bound by positive law is "a flat contradiction in terms."[89] In turn, Hägerström held this very point *against* Austin's idea of law as a form of command: since, he claims, there seems to be a "special absurdity" in the idea that "an individual can give orders to himself,"[90] there is no room for the traditional concept of autonomy and, *a fortiori*, no collective autodetermination.

The reason behind this crusade against common will presupposes an interesting standpoint as to what "will" is in general. Hägerström conceived "will" only as active capacity, characterised by a conative impulse, not as passive acceptance. To him it was absurd to claim that anyone could actually *want* a custom that only survives through absence of active desire to change things. Therefore, he also opposed another Hobbesian inheritance, namely Austin's view of tacit consent grounding

[84] Hägerström, *Inquiries, supra* note 22 at 27.

[85] *Ibid*. at 24; *cf*. Hägerström, *Är gällande rätt, supra* note 75 at 178.

[86] Hägerström, *Rätten och staten, supra* note 22 at 265; *cf*. also Axel Hägerström, *Der römische Obligationsbegriff im Lichte der allgemeinen römischen Rechtanschauung*, volume II, *Über die Verbalobligation* ed. by Karl Olivecrona (Uppsala: SKHVSU Almqvist & Wiksell, 1941) at 13.

[87] Hägerström, *Inquiries, supra* note 22 at 41.

[88] Thomas Hobbes, *Leviathan* (1651) part 2, chap. 26.

[89] Austin, *The Province, supra* note 30 at 212.

[90] Hägerström, *Inquiries, supra* note 22 at 21; *Rätten och viljan, supra* note 22 at 175.

custom: "it is a perversely modernised interpretation of the facts to say that the state gives binding force by an 'express or tacit law' to 'ancient customs.'"[91] To his eye, a custom arises from the "conditions of human social life through the direct influence which the modes of behaviour of others have on the individual,"[92] regardless of *tacitus consensus populi*.

Generally speaking, Hägerström intended "will" physiologically, in a sense not far from cognitive science;[93] on other occasions he questioned the very existence of free will: Since I decide my will without being myself under any causal law, "the idea is obviously totally absurd (…). Nothing is more illogical than the idea of free will."[94] Here we have another similitude with Hobbes, *i.e.* the interpretation of man as a machine where the causal nexus is ultimately what counts.

> It is impossible to leave unsettled the question of *what is the subject* to whom the unitary willing, which is alleged to be present in positive law, belongs. A subject which wills must be found, for willing cannot exist without one.[95]

In other words, behind the "formalistic" definition of law in terms of command we have to be able to point to a "real" (physiologic and individual) will. If no such substrate is found, the will of the state becomes indeterminate and, as we know from Hägerström's epistemological work, what lacks determinateness also falls short of reality.

In Austin's theory a real subject is indicated. Here law is identified with the will of the *de facto* power holders to whom the *bulk* of the population has a *habit of obedience*. Austin avoided the abovementioned problems: what the *de facto* power holders want is not some form of transcendent will but the desire of people in flesh and blood.

However, Hägerström's refutation of Austin's will-theory is strictly linked to his criticism of *sovereignty*. In a nutshell, he accused Austin of narrowing the focus on *rex facit legem*, forgetting the other side of the coin: *lex facit regem*. In fact, if the law equals to the sovereign's will, then, in the event of a sovereign disobeying the constitution, we would have to conclude that the constitution would no longer be in force "which in turn dissolves the existing identity between the will and the law."[96]

---

[91] *Ibid.* at 60.

[92] *Ibid.* at 63.

[93] *Ibid.* at 150.

[94] Axel Hägerström, *Moralpsykologi* ed. by Martin Fries (Stockholm: Natur & Kultur, 1952) at 185.

[95] Hägerström, *Inquiries, supra* note 22 at 36; *cf.* Hägerström, *Är gällande rätt, supra* note 75 at 191. On the analogy with the machine and its implications for SLR, see my "Social Tools and Legal Gears: Hägerström on the Nature of Law" in *Axel Hägerström and Modern Social Thought* ed. by Sven Eliaeson *et al.* (Oxford: Bardwell Press, forthcoming, 2013).

[96] Max Lyles, *A Call for Scientific Purity. Axel Hägerström's Critique of Legal Science* (Stockholm: Rönnells, 2006) at 338.

Hägerström therefore insisted that Austin's model is not grounded in constitutional states, but on despotism (*herravälde, Herrschaft*):

> It is pure despotism which serves as a model for the theory under discussion. In particular it has been occasioned by the idea (which is not adequately supported by facts) of the Roman emperor as "*princeps legibus solutus.*" It has been assumed that all law must rest upon such a power not subject to any law.[97]

Austin's theory would then imply that "the constitution, insofar as it regulates the activities of those in supreme power (…) is (…) devoid of all meaning."[98] This happens because if, in constitutional states, "the supreme authority must base itself on the established constitution in all legislation," it follows that "no constitutional rules as such can be described as a mere command or declaration of intention on the part of the possessors of power."[99]

> Must not constitutional law have first gained authority, no matter in what way this may have happened, in constitutionally governed states, in order that a certain person shall have any authority from the legal point of view?[100]

The ultimate risk of imperativism, as far as Hägerström is concerned, seems to be that it accords unclear priority to legislation among the sources of law. Consider that for instance statute law appears to be far more will-focused – thus fitting squarely into this kind of voluntaristic definition of law – than, say, *ius cogens*.

> The will-theory would still be relatively harmless, if it were not made the basis for deriving ostensibly scientific propositions with juridical content. What happens is that the supposed will of the state is used as a measuring-rod for judging the claims of other sources of law, *e.g.*, custom, the spirit of the law, the nature of the situation, equity etc., to validity, in addition to the law in the strict sense.[101]

The commonplace account of *fons iuris* covers, so to say, with apparent scientific character a State and legislation focused ideology. The sovereigns, or *de facto* power-holders, as *pouvoir constituent*, no matter how much they want something, may lose all importance after the constitution's coming into force:

> Suppose, *e.g.*, that a constitution, proclaimed by one of the heads of fortuitously collected armed forces, obtains their immediate support. Then it gains stability by causes which operate universally; *e.g.*, its approximate agreement with the national ideas of justice, the people's need of peace, the lack of organization among those classes with a rebellious tendency, etc. (…). What became the basis of the newly founded state (…) at the foundation of

---

97 Hägerström, *Inquiries, supra* note 22 at 35; Hägerström, *Är gällande rätt, supra* note 75 at 190.

98 *Ibid.* at 30; Hägerström, *Är gällande rätt, supra* note 75 at 184.

99 *Ibid.* at 34; Hägerström, *Är gällande rätt, supra* note 75 at 88. In Hägerström's jargon, a constitutional state is not a state inspired by the political doctrine of constitutionalism; it is a political organization with a developed system of sources of law where law is applied in an orderly and constant way, in opposition to pure despotism and mob-rule.

100 Hägerström, *Inquiries, supra* note 22 at 31.

101 *Ibid.* at 42.

> the American constitution, was not the *de facto* power of such and such persons. It was certain rules for exercising power within the region concerned, rules which derived their importance from being norms for the judges in carrying out the duties of their office (…). Certainly English law had no longer force in this instance. Nor did the proceedings for founding the constitution rest upon it. But there were other rules for the exercise of power which here *governed men's minds and thereby had* de facto *effectiveness* (*faktisk ideell kraft*)[[102]] (…). It was considered that the English crown had lost its rights over the colonies in question through wronging them, and that power had been transferred to its natural basis, the people. There were rules, regarded as belonging to the law of nature, according to which people themselves had certain fundamental rights.[103]

This is the critical issue with Austin's "sociological" approach to validity: its overestimation of brute force. "Law is not simply a regime of constraint."[104] To Hägerström, the forces operating in society (that jurists evasively call the "will of the state") are formed out of "a medley of all kinds of heterogeneous factors,"[105] some of which are quite close to those cited by Austin, such as:

> The habit of the people to obey decrees which present themselves with claims to authority (…) popular feeling of justice, class-interest, the general inclination to adapt oneself to circumstances, fear of anarchy, lack of organization among the discontent part of the people, and (…) the inherited custom of observing what is called the law of the land. [Hereby] law is maintained without any will intervening.[106]

5.4.2 Olivecrona Reads Austin

Olivecrona *pushed* the criticism *even further* by identifying legal positivism *tout court* with imperativism: the term 'legal positivism' – he announces – will therefore be used to denote "theories which are *professedly* built on the basic assumption that real law is the expression of the will of the supreme authority in society."[107] Imperativism is also a characteristic of natural law, implying that positivism still works within the very same framework, that of voluntarism:

> The difference between nineteenth century legal positivism and classical natural law doctrine was a difference of opinion within the framework of voluntarism (…). The voluntaristic assumption (…) has been like a signpost through which generations of philosophers and jurists have been induced to take the wrong road.[108]

---

[102] The English version states "rules that had actual power in the realm of ideas" but I prefer the original version, since the Aristotelian terms of the English translation easily mislead. Hägerström intended a form of power that Max Weber would have called "ideological." The grip of such an ideological power can be tested *de facto*, just as today we have sociological research on values.

[103] Hägerström, *Inquiries, supra* note 22 at 31–32.

[104] Hägerström, *Rätten och staten*, *supra* note 22 at 223.

[105] Hägerström, *Inquiries, supra* note 22 at 39.

[106] *Ibid.* at 38–39.

[107] Olivecrona, *Law as Fact* 2nd ed. *supra* note 25 at 43.

[108] *Ibid.* at 79–80.

At a closer look, though, Olivecrona also *restricted the scope* of the criticism of Hägerström. Indeed, while Hägerström wanted – to use Cassirer's wording – to free man from the idol of the State as God, Olivecrona noted that this deification process at hand in many forms of legal positivism cannot be found in Austin:

> The reproach that legal positivism made the state a god could only be directed against idealistic positivism. Naturalistic positivism implies no deification of the state, since it ascribes binding force to the commands of the sovereign in the sense only that the commands are accompanied by threats.[109]

Even if it is evident that "legal relations," in Austin's view, are "power relations," Olivecrona nonetheless identified Austin's weakness in that "the power of the sovereign is external only."[110] For the Austin that Olivecrona reads natural law is still clearly part of the legacy:

> The law was not invested with binding force in the usual sense. The law was only externally binding, as the teachers of natural law would have said: the commands of the sovereign were binding or obligatory in the sense only that the subjects were exposed to the threat of some evil (…). The law of nature was eliminated. But the concept of positive law current in natural law doctrine was retained. The positive law now became the naked commands of a sovereign (…) lacking the mystical power over the minds of the subjects.[111]

What left Olivecrona unsatisfied with Austin's account is that "to have a legal duty is not merely to be exposed to the risk of sanctions."[112] In fact, he insisted that duty cannot be explained in reductionist terms as a question of punishment.[113]

Consequently, Olivecrona's analysis of imperatives, in chapter five of the second edition of *Law as Fact*, is a severe criticism of Austin. We are told that, contrarily to what Austin believed, the imperative is (a) no wish; (b) no command; (c) not grounded on threats of sanction; (d) and not reducible to statements. At a first glance, this reading is unforgiving. However, at a deeper level of analysis, the "simple element" of law that Austin identified in the unconditional imperative character of rules is also for Olivecrona the very cornerstone of a sound understanding of what a norm truly is.

Olivecrona thus credited Austin with the insight that the form of expression of a rule is imperative: "Austin says that the concept of a command is the key to the science of jurisprudence and morals. There is much truth in this. The imperatives are essential both in law and morals."[114] He recognised that Austin – in *The Province of Jurisprudence Determined* – had fully realised the imperative character of law,

---

[109] *Ibid.* at 47.

[110] *Ibid.* at 32.

[111] *Ibid.* at 45.

[112] *Ibid.* at 46.

[113] Karl Olivecrona, "Legal Language and Reality" in *Essays in Honor of Roscoe Pound* ed. by Ralph A. Newman (Indianapolis, IN: The American Society for Legal History, 1962) 151–191, at 158.

[114] Olivecrona, *Law as Fact* 2nd ed. *supra* note 25 at 120.

although his error was to link the imperative features with the voluntaristic description of law. For the Swede, no will lies behind the imperativistic nature of law:

> The meaning of a law is not to say that you ought to do so-and-so if you want to reap such and such benefits, or that you ought to abstain from certain kinds of actions if you do not want to expose yourself to sanctions. The law says that you *shall* do this or that (…). The form of the law is imperative (…). The imperative is unconditional […but] we are apparently faced by a dilemma. On the one hand, the imperative character of the laws is evident (…). On the other hand, no commanding authority can be said to exist.[115]

According to Olivecrona, Austin's misstep was simply *a step too far*: it has often been added that a declaration of will, in order to be a command, "must be accompanied by a threat of some evil consequence in the case of contrary behaviour. This view on the nature of a command has been expounded in a classical way by Austin."[116] Still the imperative, on Olivecrona's reading, is *no command* in the sense that commands are those imperatives that are given by a person who stands face-to-face to the addressee.[117] Moreover, the imperative is no wish:[118]

> The relationship between a wish and such verbal expressions as Austin has in mind is misunderstood when an imperative phrase is interpreted either as a statement concerning the existence of a wish or as a direct expression of a wish (…). It should be added that a wish is a common motive for issuing a command, but by no means the only possible one (…). Giving a certain command can even be utterly distasteful to him who has given it.[119]

One of the most interesting remarks that Olivecrona makes on this occasion concerns the relationship between physical power and authority. The accusation against Austin is not – like in so many other contemporary readings – that his "naturalistic positivism" would have reduced right to might. Olivecrona's point is instead that Austin missed to see that authority has no strict and necessary link to power. Just like in Pope Gelasius I's doctrine of the two swords, *potestas* is just one of the two-headed Janus of which *auctoritas* is the second and no less important factor:

> Austin takes it for granted that an imperative phrase could have no effect unless it be accompanied by a threat which is serious because the speaker has the power of carrying it out. This is also a misconception (…). Situations occur in which a command may take effect without being backed by any power or any threats. Some people have the capability of impressing others in such a way that their commands are complied with.[120]

This authoritative element, *e.g.*, charisma, is fundamental for understanding the functioning of all sorts of normative phenomena, not only that of the law.

Another important comment that Olivecrona made here is not strictly connected to Austin. Rather, it has to do with Hart's view according to which Austin had not

---

[115] *Ibid.* at 118–120.

[116] *Ibid.* at 121.

[117] *Ibid.* at 120.

[118] *Cf.* Austin, *The Province, supra* note 30 at 21.

[119] Olivecrona, *Law as Fact* 2nd ed. *supra* note 25 at 122.

[120] *Ibid.*

realised that to command is characteristically to exercise authority over men, not power to inflict harm.[121] Olivecrona's remarks concern the relationship between authority and "the right to command", *i.e.* legitimacy. Since many maintain that a command falls flat if it does not come from an authority that can legitimately issue such commands, he noticed that "a command may be obeyed for other reasons. Fear, habit, personal respect for the commander, pure suggestion etc., or a combination of such factors, may be decisive."[122] So, command does not presuppose legitimate authority. This is an argument against Hart and in favour of Austin. In fact, Hart's reason for claiming that "we cannot profitably use, in the elucidation of law, the notion of a command" is that the notion of command implies that of authority, which in turn calls on the notion of law, so as to invalidate the whole definition. For Olivecrona, on the contrary, Hart's error is in the following:

> [Hart erroneously] rejects Austin's contention that the notion of a command is the key to the science of jurisprudence (…). The concept of command is surely most important for the elucidation of the concept of law. It has to be defined without reference to the law. Therefore, there is no circularity (as Hart seems to suggest) in explaining the nature of the law by means of the concept of (…) imperatives in general.[123]

Olivecrona still had another argument against Austin's conception of commands; these are no "constative utterances." In the view of John Austin, a command is a combination of statements of both kinds: "first a statement about the mind of the speaker, then a statement about sanctions to follow in case of disobedience."[124] To reduce imperatives to statements amounts to what Olivecrona called a "strangely rationalistic view of the causes of men's behaviour."[125] The reason is that suggestion and other subliminal stimuli motivate action far more than any "knowledge" about someone else's wishes or any "understanding" of why I would benefit from obeying.

To conclude, we might say that Olivecrona presented his analysis of Austin in order to ameliorate it and provide a more satisfying account of the imperative element in law. His *pars construens*, as commonly known, is the idea of *independent imperatives* that he developed in close dialogue with some of Austin's arguments. According to this view, the imperatives we find in the law (but not only) "may conveniently be called independent imperatives" since, he argues, they are independent of the personal relationship characteristic of a command. "They are similar to commands in the proper sense in that they serve as means of inculcating a certain behaviour in a categorical way."[126]

---

[121] Herbert L. A. Hart, *The Concept of Law* (Oxford: Oxford University Press, 1961) at 19.

[122] *Ibid*. at 124.

[123] *Ibid*. at 125.

[124] *Ibid*.

[125] *Ibid*. at 126.

[126] *Ibid*. at 129.

In this category Olivecrona included not only traditional legal formulas but also imperatives-as-non-statements, such as the presence of a fence or a lock, that are no verbal expressions but that clearly signal "hands off!" to the potential intruder.[127] The bottom line is that Austin functioned like the jumping ground that enabled Olivecrona to go beyond Hägerström's mordant criticism and develop the idea that "the clue to the riddle" of the nature of the legal rules is the concept of *independent imperatives*. "The imperative character of those rules is evident. But an imperative is no declaration of will."[128]

5.5 Core Differences

In confronting SLR and Austin, besides the explicit and specific criticisms and contrasting opinions on minor arguments (*e.g.* the doctrine of tacit consent founding custom), mention should be made of two unbridgeable divergences:

First, the view on morals; Austin embraced a form of cognitivism (that some contemporary legal scholars call objectivism,[129] but probably would go under the label prescriptivism or expressivism in contemporary meta-ethics); while the Scandinavians supported a strict form of non-cognitivism. Austin believed an ethical science to be possible that would indicate the correct rules we need to follow; the Scandinavians, on the basis of Hägerström's meta-ethical theory, denied any such possibility.

Secondly, the view on coercion: Austin claimed that law is made up out of rules which are upheld by force while the Scandinavians challenged this by considering the rules of law to concern the application of coercion. In a nutshell, force no longer qualifies *how* we define what law is, but rather *what* that law regulates. Let us start with the first point.

5.5.1 *The View of Morals*

A well-established habit in philosophy is the use of simple labels for complex traditions. In philosophy of law, this is the case of positivism, to which numerous meanings have been attached and under which multiple subcategories have been distinguished.

---

[127] *Ibid.* at 129.

[128] *Ibid.* at 130.

[129] José Juan Moreso usually uses this label and it has become legion among lawyers in the Neo-Latin speaking world: see his "Positivismo jurídico, relativismo moral y liberalismo politico" in (2012) *Teoria Politica* 103–110; and generally his *La Constitución: modelo para armar* (Madrid: Marcial Pons, 2009). I object to this position in "Doppiando il Capo Horn della scienza del diritto: Sull'oggettivismo post-metafisico quale fondamento del positivismo inclusivo" in (2012) *Teoria Politica* 143–160.

Without addressing the *vexata quaestio* of defining legal positivism, Austin's complex relation to this vast *corpus* of thought is nonetheless illuminating for introducing the first core difference dividing Austin from the Scandinavians: the view of morals.

In his 1962 book on Hobbes, Bentham and Austin, Mario A. Cattaneo made an exemplary attempt of grasping Austin's specificities with the use of simple labels:

> Austin shall thus be classified as a natural law theorist (…) in the sense of an author that establishes a series of absolute and objective principles (divine law recognizable through the principle of utility) that enables the criticism of existing law and serves for making new law. These principles determine ideal law: the legal character of positive law does not follow from them, but its potential moral value does (…). Austin is a positivist (…) insofar as he eliminates every moral element from his definition of the concept of law; he is no positivist (…) insofar as he makes the duty of obeying the law follow from their utility (and admits the principle of resistance); he is no positivist (…) since he is no ethical relativist and believes in the possibility of determining absolute and objective ethical principles.[130]

To put it succinctly: for the Scandinavians – largely inspired by the non-cognitivist and emotivist theory developed by Hägerström[131] – there are "no absolute and objective principles" enabling to assess the "moral value" of positive law. This entails four major theses that – even though this is not the place to sketch them out – do represent the very opposite of Austin's ethical theory, as anyone who has taken the trouble to read past the *Province of Jurisprudence Determined* into the *Lectures on Jurisprudence* will know:

(a) There are no moral properties (against "objectivism"[132])
(b) There can be no science in morality (against rationalism)
(c) There are no beliefs expressed in moral statements (against cognitivism)
(d) There can be no reduction of moral assessments to judgements grounded in practical reason (against Kantism).

Contrarily to these theses, Austin was deeply convinced of the importance of utilitarianism; he devoted a lengthy part of the *Lectures* to an exposition of ethical and political theories.[133] The classical reading of Austin – suggested by Lord Bryce's irritation over the space Austin accorded to the principle of utility that "has nothing to do with the Analytic Method, nor with positive law"[134] – refused to treat the ethical dimension in connection to Austin's jurisprudential work. Doing so, it opened

---

[130] Cattaneo, *Il positivismo giuridico inglese*, *supra* note 17 at 276; *cf.* Mario A. Cattaneo, "John Austin" (1978) 8:1 *Materiali per una cultura giuridica* 11–95.

[131] See Mindus, *A Real Mind, supra* note 2 in chapter 3.

[132] See note 129.

[133] Andrew D.E. Lewis, "John Austin (1790–1859) Pupil of Bentham" (1979) 2 *The Bentham Newsletter* 19.

[134] Quote from Rumble, *The Thought of John Austin, supra* note 7 at 60.

the gates for arrangements where Austin's theory is, at the same time, squeezed into the pigeonholes of both positivism and natural law, or into other incompatible groupings.[135]

Ever since Henry Maine pointed out that Austin's ideas were "consistent with *any* ethical theory,"[136] countless scholars have criticised the central chapters of Austin's *Lectures* on ethics as unrelated to his work on law. In recent years, however, a different reading has been making its way. Some scholars, such as Wilfred Rumble, have started to view Austin's work as a unified whole and not unrelated parts. In such a view:

> The impact of utilitarian arguments constitute (…) one reason for his unshakeable commitment to [the basic components of his conception of law and sovereignty]. It is difficult to understand how this conviction could fail to influence some basic concepts of his legal philosophy (…). The impact of a similar line of reasoning on his conceptions of law and sovereignty would explain why he devoted so much space to the analysis of ethics.[137]

My interest in this novel reading depends on the fact that it enables to shed light on some of the *core differences* between Austin and the Scandinavian realists. Regardless of the impact of Austin's ethical considerations on the consistency of his legal theory, what needs to be emphasised is his overall interest for ethics and belief in "absolute principles."

To Austin, in point of fact, discussions on ethical questions constitute "necessary steps" in order to engage in jurisprudence. In the *prospectus* over the remaking of *The Province of Jurisprudence Determined* – quoted by his wife in its second edition – he made it clear that his object of study was threefold, being "the principles and relations of law, morals and ethics: meaning by law *positive law*, by morals *positive morals*, and by ethics, the principles which are the test of both."[138] This enquiry into the normative side of Man's life was initiated by the inquiry into "abstract jurisprudence." For Sarah Austin, her husband felt jurisprudence and ethics to be closely related and refers that his opinion of the necessity of "an entire *refonte*" of the book arouse, in great measure, from his conviction, "which had continually been gaining strength in his mind that until the ethical notions of men were more clear and consistent, no considerable improvement could be hoped for in legal or political science."[139] Divine law (the stated foundation of his ethical system), positive law and positive morality are not separated but "connected by numerous and indissoluble ties."[140]

---

[135] Krzysztof Dybowski, "John Austin – Positivist or Utilitarist?" (1992) 78 *ARSP* 407–411; René Sève, "La théorie du droit de John Austin: le positivisme tel qu'il devrait être?" (1988) 13 *Cahiers de philosophie politique et juridique de l'Université de Caen* 69–84.

[136] Quote from Rumble, *The Thought of John Austin, supra* note 7 at 60.

[137] Rumble, *The Thought of John Austin, supra* note 7 at 107–108.

[138] Austin, *The Province, supra* note 30 at 16.

[139] *Ibid.* at 15.

[140] *Ibid.* at 14.

It is clear from these briefs observations that Austin advanced a theory radically different from the Scandinavians who developed a thoroughly non-cognitivist program. Still, it has been observed that utilitarianism offers a teleological form of ethical inquiry that has no necessary connection to so-called moral objectivism: Bentham, for instance, would not have developed an objectivist program.[141] "Austin, however, moves away from his allegedly empiricist epistemology, as he does with his legal theory and assumes the existence of ethical entities independent from human activity."[142]

There are several implications. First, Austin adopted a standpoint opposed to Hägerström's "ontological" thesis sustaining axiological nihilism *(a)*, according to which there would be no moral proprieties:

> The mere factual character of something – may it even be a question of lust and desire – does not signify value or disvalue for me observing it, unless I take a stance *vis-à-vis* the fact, liking or disliking it. For me, there are no values whatsoever in the fact that I state, because I am entirely impartial in respect of what exists in fact. Only where I critically assume a position in respect of the fact, does it acquire axiological character.[143]

Secondly, Austin held that ethics is a science the purpose of which is to determine the "nature of the index to the tacit commands of the Deity."[144] One subdivision of ethics is the science of legislation, the business of which is to determine "positive law as it ought to be", *i.e.* what we today call policy counselling. Hägerström challenged such accounts with his "epistemological" thesis (*b*), according to which there can never be any teaching *in* morality. We cannot scientifically establish the goodness of an action since there is no such thing as goodness, or any fact that entails goodness.[145]

Thirdly, since Austin was "an ardent utilitarian, he believed that evaluations of positive laws are capable of rational proofs."[146] This assumption was questioned by Hägerström's third thesis in meta-ethics (*c*) that offered a semantic form of non-cognitivism: here, moral propositions are neither true, nor false. In other words, utterances – including axiological or normative terms, such as good, bad, etc. – are not entirely susceptible of verification or falsification. For Hägerström, such statements have the same cognitive status as exclamations or interjections.

Fourthly, Austin developed a criticism of *moral sense*. He aimed to substitute intuitionism with a rational justification of moral sentiment. In Austin's view, since

[141] Moreso, "Cinco diferencias entre Bentham y Austin," *supra* note 17; José Juan Moreso, *La teoría del derecho de Bentham* (Barcelona: PPU, 1992). On Bentham and SLR, see Francesco Ferraro and Francesca Poggi, *The "Real" Bentham. Bentham and Legal Realism* (in *Analisi & Diritto*, 2012 forthcoming).

[142] Turégano Mansilla, *Derecho y moral, supra* note 59 at 445.

[143] Hägerström, *Kritiska punkter, supra* note 49 at 61–62.

[144] Austin, *The Province, supra* note 30 at 14.

[145] Axel Hägerström, *Moralfilosofins grundläggning* ed. by Thomas Mautner (Stockholm: Almqvist & Wiksell International, 1987) at 45.

[146] Rumble, *The Thought of John Austin, supra* note 7 at 76.

many of the commands of the Deity are not revealed, we need an "index" to identify what they impose: moral sense is an unreliable standard and should be reject in favour of the principle of utility. However, this principle does not apply to actions (otherwise exceptions would overflow) but to rules, leading to the elaboration of his so-called *rule-utilitarianism*:

> Utility would be the test of our conduct, ultimately, but not immediately: the immediate test of the rules to which our conduct would conform, but not the immediate test of specific or individual actions. Our rules would be fashioned on utility; our conduct, on our rules.[147]

Now, the reasons for opting for a specific set of rules will not become apparent to each single individual, hence the need for a moral authority to guide people. Most persons cannot afford to dedicate themselves to discovering ethical knowledge and therefore "many rules of conduct (…) will be taken (…) on authority."[148] This view of Austin's is at odds with a forth thesis elaborated by Hägerström according to which the nature of moral judgement is not a rational judgement or informed opinion on reality *(d)*. It is rather a mental act of a different kind, involving emotion. In this sense it is commonly claimed that Hägerström elaborated a form of emotivism. Accordingly, I cannot conceive an action to be right or wrong, without experiencing, at the same time, a feeling, which Hägerström described as a "conative impulse toward the action,"[149] *i.e.* I cannot distinguish between moral conceptions and the belief in their reality.

Generally speaking, we can say that whereas Austin was a moral objectivist and a cognitivist, Hägerström was a non-cognitivist and an emotivist. The two perspectives could not be more different.

5.5.1.1 The View of Coercion

A second core difference dividing the Austinian position from that of the Scandinavian realists concerns the view of coercion. This claim might seem a little counter-intuitive: should not the emphasis on coercion, force, and fear of sanction be a point in common? Austin was accused early on, by Maine and Bryce, of reducing law to force through the theory of sovereignty. Both Austin and the Scandinavian realist movement have been associated with the Thrasymachian slogan "Might is Right." Such accusations are hard to die: for instance, Austin has recently been portrayed as a "realist" (not in the sense of legal realism, but in the Hobbesian and Machiavellian tradition of political realism): "Austin's theory is (…) a theory of the 'rule of men': of government using law as an instrument of power."[150] In reference

[147] Austin, *The Province, supra* note 30 at 4.

[148] *Ibid.* at 60.

[149] Hägerström, *Inquiries, supra* note 22 at 152.

[150] Roger Cotterrell, *Scholar in Law: English Jurisprudence from Blackstone to Hart* (New York: NYU Press, 1996) at 70.

to the Scandinavians, similar allegations are easy to find.[151] As far as Austin is concerned, it should also be added that Arduino Agnelli insisted – half a century ago – on the inaccuracy of those accusing Austin of reductionism:

> Physical force, on which Austin's critics greatly insist, is only an instrument that authority uses in political society and does not at all establish its foundation, which, on the contrary, has to be found in the principle of utility.[152]

Nevertheless, the alleged *similarity* in equating law and force obscures a significant *difference*. I therefore claim that the view of coercion and its role in the legal theoretical architecture of the two outlooks are fundamentally different. To substantiate my claim I will be following a suggestion made by the Italian legal theorist Norberto Bobbio in a highly readable yet seldom read book from 1979 entitled *Il positivismo giuridico*.

Bobbio started by stressing the overall importance of *vis coactiva* in legal positivism:

> Legal positivism is characterized by the fact that it constantly defines law in function of coercion (…). The coercive conception of law (…) implicitly refers to the social organization that first and foremost holds this force, *i.e.* the State; hence, to define the law in function of coercion means to consider law from the point of view of the State. The coercive definition is therefore grounded on a state-centred view of law: in fact, it is coeval to the formation of the modern State, that was theorized by Hobbes in the 17th century, even though it triumphs in the era of legal positivism.[153]

Bobbio, on this occasion, also observed that the majority of those who support the classical theory of coercion "deny the legal nature of international law, [starting with] Austin who considers the international order to be positive morality."[154] On this reading, Austin represents what can be labelled the traditional doctrine of coercion: classical coercion theory claims that the law is *made up* by rules which are upheld by force, in the sense that positive law is enforced through sanctions, defined as "any conditional evil annexed to a law to produce obedience and conformity to it"[155] and thus reducible to this "essence." According to this view, we are always

---

[151] Alexander Peczenik, "Den skandinaviska rättsrealismen" in *Rättsfilosofi: samhälle och moral genom tiderna* ed. by Joakim Nergelius (Lund: Studentlitteratur, 2001) 117–127, esp. 122–124; Johan Strang, "Axel Hägerström och Gunnar Myrdal. Om den svenska värdenihilistiska traditionen" (2003) 1 *Historisk Tidskrift för Finland* 43–61, at 43; Jacob Sundberg, "A Chair in Jurisprudence" in *Perspectives on Jurisprudence – Essays in Honor of Jes Bjarup* ed. by Peter Wahlgren Scandinavian Studies in Law, vol. 48 (Stockholm: Jure, 2005) 432–464, at 434.

[152] Arduino Agnelli, *John Austin, alle origini del positivismo giuridico* (Torino: Giappichelli, 1959) at 112.

[153] Norberto Bobbio, *Il positivismo giuridico* (Giappichelli: Torino, 1979) at 172; on the centrality of sanctions in Austin and more generally in positivism, see Colin Tapper, "Austin on Sanctions" 1965 *The Cambridge Law Journal* 271–287; Frederick Schauer, "Was Austin Right After All?: On the Role of Sanctions in a Theory of Law" (2010) 23 *Ratio Juris* 1–21.

[154] Bobbio, *Positivismo giuridico, supra* note 153 at 181.

[155] Austin, *The Province, supra* note 30 at 118.

dealing with a *suffering* entailed by the sanction, even when the offence is sanctioned by nullities. There is, however, also a different, "modern" version of the theory:

> From Jhering onwards, [coercion] has been subjected to an entire development, often unconsciously, up to the point where it started to indicate *a completely different thing* (…). For the classical theory, coercion is the means through which legal norms gain validity; or, in other words, law is a set of enforced norms; for the modern theory, coercion is the object of legal norms; or, in other words, law is a set of norms regulating the use of force.[156]

Accordingly, when the State is defined as enjoying *Zwangsgewalt* (Jhering), coercion is no longer a *means* through which legal norms gain validity, but coercion is instead the *object* of these norms. More specifically, the point concerns the so-called primary and secondary norms defined by their different receivers, being the citizens in the first case and the "organs of the State" in the second case. This distinction between types of norms, on the basis of the criteria of the addressee, was another feature that Hägerström picked up, leading him towards the "modern theory of coercion" that Bobbio outlined. In the case of Jhering, only norms directed to state officials, such as judges, are to be considered as purely legal norms. Bobbio saw the inconsistency of such views:

> Is there not a contradiction between defining law as a set of norms that gain validity through enforcement and holding that legal norms are only those directed to judges? In fact the latter are not norms that gain their validity through force (they are observed following a phenomenon of spontaneous adhesion); rather such norms discipline the use of coercion on the citizens.[157]

This point was exactly what Hägerström had discovered, commenting on Jhering: State officials comply out of a *sense of duty*, whereas coercion is used primarily in other areas of the law, or in relation to those norms that are directed not to the "organs of the State" but rather to the citizens.[158] Discussing constitutional law, Hägerström distinguished between two different sorts of norms: rules for normative production and rules for the attribution of competence.

> Law is warded as follows: 1) Rules of action, really meant for the highest or higher so-called state authorities (…). These are obviously rules for the lower authorities as well. But as the authorities respond *on lower levels, the rules of action increasingly become rules for supervising and punishing transgressions* (…); 2) the system provides rules for deciding who is to be considered overall as an authority in the state and for deciding the authorities' power to declare rules included in the system, like for example, rules for deciding who is the judge and rules for deciding his competence.[159]

By pondering upon such different kinds of rules, including power-conferring rules, it becomes clear to Hägerström that coercion in the form of fear of sanction is

---

[156] Bobbio, *Positivismo giuridico, supra* note 153 at 182–83.

[157] *Ibid.* at 182.

[158] See Enrico Pattaro, "From Hägerström to Ross and Hart" (2009) 22:4 *Ratio Juris* 532–48.

[159] Hägerström, *Rätten och staten, supra* note 22 at 212–13.

not the predominant motive for obeying the law, at least not at the *higher levels of the judicial order*. On the contrary, Hägerström noted that "at the lower levels (…) the means of criminal law always acquire greater weight [than sense of duty]"[160] but, at the "higher levels" coercion no longer plays such a propulsive role. Whereas the ordinary judge holds himself to valid law because of his sense of duty, *i.e.* his unwillingness to pass unfair judgements and to be technically speaking a "bad" judge, fear of punishment lingers on the common man:

> Just like we need to presuppose that the ordinary judge does not want to pass unfair verdicts because (…) of his sense of duty, we could only presuppose that the ordinary citizen would probably not follow the constraints if the sword of law did not hang over him.[161]

Be that as it may. What seems to be emerging from the "modern theory of coercion" is that there are certain rules – regardless of whether these should be called norms[162] – such as, rules of competence and permission[163] that, say, confer on a person the power to change legal relations, that are not supported by force (*e.g.* in constitutional and administrative law). Realising this made Austin exclude such rules from being legal and this line of thought also made him develop the often-criticised view that failure to comply with such rules leads to sanctions in form of nullity. As we know, later theorists, such as Hart, would insist power-conferring rules are not commands with nullity as a sanction but need to be grasped "over and above coercive control."[164] In other words, Austin still understood the nature of law as essentially tied to its use, or probability, of sanctions, and was thus led to conclude that nullity is nothing but a kind of sanction, following a quite traditional understanding of the great divide between *ius perfectum* and *ius imperfectum*.

Even though the norm-theory in Hägerström does not at all share the complexity of late twentieth century deontic logic, it seems that his insistence on non-statute law, on the one hand, and authority-conferring rules, on the other, pushed him to the conclusion that "law is not simply a regime of constraint."[165] While legal rules might belong to a system that regulates use of power in society – following a reading often associated with the Weberian conception of the State as having *Gewaltmonopol* – all legal rules, however, are not sanction-based. It might thus well be true that law (*inter alia*) constitutes a system of social control through the determination of sanctions. But it should be clear by now that we use the law to inscribe and constitute as much as we use it to prescribe.

[160] *Ibid.* at 207.

[161] *Ibid.*

[162] See Torben Spaak, "Norms that Transfer Competence" (2003) 16 *Ratio Juris* 89–104.

[163] See Eugenio Bulygin, "On Norms of Competence" (1992) 11 *Law and Philosophy* 201–216; and Francesca Poggi, *Norme permissive* (Torino: Giappichelli, 2004).

[164] Herbert L. A. Hart, *The Concept of Law* (2nd ed.) ed. by Penelope A. Bulloch and Joseph Raz (Oxford: Oxford University Press, 1994) at 41.

[165] Hägerström, *Rätten och staten, supra* note 22 at 221.

This is precisely the point that Alf Ross picks up in his criticism of Austin. In the section on "law and compulsion" in *Towards a Realistic Jurisprudence*, Ross mentioned Austin as part of those theories that have been at pains in conciliating law and coercion:

> There are large domains, especially in constitutional law and international law, which is normally included in the sphere of law, but to which the criterion of compulsion does not seem to apply. These domains have then either been consistently kept out of the sphere of the law (*cf.* Austin) or in a more or less dextrous and convincing fashion an attempt has been made to discover the element of compulsion within these domains too.[166]

As with all progressive and gradual changes, "it is hard to establish how and when the passage from the classical to the modern theory of coercion occurred."[167] In this story, it seems that Kelsen played a somewhat ambiguous role. Bobbio claimed that in Kelsen, we would no longer be dealing with coercion as a mere means for defining what a legal rule is, but as the object that the system of law disciplines. In *General Theory of the State*, Kelsen stated the following:

> The rule of law is not a rule the efficacy of which is secured by another rule providing for a sanction (…). A rule is a legal rule not because its efficacy is secured by another rule providing for a sanction; a rule is a legal rule because it provides for a sanction.[168]

Perhaps due to Kelsen's not all too clear formulation and because of other aspects of his work,[169] including, I take it, the very theory of power-conferring rules as fragments of larger rules ultimately entailing sanctions, it is not obvious where to situate Kelsen.

Since this distinction between classic and modern theory of coercion is not common in legal theory and, if I am not mistaken, has gone unnoticed even among legal theorists who read Bobbio as standard literature, an analogy might help to grasp the point, and it ultimately has to do with the relation between law and a specific, historically determined social institution we have been calling "state" even since Machiavelli coined the expression at the start of *The Prince*. It seems to me that the analogy shows that we refer to two quite different problems when speaking of coercion.

The (classic) role of coercion in the legal system might be considered analogous to the role of electric energy in surgery. Of course, if you want to get an operation at any hospital today (the analogy excludes traditional barbers and field-surgeons), there is a need for electricity: no power, no surgery. This is the way classic theory of coercion thought of the relation between law and force: (coercive) power basically

---

[166] Alf Ross, *Towards a Realistic Jurisprudence. A Criticism of the Dualism in Law* (Copenhagen: Munksgaard, 1946) at 108–09.

[167] Bobbio, *positivismo giuridico, supra* note 153 at 182.

[168] Hans Kelsen, *General Theory of Law and State*, trans. by Anders Wedberg [first published 1945] (New Brunswick, NJ: Transaction Publ., 2006) at 29.

[169] *E.g.* see the famous remark on the Gorgon of power in Hans Kelsen, in *Veröffentlichungen der Vereinigung der Deutschen Staatsrechtslehrer* (Berlin: Gruyter, 1927) vol. 3, 54–55.

flows like (electric) power though the grid or system of law;[170] just as there can be no operation with the switches off, it is vain to call "law" the *ius imperfectum* – wishful thinking or abstract law, to adopt a more Hegelian tainted expression – of institutions lacking (or with low) enforcement-ability. Accordingly, rules of such social institutions might be moral, religious, customary, pertaining to the art of *savoir-vivre* etc., but they cannot be called legal; and, to continue with Hegel, such institutions belong to the sphere of the family and civil society, not to the State. Behind this conception of coercion, there is the Thrasymachian question, as old as philosophy itself, as Eleftheriadis correctly stresses.[171] Is it possible to reduce justice to power? This is the level of abstraction at which Austin is situated when claiming that for a law to be such a sanction has to be provided. This level of abstraction sets as observables a (determinate) law and (physical) force, *i.e.* sanction. This level of abstraction is the very same adopted by Weber in his seminal definition of the state in *Politik als Beruf*. Substitute 'state' with 'law' and 'force' (and/or 'violence') with 'sanction' and Weber sounds just like Austin:

> One can define the modern state (…) only in terms of the specific *means* peculiar to it, as to every political association, namely, the use of physical force. (…) Force is a means specific to the state. The state is considered the sole source of the 'right' to use violence. (…) The state is a relation of men dominating men, a relation supported by means of legitimate (…) violence. If the state is to exist, the dominated must obey the authority claimed by the powers that be.[172]

Power (*i.e.* the State) is here the means through which a given law gains validity and any rule that does not derive from the only social institution that (people perceive can) legitimately impose sanctions would not qualify as law – according to the tenets of the classical theory of coercion. This approach, as well known, lives on in the debates on whether moralsuasion of softlaw really is law.

A quite different level of abstraction is set in the modern theory of coercion, thus implying a different set of observables. To show this, let us go back to the chirurgical analogy: who in med school ever seriously worries about energy cuts? I take it most future surgeons focus on the kind of technicalities that need to be learnt in order to perform a specific kind of operation. Though it might be true that without electric energy none of these technicalities would matter since they could not be performed, that is not the kind of understanding that makes a surgeon; what makes a surgeon is the understanding on the technical rules of the trade – all of which, perhaps, need hospitals in order to be carried out correctly.

---

[170] Needless to add that the analogy was suggested by the famous comparison of Olivecrona in the first edition of *Law as Fact* (1939) which states that legislation is like a hydroelectric power plant; the attitudes of the 'bulk of the population' corresponds to the current; in the power plant the current is converted to electricity and distributed to the grid covering the territory of the state. This is a metaphor applied to legislation, *i.e.* to statutes originating in the state apparatus.

[171] See *infra* chapter 8.

[172] Max Weber, *Politics as Vocation* in *Essays in Sociology* ed. by Bryan S. Turner (London: Routledge Sociology Classics, 1991) 77–78.

Now the modern theory of coercion seems to presuppose that there is a (non-failed) state legislating. But the state is not just any *magna latroncina*: it cannot be replaced by just any "force" (*Macht*) – say, a bear with a club in its hands.[173] Rather, it is a legitimate power (*Herrschaft*) of the rational-legal type, pursuant to the Weberian classification in *Wirtschaft und Gesellschaft*. And it is so specifically because of the type of training that its bureaucrats have:

> The university-trained jurist, is peculiar to the Occident, especially to the European continent, and has been of decisive significance for the Continent's whole political structure. The tremendous after-effect of Roman law, as transformed by the late Roman bureaucratic state, stands out in nothing more clearly than the fact that everywhere the revolution of political management in the direction of the evolving rational state has been borne by trained jurists.[174]

In non-sociological terms, this means that what Merkel's *Stufenbau*, Hägerström's authority-conveying norms and much of later theorists' emphasis on non-sanction-backed law enable us to see is that – in Olivecrona's phrasing – "the traditional ways of defining the relationship between law and force must be discarded. It is impossible to maintain that law in a realistic sense is guaranteed or protected by force."[175]

This is so because there is a logic, typical of legal systems, that informs us *about how* it is possible to discipline power (*Macht*), which enables relatively peaceful coexistence. Any given settlement of *how* we regulate power in society can be subjected to ideological criticisms, an activity in which Hägerström engaged vigorously; that is criticisms of the reasons or motives out of which we obey "forces" that really have no physical "force" upon us; *i.e.* what Weber called "ideological power."

If we distinguish between Austin's "classical" theory of coercion and the "modern" theory that can be found, *inter alia*, in the Scandinavians, Alf Ross' otherwise rather puzzling statement becomes clear: "we must therefore insist that the relationship of the legal norms to force lies in the fact that they concern the application of force, not that they are upheld by means of force."[176]

In sum, it is an entirely different problem to inquire into what kind of procedural techniques and regulative designs are applied, *à la* Weber, in order to discipline (unregulated) power – which is the central question in the modern theory of coercion –; and to inquire on what kind of institution is able to structure our social relationships in such a way as to ensure compliance with its "laws" notwithstanding the fact that behind you no bear with a club might be standing. Austin's classical

[173] This image was suggested to me by Torben Spaak.

[174] Weber, *Politics as Vocation, supra* note 172 at 93.

[175] Olivecrona, *Law as Fact* 1st ed. 1939 at 134.

[176] Ross, *On Law and Justice, supra* note 27 at 53. Ross' embracing of the modern coercion theory also reverberated on his conception of the State, no longer reducible to Jhering's *Zwangsgewalt*: "A national law system is a body of rules concerning the exercise of physical force" (*Ibid.* at 52).

theory of coercion focuses on the second type of question and provides an answer: a law is a command coming from a specific kind of institution, *i.e.* the sovereign that is able to ensure the compliance of the "bulk of the population." The Scandinavians' modern theory of coercion instead stresses that our power-regulating technologies miss out on something crucial if defined in voluntaristic terms. Put differently, in any given hospital, surgery is performed according to technical rules that cannot be explained merely with the tricks of Edison's trade.

5.6 Conclusion

It is this "modern" theory of coercion – more than the meta-ethical theses – that pushed the realists to develop their view of the authoritative elements of law. Austin was a steppingstone for Hägerström and Olivecrona; his views were used by the Scandinavians as a foil for the elaboration and explanation of their own legal theories. By confronting Austin, they were able to blaze a new path as far as the relationship between law, force and authority is concerned. So we may rightly conclude that, to a great extent, the attack on the imperative theory of law stimulated the seminal work on the question of law's authoritative dimension in SLR; a dimension that late twentieth century philosophy of law would turn into one of its key components for understanding how the legal phenomena works and how it impacts our lives.

Acknowledgements Besides the participants in the UCL conference *John Austin and His Legacy*, I also thank the participants of the Uppsala Seminar in Philosophy of Law and the Uppsala Seminar in Practical Philosophy where previous versions of this paper were presented in 2011, and in particular I would like to thank Torben Spaak and Åke Frändberg for insightful comments.

Chapter 6
Sense and Nonsense About Austin's Jurisprudence from a Scandinavian Perspective*

Jes Bjarup

6.1 Introduction

I shall use the term "Scandinavian perspective" to refer to the so-called Scandinavian realists, the Swedes Axel Hägerström (1868–1939), Anders Vilhelm Lundstedt (1882–1955), Karl Olivecrona (1897–1980), and the Dane Alf Ross (1899–1979).[1] This division also suggest the demarcation between sense and non-sense in Austin's jurisprudence, Alf Ross holding that Austin's approach makes sense, which is vehemently denied by the Swedes. Ross applauds Austin's methodological approach and his theory of law, which I shall present in Sect. 6.2. Then I shall present Hägerström's philosophy and his view that Austin's theory exemplifies despotism and offer some critical comments in Sect. 6.3. Lundstedt's view that Austin's account is pure nonsense is dealt with in Sect. 6.4. Olivecrona follows Austin that the concept of command is essential for the understanding of law but he claims that Austin's analysis is mistaken and must be rejected in order to arrive at the theory of law as independent imperatives, which I shall deal with in Sect. 6.5. By way of conclusion I shall claim that the theory of law as independent imperatives leads to a distorted view of law and legal knowledge, and this makes room for Austin's theory of law as commands or rules of what is right and wrong conduct.

*This is a revised version of my paper presented at the conference *John Austin and His Legacy* organised by Professor Michael Freeman of the UCL Faculty of Laws, London 16th–17th December 2009. I wish to thank Michael Freeman for the invitation and Cassel Stiftelsen, Faculty of Law, Stockholm University for financial assistance.

[1] Jes Bjarup, "The Philosophy of Scandinavian Legal Realism" (2005) 18 *Ratio Juris* 1–15 for an overview.

J. Bjarup (✉)
University of Stockholm, Law School, Stockholm, Sweden
e-mail: jes.bjarup@stofanet.dk

M. Freeman and P. Mindus (eds.), *The Legacy of John Austin's Jurisprudence*, Law and Philosophy Library 103, DOI 10.1007/978-94-007-4830-9_6,

6.2 Ross on Austin

Ross studied law at the University of Copenhagen where he received the degree of law in 1922 and received a grant from the Faculty to study law abroad and went to England, France and Austria in 1923.[2] In Vienna he met Hans Kelsen and other members of the so-called Vienna School of Law and developed his interest in philosophical questions. Kelsen in particular made a deep impression on Ross as manifested in his manuscript *Theorie der Rechtsquellen* which was written during his stay in Vienna and completed in 1926, divided into a historical overview of the doctrines of legal sources in France, England, and Germany (pp. 3–192), and a systematic account of various theories of legal sources (pp. 195–434).[3] Ross subscribes to the Neo-Kantian view that philosophy is a transcendental inquiry grounded in reason concerned with the conditions of cognition in terms of categories that must be applied in order to arrive at knowledge within the various sciences. This is manifested in Kelsen's approach based upon the distinction between the category of is (*Sein*) and the category of ought (*Sollen*). The former is concerned with natural phenomenon whereas the latter is concerned with normative phenomenon, and in this respect law must be located in the category of ought in terms of positive law in relation to legal science concerned with the question what the law is as opposed to the question what the law ought to be that is not a scientific, but a political question. Since legal science is a normative science it must also be kept apart from historical, sociological and psychological inquiries, locating the law within the category of is. Thus Ross turns jurisprudence into a theory of legal cognition claiming that the traditional doctrines of the sources of law have failed to address what Ross calls "the question of the positivity of law" – that is to say the jurisprudential question what does the validity of legal system mean and the related question how is it possible to know that a legal rule exists or is a valid legal rule.[4] This is demonstrated in the historical survey with the exception of John Austin's jurisprudence dedicated to determine that "the matter of jurisprudence is positive law: law, simply and strictly so called: or law set by political superiors to political inferiors."[5]

For Ross, the merit of Austin's approach is that he has realised that the concept of law must be determined by "an a priori and deductive method as opposed to an empirical and inductive method" and the purity of his methodological approach to

---

[2] I draw upon my chapter "Alf Ross" in *Der Kreis um Hans Kelsen. Die Anfangsjahre der Reinen Rechtslehre* ed. by Robert Walter, Clemens Jabloner, Klaus Zeleny (Schriftenreihe des Hans Kelsen-Instituts, Wien: Manz, 2008) at 409–443.

[3] Alf Ross, *Theorie der Rechtsquellen. Ein Beitrag zur Theorie des positiven Rechts auf Grundlage dogmenhistorischer Untersuchungen*, in the book series *Wiener Staats- u. Rechtswissenschaftlichen Studien* (Band 13) ed. by Hans Kelsen (Deuticke: Leipzig/Wien, 1929).

[4] Ross, *Theorie der Rechtsquellen*, *supra* note 3 at 3; *cf.* 50.

[5] John Austin, *Lectures on Jurisprudence, or The Philosophy of Positive Law* ed. by Robert Campbell (4th edition, rev., London: John Murray, 1873) [Bristol: Thoemmes Press reprint, 2002], *Lecture I*, vol. I, 88.

distinguish between different inquiries into the law.[6] Ross mentions a review by John Stuart Mill but does not tell that Mill holds that Austin's concern is:

> The logic of law, as distinguished from its morality or expediency. Its purpose was that of clearing up and defining the notions which the human mind is compelled to form, and the distinctions which it is necessitated to make, by the mere existence of a body of law of any kind, or a body of law taking cognizance of the concerns of a civilized and complicated state of society. A clear and firm possession of these notions and distinctions is as important to practice as it is to science. For only by means of it can the legislator know how to give effect to his own ideas and his own purposes.[7]

This raises the question whether Austin's jurisprudence is a rational or empirical study where Ross' answer is the former whereas Mill endorses the latter in relation to Henry Maine, since:

> The subject-matter of both writers is positive law – the legal institutions which exist, or have existed, among mankind, considered as actual facts. The aim of both is to let the light of philosophy on these facts (…). Mr Maine's operation is essentially historical, not only in the mode of prosecuting his inquiry, but in the nature of the inquiry itself. He investigates, not properly the philosophy of law, but the philosophy of the history of law. (…) Austin does not specially contemplate legal systems in reference to their origin, and to the psychological causes of their existence. He considers them in respect of what may be called their organic structure.[8]

That is to say that all legal systems require a variety of conceptions based upon abstractions and expressed in names or words. Ross also quotes Maine: "to Bentham and even in a higher degree to Austin, the world is indebted for the only existing attempt to construct a system of jurisprudence by strict scientific process."[9] It is noticeable that Ross omits that Maine continues to write "and to found it, not on a priori assumption, but on the observation, comparison, and analysis of the various legal conceptions."[10] This does not square with Ross' view that Austin's method to determine the concept of law is based not upon experience but on the a priori assumption that the law must be conceptualised as commands or rules set by the will of the sovereign.

It seems to me that Ross overlooks that the starting point for Austin is the ordinary use of the word. As Austin puts it,

> A law, in the most general and comprehensive acceptation in which the term, in its literal meaning, is employed, may be said to be a rule laid down for the guidance of an intelligent being by an intelligent being having power over him.[11]

---

[6] Ross, *Theorie der Rechtsquellen*, *supra* note 3 at 79; *cf.* 87.

[7] John Stuart Mill, "Austin on Jurisprudence" printed in (October 1863) 118 *Edinburgh Review*, 439–482 [reprint Bristol: Thoemmes Press, 1996] at 441–442.

[8] *Ibid.*

[9] Ross, *Theorie der Rechtsquellen*, *supra* note 3 at 85. The reference is to Henry S. Maine, *Lectures on the Early History of Institutions* (7th ed., Murray: London, 1897) Lecture XII, "Sovereignty", 342–370, at 343.

[10] *Ibid.*

[11] Austin, *Lectures on Jurisprudence*, *supra* note 5 at 88.

These laws are laws properly so called, and embrace laws set by God to his human creatures and laws set by men to men. The former is also called "the law of nature or natural law" but this may be misleading and Austin prefers to use the term "the divine law, or the law of God." Laws set by men to men can be divided into laws properly so called or positive law set by political superiors to their subjects in an independent society and laws improperly so called or positive morality set by opinions and feelings held by people in regard to human conduct. Finally Austin refers to the metaphorical use of the term as exemplified when people talk of laws observed by animals or laws concerning the movements of inanimate bodies. Ross also mentions this division but not that Austin follows the traditional view held by Thomas Aquinas that law properly speaking belongs to will and intelligence which implies that "non-rational creatures do not hold law as perceiving its meaning, and therefore we do not refer to them as keeping the law except by a figure of speech."[12] For Austin, the essence of laws or rules, properly so called, is the concept of command "and since it is the key to the sciences of jurisprudence and morals, its meaning should be analysed with precision."[13]

If we follow Mill, Austin's jurisprudence "may be correctly characterized as being from one end to the other an analysis and explanation of a word."[14] Thus Austin sets out "to fix the meanings which the term 'command' implies" to arrive at the view that:

> The ideas or notions comprehended by the term *command* are the following 1. A wish or desire conceived by a rational being, that another rational being shall do or forbear. 2. An evil to proceed from the former, and to be incurred by the latter, in case the latter not comply with the wish. 3. An expression or intimation of the wish by words or other signs [and this implies that] *command, duty* and *sanction* are inseparably connected terms: that each embraces the same ideas as the others, though each denotes those ideas in a peculiar order or series.[15]

Austin does not mention, nor does Ross, that command is what Thomas Reid calls a social operation of the mind as opposed to solitary operations of the mind and this distinction is important for the analysis of commands.[16] As examples of solitary operations Reid mentions that "a man may see, and hear, and remember, and judge, and reason; he may deliberate and forms purposes, and execute them, without the intervention of any other intelligent being." By contrast the social operations "necessarily imply social intercourse with some other intelligent being who bears a part in them" and manifested when a man "asks a question for information, when he testifies a fact, when he gives a command to his servant, when he makes a promise, or enter into a contract." Another important difference is the following:

> In the solitary, the expression of them by words, or any other sensible sign, is accidental. They may exist, and be complete, without being expressed, without being known to any

[12] Thomas Aquinas, *Summa Theologiæ*: *Law and Political Theory* ed. by Thomas Gilby (London: Cambridge University Press, 2006) at 25 (1a2æ 90–97).

[13] Austin, *Lectures on Jurisprudence*, *supra* note 5 at 90.

[14] Mill, *Austin on Jurisprudence*, *supra* note 7 at 449.

[15] Austin, *Lectures on Jurisprudence*, *supra* note 5 at 94, his italics.

[16] Thomas Reid, *Essays on the Active Powers of the Human Mind* ed. by Baruch Brody (Cambridge, MA: MIT press, 1969) Essay V, Ch. VI, 437; *cf.* Essay II, Ch. 1, 61 ff.

other person. But, in the social operations, the expression is essential. They cannot exist without being expressed by words or signs, and known to the other party.[17]

To be sure, Austin recognises that commands imply social intercourse or communicative relations between intelligent persons and must be expressed in words. It is also the case that a command is set or posited by the will of the commanding person, but this does not imply that the command also is an expression of his will. The will is a solitary action having an object and this can only be our own actions and a person must have some understanding of what he wills. A command is a social action expressing "a signification of desire" that is distinguished from other desires "not by the style in which the desire is signified, but by the power and the purpose of the party commanding to inflict an evil or pain in case the desire be disregarded."[18] And the object and purpose of the desire is the actions of other people.

Austin proceeds upon a distinction between commands as laws and commands as "occasional or particular command" where the former "obliges a person or persons, and obliges generally to acts or forbearances of a class" and the latter is confined to a particular act performed by an individual person. Considering a law, Austin holds that it is distinct from occasional commands since "a law is a command which obliges a person or persons, and obliges generally to acts or forbearances of a class."[19] Commands make a claim to obedience and the duty to obey depends upon a sanction or "the smallest chance of incurring the smallest evil."[20] For Austin, "superiority is the power of enforcing compliance with a wish, with the power and the purpose of enforcing it, are the constituent elements of a command." This is important with respect to the positive law set by the sovereign to his subjects, using the term "power" that can be used in the sense of having authority to regulate human conduct but also in the sense of having the capacity to use force to compel people to obey the law. These are different senses and Austin is vulnerable to the objection that he conflates authority and force since his use of "power" is related to his use of "sanction" in the sense of the enforcement of obedience by means of punishment or some other evil. For Ross, the merit of Austin is that he succeeds to establish a "pure concept of duty," that is to say a concept devoid of any moral or ethical connotation, that informs the duty to obey the positive law. Since there cannot be any norms without punitive sanctions, it follows that "a categorical imperative is a meaningless construction."[21] Ross overlooks that the term "sanction" also can be used in the sense of approval or recognition concerning "the validity of laws" as Austin notices.[22] This is important with respect to constitutional law that determines the criteria that

[17] *Ibid.*

[18] Austin, *Lectures on Jurisprudence*, *supra* note 5 at 91; *cf.* 98.

[19] *Ibid.*

[20] *Ibid.* at 93.

[21] Ross, *Theorie der Rechtsquellen*, *supra* note 3 at 89.

[22] Austin, *Lectures on Jurisprudence*, *supra* note 5 at 528–530.

turn a rule into a valid legal rule or positive law. Thus Austin recognises that term "sanction" is used to signify "confirmation by some legal authority. Thus we say that a Bill becomes law when sanctioned by Parliament, and that it does not become law till it is sanctioned by the Royal assent or till it has received the Royal sanction."[23] Considering the validity of a legal rule, it seems to me that this depends upon the use of sanction in the sense of approval rather than the sense of an evil. But Austin's correlation between norm and punitive sanction implies that constitutional law is not positive law but only positive morality, at least in a monarchy. And international law does not have the status of law properly so called but is only positive morality among nations.

Ross states that "the core concept in Austin's concept of law is the concept of sovereignty" although he does not elaborate this.[24] Surely the sovereign is the legislator within a given society setting the positive law which implies that custom is not positive law until it is transformed by the sovereign's organs, in particular the courts. Austin also stresses that positive law may be created by the judges as a species of judiciary law that receives Ross' approval. This is an attack upon the prevailing view on the continent that custom is an independent source of law and confines the task of judges to find the law and never to make it. Thus Austin is able to maintain the unity of law within a state in terms of positive law set by the will of the sovereign as the ultimate source of law. In this way Austin provides the answer to the question of the positivity of the law since it is the sovereign's wish and desire that determines the validity of legal rules in terms of their form as opposed to their content. And the sovereign's will and desire also provide the epistemological foundation for knowledge of what the law is as opposed to what the law ought to be where Ross refers approvingly to what is known as Austin's *dictum*:

> The existence of law is one thing; its merit or demerit is another. Whether it be or be not is one inquiry; whether it be or be not conformable to an assumed standard, is a different inquiry. A law, which actually exists, is a law, though we happen to dislike it, or though it vary from the text, by which we regulate our approbation and disapprobation. This truth, when formally announced as an abstract proposition, is so simple and glaring that it seems idle to insist upon it. But simple and glaring as it is, when enunciated in abstract expressions, the enumeration of the instances in which it has been forgotten would fill a volume.[25]

Austin's account of law depends upon his definitions and this raises the question what sort of definition he has in mind which he does not address explicitly, but it seems to me that Robert Moles is right when he suggests that Austin proceeds upon stipulative definitions.[26] These definitions cannot be true or false but they can be evaluated as useful or useless. And it is an open question if it useful to deny the status

---

[23] *Ibid.* at 524.

[24] Ross, *Theorie der Rechtsquellen*, *supra* note 3 at 90.

[25] *Ibid*; *cf.* at 79. The reference is to Austin, *Lectures on Jurisprudence*, *supra* note 5 at 220 fn.

[26] Robert Moles, "John Austin Reconsidered" (1985) 36 *Northern Ireland Legal Quarterly* 193–221, at 213.

of law to constitutional law and international law. His definition of positive law as the commands set by the sovereign also suggests that who is sovereign and what laws are passed are empirical questions. This is Karl Bergbohm's view, praising Austin as the founder of analytical jurisprudence and referring approvingly to Austin's *dictum* but it rules out any inquiry into what the law ought to be since this is not science but legal politics.[27] Bergbohm also addresses the question of the positivity of law and his answer is experience since "it is one and the same thing to be positive law and to come into existence historically by being laid down as binding rules."[28] The positive law is brought into existence by the will of the competent authorities using a proper and public procedure to turn rules into valid legal rules that constitute the object of legal science as an empirical science. For Ross, this is a version of "naïve positivism" based upon an "uncritical empiricism" which was prevalent in French and English philosophy in the second half of the nineteenth Century.[29] Ross' objection is based upon the Kantian view that knowledge begins with experience but categories and concepts are necessary in order to make experience of the world possible. For Ross, Austin's jurisprudential concern provides an outline for a "formal theory of norms" that can be applied within legal science as a normative science concerned with presenting an account of the meaning of legal norms.

Ross' view anticipates the view put forward by Julius Stone that the purpose of Austin's theory of law is "not to provide a theory of how power was or ought to be distributed in society, but to suggest a framework for viewing the propositions of a legal order as a logically self-consistent system."[30] For Stone, Austin's theory of law is a "formal theory of law" concerned with the conceptual clarification of legal concepts in order to improve the legal terminology to be used in the making and application of legal rules as well as providing an analytical classification of legal rules that makes it possible to understand actual legal orders or aspects of them. Stone's view has been questioned by William L. Morison, claiming that Austin's jurisprudential approach leads to legal science as an empirical science, and contrary to Ross, Morison describes Austin approvingly as an "empiricist."[31] For Bergbohm, Austin's empiricism leads to legal science as legal dogmatics concerned with an account of the meaning of legal rules. For Morison, Austin's empiricism leads to legal science as legal sociology or psychology concerned with an account of the variety of factors that determine legal decision-making. Ross' objection is that this is tantamount to confuse the sociological causes to legal rules with the epistemological reasons for knowing that a rule is a legal rule.[32]

[27] Karl Bergbohm, *Jurisprudenz und Rechtsphilosophie*, Bd 1 (Leipzig: Verlag von Duncker & Humblot, 1892) at 13; *cf.* 398.

[28] *Ibid*. at 549, my translation.

[29] Ross, *Theorie der Rechtsquellen*, *supra* note 3 at *vi*; *cf.* 181.

[30] Julius Stone, *Legal System and Lawyers' Reasonings* (London: Stevens & Sons, 1964) at 74.

[31] William L. Morison, *John Austin* (London: Edward Arnold, 1982) at 189. For a response, see Stone, *Legal System*, *supra* note 30 at 90, *cf.* 83.

[32] Ross, *Theorie der Rechtsquellen*, *supra* note 3 at 91.

However, Ross claims that Austin's theory is vitiated by a fundamental mistake since he claims that positive law must be based upon something outside the law in terms of the sovereign standing behind the positive law having actual power to enforce it.[33] Another mistake is that Austin makes room for a scientific inquiry into the merit or demerit of positive law in terms of the principle of utility as manifested in the divine law as the ultimate test of positive law and positive morality. For Ross, Austin's theory of utility is superficial and without any interest for modern lawyers. In this respect, Ross endorses Maine's view that "the jurist, properly so called, has nothing to do with any ideal standard of law and morals."[34] Ross overlooks that for Austin, "jurisprudence is the science of what is essential to law, combined with the science of what it ought to be."[35]

Ross claims that Austin's approach is not followed by his successors in England and the United States where jurisprudence deteriorates as manifested in the distinction between formal and material sources of law, which Ross holds is "a methodological impossibility."[36] I beg to differ since the distinction is used to address different questions: the formal source is concerned with the existence and validity of the law whereas the material source is concerned with the content and merit of a law. Ross also overlooks that Austin's analysis of the concept of right and duties form the starting point for Wesley Newcomb Hohfeld's analysis of legal relations.[37] For Ross, Hohfeld's approach is "an interesting but unsuccessful attempt to establish a theory of knowledge of law."[38] For Ross, "Austin lived in the 19th Century but he wrote for the twentieth Century."[39] This is not reflected in the second part where Ross presents his systematic account of the doctrines of the sources of law, which does not include Austin. But it may be said that Ross introduces Austin to Kelsen, although Kelsen does not consider Austin's theory until 1941.[40]

When returning from Vienna to Copenhagen in 1926, Ross submitted his manuscript as a doctoral dissertation for the degree of doctor of law at the Faculty of Law in the University of Copenhagen, only to be rejected by the selection committee. This was a blow for Ross, since to be is to be recognised, but he did not abandon the manuscript. Ross got in touch with Axel Hägerström, holding the chair of practical philosophy at the University of Uppsala in order to submit it as a dissertation for the degree of doctor of philosophy at the University of Uppsala. This required Ross to pass the degree of philosophy and he spent the years from 1928 to 1929 in Uppsala,

---

[33] *Ibid.* at 98; *cf.* 115.

[34] Maine, *Lectures*, *supra* note 9 at 370.

[35] Austin, *Lectures*, vol. 2, "On the Uses of the Study of Jurisprudence", *supra* note 5 at 1112.

[36] Ross, *Theorie der Rechtsquellen*, *supra* note 3 at 101.

[37] Wesley N. Hohfeld, *Fundamental Legal Conceptions* (1919) ed. by Walter W. Cook, with a new foreword by Arthur L. Corbin (New Haven: Yale University Press, 1946 reprint 1964).

[38] Ross, *Theorie der Rechtsquellen*, *supra* note 3 at 76, fn 3.

[39] *Ibid.* at 85.

[40] Hans Kelsen, "The Pure Theory of Law and Analytical Jurisprudence" (1941–1942) 55 *Harvard Law Review* 44–70, at 54 ff.

graduating in philosophy and was then awarded the doctoral degree in philosophy in 1929, when the book, dedicated to Hans Kelsen, finally was published.[41]

In his later writings Ross changed his allegiance from Kelsen to Hägerström and then to logical positivism. He succeeded in receiving the degree of doctor of law at the Law Faculty of University of Copenhagen in 1934 where he was appointed professor, teaching international law, jurisprudence and constitutional law. In his textbook *Om Ret og Retfærdighed,* Austin is mentioned as a representative of analytical jurisprudence but Ross' analysis is based upon logical positivism as manifested in his definition of legal norms as "directives, that is, utterances with no representative meaning but with intent to exert influence."[42] In a later article, he presents a summary of Austin's theory which he claims he has refuted.[43]

6.3 Hägerström on Austin

According to Morris Cohen, "in nearly all modern jural and political discussion that styles itself scientific, law is defined as the will of the sovereign."[44] This is also known as the imperative theory of law or the will theory of law which Hägerström subjects to a blistering critique. For Hägerström, philosophy is concerned with the conceptual analysis of fundamental concepts in order to establish the secure foundation for scientific knowledge of nature, morality and law.[45] Hägerström is known for his rejection of metaphysics in the sense of the existence of a metaphysical or supernatural world beyond the existence of the physical or natural world in time and space. But it is often overlooked that Hägerström is committed to the ontological view that maintains the completely logical character of sensible reality which implies that nature is intelligible but not as a spiritual reality in terms of ideals but as a conceptual reality in terms of ideas embedded in things and their properties which exist apart from human mind. This informs Hägerström's conceptual analysis that the meaning of ideas consists in their relation to the impact of things and their properties upon the human mind, which

[41] See *supra* note 3.

[42] Alf Ross, *Om Ret og Retfærdighed* (København: Nyt Nordisk Forlag, 1953) Eng. trans. by Margaret Dutton, *On Law and Justice* (London: Stevens & Sons, 1958) at 1, referring to his *Theorie der Rechtsquellen* for an account of Austin's theory, and 8 for the quotation.

[43] Alf Ross, "Naturret contra Retspositivisme" [Natural Law v. Legal Positivism] (1963) *Tidskrift for Rettsvitenskap* 497–525, reprinted in Alf Ross, *Ret som teknik kunst og videnskab* ed. by Isi Foighel, Hans Gammeltoft-Hansen, Henrik Zahle (København: Jurist- og Økonomforbundets forlag 1999) 228–260, at 239–242.

[44] Morris Cohen, "'Real' and 'Ideal' Forces in Civil Law" (1916) 26 *International Journal of Ethics* 347–358, at 348.

[45] In addition to my article, "Alf Ross" *supra* note 2, see Patricia Mindus, *A Real Mind. The Life and Work of Axel Hägerström* (Dordrecht: Springer, 2009).

makes our utterances the expression of thoughts or concepts as opposed to sounds or empty words. Thus if it can be demonstrated that a word is not related to any observable feature in the external world then it must be discarded as meaningless and not fit to use in science and this is what Hägerström's philosophy, called "rational naturalism," is about. Thus he advances the naturalistic approach as the only scientific or realistic approach to the study of the world in time and place describing things and their causal relations and using the inductive method to arrive at causal laws stating necessary relations between events. His rational naturalism also informs his conceptual inquiries into morals and law. With respect to morals, Hägerstöm holds that nature is devoid of any values and this implies that there can be no moral reality independent of human beings. Values are located in the minds of people but not as beliefs but as feelings having impulsive and imperative elements. This is Hägerström's moral nihilism that denies the existence of moral obligations as well as moral or natural rights that is related to his moral scepticism that there can be no moral knowledge as expressed in normative concepts and propositions. To be sure, there can be a scientific inquiry into the use of moral vocabulary to regulate human behaviour but this is to endorse the naturalistic approach providing a description and explanation of the causal relations between the use of moral words and their effects upon human behaviour.

Hägerström's moral nihilism also informs his conceptual analysis concerned with the object of legal science that "determines the content of 'positive law'."[46] Hägerström uses the expression *gällande rätt*, in German the expression is *geltendes Recht* that is used synonymously with the expression *positives Recht*, so it seems to me that Broad's translation "positive law" is justified.[47] Hägerström mentions that law may be seen either as object of theoretical consciousness, or cognition, that determines the nature of what actually exists; or as an object of evaluating consciousness, or an apprehension, of what ought to be regardless of the actual constitution of reality. He adopts the former when he refers to the usual view in modern legal science:

> The most usual view in modern legal science and jurisprudence is the following. Law is regarded as an actual reality, as being the content of a certain will, endowed with power and active in society; that content being expressed in a certain way. Accordingly the business of legal science would be to determine the content of that will under the guidance of its pronouncements. Of course it is the positivity of the law which this view stresses against the theory of natural law.[48]

Hägerström also stresses that the question is not how law is brought into existence through human will but the question is "about positive law as such, no matter how it may have arisen. Is it, as it now exists and as legal science analyses it, the content

[46] Axel Hägerström, *Är gällande rätt uttryck av vilja?* (1916) trans. by C.D. Broad, "Is Positive Law an Expression of Will?" in Hägerström, *Inquiries into Law and Morals* ed. by Karl Olivecrona (Uppsala: Almqvist & Wiksell, 1953) at 17–55. I have modified Broad's translation.

[47] See Bergbohm, *Jurisprudenz und Rechtsphilosophie*, *supra* note 7 at 49.

[48] Hägerström, *Inquiries into Law and Morals*, *supra* note 46 at 17.

of will in the sense suggested? To determine the conditions of its origin settles nothing about its essential nature."[49] Hägerström suggests that the content of positive law may embody the will of god and this is a natural law-view, which he otherwise rejects. It is true that the truth of beliefs is independent of their origin, if that is what Hägerström means by his claim that the origin of something does not settle anything about its nature. He supports his claim by writing:

> A machine comes into existence and brought into function by a human will. But the investigation of the machine's structure and mode of operation is not, for that reason, an investigation of a certain human activity. It is concerned with a certain limited part of external nature, which works in a certain way in accordance with the laws of that nature.[50]

To be sure, machines and positive law share a common element that they are human constructions brought about by human will and intelligence. It is also the case that machines and positive law exist independently of human beings and subject to scientific investigations. Thus the scientific account of machines offers a description of its structure and its working according to causal laws. Human beings also behave according to causal laws and it is possible to present a scientific account of their behaviour, which is the concern of psychology and sociology. But human beings also have the capacity to act according to laws of their own making in terms of normative requirements that are related to the investigation of a certain human activity. It seems to me that Hägerström overlooks that there is a crucial difference between the account of machines and the account of normative requirements since the latter are the result of the will and intelligence of human beings and some are manifested in laws and the concern of jurisprudence since it raises the question whether laws are commands that embody the will of the sovereign or state which Hägerström addresses in his article.

I shall not enter into a discussion of his criticism of various German theories that law is a declaration of will, but do notice that he follows Kelsen's view that jurisprudential theories cannot be grounded in any psychological or sociological facts, yet Hägerström rejects Kelsen's theory as circular since the will is determined by law.[51] By contrast, Austin's theory is not circular since

> Law can be defined without circularity as a system of imperatives or declarations of intention issuing from certain independently authoritative persons or complexes of persons in a society who are in position to carry out the intentions thus expressed because the members of the society regularly obey them.[52]

For support, Hägerström refers to Austin who defines the sovereign as the source of positive law in the following way:

> If a determinate human superior, not in a habit of obedience to a like superior, receive habitual obedience from the bulk of a given society, that determinate superior is sovereign

[49] *Ibid.* at 18.

[50] *Ibid.*

[51] *Ibid.*

[52] Hägerström, *Inquiries into Law and Morals*, *supra* note 46 at 28.

in that society, and the society (including the superior) is a society political and independent.[53]

Hägerström omits the last sentence, and it seems to me that he relies upon Maine's account when quoting Austin since he only refers to "the last of his (*i.e.* Austin) *Lectures*."[54] As noticed above, Ross claims that it is a mistake to define the law in terms of something outside the law, whereas Hägerström holds that this is merit. This leads Ross to claim that Hägerström follows Maine and considers Austin from a psychological and sociological perspective that ignores his epistemological and jurisprudential perspective.[55] It seems to me that Ross has a point since Hägerström endorses Maine's view "that this or that resolution of a majority in the representative assembly should be regarded as an expression of its unitary will is nothing but a juridical fiction" and this implies that Austin's theory "is a gross logical circle."[56] If so, then Hägerström is also involved in a logical circle since the law cannot be defined in terms of the will of the sovereign. Hägerström relies upon the view that for a person to will something implies that the person must also have some understanding of what it wills and most members of a parliament voting for a bill lack any understanding of the content of the bill. The rejoinder is that the sovereign, be it a king or members of parliament, need not understand the content of the law but only need to know that he is engaged in the intentional activity of making the law. Another of his objections is that Austin's account of the persistence of the positive law through time is defective since the present sovereign is not the author of laws passed by his predecessors. Austin appeals to the Hobbesian view that "the legislator is he, not by whose authority the law was first made, but by whose authority it continues to be a law."[57] And the authority of the present legislator depends upon that he is a determinate person who is recognised by other persons to have the capacity to make and apply the law as positive or valid law, setting the measures of legal justice and injustice that can be enforced, if necessary, by the courts.

Although Maine quoted Austin's account of sovereignty, he states it in a different way:

> More popularly, though without, I think, any substantial inaccuracy. It is as follows: there is, in every independent political community – that is, in every political community not in the habit of obedience to a superior above itself – some single person or some combination of persons which has the power of compelling the other members of the community to do exactly as it pleases.[58]

[53] *Ibid.* at 29.

[54] *Ibid.* See also Maine, *Lectures*, Lecture XII "Sovereignty", *supra* note 9 at 348; Austin, *Lectures*, Lecture VI, *supra* note 5 at 226.

[55] Ross, *Theorie der Rechtsquellen*, *supra* note 3 at 113 fn 89a.

[56] *Ibid.* at 34.

[57] Austin, *Lectures on Jurisprudence*, *supra* note 5 at 226; *cf.* 337.

[58] Maine, *Lectures*, Lecture XII, *supra* note 9 at 349. Maine's statement is misleading, see John Dewey, "Austin's Theory of Sovereignty" (1894/1895) 9 *Political Science Quarterly* 31–52.

Maine is followed by Thomas Hill Green, holding that Austin "only recognizes sovereignty in a determinate person or persons, and it considers the essence of sovereignty to lie in the power, on the part of the such determinate persons, to put compulsion without any limit on subjects, to make them do exactly as it pleases."[59] Hägerstöm follows suit when he claims that Austin's view implies that the constitution, "*according to its own meaning*, cannot be applied to those in supreme authority. These may do whatever they please, they may arbitrarily infringe as much as they like the so-called fundamental laws, and yet they will not be breaking any rules which are contained in the constitution as part of its meaning."[60] Thus Hägerström arrives at the conclusion that "it is pure despotism which serves as a model for the theory under discussion."[61] Hägerström fails to mention that Austin also considers the difference between free and despotic governments, claiming that:

> Every supreme government is free from legal restraints, or (what is the same proposition dressed in different phrase) every supreme government is legally despotic. The distinction, therefore of governments into free and despotic, can hardly mean that some of them are freer from restraints than others: or that the subjects of the governments which are denominated free, are protected against their governments by positive law.[62]

He continues to remark that the use of the terms "free" and "despotic" expresses value judgements of praise and blame implying that a free government is better than a despotic government. This is also Hägerström's view, and if we follow his analysis of value judgements then value judgements do not express judgements or propositions that can be true or false but are only the use of words expressing feelings that a government is disliked as opposed to being liked as a constitutionally governed state.

Hägerström's understanding of Austin's account of constitutional law can also be questioned. For Austin, constitutional law "fixes the structure of the given supreme government and determines the character of the person, or the respective characters of the persons, in whom, for the time being, the sovereignty shall reside."[63] However, constitutional law cannot be legally enforced and this implies that it cannot be conceptualised as positive law but only as positive morality. It follows that "supreme power limited by positive law, is a flat contradiction in terms."[64] It does not follow that the supreme power can do whatever it pleases, as Hägerström suggests. Moreover, he fails to notice that Austin recognises that the sovereign appeals to constitutional rules in order to make and enforce valid legal rules. Constitutional law as positive morality is guarded by moral sanctions in terms of sentiments current in the given society in relation to the proper end of a sovereign

---

[59] Thomas Hill Green, "Lectures on the Principles of Political Obligation" in *Philosophical Works*, vol. 2 [first published 1888] (reprint London: The Lawbook Exchange, 2006) at 95, referring to Maine's account of Austin's theory in *Lectures*, see note 32 *supra*.

[60] Hägerström, *Inquiries into Law and Morals*, *supra* note 46 at 30, his italics.

[61] *Ibid.* at 35.

[62] Austin, *Lectures on Jurisprudence*, *supra* note 5 at 283.

[63] *Ibid.* at 274.

[64] *Ibid.* at 270. This is false, but I shall not enter into a discussion.

government, that is to say "the purpose or end for which it ought to exist" which Austin holds is not the Kantian idea of allowing the greatest possible human freedom in accordance with laws by which the freedom of each is made to be consistent with that of all others but "the greatest possible advancement of human happiness."[65] Thus Austin recognises that political institutions are controlled by moral considerations, in Austin's case his utilitarian morality based upon the divine law, and this implies that the sovereign's power necessarily is restrained as a matter of fact, as Austin duly recognises, but Hägerström overlooks. His critique is misplaced since Austin recognises that the sovereign may break constitutional law. An act of the sovereign which violates constitutional law cannot be considered as an infringement of law and styled illegal, but it "may be styled with propriety unconstitutional" thus "would not be legally binding, and disobedience to that command would therefore not be illegal."[66]

Another question is whether there is a duty to obey a valid but immoral law, which Austin claims is a legitimate question to be answered by reference to utilitarian considerations.[67] By contrast, Hägerström's moral nihilism implies that the question does not make sense since there are no moral duties. Austin also recognises that people may obey the sovereigns for a variety of reasons but that does not impair their sovereignty since the people is an indeterminate body of persons as opposed to the sovereign as a determinate person or body of persons. This is not mentioned in Hägerström's account where he uses the term "will of the state" as "an anthropomorphization of the various forces which maintain the legal system."[68] This implies that Hägerström has changed the subject from being an inquiry into the content of legal rules as commands or normative requirements to be an inquiry into "the force which commonly keeps in existence an already existing law."[69] Hägerström's answer is "a medley of all kinds of heterogeneous factors" which turns legal rules into causal regularities between the use of words and human behaviour. Hägerström's understanding that "it is pure despotism which serves as a model" for Austin's theory can be seen as anticipation of Herbert L. A. Hart's understanding of Austin in terms of the model of the sovereign as the gunman setting orders backed by threats to his subjects which Ross also endorses in his review of Hart.[70]

---

[65] *Ibid.* at 298.

[66] *Ibid.* at 279.

[67] *Ibid.* at 121.

[68] Hägerström, *Inquiries into Law and Morals*, *supra* note 46 at 37 ff.

[69] *Ibid.* at 39.

[70] Herbert L. A. Hart, *The Concept of Law* (2nd ed.) ed. by Penelope A. Bulloch, Joseph Raz (Oxford: Oxford University Press, 1994) at 35–42. See also Alf Ross, "Review of H. L. A. Hart, The Concept of Law" (1962) 71 *The Yale Law Journal* 1185–1190, 1185; Moles, "John Austin Reconsidered" *supra* note 26, for the critique according to which Hart misunderstands Austin.

In his lectures *State and Forms of State* delivered in 1921, Hägerström considers Austin's theory only to reject it, but his arguments add nothing new.[71] For Hägerström, the positive law is saturated with magical ideas and the legal vocabulary does not consist in concept but in the use of words to regulate human behaviour. This is in turn important for the scientific study of law since this cannot be concerned with presenting an account of the conceptual meaning of legal rules when they lack any conceptual meaning. If we follow Hägerström's naturalistic approach the scientific study of law must be an empirical study presenting a description of the use of the legal vocabulary to regulate human behaviour and to provide explanations in terms of causal laws, but Hägerström did not elaborate this.

6.4 Lundstedt on Austin

In 1914, Lundstedt was appointed professor in civil law at the Faculty of Law at the University of Uppsala where he was introduced to Hägerström and converted to his philosophical views. In his writings on jurisprudential and legal questions Lundstedt quotes extensively Hägerström's German writings and provide translations of his Swedish writings and this contributes to make Hägerström's philosophy known to a wider audience not only nationally but internationally.[72] Thus it is thanks to Lundstedt that Hägerström's philosophy is known; something Hägerström also recognises. Lundstedt's concern is to establish the study of law as a scientific study and he endorses rather uncritically Hägerström's epistemological and ontological view that confines scientific knowledge to natural and social science rejecting "all that is called *Geisteswissenschaft* – whether it concerns the I, society, the state, morality, or religion – is only an intellectual play with expressions of feeling, as if something real were designated thereby."[73]

Turning to the law, Lundstedt endorses Hägerström's rejection of natural law and natural right theories, and his view that the imperative or will theory is an absurdity since the will of the sovereign or state lacks any basis in reality. Lundstedt's target is the theories put forward by Bergbohm and Austin and he uses the opportunity to draw attention to that Ross, "a 'modern' Scandinavian lawyer" praises Austin for his achievements that the positive law is set by the sovereign as the ultimate source

[71] Axel Hägerström, "Stat och Statsformer" (1921), now in *Rätten och staten. Tre föreläsningar om rätts- och statsfilosofi* [The Law and the State. Three Lectures on Philosophy of Law and State] ed. by Martin Fries (Stockholm: Natur & Kultur, 1963) at 119–173.

[72] See Vilhelm Lundstedt, "Ausführungen von Hägerström" [Hägerström's statements] in *Die Unwissenschaftlichkeit der Rechtswissenschaft*, Bd. 1, *Die Falschen Vorstellungen von objektiven und subjektiven Rechten* (Berlin: Rothschild, 1932) at 217–231.

[73] Axel Hägerström, *Selbstdarstellung* (1929) transl. Robert T. Sandin as "Summary of My Own Philosophy" in *Philosophy and Religion* ed. by Robert T. Sandin (London: Allen & Unwin, 1964) at 74.

of law that also serves as the epistemological foundation for legal knowledge and draws a comparison with Kant, whereas the truth is that "it is impossible to find a single thought in Austin's work that stands to common sense and his thinking is nothing but pure Scholasticism."[74] Lundstedt is at pains to emphasise that his claim is not that Austin lacks common sense, only that his theory is devoid of meaning which Lundstedt supports by long quotations from Austin's *Lectures*. It should be noticed that Lundstedt does not mention Ross' critique of Austin and he takes Ross to task for holding that, thanks to Austin's theory, British jurisprudence has eschewed natural law that still dominates on the continent. To be sure, the latter is true but natural law thinking in the sense of superstitious ideas still flourish in Britain as Austin's theory exemplifies since legal rules are derived from the will of the sovereign which is "pure phantasy."[75] Austin's series of empty phrases leads Lundstedt to object that laws are not commands of the sovereign since the sovereign has no knowledge of them, that it is circular reasoning that commands create duties which are conditioned by sanctions, and it is false that duties create rights. Austin fails to recognise that his distinction between legal and moral rules does not make sense since both are just empty words, and he has "no idea of what establishes and maintains the so-called law and morality and the real relations between them."[76] Lundstedt's arguments do not add much to Hägerström's arguments so he is vulnerable to the criticism of Hägerström's position.

The result of Lundstedt's analysis is that lawyers and legal scholars have failed to realise that "the jurisprudential concept of positive law does not exist."[77] Thus there are no written or unwritten legal rules that must be obeyed by people, being binding for the making of decisions by courts and other legal officials because the rules have no basis in reality and therefore are unthinkable. As he puts is, "the words in the sentence 'this rule is a valid legal rule' have no conceptual content" because there are no thoughts behind the words.[78] This also applies to legal concepts like right and duty, guilt and liability that are metaphysical ideas devoid of any conceptual meaning. Hägerström's moral philosophy leads to moral nihilism and moral scepticism. Lundstedt's understanding of Hägerström's philosophy leads to legal nihilism, there is no such thing as legal rules, legal rights and duties. This is, in turn, related to legal scepticism: there is no such thing as legal science. This is radical view that raises a serious question for legal science, which, according to Lundstedt, has the responsibility for the form of life within a state and for the development of relations among states. He rejects the traditional view of legal science since it is based upon metaphysical ideas and assumptions. Legal science must be based upon facts, and the facts are psychological elements in terms of feelings and social instincts. This is the reality

[74] Lundstedt, *Die Unwissenschaftlichkeit der Rechtswissenschaft*, *supra* note 72 at 196.

[75] *Ibid.* at 197.

[76] *Ibid.*

[77] Lundstedt, *Die Unwissenschaftlichkeit der Rechtswissenschaft*, *supra* note 72 at 257; *cf.* 320.

[78] *Ibid.* at 253.

behind the expression that a legal rule is a valid rule if legal officials, in particular judges, in certain situations, will behave regularly and render decisions that are useful in the state.

For Lundstedt, the terms "legal order" and "legal rule" are not concepts but merely words and should be replaced with the "legal machinery" referring to the psychological factors that determine human behaviour in relation to the use of the legal vocabulary. Legal concepts, *e.g.* "right" and "duty," are also devoid of any conceptual meaning and should be abandoned, but Lundstedt admits that it is impossible to eradicate them since they are used to regulate human behaviour and have a place within legal science provided the use of quotations marks to indicate that they are not concepts but just empty words. If we follow Lundstedt, legal science is reduced to a branch of psychology or social-psychology, fitting with Hägerström's naturalistic approach. However, Lundstedt does not enter into any empirical inquiries into the maintenance of the legal machinery in terms of rules as behavioural regularities as opposed to rules as normative requirements. This distinction is blurred when Lundstedt appeals to what he calls "the method of social welfare" to be used by legal officials operating the legal machinery and by legal scholars to offer solutions to legal question. This is a matter of value judgements that puts Lundstedt's legal science in jeopardy; since value judgements are not scientific judgements but, according to Hägerström, an intellectual play with expressions of feeling, as if something real were designated thereby. By contrast, Austin makes room for moral science because the goodness or badness of positive law is objectively determinable facts based upon experience.

6.5 Olivecrona on Austin

Olivecrona was professor of procedural law at the Faculty of law, University of Lund and like Lundstedt he was a disciple of Hägerström as his "revered and beloved master" and his "endeavour to treat law as fact could not have been made without the basis supplied by Hägerström's work."[79] Thus he follows Hägerström in that the conceptual meaning of words consists in their relation to observable elements in the external world making an impact upon human minds that turns words into concepts. Olivecrona applies this analysis to the traditional view that the law has binding force, which means that there is a duty to obey the law and demonstrates to his own satisfaction that it is impossible to find any observable facts that correspond to the words and this implies that "the law is endowed with a super-natural power.

[79] Karl Olivecrona, *Law as Fact* 1st ed. (London: Humphrey Milford, 1939) *Preface*. Olivecrona was also instrumental for publication of Hägerström's articles; see his introduction to Hägerström, *Inquiries*, *supra* note 44 at x–xxvii. See also Torben Spaak, "Olivecrona's Legal Philosophy. A Critical Appraisal" (2011) 24 *Ratio Juris* 156–193.

Otherwise the words are empty, being used according to a secular habit without a real thought behind them."[80] For Olivecrona, the former view is pure superstition based upon a metaphysical view that must be replaced by realism and the scientific view that the "binding force" of the law is a reality merely as an idea in human minds. There is nothing in the outside world that corresponds to this idea. Thus his examination of the moral vocabulary demonstrates that it does not correspond to observable facts in the external world in time and space and this implies that it cannot be used to express moral beliefs in terms of concepts and judgements. This is tantamount to endorse Hägerström's moral nihilism that human beings have no moral duties. It does not follow that people are at liberty to act as they please and in this respect the words expressing the imaginary ideas of binding force or duty are important, because they can be used by the legislators to impress certain behaviour on people. It is sheer nonsense to say that they signify a reality. "Their sole function is to work on the minds of people, directing them to do this or that or to refrain from something else – not to communicate knowledge about the state of things."[81]

This way the law is like a link in the chain of cause-and-effect: it is positive law created by human beings; thus a product of natural causes, having natural effects. In fact, human beings use these words to maintain the law to regulate human behaviour. In this respect, it seems to me that Olivecrona is wrong when he suggests that the empty words are used according to *a secular habit without a real thought behind them*. Surely, when used by legislators and legal officials to maintain the law, there are thoughts behind the words.

Olivecrona also discusses the question of the binding force in his second edition of *Law as Fact*, making a distinction between what he calls "naturalistic legal positivism because it purports to give a purely factual, naturalistic explanation of the nature of law" and "idealistic legal positivism [that] contains an idealistic element in the obligatory force is supposed to be a property of the law."[82] The latter is represented by German authors, whereas Bentham and Austin would subscribe to the former as they claim that "the law was not invested with binding force in the usual sense."[83] It seems to me that Olivecona's understanding of Bentham and Austin is false. Bentham is committed to the view that the positive law has binding force in the sense that there is a moral obligation to obey the law. As Bentham puts it, "under a government of laws, what is the motto of a good citizen? To obey punctually, to censure freely."[84] As noticed above, Austin also holds that the concept of command implies a duty to obey and he endorses the traditional view "that obedience to established government is enjoined generally by the Deity."[85] Both Bentham and Austin

[80] Olivecrona, *Law as Fact* 1st ed., *supra* note 79 at 17.

[81] *Ibid.* at 21.

[82] Karl Olivecrona, *Law as Fact* 2nd ed. (London: Stevens & Sons, 1971) at 40.

[83] *Ibid.* at 45.

[84] Jeremy Bentham, *A Fragment on Government* (1776) in *The Collected Works of Jeremy Bentham* ed. by James H. Burns, Herbert L. A. Hart (London: The Athlone Press, 1977) at 399.

[85] Austin, *Lectures on Jurisprudence*, *supra* note 5 at 121.

hold that reason for obedience is grounded in the principle of utility but they differ since Austin makes room for disobedience in cases where government "vex us with needless restraints and load us with needless restraints."

Having dismissed the binding force of law, Olivecrona considers the traditional view of the nature of law as commands, by claiming "the concept of command is surely most important for the elucidation of the concept of law."[86] Austin shares this view and he would agree with Olivecrona that commands involve relations between the law-givers and people where the former want to influence the conduct of the latter. Olivecrona proceeds upon a distinction between the content and form of commands, which he later replaces with the technical expressions *ideatum* and *imperatum*.[87] The *ideatum* is concerned with the law-givers and their "ideas of imaginary actions by people (*e.g.* judges) in imaginary situations" whereas the *imperatum* is "using the imperative mood to call up the idea that this line of action must, unconditionally, be followed." Olivecrona considers Austin's analysis of command only to reject it as mistaken. Thus Austin commits a "grave fallacy" by holding that the content or *ideatum* is a declaration of the legislator's will.[88] Olivecrona's argument is that the command is issued by the will of the legislator, but it does not follow that the command itself expresses his will. I fail to see that Austin commits a fallacy since his claim is that the command is not a declaration of the will but a signification of the sovereign's desire to the people. The command is issued by the will of sovereign, but his will is a solitary act concerning his own actions, and one cannot will the actions of other people. But the sovereign may desire or wish that other people perform various actions, which is expressed in the command. As noticed above, commands are social acts of the kind that imply that there are communicative relations between intelligent persons, in terms of legal rules expressing the sovereign's signification of desire.

> [The latter] is distinguished from other significations of desire, not by the style in which the desired is signified, but by the power and the purpose of the party commanding to inflict an evil or pain in case the desire be disregarded.[89]

For Austin, the purpose of making laws is to guide and inform people about the right and wrong conduct, expressed by what Olivecrona calls *ideatum*. The sovereign's wish or desire is not a statement about his own mind but a statement about other people's behaviour. This is not far from Olivecrona's own view that a command is "an instrument used in order to obtain the fulfilment of a wish, a tool in the hands of the speaker."[90] For Olivecrona, the purpose of the law-givers is to

---

[86] Olivecrona, *Law as Fact* 2nd ed., *supra* note 82 at 125.

[87] Olivecrona, *Law as Fact* 1st ed., *supra* note 79 at 28, 31; see 2nd ed., *supra* note 82 at 120–126. Karl Olivecrona, "The Imperative Element in Law" (1964) 18 *Rutgers Law Review*, 794–810 introduces the distinction between ideational and imperative elements in a command.

[88] Olivecrona, *Law as Fact* 1st ed., *supra* note 79 at 32.

[89] Austin, *Lectures on Jurisprudence*, *supra* note 5 at 91.

[90] Olivecrona, *The Imperative Element*, *supra* note 87 at 796.

regulate human conduct: "in their imagination they conceive a picture of the conduct desired which is then conveyed to the people concerned in some suitable way."[91] Yet Olivecrona and Austin differ concerning their understanding of the *ideatum*. For Austin, it consists of the sovereign's utterances, expressing concepts and propositions, that are addressed to the intellect of the receivers in order to inform them about what conduct is right and wrong. By contrast, Olivecrona holds that the *ideatum* consists of empty words and suggestive sentences that do "not serve to convey information" but are "mere sting of words, working on us by suggestion."[92]

Thus he claims that Austin commits another mistake as commands are "not intended to impart knowledge but to influence the will."[93] Olivecrona follows the Humean view that the intellect does not move the will but desires do; this explains his view that commands are addressed to the will of the receivers as well as his claim that Austin has overlooked "the suggestive character of commands."[94] The rejoinder is that the will can only pursue what the intellect can understand and this requires that they need to understand the meaning of the words set out in the *ideatum* which Austin stresses at the expense of the *imperatum*, writing that "the evil to be incurred, with the chance of incurring it, are kept (if I may so express myself) in the background of my picture."[95]

Olivecrona, on the contrary, is interested in the *imperatum* at the expense of the *ideatum* which leads him to claim that Austin commits a mistake when he explains the nature of the *imperatum* in terms of "threats, which are often added to the command but must be distinguished from the command itself."[96] The rejoinder is that Austin proceeds on a distinction between, on one hand, legal rules and, on the other, sanctions in the sense of evil. However, the sanction does not serve as motivation for obedience: it is a means to determine the existence of the duty to obey the law. Olivecrona has already rejected the existence of the duty to obey the law as an illusion and what matters is to supply another motive for people to follow the law. Hence the importance of the *imperatum*, that is to use the imperative form to "create and maintain a feeling that the rules should be obeyed unconditionally."[97] The legal rules are concerned with imaginary ideas about human behaviour and these rules are at the same time rules about the use of force by legal officials. This is akin to Austin's view that the enforcement of law depends on the sovereign's power using the concept of power in the sense of physical force. However, the concept of power can also be used in the sense of the right or authority to command or rule which

[91] Olivecrona, *Law as Fact* 1st ed., *supra* note 79 at 28.

[92] *Ibid*. at 47; *cf*. 2nd ed., *supra* note 82 at 127.

[93] Olivecrona, *Law as Fact* 1st ed., *supra* note 77 at 33.

[94] *Ibid*. at 213.

[95] Austin, *Lectures on Jurisprudence*, *supra* note 5 at 94.

[96] Olivecrona, *Law as Fact* 1st ed., *supra* note 77 at 213.

[97] *Ibid*. at 133.

Olivecrona holds "is an absurd supposition. Speaking rationally, there can only be a question of the psychological requirement for the efficacy of a command."[98]

Olivecrona finds Austin's analysis of command wanting, not merely out of its mistakes but also because "the concept of command has to be defined without reference to the law."[99] His concern are rules, made by human beings, that should be distinguished into rules made by personal and impersonal agents; this, in turn, raises the question which category the law belongs to. Austin holds that constitutional law is not law properly speaking, but only positive morality, and this may suggest that the sovereign is a personal agent. This is Hägerström's understanding and Olivecrona follows suit. However, Austin's definition of the sovereign as "a determinate and common superior person or body of persons" makes room for the idea that these persons are impersonal agents.[100] For Olivecrona, the positive law is also made by impersonal agents or as he puts it "by people occupying a network of positions of power."[101] In contrast to Austin, Olivecrona suggests that the law is made by an indeterminate body of people and even goes as far as claiming that there is no need for any agent or "imperator" at all.[102]

Olivecrona introduces another distinction between commands in the proper sense and independent imperatives.[103] Commands in the proper sense imply personal relations between the giver and the receiver in terms of face-to-face commands that are issued by the giver to produce a particular action by the receiver. By contrast, independent imperatives do not imply any personal relations between sender and receiver, nor are they addressed to any particular person. This leads Olivecrona to reject Austin's view that legal rules are commands in favour of his view that legal rules must be conceptualised as independent imperatives.[104] Olivecrona's definition of command is what Austin calls an occasional or particular command that must be kept apart from commands in the sense of laws or rules. Olivecrona fails to appreciate Austin's distinction. This may have led him astray in holding that Austin equates occasional commands with rules. Olivecrona also refers to Hart's criticism, according to which Austin's doctrine should be amended by the introduction of "the notion of a rule" instead of the notion of command, and he endorses Hart's criticism that it is misleading to call commands "orders backed by threats."[105] The criticism, however, overlooks that Austin uses the concept of command in the sense of rule or law, whereas Hart uses it in the sense of orders backed by threats to arrive at the gun-man model of positive law. So Hart's account of Austin is misleading because Austin

[98] Olivecrona, *Law as Fact* 2nd ed., *supra* note 82 at 124.

[99] *Ibid.* at 125.

[100] Austin, *Lectures on Jurisprudence*, *supra* note 5 at 227.

[101] Olivecrona, *Law as Fact* 1st ed., *supra* note 79 at 219.

[102] Olivecrona, *Law as Fact* 2nd ed., *supra* note 82 at 129.

[103] Olivecrona, *Law as Fact* 1st ed., *supra* note 79 at 43; 2nd ed., *supra* note 82 at 28.

[104] Olivecrona, *Law as Fact* 1st ed., *supra* note 79 at 43; 2nd ed., *supra* note 82 at 130.

[105] Olivecrona, *Law as Fact* 2nd ed., *supra* note 82 at 82; *cf.* 124.

holds that legal rules as commands are normative propositions that serve as reasons for belief and action. The gun-man model is rather exemplified by Olivecrona's theory of law as independent imperatives that are devoid of any cognitive meaning, serving only as a means of inculcating patters of behaviour in a categorical way. I cannot follow Lloyd and Freeman in that Austin is "justified in classifying legal rules as imperative statements" since this implies that Austin holds that legal rules are devoid of cognitive meaning and this is false.[106]

For Olivecrona, law is positive law set by human beings occupying various positions of power within a given state as a means to further their interests as manifested in the content or *ideatum* of rules in terms of imaginary ideas about human actions. The ideas do not express concepts but imperative feelings through empty words. In addition, there is the form, or *imperatum*, that the imagined action must be performed. However, the *imperatum* hangs in the air since the *ideatum* does not offer any information: the ideas are devoid of cognitive meaning. Thus the individual addressees cannot understand the rules as normative requirements in terms of reasons for belief and action. What the individuals experience is only the impact of suggestive words upon the mind causing the appropriate behaviour. This is social conditioning by means of hollow words where the important fact is that the utterances have a suggestive force that, in the end, is related to the regular use of physical force by legal officials in order to make people comply with the rules. Olivecrona's theory conceptualises legal rules as independent imperatives and this leads him, in turn, to claim that positive law can only be conceived as "a system of organised force."[107]

6.6 Conclusion

The theory of law as independent imperatives is based upon a jurisprudential analysis that denies the existence of legal concepts and rules, which is a version of legal nihilism that is related to legal scepticism. The theory implies that legal rules are deprived their normative character as reasons for belief and action and the related view of legal science as a normative science concerned with an account of what the positive law is and what it ought to be is dismissed as non-scientific. The theory of law as independent imperatives holds that legal rules are nothing but strings of empty words that are used to cause human behaviour as the effect. In this way the positive law is located within the world in space and time that is related to the scientific study of law as an empirical science concerned with the description of legal rules in terms of social conditioning to arrive at rules as behavioural regularities.

---

[106] Lloyd's *Introduction to Jurisprudence* ed. by Michael D.A. Freeman (7th ed., London: Sweet & Maxwell, 2001) at 208.

[107] Olivecrona, *Law as Fact* 1st ed., *supra* note 79 at 185; Olivecrona, *Law as Fact* 2nd ed., *supra* note 82 at 171. Alf Ross also follows suit endorsing Olivecrona's theory but instead of using the term "independent imperatives" Ross prefers to use the technical term "directives."

Although the Scandinavians advance their theory as the only scientific or realistic approach, they never enter into any empirical inquiries but continue to follow the traditional approach when writing their textbooks. Now there are many versions of realism as Albert Koucerek points out, and "the particular type of realism supported by Hägerström and Lundstedt (…) may, to borrow from the fine arts, be called 'surrealism.'"[108] Now Lundstedt's view that there are no legal rules is rejected by Olivecrona and Ross in favour of their view that there are legal rules in terms of independent imperatives or directives. But then their approach presents another surrealist view that independent imperatives or directives are devoid of any meaning which implies that there is no legal knowledge. It seems to me that we are better off with Austin's theory of law as commands or rules that determine what is right and wrong conduct and his view of jurisprudence as the science of what is essential to law, combined with the science of what it ought to be.

[108] Albert Koucerek, "Review of Heinz Lunau" (1939–1940) 34 *Illinois Law Review* 637–640, at 638.

Chapter 7
Did Austin Remain an Austinian?

Wilfrid E. Rumble

7.1 Introduction

Although much has been written about Austin in the last century and a half, more remains to be done. While different scholars may well disagree about the precise agenda, it includes, it seems to me, the resolution of this issue: did Austin cease being an Austinian? To be sure, most commentaries on his legal philosophy (including my own) assume that it did not change after 1832,[1] the year that he published

[1] My survey of the literature about Austin is highly selective. The textbooks on English jurisprudence written in the late nineteenth and first half of the twentieth century that I have consulted almost invariably tend, without discussion, to assume that his legal philosophy did not change in the latter stages of his life. For a few examples, see Sir William Markby, *Elements of Law Considered with Reference to Principles of General Jurisprudence* (6th ed., Oxford: Clarendon Press, 1905); Sir Thomas Erskine Holland, *The Elements of Jurisprudence* (13th ed., Oxford: Clarendon Press, 1924); Sir Carleton Kemp Allen, *Law in the Making* (6th ed., Oxford Clarendon Press, 1958) [first published in 1927]; and Sir John Salmond, *Jurisprudence* (7th ed., London: Sweet & Maxwell, 1924) [first published in 1902]. The more recent literature of the last 50 or 60 years is more varied in this respect. Analyses of, or comments on, Austin that assume that his legal philosophy did not change include these works by Herbert L. A. Hart: "Introduction" John Austin, in *The Province of Jurisprudence Determined* (London: Weidenfeld and Nicolson, 1954); and *The Concept of Law* (2nd ed.) ed. by Penelope A. Bulloch, Joseph Raz (Oxford: Clarendon Press, 1994). Other authors who make a similar assumption include William L. Morison, *John Austin* (Stanford, CA: Stanford University Press, 1982); Wilfrid E. Rumble, *The Thought of John Austin* (London: Athlone Press, 1985); Simon Honeyball, "Defences of Austinian Commands" 54 (2003) *Northern Ireland Legal Quarterly*, 254; Neil Duxbury, "English Jurisprudence Between Austin and Hart" (March, 2005) 91 *Virginia Law Review* 1–91; Richard T. Bowser, J. Stanley McQuade, "Austin's Intentions: A Critical Reconstruction of His Concept of Legal Science" 29 (2006) *Campbell Law Review* 47; Brian H. Bix, *Jurisprudence: Theory and Context* (5th ed., Durham, North Carolina: Carolina Academic Press, 2009); and Suri Ratnapala, *Jurisprudence* (Cambridge: Cambridge University Press, 2009). Richard A. Cosgrove appears to accept the Hamburgers' argument.

W.E. Rumble (✉)
Department of Political Science, Vassar College, New York, USA
e-mail: wirumble@vassar.edu

M. Freeman and P. Mindus (eds.), *The Legacy of John Austin's Jurisprudence*, Law and Philosophy Library 103, DOI 10.1007/978-94-007-4830-9_7,

The Province of Jurisprudence Determined.[2] Still, this assumption has been challenged by Lotte and Joseph Hamburger in their justly acclaimed biography of the Austins, *Troubled Lives*.[3] The Hamburgers argue that, by the end of his life, Austin had abandoned the legal philosophy set forth in his book, the only one that he published in his lifetime. Since they make this argument more fully than any other scholars, I am going to focus in this paper on their development of it.[4] Admittedly, their book was published over 25 years ago. Nevertheless, legal scholars have tended to pay relatively little attention to their interpretation of Austin's legal philosophy. If I am critical of this aspect of their study, however, I have nothing but praise in general for their biography of the Austins. It is an outstanding achievement that will long remain the seminal work on the subject. Indeed, this is one reason why their interpretation of Austin's change of heart must be taken seriously and examined carefully.

There are also other reasons. They are reasons that explain the importance of determining whether Austin ceased being an Austinian. To begin with, the question is important because historical accuracy is important. If the Hamburgers' interpretation of Austin is sound, it would dramatically modify our understanding of his jurisprudence. No doubt, in one respect whether he modified his legal philosophy towards the end of his life does not matter. The modifications would have no bearing on the

See his *Scholars of the Law: English Jurisprudence from Blackstone to Hart* (New York: New York University Press, 1996) at 98–99. Raymond Wacks argues that Austin "eventually came to disown the principle of utility and to doubt the value of his own 'expository' jurisprudence" in *Understanding Jurisprudence: An Introduction to Legal Theory* (2nd ed., Oxford: Oxford University Press, 2009) at 82. Ian Duncanson also appears to accept the Hamburgers' interpretation of Austin's conception of sovereignty: see his "Law, History, and Postcolonial Theory and Method: Writing and Praxis" (2003) *Law Text Culture* 31. Wayne Morrison thoughtfully discusses two possible explanations of why Austin did not revise and extend his lectures: See his *Jurisprudence: from the Greeks to Post-Modernism* (London: Cavendish Publishing Limited, 1997) at 244–245.

[2] See John Austin, *The Province of Jurisprudence Determined* ed. by Wilfrid E. Rumble (Cambridge: Cambridge University Press, 1995) [A Cambridge Text in the History of Political Thought]. Hereinafter cited as *The Province.*

[3] See Lotte and Joseph Hamburger, *Troubled Lives: John and Sarah Austin* (Toronto: University of Toronto Press, 1985).

[4] Eira Ruben agrees with the Hamburgers that Austin rejected utilitarianism in *A Plea for the Constitution*. She claims that he did so because he saw the principle of utility as a "potentially radical doctrine." See her essay, "John Austin's Political Pamphlets 1824–1859" in *Perspectives in Jurisprudence* ed. by Elspeth Attwooll (Glasgow: University of Glasgow Press, 1977) at 28–29, as well as at 25 and 37–38. Although the Hamburgers agree with Ruben *that* Austin ended up abandoning utilitarianism, they claim that she "exaggerates the unity of Austin's thought and tendentiously attributes to him an ideological defense of the middle classes" which is difficult to document and, if Austin's own words are used, easy to contradict. See *Troubled Lives: John and Sarah Austin*, *supra* note 3 at 244, fn 11. For a much more detailed critique of Ruben's interpretation of Austin, see William L. Morison, *John Austin* (Stanford: Stanford University Press, 1982) at 122–132. In any case, Ruben does not discuss Austin's legal philosophy *per se* and whether it changed in the final years of his life.

influence of what may be called the historical Austin. *That* Austin was the author of *The Province* and his *Lectures on Jurisprudence*.[5] Still, the alleged changes would require us to revise not only our *understanding* of Austin's legal philosophy, but our *evaluation* of it. If he no longer were an Austinian, then he would be the author of two different legal philosophies, each of which would have to be evaluated separately.

Aside from this, the literature about Austin is divided on whether he ceased to be an Austinian. The older works, and much of the more recent scholarship, assume that his legal philosophy did not change.[6] Some of the more recent studies, however, appear to agree with the Hamburgers.[7] The same can be said of four reviews of *Troubled Lives*.[8] Nowhere, however, is the issue of whether Austin remained an Austinian systematically discussed, a gap that my paper attempts to fill.

Finally, the supposed changes in Austin's legal philosophy could help to answer a puzzling question. After 1832 he published nothing that focused on jurisprudence, and relatively little on anything else. The question is, why? According to the Hamburgers, because "it became evident that it would be difficult to make his new political views compatible with his jurisprudence. This erosion of Austin's early confidence in the validity of his jurisprudence may also have been an obstacle to his completing the work."[9]

Granted that this interpretation of Austin is important, is it accurate? How strong a case can be made in support of the contention that in the final years of his life he no longer believed in the major tenets of his legal philosophy as expressed in his lectures? In short, how persuasive is the argument that he ceased being an Austinian? I intend to address this question by discussing the following four issues: first, what exactly is the argument of the Hamburgers? Second, what does it mean to be an Austinian? Third, does Austin's rejection of requests to reprint *The Province* shed any light on alleged changes in his legal philosophy? What about the new and larger work that he envisaged, but never started, as far as we know? Finally, does *A Plea for the Constitution*[10] really support the notion that he no longer remained an Austinian?

---

[5] See John Austin, *Lectures on Jurisprudence or the Philosophy of Positive Law*, 2 vols. (5th ed., London: John Murray, 1885). Hereinafter cited as *Lectures*.

[6] See the literature cited *supra* note 1.

[7] *Ibid*.

[8] See Rosemary Ashton, [review of *Troubled Lives*] (1985, Oct. 17) 7:18 *London Review of Books* 20; Shirley Robin Letwin, [review of *Troubled Lives*] (1985, 29 June) *The Spectator* 25; William Thomas, "A Moper and His Helpmeet" 1985, Nov. 8 *Times Literary Supplement*, 1253; and Patrick Brode, [review of *Troubled Lives*] (1986–87) 51 *Saskatchewan Law Review* 341.

[9] See Lotte and Joseph Hamburger, *Troubled Lives*, *supra* note 3 at 178.

[10] John Austin, *A Plea for the Constitution* (2nd ed., London: John Murray, 1859) [hereinafter cited as *A Plea*].

7.2 The Text Behind Hamburgers' Argument

The primary textual basis for the Hamburgers' argument is *A Plea for the Constitution*, a very conservative pamphlet that Austin published in 1859.[11] There is no denying that in this short work – it is only 42 pages long – he did express some political opinions that were very different from those that he held earlier in his life. As a young man he was an ardent radical who in 1819 described himself as a "disciple" of Jeremy Bentham.[12] His doctrines had "long" inflamed Austin, the latter wrote, "with an earnest desire to see them widely diffused and generally embraced."[13] Indeed, Austin indicated that once he was able to support himself and his wife in "independence and comfort," he would feel "no violent desire for any other object than that of disseminating [... Bentham's] doctrines."[14] In any case, Austin harshly condemned "aristocratical ascendancy and aristocratical misgovernment."[15] This highly critical attitude was a major reason for his rejection of primogeniture, which not only perpetuates "aristocratical power," but leads to "a most terrible abuse" of it.[16]

By 1859 Austin's political outlook could hardly be more different from this. Instead of condemning the aristocracy, he extolled the virtues of the "aristocracy of independent gentlemen" who constitute a majority of the members of the House of Commons.[17] He particularly praised the landed gentry and the men connected, by various family relations, to it and the members of the House of Lords.[18] Precisely how long he had held his new opinions is impossible to say. He did indicate that he had "long entertained" the view that "all" of the consequences of Parliamentary reform are "mischievous."[19] He described the evolution of his thinking in these terms:

> By my reverence for Mr. Bentham as a writer on law and legislation, I was naturally led (being then young) to accept his political opinions without sufficient examination (...). Even before the Reform of 1832, I had rejected his *radical* politics; and had returned to the opinion (Whiggism, Liberal Conservatism, or whatever else it may be called) which is held, with shades of difference, by the generality of instructed Englishmen. I have since resided in Germany and France, and studied and observed their political institutions and condition;

---

[11] *Ibid.*

[12] See his letter to Bentham, 20 July 1819, in *The Correspondence of Jeremy Bentham* ed. by Stephen Conway (Oxford: Clarendon Press, 1989), vol. 9, at 337.

[13] *Ibid.* at 336.

[14] *Ibid.* at 337.

[15] John Austin, "Disposition of Property by Will – Primogeniture" (Oct., 1824) LXXX *Edinburgh Review* 546.

[16] *Ibid.* at 512.

[17] Austin, *A Plea*, *supra* note 10 at 11.

[18] *Ibid.* at 12.

[19] *Ibid.* at *iii*.

> and I therefore am better qualified than most of my countrymen, to appreciate the matchless union of order and liberty for which we are indebted to our present incomparable Constitution.[20]

The Hamburgers argue that the corollary of this sea change in Austin's political faith was an equally profound transformation of his legal philosophy. Their argument is not merely that some of the ideas that he expressed in *A Plea* are inconsistent with views he developed in his lectures on jurisprudence. Rather, they make a stronger claim about the content of Austin's mind, what he actually believed. The essence of it is that by the end of his life he had abandoned his earlier legal philosophy. The Hamburgers' commitment to this position is particularly evident in the final paragraph of the chapter in their book addressing the question of whether Austin remained an Austinian.[21] They write that he "had sacrificed decades of thought and labour to a science of jurisprudence whose foundations he now *recognized* to be feeble."[22] They also claim that Sarah Austin perpetuated John's "reputation as one of the founders of analytical jurisprudence long after he ceased to *believe* in it."[23] Instead, he began to move "in the direction of the historical school, which emphasized the importance of continuity and tradition."[24] This is apparent, the Hamburgers argue, from the greater importance that he attached to positive morality, his new emphasis on gradual improvement and continuity with the past, and his heavy stress on "feelings, sentiments, and attachments."[25]

7.3 What Does It Mean to Be an Austinian?

In order to know whether Austin ceased being an Austinian, it is first necessary to know *what* it is that he ceased being. What then does it mean to be an Austinian? It should be acknowledged at the outset that any attempt to answer the question may

---

[20] *Ibid.* at *vi*. Austin's residence in Paris during the French Revolution of 1848, to which he reacted very negatively, particularly influenced his "turn to the right." He was especially disturbed by the social egalitarianism of the French revolutionaries. It is "important to recollect" he claimed, "that the present revolutionary tendencies [in France] are social rather than political; aiming at equality of possessions, or an equal distribution of revenue, rather than the mere establishment of democratical constitutions. This is the alarming feature in the present condition of France." Excerpt from a letter to Lady Duff Gordon, 1848, as quoted in Janet Ross, *Three Generations of English Women: Memoirs and Correspondence of Susannah Taylor, Sarah Austin, and Lady Duff Gordon* (a new, revised, and enlarged edition; London: T. Fisher Unwin, 1893) at 98. Also see Sarah Austin's comments, *Lectures*, *supra* note 5 at 18, and her report of her husband's reaction, *Three Generations of English Women*, at 222.

[21] Also see Lotte and Joseph Hamburger, *Troubled Lives*, *supra* note 3 at *xi*, where they write that Austin's "conservatism ultimately led to a recantation of parts of his jurisprudence."

[22] *Ibid.* at 191, emphasis added.

[23] *Ibid.*, emphasis added.

[24] *Ibid.* at 189.

[25] *Ibid.* at 190.

be analogous to trying to walk barefoot and unscathed on hot coals. No two Austin scholars would be likely to give exactly the same answer to the query. To be sure, their responses would no doubt overlap to a very great degree. For example, any satisfactory explanation of "Austinian" would have to include, it seems to me, at least the first five of the principles, notions, and distinctions enumerated below. There might be some disagreement, however, about *which* other ideas (if any) should be added to the list. There might also be differences of opinion about whether some of the ideas listed are "major" or "minor" elements of his legal philosophy. After all, Austin did not tell us, explicitly, what the major elements of his legal philosophy are. Any attempt to identify, or, even more so, to interpret, them, involves choices about which equally well-informed scholars may disagree. In short, there is an inescapably personal element to any interpretation of "Austinian." Moreover, a wholly satisfactory analysis would require vastly more pages than I can devote to it here. Nevertheless, it is possible and desirable at least to stipulate what one means by "Austinian." Otherwise, it would be unclear exactly what Austin allegedly no longer believed in by the end of his life. Unfortunately, lack of clarity on this front is one of the limitations of the Hamburgers' interpretation. They never really explain what they mean by "Austinian."

I think that to be an Austinian is to accept the major ideas of Austin's legal philosophy (By this I mean what *he* regarded as the major ideas). My list of such ideas embraces *nine* principles, notions, and distinctions that he expounded. Leaving aside the question of methodology, they are:

1. a particular conception of jurisprudence, what Austin called "general jurisprudence;"[26]
2. the command conception of a law[27]
3. the notion of a positive law as the command of the sovereign;[28]
4. the idea of sovereignty;[29]
5. a sharp distinction between law and morality (the words "distinction between" law and morality are a much more accurate representation of Austin's views than the more frequently used "separation of" the two);[30]

---

[26] His best explanation by far of this notion occurs in "On the Uses of the Study of Jurisprudence" in *Lectures*, *supra* note 5 at 1071–1091.

[27] See Austin, *The Province*, *supra* note 2 at 18–37.

[28] *Ibid.* at 106–122 and 164–65.

[29] *Ibid.* at 165–293.

[30] The problem with the use of the word "separation" in this context is that it tends to conceal the many links that Austin recognized between law and morality. For example, he claimed that positive law, positive morality, and ethics "are the inseparably-connected parts of a vast organic whole." See Austin, *Lectures*, *supra* note 5 at 16. He also indicated that the positive law of a nation is "in a great measure" founded on its positive morality as well as "international morality." (*Lectures*, *supra* note 5 at vol. 2, 754 and 636, and *infra* 7.4). Despite this, if not because of it, Austin insisted that law and morality are all-too-frequently confused and must be distinguished. In reality, "a law, which actually exists, is a law, though we happen to dislike it, or though it vary from the text, by which we regulate or approbation and disapprobation" (*The Province*, *supra* note 2 at 157). To argue that a human law that conflicts with the divine law is not binding, or a law, is to talk 'stark

6. harsh criticism of the concept of natural law and rights;[31]
7. a particular conception of liberty;[32]
8. various classifications of the law, most notably the distinction between the law of things and the law of persons,[33] and primary and secondary rights and duties;[34]
9. and a strong commitment to codification.[35]

Although Austin's utilitarianism is the lodestar of his *ethical*, as distinguished from his *legal*, philosophy, it heavily influenced certain of his ideas about law. For example, he claimed that the principle of utility has "usually been the principle consulted in making laws;"[36] that perceptions of utility help to explain the habitual obedience of the bulk of the population to the sovereign;[37] and developed a utilitarian theory of

nonsense'" (*ibid.* at 158). The right of a master to the labour of his slave is an example. Pernicious as the right is, to deny its existence or possibility is "to talk absurdly" (*ibid.* at 159).

[31] See *infra*, 7.3.3.

[32] See *infra*, 7.3.2.

[33] He indicated that the terms themselves "were devised by the Civilians of the Middle Ages, or arose in times still more recent." (*Lectures*, *supra* note 5 at vol. 1, 369). He claimed, however, that what the two bodies of law are called is "*insignificant*" (*ibid.* at vol. 2, 734). What is crucial is to recognize that the difference between them lies in their *compass*, not their *subject-matter* (*ibid.* at vol. 1, 369). Rights *in rem* are not rights over things. Rather, they are rights that avail against the world at large, or persons generally. In contrast, rights *in personam* avail "*exclusively* against a *determinate* person, or (…) *determinate* persons" (*ibid.* at 370). The duties that correlate with "rights *in rem*, are always *negative*: that is to say, they are duties to forbear or abstain. Of the obligations which correlate with rights *in personam*, *some* are negative, but *some* (and most) are *positive* — that is to say, obligations to do or perform" (*ibid.* at 371). For this reason, the terms "'*General and Particular*' would suffice" as names for the two kinds of rights (*ibid.* at vol. 2, 734). Whether a specific right belongs to the law of things or the law of persons depends, however, on how it is viewed. The right of a father to the custody and education of a child is an example. As against the child, in case he or she deserts the father, it is a right *in personam*. The father may compel the child to return. Yet, as against the world at large, the right of the father belongs to the law of things. It is not so much a right to the custody and education of the child as it is a right to "the *exercise* of such rights *without molestation by strangers*" (*ibid.* at vol. 1, 384–85). Overall, the law of things *is* the law, minus those parts of it affecting particular classes of persons (*ibid.* at vol. 2, 687). Although Austin attached great importance to this classificatory scheme, he denied that it is essential, necessary, or perfect. Rather, he regarded it as the most convenient, or least inconvenient, of the possible classifications of the law (See *Lectures*, *supra* note 5 at vol. 1, 41–42, and vol. 2, 689, 691, 721).

[34] Primary rights are not consequences of delicts, or not direct or immediate consequences, while secondary rights are (*Lectures*, *supra* note 5 at vol. 2, 764). Their purpose is two-fold: to deter violations of rights and duties, and to provide remedies if they occur. According to Austin, "the law which gives the remedy, or which determines the punishment, is the only one that is absolutely necessary. For the remedy or punishment implies a foregone injury, and a foregone injury implies that a primary right or duty has been violated. And, further, the primary right or duty owes its existence as such to the injunction or prohibition of certain acts, and to the remedy or punishment to be applied in the event of disobedience (…). The essential part of every imperative law is the imperative part of it" (*ibid.* at 767).

[35] See Austin, *Lectures*, *supra* note 5 at vol. 2, 653, 660–681, 1021–1039, 1092–1102.

[36] See Austin, *The Province*, *supra* note 2 at 58.

[37] Austin, *The Province*, *supra* note 2 at 247.

ethically justifiable resistance to government.[38] Most important of all, perhaps, he contended that the very possibility of general jurisprudence is dependent upon the principle of utility. It is because some of its dictates are "always and everywhere the same, and are also so plain and glaring that they hardly admit of mistake, [that] there are legal and moral rules which are nearly or quite *universal*."[39]

These considerations help to explain why Austin regarded his lengthy exposition of ethical theories in *The Province* as a "necessary link" in "a chain of systematical lectures concerned with the *rationale* of jurisprudence."[40] Some discussion of his utilitarianism has to be included therefore in any satisfactory account of his philosophy of law. Of course, it could be argued that it does not matter, for the purpose of this paper, whether he remained a utilitarian in the final years of his life. Such is the case because his utilitarianism is *not* part of his *legal* philosophy. Loss of faith in the one does not signify therefore abandonment of the other. The heavy emphasis of the Hamburgers upon Austin's ultimate rejection of utilitarianism is therefore misplaced. Even if he no longer believed in it, that fact does not demonstrate that he was not an Austinian.

The problem with this argument is its deemphasis of Austin's insistence on the *links* between jurisprudence and legislation. To be sure, he did sharply distinguish between them. The focus of the former is the law as it is, while that of the latter, a branch of the science of ethics, is the laws that ought to be. Nevertheless, he emphasized the relationships between the two sciences. They are, he claimed, "connected by numerous and indissoluble ties."[41] To this extent, it *does* matter whether Austin remained a utilitarian throughout his life.

In any event, it is not necessary here to elucidate all of the different components of Austin's legal philosophy. Such is the case because he rarely discusses legal philosophy in *A Plea*. Whatever he says about it is also very brief and incidental to the political themes that are the *raison d'être* of the work. In fact, only three of the nine principles, notions, and distinctions that I have listed are discussed.[42] Whether he still believed in the other tenets of his legal philosophy is therefore impossible to determine from his pamphlet. The well is dry. It is necessary, however, to elucidate how he conceived in his books of the small number of the basic elements of his legal philosophy that he does allude to in his pamphlet. Only then can it be determined whether they are consistent with what he says about them in *A Plea*.

7.3.1 The Conception of Sovereignty

According to Austin, every independent political society not only in fact has, but must have, a sovereign. This person, or body of persons, is the ultimate source of the positive law of that society. He, she, or it is identifiable on the basis of two "marks." One is positive

[38] *Ibid.* at 53–55.

[39] *Ibid.* at 153.

[40] *Ibid.* at 13.

[41] *Ibid.* at 14.

[42] See *supra* 7.3.

and consists of the receipt of habitual obedience from the bulk of the population. The other is negative and signifies the absence of habitual obedience to any other determinate human superior.[43] The powers of the sovereign are, and must be, legally illimitable. To say that supreme power can be limited by positive law is, according to Austin, a "flat contradiction in terms."[44] Moreover, the notion that the power of the sovereign is incapable of legal limitation holds "universally or without exception."[45] It is for this reason, among others, that neither international law nor constitutional law, is law "properly so-called." Both attempt to impose limits on what the sovereign can do and are therefore "nearly in the same predicament. Each is positive morality rather than positive law. The [one…] is guarded by sentiments current in the given community, as the [other…] is guarded by sentiments current amongst nations generally."[46]

Austin not only developed this general theory of sovereignty, but also identified the British sovereign (among others). His contention was that sovereignty in Great Britain does *not* lie with Parliament, *i.e.* with the Crown, the House of Lords, and the House of Commons. Rather, it "always resides in the king and the peers, with the electoral body of the commons."[47] He justified this highly unusual doctrine, strongly criticized by Dicey,[48] on the ground that the members of the House of Commons are merely trustees for the electorate. Austin claimed that the notion of a trust is implied by "the correlative expressions *delegation* and *representation*. It were absurd to suppose that the delegating empowers the representative party to defeat or abandon any of the purposes for which the latter is appointed."[49] At the same time he acknowledged that this trust is "general," "vague," and "tacit."[50] Also, it is enforced by moral rather than legal sanctions, by fear of offending "the bulk of the community."[51] The duties of the representative body towards the electorate constitute "positive morality merely."[52] Indeed, Austin argued that "all constitutional law, in every country whatever, is, as against the sovereign, in that predicament."[53]

7.3.2 The Conception of Liberty

Another element of Austin's philosophy of law discussed in *A Plea* is what may be called his negative and instrumental notion of liberty. It is a conception that contrasts

---

[43] See Austin, *The Province*, *supra* note 2 at 166.

[44] *Ibid.* at 212.

[45] *Ibid.*

[46] *Ibid.* at 219.

[47] *Ibid.* at 194.

[48] See Albert Venn Dicey, *Introduction to the Study of the Law of the Constitution* (8th ed., Indianapolis, Indiana; Liberty Classics, 1982) at 26–29.

[49] See Austin, *The Province*, *supra* note 2 at 194.

[50] *Ibid.*

[51] *Ibid.* at 193–194.

[52] *Ibid.* at 194.

[53] *Ibid.*

sharply with the view of, say, archdeacon William Paley, the eighteenth-century English theologian. He had defined civil liberty as "*the not being restrained by any Law, but what conduces in a greater degree to the public welfare*."[54] In sharp and explicit criticism of Paley's notion of liberty, Austin claimed that "restraint is restraint although it be useful, and liberty is liberty though it may be pernicious."[55] "When liberty is not exactly synonymous with right," he argued, it "means, and can mean nothing else, but exemption from restraint or obligation."[56] As such, it is neither intrinsically good nor bad. "Political or civil liberty, like political or legal restraint," he argued, "may be generally useful, or generally pernicious; and it is not as being liberty, but as conducing to the general good, that political or civil liberty is an object deserving praise."[57] To argue that either political liberty or legal restraint ought to be the principal end of government is therefore "to talk absurdly: for each is merely a means to that furtherance of the common weal, which is the only ultimate object of good or beneficent sovereignty."[58]

Austin did add that to claim that legal restraint is the end of government is less absurd than to say that political liberty is the end.[59] The reason for this is simply that in general a person's enjoyment of civil or political liberties depends upon others being restrained from interfering with them. For example, the liberty to move from one place to another would be of little value unless others were obligated not to assault and imprison the person exercising the liberty.[60] To this extent, Austin argued, "political liberty is fostered by that very political restraint from which the devotees of the idol liberty are so fearfully and blindly averse."[61]

7.3.3 A Critique of Natural Law and Rights

A third conspicuous dimension of Austin's legal philosophy, as developed in his lectures, is a highly critical analysis of natural law and rights. He condemned the latter as consisting of "unmeaning abstractions" and "senseless fictions."[62] Also, their use in law and politics makes compromise, trade-offs, and peaceful resolution of differences difficult, if not impossible.[63] Although his attitude towards natural

[54] William Paley, *The Principles of Moral and Political Philosophy* (9th American ed., Boston: West and Ricardson, 1818) at 311.

[55] See Austin, *The Province*, *supra* note 2 at 160.

[56] *Ibid.*

[57] *Ibid.* at 223–24.

[58] *Ibid.* at 224.

[59] *Ibid.*

[60] *Ibid.* at 225.

[61] *Ibid.*

[62] *Ibid.* at 55.

[63] *Ibid.*

law was somewhat more favourable, he was also highly critical of it. He assailed the term itself as "ambiguous and misleading."[64] He also argued that to claim that any human law contrary to the will of God is void is "to preach anarchy, hostile and perilous as much to wise and benign rule as to stupid and galling tyranny."[65] Finally, he regarded the notion of natural law as closely connected with theories of the moral sense, or instinct, or "innate practical principles."[66] Austin objected very strenuously to these ideas, which he assailed as ambiguous, "misleading," and "pernicious jargon."[67] Since they are "closely allied" with the notion of natural law, he claimed, it "ought to be expelled (…) from the sciences of jurisprudence and morality."[68]

7.3.4 The Principle of Utility

The importance that Austin attached to this idea is indicated by how much of *The Province* he devoted to it. Three of its six "lectures," or about 23 % of the entire book, are an explanation and defence of the principle. He conceived of it, to oversimplify, as the notion that whether actions are right or wrong depends upon their "probable effects (…) on the greatest happiness of all, or […their] tendencies (…) to increase or diminish that aggregate."[69] What counts for Austin is, however, the tendencies of the class of actions to which a specific action belongs, not the effects of the specific action itself. The individual should not decide how to act by applying the principle of utility directly to his or her situation. Rather, he or she should decide what to do by deducing the decision from a rule grounded in the principle of utility. In short, Austin was a rule-, rather than an act-utilitarian. His defence of rule-utilitarianism rests in large part on the claim that the direct application of the principle of utility to specific cases as a means to determine what ought to be done is "too slow and uncertain to meet the exigencies of our lives."[70] Indeed, he went so far as

---

[64] *Ibid.* at 19.

[65] *Ibid.* at 159.

[66] See Austin, *The Province*, *supra* note 2 at 153.

[67] *Ibid.*

[68] *Ibid.*

[69] *Ibid.* at 41. The statement in the text is an oversimplification because Austin was a theological utilitarian. As such, he claimed that divine laws are the ultimate test of the rightness or wrongness of human actions. He distinguished, however, between two types of the laws of God. Some consist of His express commands, which are uttered by God directly, or "by servants whom he sends to announce them" (Austin, *Province*, *supra* note 2 at 39). These laws are known by revelation and are, according to Austin, "stated distinctly and precisely" (*ibid.*). He never explains, however, which of God's many and quite different servants announce or state these laws. As a matter of fact, he says very little about revelation and tends to focus on the second kind of divine laws. They consist of the tacit commands of God, the index to which is the principle of utility. Whether what he says about it is ultimately consistent with his notion of revelation is a large question that I hope to explore in the future.

[70] *Ibid.* at 50.

to argue that *if* this process were required by utilitarianism, the principle of utility would be "a halting and purblind guide."[71]

Austin's defence of rule-utilitarianism thus reflects his keen perception of certain limitations of the principle of utility. This perception is also apparent from other strands of his thought. They include his contention that even utilitarians might disagree about the utility of particular laws. Such is the case because conceptions of "the proper absolute end of a sovereign political government," including the principle of utility, are "*inevitably* conceived in a form, or is *inevitably* stated in expressions, *extremely* abstract and vague."[72] He gave the example of a law enacted *ex post facto*. People who agree that utility is the purpose of government might assess such a measure very differently.[73] The same is true of resistance to government. Although Austin maintained that obedience to laws should be the rule, he admitted that resistance to them is sometimes ethically justifiable on utilitarian grounds. He acknowledged, however, that even utilitarians might disagree about *whether*, and *when*, such resistance is warranted. The fact of the matter is that assessments of its utility "would probably be a difficult and uncertain process. The numerous and competing considerations by which the question must be solved, might well perplex and divide the wise, and the good, and the brave."[74]

Despite these difficulties, however, Austin remained a convinced utilitarian. For one thing, he insisted that the cases in which the principle of utility must be directly applied are "comparatively few."[75] Most of the time, rules suffice. For another thing, even if it must be directly applied, the principle of utility is preferable to the alternatives. As he put it, we "must pick our scabrous way with the help of a glimmering light, or wander in profound darkness."[76] While the principle of utility would provide "no certain solution," at least it would provide an intelligible test.[77] Its use would also be likely to encourage peaceful compromise of differences, a point that Austin heavily emphasized. If the appeal were to inalienable rights, the sacred rights of sovereigns, basic liberties, or an original contract, however, such a fact-based, cost-benefit approach would be impossible.[78] The only option for parties who disagree would then be to "take to their weapons, and fight their difference out."[79] According to Austin, England's "needless and disastrous" war with her American colonies illustrates the problem.[80]

[71] *Ibid.* at 49.

[72] *Ibid.* at 262, emphasis added.

[73] *Ibid.*

[74] *Ibid.* at 54.

[75] *Ibid.* at 57.

[76] *Ibid.* at 48.

[77] *Ibid.* at 54.

[78] *Ibid.* at 55.

[79] *Ibid.*

[80] *Ibid.*

Although Austin acknowledged even more serious limitations of the principle of utility in *A Plea*, he still retained a belief in it as an ultimate standard. Or so I will argue in a subsequent section.

7.4 Basis for Alleged Changes in His Legal Philosophy

Before addressing the question of whether, or how, Austin modified his legal philosophy in *A Plea*, a brief discussion of two other matters is desirable. Both shed some light on, though they do not resolve, the question of whether he had ceased to be an Austinian. One is his refusal to permit a reprint of *The Province*. The other is the nature of the larger book on jurisprudence and ethics that he contemplated, but never wrote.

According to Sarah Austin, in the mid-1830s and again in 1844, her husband received numerous entreaties to publish a second edition of his book or simply reprint it.[81] He refused these requests, which probably would have delighted most authors. He did so, according to Sarah, on the ground that he "had discovered defects in [...the book] which had escaped the criticism of others; and with that fastidious taste and scrupulous conscience which it was impossible to satisfy, he refused to republish what appeared to him imperfections."[82] His view was that the elimination of these flaws would require that his book "be entirely recast and rewritten, and that there must be at least another volume."[83]

There is, thus, little doubt that Austin became dissatisfied with *The Province*, a point the Hamburgers understandably emphasize. The key question, however, is the nature of his dissatisfaction with it. Specifically, why did he believe that the book must be entirely recast or rewritten, and what exactly did he think the defects in it were? Were they the core elements, or any elements, of his legal philosophy, or something else? According to Sarah Austin, her husband believed that an "entire *refonte*" of the book was necessary largely because of "the conviction, which had continually been gaining strength in his mind, that until the ethical notions of men were more clear and consistent, no considerable improvement could be hoped for in legal or political science, nor, consequently, in legal or political institutions."[84] Unfortunately, she did not explain what her husband regarded as the basis of this conviction. However, it is not inconsistent with *any* of the crucial elements of his *legal* philosophy as developed in his *Lectures*. Although Austin sharply distinguished between law and morality, for example, he also pointed out the various connections between them. As he put it, in a very meaningful passage, there are "numerous cases wherein law and morality are so intimately and indissolubly allied, that, though they

[81] See Austin, *Lectures*, *supra* note 5 at vol. 1, 14–15.

[82] *Ibid.* at 16.

[83] As summarized by Sarah Austin. *Ibid.*

[84] *Ibid.*

are of distinct natures and ought to be carefully distinguished, it is necessary nevertheless to consider them in conjunction."[85] Moreover, *The Province* hardly ignored ethical notions, discussion of which takes up almost one-quarter of the book.

There is also no incompatibility between the views expressed in Austin's *Lectures* and the much larger work that he contemplated writing. Although we do not know much about the projected contents of these volumes, we do know something. The major source of information is a *prospectus* for the book (date not indicated) that Sarah Austin reprinted in her Preface to her edition of her husband's lectures.[86] The other source is a letter, also undated, that he had written to Sir William Erle.[87] The *prospectus* is three paragraphs long and indicates that the title of the new work would be *The Principles and Relations of Jurisprudence and Ethics*. According to Austin, it would cover the same "subject" as *The Province*, but go "more profoundly into the related subject of Ethics."[88] The purpose of the work was to explain the nature and common relations of positive law, positive morality, and "the principles which form the text [I think that Austin meant "test"] of both."[89] All of them are, he wrote, "the inseparably connected parts of a vast organic whole."[90]

Austin indicated that his new work would be divided into two parts. The first would be an exposition of general jurisprudence. It would go into the detail indicated by his "Outline of a Course of Lectures on General Jurisprudence." He had published this Outline in 1831 and subsequently attached an enlarged version of it to *The Province*.[91] The second part of the treatise would focus on ethics. Positive morality would not receive separate treatment, but would be discussed in connection with jurisprudence and ethics.[92]

In his letter to Sir William Erle, an old friend, Austin described his new volumes in much the same terms as the *prospectus*. He wrote:

> I intend to show the relations of positive morality and law (…) and of both, to their common standard or test; to show that there are principles and distinctions common to all systems of law (or that law is the subject of an abstract science); to show the possibility and conditions of codification; to exhibit a short scheme of a body of law arranged in a natural order; and to show that the English Law, in spite of its great peculiarities, might be made to conform to that order much more closely than is imagined.[93]

Do any of these ideas conflict with, or substantially modify, any of the elements of Austin's legal philosophy enumerated previously in this paper? The answer to this question seems to me to be an unqualified "no." Rather, his very brief account of his contemplated work indicates that it would differ from *The Province* in essentially three respects. In the

---

[85] *Ibid.* at vol. 2, 746.

[86] *Ibid.* at vol. 1, 16–17.

[87] *Ibid.* at 17.

[88] *Ibid.* at 16.

[89] *Ibid.*

[90] *Ibid.*

[91] See Austin, "Outline of the Course of Lectures" in *Lectures*, *supra* note 5 at vol. 1, 31–73.

[92] *Ibid.* at 17.

[93] *Ibid.*

first place, it would be a more detailed analysis than was possible in his book of the matters suggested by the Outline for his course. In the second place, it would go much more fully into the subject of ethics. Finally, the new work would analyze in more detail than his book the relationships between positive law, positive morality, and the principles of ethics that are the test or measure of both. The two projected volumes were not, thus, based upon Austin's *rejection* of the principles, notions, and distinctions set forth in *The Province* and the Outline for his course. Instead, the work that he visualized presupposes these ideas, which he would build upon.

Finally, Austin's inability to get this project off the ground could be explained on bases other than changes in his legal philosophy. One such explanation was offered by Sarah Austin. The short of it was a reluctance of her husband to return to a subject from which he had been diverted. According to Sarah, it "seemed as if he had a sort of dread of the labour and tension to which, when it had once taken hold on him, it would inevitably subject him."[94] This dread may have been particularly acute in his final 12 years, the "happiest period of his life."[95] Another factor could have been discouragement at what he perceived to be the unenthusiastic reaction to *The Province*. Although his perception was not accurate,[96] his book was not reviewed by the two most influential journals of the day, the *Edinburgh Review* and the *Quarterly Review*. Certain limitations of his character as well as recurring bouts of ill-health could also have contributed. If Sarah Austin is correct, his poor health was secondary.[97] Indeed, Austin himself wrote in 1811 that "indolence" was "always the prominent vice of my character."[98] Then, too, there is the extraordinary difficulty of what he was proposing to do, of which he was well-aware.[99] To explain the nature and common relations of positive law, positive morality, and the principles that are presumably the common measure or test of both is a Herculean task, mind-boggling in its vastness and complexity. It is no wonder that he never wrote the volumes that would furnish such an explanation.

7.5 What About the Work He Never Started?

The case for claiming that Austin did not remain an Austinian must rest, thus, on *A Plea*. Neither his correspondence, nor the two articles on free trade and centralization that he published in 1842 and 1847,[100] provide any evidence of changes in his legal philosophy. Indeed, the Hamburgers admit that in the article on centralization Austin "used the

[94] *Ibid.* at 14.

[95] *Ibid.* at 18.

[96] See Wilfrid E. Rumble, *Doing Austin Justice: The Reception of John Austin's Philosophy of Law in Nineteenth-Century England* (London: Continuum, 2005) at 57–74.

[97] Letter to M. Guizot, March 17, 1857, in Janet Ross, *Three Generations of English Women*, *supra* note 20 at 325.

[98] As quoted in Lotte and Joseph Hamburger, *Troubled Lives*, *supra* note 3 at 5.

[99] See Austin, *Lectures*, *supra* note 5 at vol. 1, 16.

[100] See John Austin, "List on the Principles of the German Customs-Union" (1842) 75 *Edinburgh Review*, 515–56, and "Centralization" (1847) 85 *Edinburgh Review* 221–58.

concepts and distinctions laid out" in *The Province*.[101] Nor do Austin's notes or memoranda on his lectures provide any evidence, apparently, of his abandonment of his legal philosophy. At least Sarah Austin made no mention of any such abandonment in her editions of John's works. Yet, she indicated that she "preserved the traces of the questionings which continually suggested themselves to his penetrating and sincere mind; and with which he was careful to qualify and limit his assertions, so long as the shadow of a doubt remained."[102]

In any event, *A Plea* seems to me to provide relatively little evidence of changes in Austin's legal philosophy. To begin with, in this work he discusses very few elements of his philosophy of law. He says nothing about his conception of general jurisprudence, the command conception of law, the nature of a positive law, the distinction between law and morality, the classification of law into the law of things and the law of persons, and codification. Nor is it surprising that he did not discuss these ideas. *A Plea* is an avowedly political pamphlet, the purpose of which is to express Austin's opposition to the reform of Parliament. To say this is not in any way to denigrate the pamphlet, but simply to characterize it.

Austin does discuss in *A Plea* three elements of his legal philosophy. One is sovereignty, which he only mentions briefly. What he says about it is illustrated by these four short quotations from the work:

> As freedom from legal restraints is of the essence of sovereignty, all sovereign governments are free or independent.[103]
>
> As sovereign, [Parliament…] has all political powers actual and possible; and all the political powers which are vested in other authorities (…) are emanations from that sovereign authority and held in subordination to it.[104]
>
> The sovereignty [in the United Kingdom] resides in the King, the House of Lords, and the electoral body of the Commons.[105]
>
> According to the true theory of the British Constitution, the powers residing in the electoral body of the Commons are completely delegated to the Commons' House.[106]

Whatever one may think of these notions of sovereignty or the British sovereign, they reiterate positions that Austin had staked out in *The Province*. The same is true of the conception of liberty that he develops in *A Plea*. Although he does not discuss it at any length in the pamphlet, what he does say is consistent with his analysis of it in his book. For example, he claims that a free government is one "which permits to its subjects a large measure of *useful* liberty, or a large measure of *that* liberty which consists with the purposes of political society."[107] In a passage that could have been lifted *verbatim* from *The Province*, he maintained that:

> Freedom from legal restraints is an evil rather than a good, unless it promotes the purposes of the political union; unless the rights imparted by the government to its subjects, be not

---

[101] Lotte and Joseph Hamburger, *Troubled Lives, supra* note 3 at 179.

[102] See Austin, *Lectures*, *supra* note 5 at vol. 1, 28.

[103] See Austin, *A Plea*, *supra* note 10 at 14.

[104] *Ibid.* at 3.

[105] *Ibid.* at 9.

[106] *Ibid.* at 23.

[107] *Ibid.* at 14–15.

> only consonant to public utility, but be also protected by the government from unlawful infringement. In short, the only freedom which a rational people would aim at, is a legal order commended by public utility, and coupled with all the freedom which that order will allow.[108]

The third element of his legal philosophy that Austin briefly discusses in *A Plea* is the notion of natural law and rights. If anything, he was even more critical of them than he had been in *The Province*. This is apparent from his indictment of political instability in the United States and France. He argued that in America the root of the problem is the provision in the federal constitution, and most state constitutions, for amending the fundamental law through constitutional conventions. According to Austin, the effects of these various provisions are disastrous:

> This frequent meddling with the fundamentals of the political order must gradually eradicate from the hearts of the people all respect for their positive institutions. They become familiar in practice with the absurd and anarchical notion, which, in the declaration of rights prefixed to many of their constitutions, is expressly or implicitly adopted: the notion of a natural law, superior to positive ordinances, which justifies the [sic] resisting them, or the setting them aside, whenever they conflict with that paramount authority. As the notion is utterly indefinite, it would justify resistance to government under any pretext whatever.[109]

Austin applied much the same analysis to his critique of political instability in France. The French people, he argued, "attempted to build a constitution on the natural rights of man and the natural sovereignty of the people: a jargon involving stupendous absurdities, admitting of any interpretation, and offering pretexts for rebellion against any government whatever."[110]

7.6 Is *A Plea for the Constitution* Non-Austinian?

This leaves the principle of utility, which Austin discusses at much greater length in *A Plea* than the other three notions. His discussion of it also provides some evidence for the Hamburgers' interpretation. Their argument is *not* that he explicitly and categorically rejected it. Instead, they maintain that he continued "to pay lip service" to the principle and was "unable entirely to cast aside the language of utilitarianism."[111] Nevertheless, doubts about it had "crept into his thinking"[112] and he heavily emphasized its limitations. In particular, he no longer believed in its applicability to the

[108] *Ibid.* at 15.

[109] *Ibid.* at 38–39.

[110] *Ibid.* at 40–41.

[111] Lotte and Joseph Hamburger, *Troubled Lives, supra* note 3 at 183.

[112] *Ibid.* at 182.

"realm" of the constitution and positive morality.[113] The Hamburgers particularly emphasize statements such as this by Austin:

> Applied to so vast a subject as the government of a great country, public utility (though not involving absurdities), leads to differences of opinion that are all but invincible. A government adapted to so complicated a thing as the situation of a great country, is a work for generations; and the creation of such a government in pursuance of a plan, would suppose on the part of its authors a range of intelligence more than human.[114]

In *A Plea*, Austin thus rejected the principle of utility as a basis for the creation of the government of a great country. Instead, he emphasized the necessity for stable government of what he called "*the sentiment of constitutionality*." He defined it as "the peculiar attachment of a people to the constitution of their sovereign government."[115] He sharply distinguished it from their rational or "reflective attachment" to a government based upon their belief in its tendency to promote their well-being. He put it this way:

> To a people in whom this feeling is deep and general, the constitution of their sovereign government, *in and for itself*, is an object of love and veneration. Although it may involve a belief in the beneficent tendencies of the constitution, their attachment rests directly on authority and habit; and, speaking generally, the object of their disinterested feeling is not a constitution of recent origin, but one which has descended to them from preceding generations.[116]

The sentiment of constitutionality was for Austin the only opinion supportive of the constitution that the bulk of the people can share. As such, it is the basis of a stable and efficient government. The prevalence of the sentiment among the English people largely explains, he argued, their "signal success"[117] in their long and gradual attempts to reform their political institutions. Since they had a definite constitution which they tended to venerate, they wished only to modify rather than radically change it. They have thus "kept within the limits of the positive and the practical, and have not ventured on the ocean of purely speculative innovations."[118] He sharply contrasted the political situation in England in this respect with that of the United States and France. Although he had praised both countries highly in his first published article on primogeniture,[119] his attitude towards them had changed drastically by

[113] *Ibid.* at 183.

[114] *Ibid.* The quotation from *A Plea*, *supra* note 10 at 41.

[115] *Ibid.* at 37.

[116] *Ibid.*

[117] *Ibid.* at 38.

[118] *Ibid.*

[119] See Austin, "Disposition of Property by Will – Primogeniture" *supra* note 15 at 503–53. For his very favourable comments on the United States, where "the *people reign*" (see *ibid.* at 551 fn). He particularly praised the "glorious administration" of Thomas Jefferson for repealing the "odious Law" of political libel and permitting "that unbounded censure of public men and measures which has ever since been exercised by writers of all parties" (*ibid.*). Although Jefferson did not "repeal" the Sedition Act of 1798, which expired on the last day of the Adams Administration, he was strongly opposed to it. For an excellent and lively discussion of the Act – its enactment, enforcement, and limitations – see Geoffrey R. Stone, *Perilous Times: Free Speech in Wartime from the Sedition Act of 1798 to the War on Terrorism* (New York: W.W. Norton & Co., 2004) at 16–78.

1859. He also attributed the alleged political instability of both nations to their lack of the sentiment of constitutionality.[120]

The Hamburgers conclude that if these ideas of Austin do not constitute an "abandonment" of his earlier position, at least they amount to "a major retreat."[121] But do they? I do not think that they do and for basically four reasons. To begin with, Austin's analysis of utilitarianism in *A Plea* is not that different from his discussion of it in *The Province*. To be sure, there are differences. In his book he does not argue that the principle of public utility is unable to provide a basis for stable government. Nor does he claim that the only opinion favourable to their constitution that the bulk of the people can hold in common is the sentiment of constitutionality, or that the application of the principle of public utility leads in general to an "invincible" diversity of opinions.[122] Still, even in *The Province* he did not represent ethical decision-making as solely a matter of rational calculation. Such calculation is involved, but remotely rather than immediately. To think therefore that "the theory of utility would *substitute* calculation for sentiment, is a gross and flagrant error."[123] Aside from this, as was pointed out in a previous section, he was acutely aware of what he perceived to be the limitations of the principle of utility.[124] They include its extremely abstract and vague character, his perception of which underlies his heavy emphasis upon rules.

There is a second reason for believing that Austin did *not* make a "major retreat" from utilitarianism in *A Plea*. Throughout the pamphlet, he evaluated parliamentary reform and other political matters from a utilitarian perspective. In the very first sentence of the work he indicated that:

> Before we can decide on the *expediency* of Parliamentary Reform in general, or of any specific alteration in the present constitution of Parliament, we must determine its *probable effects* on the whole of the Parliamentary system, and, through the Parliamentary system, on the general condition of the country.[125]

Moreover, he employs "public utility" as his standard for evaluating laws,[126] political parties,[127] stable cabinets,[128] inequalities in the size and population of parliamentary constituencies,[129] and the great variety of electoral qualifications.[130]

---

[120] See Austin, *A Plea*, *supra* note 10 at 38–42. Austin was also critical of the "gradual growth of fraud, lawlessness, and brutality" in the United States. As quoted by Sarah Austin, in a letter to M. Guizot, Dec. 7, 1861, as reprinted in Janet Ross, *Three Generations of English Women*, *supra* note 20 at 380.

[121] Lotte and Joseph Hamburger, *Troubled Lives*, *supra* note 3 at 183.

[122] See Austin, *A Plea*, *supra* note 10 at 37.

[123] See Austin, *The Province*, *supra* note 2 at 52.

[124] See *supra* 7.3.4.

[125] See Austin, *A Plea*, *supra* note 10 at *iii*, emphasis added.

[126] *Ibid.* at 16.

[127] *Ibid.* at 34.

[128] *Ibid.* at 36.

[129] *Ibid.* at 29.

[130] *Ibid.*

This approach indicates to me that Austin paid more than "lip service" to the principle of utility in *A Plea*. To be sure, one person's "lip service" may be another person's "profound commitment." Nevertheless, he did use utility, or "public utility," as *the* ultimate standard of political judgement.

A third reason to claim that Austin did not abandon utilitarianism is his analysis of the relationship between the principle of utility and the sentiment of constitutionality. The question is whether this sentiment serves the utilitarian end of the "greatest happiness of all."[131] In *A Plea* Austin insisted that it did: "though not reposing directly and exclusively on considerations of public utility, the feeling is not rejected by that ultimate test; and is, indeed, an imperative condition of steady political and social advancement."[132]

This language is admittedly not as strong as it might have been. Although Austin refers to public utility as the "ultimate test," he articulates its relationship to the sentiment of constitutionality in negative terms. The one is "not rejected" by the other. For this reason what he says in the final pages of the pamphlet is more conclusive evidence of the priority that he gave to public utility. His point was that "extraordinary" cases occur in which:

> The authority of the ultimate principle [public utility] ought to silence the sentiment [of constitutionality]: in which the end of the constitution, and of the feeling guarding it from infringement, would be manifestly defeated by an inflexible adherence to it. By the ancient partisans of divine right, and by the modern legitimists, this indispensable limitation to the authority of the sentiment has been absurdly rejected (…). By erecting the sentiment into an ultimate principle not permitting an exception in any extremity whatever, they have turned an elevated feeling sanctioned by public utility into a groundless and untenable superstition.[133]

It is difficult for me to imagine a clearer affirmation of the priority that Austin continued to give to public utility in his final work. The testimony of two persons who knew him very well constitutes a fourth and final reason for concluding that he remained a utilitarian. John Stuart Mill not only was a friend and admirer of Austin's, but was tutored by him in Roman law, took his course at the University of London, and reviewed his books on jurisprudence as well as *A Plea*.[134] In addition, Mill was the author of a classic essay on utilitarianism.[135] In short, he was very familiar with

---

[131] See Austin, *Province*, *supra* note 2 at 41.

[132] See Austin, *A Plea*, *supra* note 10 at 37.

[133] *Ibid*. at 37–38.

[134] See "Austin's Lectures on Jurisprudence" (Dec., 1832) II *Tait's Edinburgh Magazine* 343–348, as reprinted in *Collected Works of John Stuart Mill* ed. by John M. Robson (Toronto: University of Toronto Press, 1984), vol. XXI, 51–60; "Austin on Jurisprudence" *Dissertations and Discussions*, (1867) III, 206–74, as reprinted in *Collected Works of John Stuart Mill* ed. by John M. Robson, vol. XXI, 166–205; and "Recent Writers on Reform" (April, 1859) *Fraser's Magazine* 489–508, in *Collected Works of John Stuart Mill* ed. by John M. Robson (Toronto: University of Toronto Press, 1977), vol. XIX, 343–370.

[135] See John Stuart Mill, *Utilitarianism* (1861), in *Collected Works of John Stuart Mill: Essays on Ethics, Religion and Society* ed. by John M. Robson (Toronto: University of Toronto Press, 1969), vol. X, 205–259.

Austin's mind-set, the subject of utilitarianism, and, it is reasonable to assume, *A Plea*. I find it difficult to believe, in light of all of this, that Mill would have missed it if Austin had abandoned utilitarianism. According to Mill, "like me, he [Austin] never ceased to be an utilitarian."[136] Sarah Austin expressed a similar opinion about her husband's commitment to utilitarianism. Her views merit close attention because, she has written, she was "the one person to whom [her husband…] ever talked freely of himself."[137] According to Sarah, he read and talked to her "on the subjects which engrossed his mind."[138] If he had abandoned utilitarianism, it seems very strange that he would not have disclosed it to Sarah. Yet, she makes no mention of any such thing and, in fact, after his death reaffirmed his commitment to utilitarianism. This is evident from her correspondence with Francois Guizot, the French historian and statesman. In 1862 he asked Sarah whether her husband was a disciple of Bentham. Her initial answer was that he definitely was *not* in so far as Bentham's politics and philosophy were concerned, admirable though they were in some respects.[139] Rather, "it was as a Jurist, or rather as the most original and inventive of all writers on Law, that he looked up to him with profound veneration."[140] In a subsequent letter, however, she qualified her comment about John Austin's dissent from Bentham's philosophy. Although her husband did dissent from parts of it, she wrote, as Bentham's "exposition of the doctrine of *utility* is by many regarded as his master-work, it would be wrong to say that he differed wholly from Bentham's philosophy, of which *that* must be regarded as a main feature."[141] Indeed, the entire structure of Austin's jurisprudence has as its foundation "the only sure test to which the goodness or badness of laws can be brought."[142] To be sure, Austin eventually became critical of numerous of Bentham's ideas even about law.[143] Nevertheless, these criticisms do *not* include censure of Bentham for his adoption of the principle of utility for evaluating laws.

---

[136] John Stuart Mill, *Autobiography and Literary Essays*, in *Collected Works of John Stuart Mill* ed. by John M. Robson and Jack Stillinger (Toronto: University of Toronto Press, 1963), vol. 1, 185. Although Mill was quite critical of the conservative thrust of *A Plea,* he agreed with Austin that until human beings are much better than "there is any present hope of, even good political institutions cannot dispense with the support afforded by traditional sentiment" (*Collected Works, supra* note 134 at vol. XIX, 352). Given the limitations of the principle of public utility, an attachment "resting on authority and habit to the existing constitution 'in and for itself' is, as Mr. Austin remarks (…) in the existing state of the human mind, an almost indispensable condition of the stability of free government" (*ibid.*).

[137] See Austin, *Lectures, supra* note 5 at vol. 1, 12.

[138] *Ibid.* at 23.

[139] Letter to M. Guizot, Dec. 18, 1861, as reprinted in Janet Ross, *Three Generations of English Women, supra* note 20 at 382.

[140] *Ibid.*

[141] Letter to M. Guizot, Jan. 3, 1862, *supra* note 139 at 383.

[142] *Ibid.* at 384.

[143] In the Preface to *A Plea* for example, Austin stated his position in these terms: "I have (…) dissented from many of his views of law and of the various subjects immediately connected with it; although my admiration of his genius has increased in intensity as my increasing knowledge has

There are, thus, many reasons for holding that Austin remained a utilitarian. The undeniable and very substantial change that occurred in his political views did not cause him to abandon the principle of utility. He may have emphasized different limitations of it than he had stressed in his book, but he remained committed to it as the "ultimate principle"[144] or "ultimate test."[145] The changes in his political outlook were due to his different calculation of how this ultimate end can best be realized. No doubt, his arguments may not be convincing from a utilitarian (or some other) perspective. Whether they are is an entirely different question from the central issue discussed here, which is whether Austin remained a utilitarian. Admittedly, too, there is an irony in a utilitarian arguing that the ultimate end can best be achieved if the members of a society do not view their constitution as a means to an end, but love and venerate it for itself. An irony is not, however, a contradiction. And there is no contradiction is arguing that the effects of this veneration are beneficial for society. Why people obey is one thing; whether their obedience is justifiable on utilitarian grounds is another. After all, what counts for a utilitarian *is* effects, not motives.

7.7 Conclusions

The bulk of the evidence fails, thus, to substantiate the claim that Austin did not remain an Austinian. Of course, he did acknowledge that *The Province* had defects that required it to be entirely recast and rewritten. While these flaws could have been in the core elements of his legal philosophy, there is little evidence that they were. Such an interpretation would have to be based upon *A Plea*, but this pamphlet does not provide convincing support for it, or so I have argued.

In short, there is no compelling reason to doubt the traditional assumption that Austin remained an Austinian. The Hamburgers' interpretation of his abandonment of the legal philosophy developed in *The Province* cannot be sustained. To say this is not in any way to deny the high quality of their biography of John and Sarah Austin. The Hamburgers' contribution in this respect is invaluable and all students of Austin are indebted to them. In addition, they are to be applauded for emphasizing his eventual dissatisfaction with *The Province*, an emphasis which has not received the attention that it deserves. It is also conceivable that this dissatisfaction could have expressed itself in the abandonment of core elements of his legal philosophy. There is little or no evidence, however, that it in fact had this effect.

---

rendered it less undiscerning" (*ibid.* at *vi*). Austin's dissent from some of Bentham's opinions long antedated *A Plea*. For discussion of the differences between the two leading utilitarians, see Wilfrid E. Rumble, *The Thought of John Austin*, *supra* note 1 at 25–26.

[144] See Austin, *A Plea*, *supra* note 10 at 37.

[145] *Ibid.*

If I am correct, then, we are left with the Austin whose legal philosophy must be reconstructed primarily from his books. Although this conclusion simplifies the task of understanding his ideas, the task itself is by no means simple. Many problems remain to be resolved. Such is the case; at least, if I am justified in believing that Austin is a more complex thinker than he has frequently been represented to be. The problems do *not* include, however, whether he remained an Austinian.

Chapter 8
Austin and the Electors*

Pavlos Eleftheriadis

8.1 Introduction

In the era of the Roman Empire, John Austin tells us, the Roman Emperors or Princes "did not succeed to the sovereignty of the Roman Empire or World by a given generic title: by a mode of acquisition given or preordained, and susceptible of generic description."[1] The pretenders to this office did not claim they were descendants of Julius Caesar or Augustus, or that they were appointed by the last possessor to the throne or that they were appointed or nominated by the Roman people or senate. Their success was based on brute force:

> Every successive Emperor acquired by a mode of acquisition which was purely anomalous or accidental: which had not been predetermined by any law or custom, or by any positive law or rule of positive morality. Every actual occupant of the Imperial office or dignity (...) was obeyed, for the time, by the bulk of the military class; was acknowledged, of course, by the impotent and trembling senate; and received submission, of course from the inert and helpless mass which inhabited the city and provinces. By reason of this irregularity in the succession to the virtual sovereignty, the demise of an Emperor was not uncommonly followed by a shorter or longer dissolution of the general supreme government. Since no one could claim to succeed by a given generic title, or as answering for the time being to a given generic description, a contest for the prostrate sovereignty almost inevitably arose between the more influential of the actual military chiefs. (...) There was not, in the Roman World,

* An earlier draft was presented at the conference "John Austin and his Legacy" at University College London, 16–17 December 2009. Many thanks to all participants for their comments and suggestions and especially to Brian Bix, David Dyzenhaus, Michael Freeman, George Letsas, Patricia Mindus, Stanley Paulson, James Penner, Frederick Schauer, Lars Vinx and Emmanuel Voyiakis.

[1] John Austin, *Province of Jurisprudence Determined* ed. by Wilfrid E. Rumble (Cambridge: Cambridge University Press, 1995) at 132.

P. Eleftheriadis (✉)
University of Oxford, Mansfield College, Oxford, UK
e-mail: pavlos.eleftheriadis@law.ox.ac.uk

M. Freeman and P. Mindus (eds.), *The Legacy of John Austin's Jurisprudence*, Law and Philosophy Library 103, DOI 10.1007/978-94-007-4830-9_8,

any determinate person, whom positive law or morality had pointed out to its inhabitants as the exclusively appropriate object of general and habitual obedience.[2]

Those familiar with Austin's theory of law and of H. L. A. Hart's criticisms of it will find this passage very strange. Austin speaks here dismissively of the practice of assuming power by force. It is, he says, "anomalous or accidental." He observes on the same page that the resulting system of government suffers from instability and strife. Austin's readers will be surprised by these comments because at the very beginning of his book Austin tells us that sovereignty is not supposed to be a matter of title at all, either legal or moral. There is no appropriateness in sovereignty. This is precisely the point at which Hart criticised the command theory of law. Since it reduced law to power, it could not explain the nature of the succession of political power. Sovereignty is a matter of fact, a fact of brute force. Or so we thought.

In the first few pages of the book Austin insisted that the superiority of the sovereign was, literally, only a matter of "might." He said there that "taken with the meaning wherein I here understand it, the term *superiority* signifies *might*: the power of affecting others with evil or pain, and of forcing them, through fear of that evil, to fashion their conduct to one's wishes."[3] That power was not a matter of title, but a matter of fact:

In short, whoever can *oblige* another to comply with his wishes, is the *superior* of that other, so far as the ability reaches: the party who is obnoxious to the impending evil, being to that extent, the *inferior*.[4]

There is no doubt that this is the meaning Austin gives to sovereignty, because he repeats it at the beginning of Lecture VI. The sovereign emerges through the habit of obedience of his subjects:

If a *determinate* human superior, *not* in a habit of obedience to a like superior, receive *habitual* obedience from the *bulk* of a given society, that determinate superior is sovereign in that society.[5]

This account follows that of Bentham, who wrote that:

By a sovereign I mean any person or assemblage of persons to whose will a whole political community are (no matter on what account) supposed to be in a disposition to pay obedience: and that in preference the will of any other person.[6]

If this is sovereignty, then what is wrong with the Roman succession? There cannot be any anomaly, under Austin's theory of law. According to the Command theory the Roman legal system works through (although not necessarily because of) the brute fact of power and the series of commands backed by threats that it brings about.

---

[2] Austin, *Province supra* note 1 at 133–4.

[3] *Ibid*. at 30.

[4] *Ibid*. at 30.

[5] *Ibid*. at 166.

[6] Jeremy Bentham, *Of Laws in General* ed. by Herbert L. A. Hart (London: Athlone Press, 1970) at 18.

Austin nevertheless says that the anomaly in succession makes the legal system precarious. He notes that "by reason of this irregularity in the succession to the Imperial office, the general and habitual obedience to an actual occupant of the office was always extremely precarious."[7] And a few lines later he gives the following advice:

> Unless the members of the supreme body hold their respective stations by titles generic and fixed, the given supreme government must be extremely unstable, and the given society wherein it is supreme must often be torn by contests for the possession of shares in the sovereignty.[8]

But is power not always precarious?

Austin's concern with the instability of the Roman system seems very odd. The whole idea of his book is that law is a fact. It is a matter independent of political philosophy or political advice. His theory offers an account of positive law, not of positive morality. So one would be inclined to think that what makes for stable or unstable government is not part of the philosophy of positive law. There will be different political ways in which "sovereignty" is established. None of them are part of jurisprudence. For jurisprudence, Austin seems to be telling us, is happy to start with the fact of domination. The philosophy of positive law is not interested in justifications or techniques of persuasion. Legal philosophy in Austin and Bentham's sense, *i.e.* the philosophy of positive law, requires the philosopher to be the "expositor" and not the "censor" of the law.[9]

It is further striking, however, that Austin sets out to solve the problem faced by the Romans. So he writes that "[i]n order that a given society may form a society political, the generality or bulk of its members must habitually obey a superior determinate as well as common."[10] He spends a lot of energy explaining how a body of persons, as opposed to a real person, can be a determinate agent. He argues at length for a determinate corporate body as the bearer of the sovereignty in Great Britain and he concludes that in the United Kingdom "speaking accurately, the members of the commons' house are merely trustees for the body by which they are elected and appointed: and consequently, the sovereignty always resides in the king and the peers, with the electoral body of the commons."[11] The sovereign body consists of the King, the members of the House of Lords and the Electors.[12] The electors in

---

[7] Austin, *Province*, *supra* note 1 at 133.

[8] *Ibid.* at 134.

[9] Jeremy Bentham, "A Fragment on Government" in J. Bentham, *A Fragment on Government with An Introduction to the Principles of Morals and Legislation* ed. by Wilfred Harrison (Oxford: Blackwell, 1967) at 7.

[10] Austin, *Province*, *supra* note 1 at 169.

[11] *Ibid.* at 194.

[12] He gives a similar answer as to the sovereignty of the United States: "I believe that the sovereignty of each of the states and also of the larger state arising from the federal union, resides in the states' governments as forming one aggregate body: meaning by a state's government, not its ordinary legislature, and which, the union apart, is properly sovereign therein" (Austin, *Province*, *supra* note 1 at 209).

particular sit very uneasily in Austin's scheme. They do not even participate in the drafting of laws. They may have voted for the losing party and be vehemently opposed to the decisions ultimately reached in their name. Their role is merely in electing the MPs. How can that be an exercise of sovereignty?

This is a very different account of sovereignty, because it is based not on power but on a moral relation, the relation of trust between represented and representative. The Electors are part of the sovereign body, but do not exercise any active power. Austin writes:

> That a trust is imposed by the party delegating, and that the party representing engages to discharge the trust, seems to be imported by the correlative expressions *delegation* and *representation*.[13]

The result is that the relationship is defined by constitutional law, which is "positive morality merely." The trust is enforced by means of moral, not legal, sanctions. Nevertheless, the model here is very complex and is quite far from the model announced in Lecture I. For the electors are both holders of sovereignty and subjects to it. So it cannot be true that subjects obey and the sovereign commands. It appears that the electors are both sovereign and subject at the same time:

> Generally speaking, if a member of a sovereign body, taken or considered severally, be not amenable to positive law, it is merely as a member of the body that he is free from legal obligation. Generally speaking, he is bound, in his other characters, by legal restraints.[14]

The exercise of sovereignty here is not a matter of force. It is a matter of legal standards and distinctions. We obey in our "character" as subject. We command in our "character" as electors and members of the sovereign body.

Austin appears, thus, to hold two inconsistent views about sovereignty. First, sovereignty is a matter of brute force. Second, sovereignty is not a matter of brute force but a matter for the electors. It is only in the second sense that the electors are sovereign. And as a result of this accommodation of the electors, Austin's whole theory of law becomes, in my view, hopelessly inconsistent. And its inconsistency is instructing for it shows the limitations of any theory of law that tries to pursue the intellectual project that Austin was engaged in, namely "empirical positivism."

8.2 Two Theories of Sovereignty

In the course of the book Austin suggests that a sovereign can be both a person and a body of persons. He appears to be thinking that it is the same theory of sovereignty that supports the two options. But the two options are two entirely different theories of sovereignty.

---

[13] Austin, *Province*, *supra* note 1 at 194.

[14] *Ibid.* at 221.

8.2.1 The First Theory: Personal Sovereignty

The first theory is the theory that Austin outlines as his own. It is a theory based on the reality of power as a feature of persons. The sovereign is a person to whom "the bulk of the given society are in a *habit* of obedience or submission" and who "is *not* in a habit of obedience to a determinate human superior."[15] What is submission and obedience? This is defined in Lecture I as follows: "being liable to evil from you if I comply not with a wish which you signify, I am *bound* or *obliged* by your command, or lie under a duty to obey it."[16] It is not enough that compliance may be induced by the incentive of a benefit. Command and obedience are the result of fear for a loss:

> I am also determined or inclined to comply with the wish of another, by the hope of advantage or good. But it is only by the chance of incurring *evil*, that I am *bound* or *obliged* to compliance. It is only by conditional *evil*, that duties are *sanctioned* or *enforced*. It is the power and the purpose of inflicting eventual evil, and not the power and the purpose of imparting eventual good, which gives to the expression of a wish the name of a command.[17]

Austin's analysis has a very obvious psychological element. A law exists if a set of beliefs are true.

A command is a wish or desire conceived by a rational being that another rational being shall do or forbear, "with an evil to be inflicted and incurred in case the wish be disregarded." A command is a duty, when it is backed by a sanction. There are two possible readings of this, both psychological in a different way. The first, objective, reading would be that a command is a law, if the commander is as a matter of (observable, empirically verifiable) fact powerful in the way of a sovereign. But he will be powerful in a way of a sovereign if the subjects have a habit of obedience based on a set of beliefs about his powers. A second reading is more subjective: a command is a law if the person to whom it is addressed believes that the commander is powerful in the way of a sovereign, *i.e.* if he believes that others have a habit of obedience etc.

The idea of the habit of obedience is psychological in both cases. In the first case it arises from the observable fact (if it is a fact) that there is a state of mind of submission and therefore obedience to the sovereign. In the second it arises from the observable belief (if it is a belief) that there is a general state of mind of submission and therefore obedience to the sovereign. The habit of obedience is, in both cases, the essential psychological ingredient. So Austin says that "taken with the meaning wherein I here understand it, the term superiority signifies might: the power of affecting others with evil or pain, and of forcing them through fear of that evil, to fashion their conduct to one's wishes."[18] This is the psychological relation at the heart of sovereignty: the power "of affecting others with evil or pain." This is the core of the "personal" understanding of sovereignty that Austin relies on. This is

[15] *Ibid.* at 166.

[16] *Ibid.* at 22.

[17] *Ibid.* at 24.

[18] *Ibid.* at 30.

also the darker reading of sovereignty, because it is wholly neutral. It includes all the cruel manifestations of human submission.

8.2.2 The Second Theory: Impersonal Sovereignty

Austin believes that this same sense of sovereignty can accommodate the idea of a determinate body as sovereign. Throughout the book Austin speaks as if the difference between a personal sovereign and a corporate sovereign is not essential. But, as I will try to show in this section, the difference is essential because the way in which a corporate body is perceived is entirely different. The psychological element is here entirely different.

Austin defines a "determinate body" as follows: "if a body of persons be determinate, *all* the persons who compose it are determined and assignable, or *every* person who belongs to it is determined and may be indicated."[19] Austin assumes rules of composition that either identify members of the body by virtue of "generic descriptions" or by way of "specific or appropriate character." He then concludes that once we have solved the problem of the determinacy of the body, then it can be sovereign. The theory as applicable either for a person or body as sovereign:

> Every positive law (…) is set, directly or circuitously, by a sovereign person or body, to a member or members of the independent political society wherein that person or body is sovereign or supreme. Or, (changing the expression) it is set, directly or circuitously, by a monarch or sovereign number, to a person or persons in a state of subjection to its author.[20]

But it is evident that one cannot have the same psychological attitude of obedience to a "determinate body" of persons. Austin assumes that once the composition of the body is fixed, the relationship of obedience is the same. One has the habit of obeying a sovereign body.

But even if the membership of the body is fixed without any doubt, its rules of procedure and conduct may not be. Before one can ascribe intention and will to a corporate body, one needs to have a theory of its procedures. We need to know when the body has acted in ways relevant to law. This theory cannot turn on a psychological pattern of obedience. It will be in effect an impersonal theory of validity, because it will have to address both the problem of the composition of the body and of its appropriate procedures. We cannot identify the law made by this body without knowing in full its theory of its composition and procedure. If the body fails to meet these constitutive rules, it fails to legislate.[21]

Austin is not unaware of this dimension added by the idea of a sovereign body, whose procedures may occasionally fail to be observed:

---

[19] *Ibid.* at 127.

[20] *Ibid.* at 212.

[21] The problem of having procedure for making law is highlighted by Joseph Raz as follows: "it is usually the case, even in states where sovereignty is in the hands of a single person, that laws are created only when the sovereign follows a certain accepted procedure of legislation. But according

> If a [member of a sovereign body] affected to issue a command, which it is not empowered to issue by its constitutional share in the sovereignty, its unconstitutional command would not be legally binding, and disobedience to that command would therefore not be illegal (…). For example: if the king or either of the houses, by way of proclamation or ordinance, affected to establish a law equivalent to an act of parliament, the pretended statute would not be legally binding, and disobedience to the pretended statute would therefore not be illegal.[22]

If the body violated its own procedures, it would not produce law. Why is this the case? How can a command issued by the relevant persons and apparently backed by the same treat of a sanction fail to be law? This meets all the empirical conditions Austin had set out for the existence of law. Austin seems to be adding a new criterion. This is a criterion of validity or appropriate procedure. Austin here says that those who appear to hold the power as representatives of the sovereign body, are themselves under a disability, defined by the body's own procedures. Even if the body is represented by the person who is ordinarily its spokesperson and leader, it will fail to produce a relevant law if it fails to comply with the relevant procedures. When sovereignty belongs to a body and not a single person, whether law exists or not does not depend just on a psychological relationship with him. It depends on criteria of validity. This is the essence of Hart's criticism of the command theory as a whole.

Austin glosses over the problem of what exactly this theory of the validity of the corporate body's actions should be. He says very little about the appropriate *procedures* by which a sovereign body may or may not act and legislate. He just focuses on its composition. He says:

> A determinate body of persons is capable of *corporate* conduct, or is capable, as a body, of positive or negative deportment. Whether it consists of persons determined or defined by a character or characters generic, every person who belongs to it is determined and may be indicated.[23]

He says that once we sort out the composition, the rest remains the same. The body can be as determinate as the personal holder of sovereignty. But that cannot be enough. By invoking the idea of a corporate body as sovereign, he invites an entirely new theory of sovereignty.

The composition of the body does not solve the problem. The United Kingdom constitution identifies ways in which the relevant bodies meet in order to issue Acts of Parliament. It does not just outline their membership.[24] It is obvious that what counts as an Act of Parliament is not based on a psychological relationship of

---

to Austin every expression of the sovereign's desire which is a command is law, so he does not allow for the fact that sovereign can command in ways which differ from the accepted procedure, in which case his command is not a law" (Joseph Raz, *The Concept of a Legal System*, 2nd ed., Oxford: Clarendon Press, 1980 at 38).

[22] Austin, Province, *supra* note 1 at 221.

[23] *Ibid*. at 130.

[24] For a criticism of Dicey and Austin on this see Pavlos Eleftheriadis, "Parliamentary Sovereignty and the Constitution" (2009) 22 *Canadian Journal of Jurisprudence* 267–290.

obedience to anything the members of these bodies say, but on the fact that the technical rules of procedure are respected to the full. It is not relevant here whether these rules are legal or not. What matters is their nature as standards of conduct. One identifies the law, *i.e.* the Act of Parliament, by comparing the actions of the members of the sovereign body with the standards they are supposed to obey. If they fail to comply with them, we must say there is no law.

This is in fact a theory of law that is very different to the one proposed at the beginning of Austin's book. Here we do not identify the law by perceiving a command issued by the person, whom take to be sovereign on account of the habits or beliefs of his subjects. We identify the law by means of a cognitive process of reasoning on the basis of some standard of decision-making. This is not a matter of a pattern of conduct, of habitual obedience. It is a matter of a theory of law. The result is much closer to Hart's rule of recognition than to the idea of a habit of obedience. And this is implicit in Austin's own account of the sovereign body. So Austin's account of impersonal sovereignty, the sovereignty of the determinate corporate body, is inconsistent with the rest of Austin's command theory. The law is identified by means of the powers and disabilities of the corporate body. It is not identified by means of commands, threats and sanctions.[25]

8.3 Sovereignty and Publicity

Explaining Austin's inconsistency on the content of sovereignty sheds some light on his treatment of the Roman succession. Austin deploys his second sense of impersonal sovereignty in order to criticise the Roman example. He does not seem to see that what he describes as the problematic Roman case is precisely a model of his own theory of law, a result of his own first sense of personal sovereignty.

I think that this inner tension appears even earlier in Austin's *Lectures*. I want to draw attention to two other aspects of the theory: the generality of laws and the superiority of the law-makers. Both are requirements for law but both seem redundant from the point of view of the first theory of sovereignty. They are not redundant from the point of view of the second theory.

8.3.1 Generality of Laws

When he outlines the command theory in Lecture I, Austin explains that a proper law is to be "general not particular." He explains that a command is a law or rule

[25] I outline this argument in greater detail in Pavlos Eleftheriadis, "Law and Sovereignty" (2010) 29 *Law and Philosophy* 535–569.

only if "it obliges generally to acts or forbearances of a class."[26] He then explains how some particular whim of a sovereign would not be counted as law.

> An act which is not an offence, according to the existing law, moves the sovereign to displeasure: and, though the authors of the act are legally innocent or unoffending, the sovereign commands that they shall be punished. As enjoining a specific punishment in that specific case, and as not enjoining generally acts or forbearances of a class, the order uttered by the sovereign is not a law or rule.[27]

It is very hard to reconcile this condition with the theory as a whole. Why should laws be general? They ought to be general from the point of view of the rule of law. But this criterion of generality is not entailed at all by the command theory: a law is a command issued by the sovereign backed by a sanction. Commands can easily be general and particular.

8.3.2 *Superiority*

Austin insists that laws are commands issued by superiors that bind or oblige inferiors.[28] But when we look at the command theory more closely, the requirement is redundant. A command is "distinguished from other significations of desire, not by the style in which the desire is signified, but by the power and the purpose of the party commanding to inflict an evil or pain in case the desire be disregarded."[29] The power and purpose of the party commanding is necessary for the command to exist. But it does not entail that the commander is "superior" to the subject. If someone has power, they have power. They may have power because the sovereign has delegated his power to them just for this instance. To say that they are superior is to insert, once again, an element of permanence and generality that it is not necessary from the logic of the command theory.

Notice also how Austin speaks of an order of delegation in the law. He assumes that in a society of any complexity "the intervention of representatives" of the sovereign will be necessary.[30] He then allows that we divide powers into supreme and subordinate. The supreme powers are the "political powers, infinite in number and kind, which, partly brought into exercise, and partly lying dormant, belong to a sovereign or state."[31] But the subordinate powers are those "portions of the supreme powers which are delegated to political subordinates." Nevertheless, delegation cannot happen in this way according to the command theory. Power cannot be delegated to a person from the sovereign directly. If the command theory is correct, delegation

---

[26] Austin, *Province*, *supra* note 1 at 25.

[27] *Ibid*. at 27.

[28] *Ibid*. at 29.

[29] *Ibid*. at 21.

[30] *Ibid*. at 190.

[31] *Ibid*. at 199.

can only work if the sovereign first asks the subject to obey the minister as a duty. Delegation must be the result of a command (and here Hart's criticism of the command theory has real bite). Nevertheless, it is clear that Austin relies on an idea of a public delegation of power that leads to some sort of "superiority." But the sovereign can only create a class of "superiors" if he is legislating by means of secondary rules, not by means of commands backed by sanctions.

8.3.3 Publicity

Clearly, the two criteria, namely the generality of law and the superiority of the person commanding, introduce an element of publicity to the law that would otherwise be lacking. They are designed to make the law intelligible as a system of classifications and reasoning. The same virtues are served by the idea that the sovereign body needs to be carefully defined by rules that render it "determinate." For what is a determinate body, if not a body whose actions are public and intelligible? This emphasis on the publicity of law as a system of reasoning is what guides Austin's criticism of the Roman succession:

> There was not, in the Roman World, any determinate person, whom positive law or morality had pointed out to its inhabitants as the exclusively appropriate object of general and habitual obedience.[32]

There was no public way of resolving the problem of succession and of publicly explaining that solution to the all citizens. So when Austin speaks of the sovereign issuing general laws, of being a superior person or body (after an appropriately public scheme of delegation) and of being an "appropriate object of general and habitual obedience" he has in mind to satisfy the requirement that a theory of law that achieves this kind of public guidance. Sovereignty serves as a public theory of power.

But why should this be the case? If we turn our attention to the first sense of sovereignty, *i.e.* to "personal" sovereignty, we see that sovereignty need not be public. A person may be habitually obeyed by everyone, without all the others knowing that this person is actually the sovereign. The same may be true while there is an external *façade* of a supposedly sovereign body. So we may say that the electors and parliament are the apparent sovereigns but power really lies with politician A or politician B. It may also be (as it probably is the case) that the balance of power changes every week. The sovereign need not be permanent for law to exist. There will be law, even if it is hard to follow or it is impractical. The sovereign, thus, does not need to issue general laws in order to meet Austin's criteria. He need not delegate his powers to a structure of superiors, but may delegate on an *ad hoc* basis, issuing commands here and there to obey such and such a person. He may change his mind frequently.

[32] *Ibid.* at 133–4.

He may thus cause hopeless instability. Clearly such a system of government would be appallingly oppressive. But was not Austin's theory supposed to be neutral between political theories?

Austin's empiricist theory of law could perhaps accommodate the oppressive model of secret sovereignty. Such a system may well be an order of power and therefore an order of law. Such a system was perhaps the system of the Roman Empire. Why does Austin rule out a system of hopeless instability from the realm of law? He does say at the end of the book that the real foundation for his theory of law is *utility*:

> The habitual obedience to the government which is rendered by the bulk of the community, partly arises (…) in almost every society, from the cause which I now have described: namely, a perception, by the bulk of the community, of the utility of political government, or a preference by the bulk of the community, of any government to anarchy.[33]

But a theory of utility cannot be a defence of the command theory of law. A defence of this nature would be conflating the description of the law with its justification. It would not be an empirical theory of law, neutral between all moral theories.

It is obvious that Austin does not feel entirely at ease with this kind of – self-imposed-neutrality. He returns again and again to the themes of the stability and publicity of the institutions of law. Austin's faces a dilemma here that any "empiricist" theory of law has to deal with. Is law – as most people take it to be – a public order of standards of conduct aiming to guide behaviour? Is this moral purpose to be taken seriously by any legal philosophy? If so, then law is a moral idea (in the succinct phrase used by N. E. Simmonds) and "sovereignty" as the core of legal theory ought to be public and intelligible.[34] Sovereignty and publicity ought to go together. For the neutral reading, by contrast, sovereignty need not entail publicity or the rule of law at all. Law is an order of power, which may remain unpredictable, fluid and useless. Sovereignty may well remain a mystery to those living under it, accessible only after the event by the expert legal philosopher.

Some modern legal philosophers cheerfully accept this conclusion. Such modern legal positivists would presumably criticise Austin for what they take to be a lapse of methodology. They would say, perhaps, that law and sovereignty are "normatively inert," and because they are so inert his theory should perhaps accommodate the idea of a secretive and unpredictable order of power that Austin was so careful to exclude.[35] But Austin does not agree with these modern followers. Austin's second theory of sovereignty is aimed at satisfying a practical requirement of law (and of jurisprudence itself), *i.e.* to be in the position of publicly guiding conduct.

---

[33] *Ibid.* at 247.

[34] See N. E. Simmonds, *Law as a Moral Idea* (Oxford: Oxford University Press, 2007).

[35] The phrase belongs to John Gardner. See Gardner, "Legal Positivism: 5 1/2 Myths" (2001) 46 *American Journal of Jurisprudence* 199.

8.4 "An Enemy to Itself"

Austin seems torn between his methodological empiricism and his common sense. He wishes to describe law as an order of power, yet he cannot bring himself to do so with the thoroughness we have come to expect from an otherwise meticulous scholar. As we have seen, he has introduced some wholly unwarranted conditions, namely publicity, stability, order of rules. But is the choice between the first, theory of "personal" sovereignty and the second, public theory of "impersonal" sovereignty a choice between methodological neutrality on the one hand and moral and political philosophy on the other? It may seem that the two versions talk about two different things: a descriptive theory on the one hand and a moral theory on the other. It is tempting to see it this way, splitting the difference, so to speak, between Austin and his critics. Perhaps Austin was engaged in both a descriptive and a separate normative project about law. But I do not think it can be done that way. I think Austin was right to abandon the theoretical project of neutrality. The reason is implicit in his book, but is much more clearly expressed in the classics of political philosophy.

Austin tries to say that law is merely a matter of power: naked, raw, fluid unpredictable, self-seeking, morality-busting power. But he also wants to say that public institutions organised by means of public rules are the appropriate bearers of sovereignty, of law-making power that secures continuity and stability. How can the two be reconciled? In the process he tells us that the sovereign body is a kind of person, a person imposing or inspiring obedience in other persons, just like any other. It is hard to see, however, how that body can hold this kind of power and, more importantly, how a body can be the ultimate origin of law by means of imperatives backed by sanctions. The very constitution of that body depends on rules of composition and procedural rules determining its identity and form. These rules make the analogy with a single person unworkable. Austin is guilty of an error of anthropomorphism. The body is not a person and drawing analogies with the actions of persons is bound to mislead.

The argument against this kind of personification is very old. It forms one part of Plato's argument against Thrasymachus. Offering an argument for the superiority of unjust action over just action, Thrasymachus famously argued that justice was "nothing other than the advantage of the stronger."[36] It is close to what Austin is saying.

There should be no doubt that when Plato writes here about "justice" he means a combination of moral practice and legislation. For immediately Thrasymachus adds:

> Democracy makes democratic laws, tyranny makes tyrannical laws, and so on with the others. And they declare what they have made – what is to their own advantage – to be just for their subjects, and they punish anyone who goes against this as lawless and unjust. This, then, is

[36] Plato, *The Republic*, trans by G. M Grube, rev. by C. D. C Reeve, in Plato, *The Complete Works* ed. by John Cooper (Indianapolis: Hackett, 1997) at 971, R 338c.

> what I say justice is, the same in all cities, the advantage of the established rule. Since the established rule is surely stronger, anyone who reasons correctly will conclude that the just is the same everywhere, namely the advantage of the stronger.[37]

So Thrasymachus makes an argument that is very close to that of Austin, although it says more than Austin. He says that the law is made by the stronger, in order to serve the interests of the stronger. When Socrates asks him, he affirms that as a result there is a duty to follow the law of the stronger: "and whatever laws they make must be obeyed by their subjects, and this is justice? Of course."[38] Thrasymachus is caught out by Socrates when he is confronted by the fact that laws sometimes work to serve the interests of the stronger and sometimes they do not. So justice, even if it is shaped by the stronger, is not always in his interest. After all, it is made by fallible self-seekers. But Austin's more austere formulation is unaffected: the laws are made by the stronger – for whatever reason – and they are laws just because they are so made. And laws are to be followed for that reason alone.

Socrates' next argument, however, undermines the Austinian theory in equal measure. He notes that if everyone endorsed the non-moral attitude, then no group of people could ever work together. If they do not respect common ground rules of conduct and communication in order to establish at least some basic trust, all co-operation between them will fail. So Socrates asks:

> Do you think that a city, an army, a band of robbers or thieves, or any other tribe with a common unjust purpose would be able to achieve it if they were unjust to each other?[39]

The body would hardly exist without common rules that everyone obeyed: "injustice, Thrasymachus, causes civil war, hatred, and fighting among themselves, while justice brings friendship and a sense of common purpose. Isn't that so?"[40] Thrasymachus agrees and helps Socrates into this conclusion:

> Apparently, then, injustice has the power, first, to make whatever it arises in – whether it is a city, a family, an army, or anything else – incapable of achieving anything as a unit, because of the civil wars and differences it creates, and, second, it makes that unit an enemy to itself and to what is in every way its opposite, justice.[41]

So a group of people trying to become a body but consisting of principled immoralists that set out only to serve their self-interest with utter disregard of what justice requires of them, will fail to constitute a parliament or an army or even a band of

---

[37] R 338e-339a. The word translated as "justice" is *δίκαιον*, which is to be contrasted to statute, *i.e. νόμος*. So the idea of justice in Plato is complex in that it is a blend of moral principle and legislative action. One plausible interpretation is that justice (*díkaion*) is a moral idea separate both from personal virtue (*agathòn*) and from the content of a statute (*nomos*). For this exchange see Bernard Williams, "Plato Against the Immoralist" in Bernard Williams, *The Sense of the Past: Essays in the History of Philosophy* ed. by Myles Burnyeat (Princeton: Princeton University Press, 2008) at 97–107.

[38] R 339c.

[39] R 351c.

[40] R 351d.

[41] R 352a.

robbers. Their incompatible ends will drive them to strife and oblivion. Remember that here Plato is not speaking of virtue. He is speaking of principles of just conduct that can publicly be formulated by the legislator. These standards of justice, these public rules, are required for a body to exist. Without the practice of justice, there is no collective agent.[42]

But Plato's argument says more. It is not that it is inconsistent to assume that a body can exist without rules of composition and procedure. His argument is also meant to suggest that those involved in the composition of the body that exercises political power cannot co-operate sufficiently without a conception of justice. Notice what Plato says. It is not enough that someone issues directives about what to do. We need general principles by which we shall understand and interpret the directions, such as they are. There are numerous problems of coordination in any collective decision-making exercising political dominion. Later in the *Republic* he will show that it is not enough to pretend that we are committed to a set of principles. We must seek to understand and follow them for their own sake.

Austin seems to agree. He is offering us a practical theory that explains the structure of the law as an element of the civil condition, *i.e.* as a public order of rules. He says that in the United Kingdom and in the United States there is an elaborately defined sovereign body that issues general and intelligible rules of law and whose major component is the body of the electorate – and whose animating theory is democracy. The will of the majority is the theory that gives meaning and procedural content to the law. Law is not a haphazard order of commands of the powerful. If it was such a haphazard order, it would also become "an enemy to itself." Austin goes further than Thrasymachus' concessions. He offers not just an austere theory of law, but also the preliminaries of a theory of government. Otherwise, he would not have spoken of the electors and would not have complained of the Roman succession.

8.5 Conclusion

Why did Austin attempt such an unlikely reconciliation between sovereignty and political philosophy? I think he did so in order to make sure that law does not become "an enemy to itself." The argument from the electors undermined the simplicity of the theory. It contradicted some of the early basic assumptions of the idea of law as a command. And it made the command theory, ultimately, incoherent as a theory of law.

Why did Austin venture that far from "empirical positivism"? It is for the reasons Plato gives us. A state cannot exist if its members are not guided by some basic understanding of the public role of institutions and some conception of justice. Without them, sovereignty is useless and self-destructive. Without them, the civil condition disintegrates. In this sense, law is a normative ideal, perhaps identical to that of justice. Even Austin could not escape the force of this basic truth.

[42] See Williams, "Plato Against the Immoralist" at 97–98.

Chapter 9
Positive Divine Law in Austin*

James Bernard Murphy

9.1 The Last of the Schoolmen

John Austin is much better understood as the last of the schoolmen rather than the first of the Benthamites.[1] We must take seriously Austin's elegiac reflection: "I was born out of time and place. I ought to have been a schoolman of the twelfth century—or a German professor."[2] Austin's discourse of positive law reveals that, in many respects, he was a twelfth-century schoolman, by way of being a German professor. Austin tells us that he borrowed the subtitle of his lectures on jurisprudence,

*In this paper I draw freely on my book *The Philosophy of Positive Law: Foundations of Jurisprudence* (New Haven: Yale University Press, 2005), especially Chapter 4: Positive Law in the Analytical Positivism of John Austin.

[1] Many commentators describe Austin simply as a disciple of Bentham: "Austin followed very much in Bentham's footsteps, though he did not command his master's powers of innovation in logic." See Herbert L. A. Hart, "Jhering's Heaven of Concepts" in *Essays in Jurisprudence and Philosophy* (Oxford: Clarendon Press, 1983) 265–277, at 273. Obviously Hart is aware that, after the publication of his first lectures on jurisprudence, Austin distanced himself radically from Bentham's politics. For an assessment of this distance, see Lotte and Joseph Hamburgers' *Troubled Lives: John and Sarah Austin* (Toronto: University of Toronto Press, 1985), chap. 9: "Did Austin remain an Austinian?" But even in his early lectures on jurisprudence, Austin's commitment to rule utilitarianism and his grounding of moral and legal duty in divine law show him marching out of step with Bentham. See Wilfrid Rumble's *The Thought of John Austin* (London: Athlone Press, 1985), chap. 3: "Divine law, utilitarian ethics, and positivist jurisprudence." Austin later said of his relationship to Bentham: "I have since [my youth] dissented from many of his views of law and of the various subjects immediately connected with it." *Cf.* John Austin, *A Plea for the Constitution* (London: John Murray, 1859) at *vi*.

[2] John Austin's confession here is reported by Sarah Austin in her "Preface" to his *Lectures on Jurisprudence: Or the Philosophy of Positive Law* [hereafter *Lectures*], ed. by Robert Campbell (5th ed., London: John Murray, 1885) at 12.

J.B. Murphy (✉)
Department of Government, Dartmouth College, Hanover, NH, USA
e-mail: jamesbemardmurphy@gmail.com

M. Freeman and P. Mindus (eds.), *The Legacy of John Austin's Jurisprudence*, Law and Philosophy Library 103, DOI 10.1007/978-94-007-4830-9_9,

"the philosophy of positive law," from the German jurist Hugo.[3] Austin's kinship with the medieval scholastics extends far beyond his passion for hair-splitting: by defining his jurisprudence as a philosophy of "positive law," an expression studiously avoided by his first masters in law, Bentham and Blackstone,[4] Austin placed himself in the medieval and early modern natural law tradition of moral and theological reflection on law. Austin's commentators have long puzzled over why he devotes so much of his exposition of the philosophy of positive law to the topics of moral truth and divine law.[5] But these puzzles vanish when we situate his jurisprudence in its proper context. For the schoolmen, positive law could be illuminated only in relation to the moral truth of the natural law and the claims of divine law.

Austin develops a divine-command theory of moral and legal obligation without any attempt to provide support or evidence for his theological premises. So although he devotes immense labour to securing the superstructure of his theory to its base, he makes no effort whatever to secure the very foundation of his moral and legal theory. This curious fact has led most of his commentators simply to set aside his theological claims on the grounds that they are either superfluous or that they are insincere. I make no attempt to judge Austin's sincerity, but I will argue that his theological claims are not superfluous to his account of moral and legal obligation. He may not have a right to his theological premises, since he makes no effort to support them, but they are nonetheless central to his theory.

9.2 Is There a Positive Divine Law?

The medieval discourse of positive law stems from ancient Greek debates about the nature of language.[6] In Plato's *Cratylus*, for example, Hermogenes tells Socrates that according to Cratylus, words get their meaning by nature (*physei*), both in the

---

[3] Austin, *Lectures*, *supra* note 2 at 32.

[4] Blackstone and Bentham fail to avoid "positive law" entirely. For Blackstone's contrast of "natural duties" to "positive [legal] duties" and for his contrast of positive and common law, see William Blackstone (Dublin: 5th edition, 1773) Introduction, sec. 2, at 57–58 and sec. 3.10 (at 92); for Bentham's very rare use of "positive law" see Jeremy Bentham, *Deontology Together with A Table of the Springs of Action and the Article on Utilitarianism* ed. by Amnon Goldworth (Oxford: Clarendon Press, 1983) at 34 and *Legislator of the World: Writings on Codification, Law and Education* ed. by Philip Schofield and Jonathan Harris (Oxford: Clarendon Press, 1998) at 29 and 203.

[5] Henry Sumner Maine led a chorus of complaints that Austin's lectures on utilitarianism were "the most serious blemish in the *Province of Jurisprudence Determined*" because "it is a discussion belonging not to the philosophy of law but to the philosophy of legislation." See Henry Sumner Maine, *Lectures on the Early History of Institutions* (New York: Henry Holt, 1975) at 369–370. Even today, Michael Lobban complains: "Austin created confusion by spending much time in the *Province of Jurisprudence Determined* discussing utilitarian theory. Yet this was irrelevant to *jurisprudence*. (…) Utility was clearly part of the science of ethics, and had nothing to do with law *as* law." See Michael Lobban, *The Common Law and English Jurisprudence 1760–1850* (Oxford: Clarendon Press, 1991) at 246 and 254.

[6] *Quod P. Nigidius argutissime docuit nomina non positiva esse, sed naturalia*: Gellius then points to the Greek origin of this debate: "Quaeri enim solitum aput philosophos, *physei ta onomata* sint

sense that words were originally transparent to their meanings, as in *onomatopoeia*, and in the sense that words arose spontaneously. Hermogenes then argues that Cratylus is wrong. Words, he says, get their meaning by convention (*thesei*), both in the sense that there is no necessary connection between the sound of word and its meaning and in the sense that the meaning of words did not arise spontaneously but was imposed by human agreement. Socrates then dialectically transcends this antithesis by arguing that Cratylus is right that words are natural in the sense that they originally were and ought to be transparent to their meanings and that words are conventional in the sense that their meanings were imposed by an original word-smith. What Socrates reveals is that to say that language is positive, rather than natural, involves two very different claims: first, language in positive because words are not transparent to their meanings, that is, there is no necessary connection between the sound of a word and its meaning; second, language is positive because those meanings were deliberately imposed by a word-smith. Socrates brilliantly shows that we can separate these claims to argue that language can be both natural in its transparency to meaning and positive in how those meanings were originally imposed.

When the twelfth-century humanists of the cathedral school of Chartres first distinguished natural from positive justice,[7] they and their successors defined positive law by two sets of contrasts: first, positive law was contrasted with natural and customary law in the sense that positive law is deliberately imposed by a legislator, while natural and customary law grow up spontaneously; second, positive law is contrasted with natural law in the sense that natural law norms are transparent to their moral rationale ("you shall not kill") while positive law norms lack this intrinsic moral force ("you shall not wear garments of linen and wool sewn together"). The first sense of positive law is a descriptive claim about the origin of a legal norm in an act of deliberate legislation; the second sense of positive law is a normative claim about the moral force of a law. Unfortunately, in the discourse of positive law from Aquinas to Austin, these two very different senses of positive law were never explicitly distinguished, reflecting the tacit assumption that what is positive in moral content

thesei." Aulus Gellius, *Noctes Atticae* ed. by Peter K. Marshall (Oxford: Clarendon Press, 1990), vol. 1, X, 4 (at 307). Other variants of *pono*, later used to describe positive law, were also derived from Greek debates about language: "illi qui primi nomine imposuerunt rebus fortasse an in quibusdam sint lapsi (…)." See Varro, *De Lingua Latina*, L. 8, 7: "qui primus, quod summae sapientiae Pythagorae visum est, omnibus rebus imposuit nomina." See also Cicero, *Tusculan Disputations*, I, 25, 62.

[7] Stephan Kuttner has traced the origin of "positive law" to the rediscovery of Chalcidius's commentary on Plato's *Timaeus* in the twelfth century in Latin (possibly a translation of a Greek original); on Chalcidius's reliance on Gellius, see Stephen Kuttner, *Repertorium der Kanonistik* (1140–1234), vol. 1 (Vatican City: Biblioteca Apostolica, 1937) at 176: "Aus welchen Quellen de französische Scholastik und Dekretistik den Ausdruck 'positives Recht' bildete – es wäre z. B. an des Chalcidius Kommentar au Platons Timäus zu denken – bedarf noch philosophiegeschichter Erforschung"; and at 176 fn. 2: "Da der Kommentar selber wohl nur eine Uebersetzung einer griechischen Kommentarkompilation ist, lässt sich vermuten, dass das Begriffspaar 'naturalis – positiva' eine Latinisierung von *physei* – *thesei* ist, wie sie auf grammatisch-sprachlogischem Gebiet schon bei Gellius (…) begegnet." See Stephen Kuttner, "Sur les origines du terme 'droit positif'" (1936) 15 *Revue historique du droit français et étranger* 728–740 at 739.

must be deliberately imposed while what is morally natural must arise spontaneously. In this tradition of legal discourse there has been no Socrates to argue that natural norms might well be deliberately enacted, as with the second table of the Decalogue or the preface to the German Constitution, while norms purely positive in content might well arise spontaneously in custom. Law can be both natural and positive.

The contrast of natural and positive law was first developed by medieval theologians attempting to grapple with the challenge posed by Mosaic law. Of the 613 commandments in the Torah, which precepts are natural (and, hence, binding on Christians) and which are merely positive (and, hence, binding only on ancient Israel)? Since all of these commandments were thought to be deliberately imposed by God through Moses, they were all positive in the sense of enacted. So the division of Mosaic precepts into natural and positive law was necessarily on the basis of their moral content. Thomas Aquinas devoted the bulk of his treatise on law to the project of distinguishing Mosaic law into natural or moral precepts, ceremonial or positive precepts, and judicial or mixed precepts.[8] In short, divine law included both natural and positive legal norms, depending upon whether the content of those norms possessed intrinsic moral force or not. The prohibition on shaving was described as positive law while the prohibition on stealing was described as natural law. This analysis of divine law into natural and positive law continued through Thomas Hobbes, who distinguished God's natural kingdom over all of mankind from God's prophetic kingdom over the Jews.[9] According to Hobbes, God rules us both by natural and by positive divine law.

Austin fits squarely within this scholastic discourse of positive law. As I demonstrate elsewhere, Austin defines positive law as law existing by imposition (he twice uses the Latin *positum*) by contrast to custom.[10] But then he also defines positive law and positive morality as norms lacking in moral necessity by contrast to natural and divine law; in this sense, positive law and positive morality have no necessary connection to moral truth. In the first sense, Austin defines positive law by reference to its pedigree in an act of legislation; in the second sense, Austin defines positive law and positive morality by reference to its content: he says that divine law is the infallible moral standard of the morally dubious positive law and positive morality. Austin even tells us that within positive law (existing by imposition) we may distinguish natural from positive law on the basis of the normative content of that law, revealing that he must implicitly mean two very different things by positive law.[11] Unfortunately Austin never acknowledges his own inconsistent uses of his most basic jurisprudential term. There is something poignant, to put it delicately, to see the philosopher of

[8] Thomas Aquinas, *Summa Theologiæ* I-II, QQ. 98–105.

[9] Thomas Hobbes, *Leviathan*, chap. 31.

[10] John Austin, *The Province of Jurisprudence Determined* (hereafter *Province*) ed. by Herbert L. A. Hart (London: Weidenfeld and Nicolson, 1954) at 365; See also Austin, *Lectures*, *supra* note 2 at 548.

[11] Austin, *The Province*, *supra* note 10 at 179.

positive law fumble his own central concept when he devoted such immense and tedious labour to verbal and conceptual precision and poured such scorn on the verbal and conceptual muddles of other writers.

It is puzzling that Austin is so determined to avoid describing any part of divine law as positive: after all, divine law is imposed by sovereign command and much of it lacks intrinsic moral force. Yet, in his official classification of law, Austin sharply distinguishes positive human law from divine law on the basis of normative content: divine law, he says, is objective moral truth while positive law is the morally dubious product of sovereign enactment. Law imposed by the civil sovereign differs from divine law, not because it is imposed, but because its content is morally contingent and adventitious:

> As opposed to the law of nature (meaning the law of God), human law of the first capital class [law imposed by the civil sovereign] is styled by writers on jurisprudence '*positive* law'.[12]

He tells us that the application of the term "positive" here is meant to obviate the confusion of human law with divine law, which is the test of human law.[13]

Yet when he focuses, not on the content of law, but on its source, he directly contradicts his official classification of laws by claiming that divine law is positive law:

> Strictly speaking, every law properly so-called is a *positive* law. For it is *put* or set by its individual or collective author, or it exists by the *position* or institution of its individual or collective author.[14]

We should note that, in this sense of positive, all divine law is positive law. Austin cannot decide if "positive law" names the genus of law properly so-called or just one species of that genus, namely, law imposed by a civil sovereign.

As Edwin Charles Clark says, in distinguishing the content of positive law and positive morality from divine law, "the term *human* would seem a better one, to express the distinction intended, than *positive*."[15] As it turns out, Austin's equation of what is positive with what is human finds its origin in the very earliest uses of the expression *justitia positiva* among the theological humanists at Chartres.[16] And even Aquinas, in his mature legal theory of the *Summa Theologiae*, generally restricts the expression "positive" law to human law. Still, the term "positive" is poorly suited to mark the distinction between divine and human law since, according to both Aquinas and Austin, divine law is imposed by God and includes precepts that lack moral necessity.

---

[12] Austin, *The Province*, *supra* note 10 at 124.

[13] *Ibid.* at 124.

[14] *Ibid.* at 124.

[15] Edwin Charles Clark, *Practical Jurisprudence: A Comment on Austin* (Cambridge: Cambridge University Press, 1883) at 132.

[16] Recall that in William of Conches's commentary on Calcidius we read: "Positive [justice] is that which is contrived by men (*ab hominibus inventa*), such as the hanging of a thief" (Latin text in Sten Gagnér, *Studien zur Ideengeschichte der Gesetzgebung*, Stockholm: Almqvist and Wiksell, 1960 at 231).

At the same time, Austin often suggests that all of divine law is natural, in the sense of morally necessary, as when he frequently says that "the divine law is the measure or test of positive law"[17] or when he says that the expression "natural law" has literal sense only if it means "the divine law."[18] These passages seem to deny any conceptual space for a positive divine law. But in other passages, Austin clearly creates space for a positive divine law: "the whole or a portion of the laws set by God to men is frequently styled the laws of nature."[19] At a minimum, Austin's language is often inconsistent on the question of whether there is a positive divine law.

9.3 Revealed and Unrevealed Divine Law

Nowhere does the Benthamite reading of Austin distort his thought more than in relation to divine law. Bentham simply sets aside the revealed will of God, and he treats God's unrevealed law as merely redundant of the conclusions of utility.[20] John Stuart Mill pioneered the Benthamite misreading of Austin by warning us not to conclude that Austin "regarded the binding force of the morals of utility as depending altogether upon the express or implied commands of God." Mill seeks to reassure us that Austin does not harbour a dark view about God's unfathomable will being the source of moral and legal obligation. Mill says that for Austin, the distinction between right and wrong is not constituted by the divine will; rather the divine will merely recognizes and sanctions the conclusions of utility.[21] Lest we fear that Austin believes that whatever God wills is right because he wills it, Mill assures us that Austin follows Bentham's complacent view that "whatever is right is conformable to the will of God." Once we are sure that God simply sanctions what we know from utility to be right, then we may quietly set aside the whole question of what the divine will is and how we might discover it.

---

[17] Austin, *The Province*, *supra* note 10 at 6.

[18] Austin rejects the misleading connotations of the expression "natural law" but he thinks it intelligible when we take it to mean divine law: "rejecting the appellation Law of Nature as ambiguous and misleading, I name those laws or rules, as considered collectively or in a mass, the *Divine law*, or the *law of God* (…) as contradistinguished to *natural* law, or to the law of *nature* (meaning, by those expressions, the law of God)": Austin, *The Province*, *supra* note 10 at 10–11.

[19] Austin, *The Province*, *supra* note 10 at 10.

[20] Bentham *An Introduction to the Principles of Morals and Legislation* ed. by James H. Burns and Herbert L. A. Hart (University of London: Athlone Press, 1970) at 31: "The *will* of God here meant cannot be his revealed will, as contained in the sacred writings" and "we may be perfectly sure, indeed, that whatever is right is conformable to the will of God."

[21] Mill says of Austin: "If he could have been suspected of encouraging a mere worship of power, by representing the distinction of right and wrong as constituted by the Divine will, instead of merely recognized and sanctioned by it." See John Stuart Mill, "Austin on Jurisprudence" in (1863) 118 *The Edinburgh Review* 222–244 at 228.

Nonetheless, Austin does not set aside or dismiss the independent moral force of the divine will. As we shall see, Austin claims that since all duty or obligation (terms which we shall follow Austin in using interchangeably) stems from a command, and since duties are ranked according to the severity of the sanction annexed to the command, our paramount duties are necessarily to obey the commands of Almighty God. But does God merely enforce the norms discovered by utility? Here we must follow Austin's distinction between God's revealed and his unrevealed law. Since God's revealed law is a more certain sign of his will than our presumptions of his unrevealed law, our conduct must be guided in the first place by his revealed law, and only then – where that revealed law is fatally uncertain or silent – by his unrevealed law. God's revealed law provides its own moral content to our duties quite apart from the deliverances of the utility calculus. But God's revealed law is not good because God wills it: even his revealed law is good only if consistent with utility.[22] Still, the existence of a law is one thing; its merit or demerit quite another. God's revealed law imposes moral obligations paramount to all others, whether we judge them good or not. So Mill is right that Austin does not look to God's will as the basis of what is good or bad, but Mill is wrong to argue that Austin does not look to God's will as the basis of all obligation. For Austin, might does not make right, but might does make duty.

Just as the medievals and Hobbes distinguished natural from positive divine law, so Austin distinguishes unrevealed from revealed divine law. Although the basic distinction between natural and positive divine law is medieval, Austin's language of "express" or revealed and "presumptive" or unrevealed divine law comes from William Paley, whose theological utilitarianism exerted considerable influence on Austin, both directly and through Bentham.[23] Paley pioneered a divine-command version of utilitarianism in which the content of moral rules stems from the happiness principle while the obligatory force of moral rules stems from divine command.[24] Paley argues that since all moral duties stem from God's will, we must find a way to discern that will. Paley illustrates these two ways to discover God's will by means of an example of the relation between an ambassador and his sovereign. If an ambassador, he says, has been given written or what Paley tellingly calls "positive" instructions, he will consult them first, since they are the surest sign of the sovereign will. But if those written instructions are silent or dubious upon a point of decision, then the ambassador consults the presumed will of his sovereign, based on the totality of what he knows about his sovereign's purposes.[25]

[22] "To say that they are good because they are set by the Deity, is to say that they are good as measured or tried by themselves. But to say this is to talk absurdly." See Austin, *The Province*, *supra* note 10 at 129.

[23] William Paley, *Principles of Moral and Political Philosophy* (London: Faulder, 1799) vol. 1 at 63.

[24] Although in contemporary philosophical ethics, utilitarian theories and divine-command theories are usually thought to be very different, one recent philosopher has shown the many structural parallels between them. See Edward Wierenga, "Utilitarianism and the Divine Command Theory" in (Oct. 1984) 21/4 *American Philosophical Quarterly* 311–318.

[25] "He will be directed by both rules: when his instructions are clear and positive, there is an end to deliberation, (…) when his instructions are silent or dubious, he will endeavor to supply or explain

In the case of God's presumed or unrevealed law, Paley says that we must consult "the light of nature." Similarly, by unrevealed divine law Austin clearly means natural law: unrevealed divine law is simply another expression for objective moral truth. But does revealed divine law mean positive law? Why would these norms need to be revealed if they were natural and hence accessible to unaided human reason? "Of the Divine laws, or the laws of God, some are *revealed* or promulged, and others are *unrevealed*."[26] He also says that some divine law is express and other divine law is tacit.[27] Austin is clear that the unrevealed or tacit divine law is natural law;[28] is the revealed or express divine law positive? Austin's description of the relation of revealed to unrevealed divine law very closely parallels a traditional juristic description of the relation between positive and natural law. For example, natural law is traditionally permitted to be enforced as law at the interstices or in the absence of positive law, *cum deficit lex*. Thus, Austin says of the unrevealed divine law:

> These laws are binding upon us (who have access to the truths of Revelation), in so far as the revealed law has left our duties undetermined. For, though his express declarations are the clearest evidence of his will, we must look for many of the duties, which God has imposed upon us, to the marks or signs of his pleasure which are styled the *light of nature*.[29]

In the revealed will of God, we expect the specific provisions characteristic of positive law ("you shall not boil a kid goat in its mother's milk"), whereas the unrevealed law of God necessarily takes the form of general moral principles ("obey your sovereign"). To begin with, the unrevealed law, grasped by inferences from utility and available to all men by natural reason, is inherently a matter of general principles, not the detailed specifications of positive law: "if the tendencies of actions be the index to the will of God, it follows that most of his commands are general or universal."[30] These general principles of utility need not be expressly revealed because they are available through natural reasoning about the tendencies of classes of acts. What matters for the grasp of natural law is not the interpretation of express language, but the discovery of whether the tendencies of classes of acts are conducive to the general happiness or not. On the other hand, the revealed law of God need not be general or universal in scope; indeed, we would expect the revealed law of God to be highly specific and targeted to particular communities, for if the revealed divine law were general and universal, then it would be merely redundant of or inconsistent with unrevealed divine law. Austin tells us that the revealed law is not inconsistent with unrevealed divine law, since both kinds of divine law aim at "the *general happiness* or *good* which is the object of the Divine Lawgiver in all his

---

them, by what he has been able to collect from other quarters of his master's general inclination or intentions." Paley, *Principles of Moral and Political Philosophy*, *supra* note 21, vol. 1 at 63–64.

[26] Austin, *The Province*, *supra* note 10 at 34.

[27] *Ibid*. at 34 and 104.

[28] *Ibid*. at 34.

[29] *Ibid*. at 35.

[30] *Ibid*. at 40.

laws and commandments."[31] Nor is revealed divine law wholly redundant of unrevealed divine law, since the revealed law, he says, is available only to those with access to Revelation.[32] Austin never explicitly acknowledges that revealed divine law might well in part serve merely to reinforce and to clarify the conclusions of the unrevealed law discovered by utility, as in the second Table of the Decalogue.

Moreover, we grasp the revealed divine law, not by reasoning from principles of utility, but by the literal construction of the exact language of the revealed statutes: "in so far as the laws of God are clearly and indisputably revealed, we are bound to guide our conduct by the plain meaning of their terms."[33] Since the moral authority of the revealed law of God rests upon the precise language of its expression in Scripture, this revealed law must be at least partly positive in content, in the sense of specific and morally contingent (only binding at least in part because commanded by God). The commandment "keep holy the Sabbath" would seem to exemplify what Austin means by revealed divine law. Unrevealed or natural divine law might lead us to recognize a duty to honour God,[34] but only through knowledge of God's express commandment could we know that honouring God requires a specific day of rest. Since God's will is more certain in the case of express statutes, constructed literally, than in our inferences to his will based on the utility calculus, our conduct must be guided in the first place by God's express or positive law; we resort to utility only where God's express law is silent. As Austin says, "the *whole* of our conduct should be guided by the principle of utility, in so far as the conduct to be pursued has not been determined by Revelation."[35]

Thus, Austin collapses the traditional distinction of natural and positive divine law into his distinction of unrevealed and revealed divine law. No one has argued that positive divine law could be unrevealed, since what is positive in content lacks intrinsic moral force and must get its force from its deliberate enactment. So Austin seems justified in suggesting that all positive divine law must be revealed. However, Aquinas, Hobbes, and many other theorists of positive law have claimed that God's revealed law includes both natural and positive precepts. Austin points out that the Bible itself says little about the unrevealed divine law, though he could have cited Romans (2:14) where Paul argues that even those without access to revelation are guided by the law of nature written on the human heart.[36] Revealed divine law gets its priority over unrevealed divine law for the same reason that we normally give priority to the express and specific provisions of a statute or a written contract over

[31] *Ibid.* at 42–43.

[32] *Ibid.* at 35.

[33] *Ibid.* at 42.

[34] Austin includes in natural law "the dictates of natural religion" in Austin, *The Province*, *supra* note 10 at 34.

[35] *Ibid.* at 43.

[36] Austin says that Revelation tells us next to nothing about the unrevealed divine law: "These [rules known by "the light of nature or reason"] the revealed law supposes or assumes. It passes over them in silence, or with a brief and incidental notice": Austin, *The Province*, *supra* note 10 at 35.

the general and tacit principles of natural equity. Where express language is silent or obscure, we rightly presume that the legislator intends natural equity.

Because Austin says relatively little about revealed divine law and because he ventures not even one explicit example of a precept of biblical law, it is tempting to infer that Austin has simply found a decorous way to follow Bentham by setting aside the revealed divine law. After all, Austin says that we are bound by biblical law "in so far as the laws of God are clearly and indisputably revealed";[37] yet, notoriously, many biblical laws have been disputed in endless sectarian controversy. Hobbes's manifest failure to consistently distinguish natural from positive divine law, despite his Herculean labours of biblical exegesis, was a cautionary tale for Austin. Far from saying that the general happiness is good only because God commands it, Austin says that God's commands are good only because they are consistent with utility:

> If the laws set by the Deity were not generally useful, or if they did not promote the general happiness of his creatures, or if their great Author were not wise and benevolent, they would not be good, or worthy of praise, but were devilish and worthy of execration.[38]

Of course, given Austin's sharp distinction between law as it is and law as it ought to be, the fact that divine law might turn out to be devilish and execrable in no way diminishes our duty to obey it. The sanctions associated with divine law give us a rational motive for obedience "paramount to all others."[39]

Bentham dismissed appeals to the revealed divine law by reason of the uncertainty of that law made manifest by the endless interpretive disputes among divines.[40] Austin admits this uncertainty but draws very different conclusions from it: "the laws of God are not always certain. All divines, at least all reasonable divines, admit that no scheme of duties perfectly complete and unambiguous was ever imparted to us by revelation."[41] To say that revelation does not provide a perfectly complete and unambiguous scheme of duties is far from asserting that revelation is irrelevant to the determination of our fundamental moral duties. Even this modest degree of uncertainty might amount to a serious disability if we had a more certain index of divine law by means of the science of utility, but Austin admits the grave uncertainty of utility: "as an index to the Divine will, utility is obviously insufficient. What appears pernicious to one person may appear beneficial to another."[42] Austin has hopes for gradual improvements in the science of utility: "But, though they [principles of utility] may constantly approach,

---

[37] Austin, *The Province*, *supra* note 10 at 42.

[38] *Ibid*. at 129.

[39] *Ibid*. at 42 and 186.

[40] Bentham on revealed divine law: "(…) before it can be applied to the details of private conduct, it is universally allowed, by the most eminent divines of all persuasions, to stand in need of pretty ample interpretations; else to what use are the works of those divines?" Thus, he says, "setting revelation out of the question." See Bentham, *An Introduction to the Principles of Morals and Legislation*, *supra* note 18 at 31.

[41] Austin, *The Province*, *supra* note 10 at 185–186.

[42] *Ibid*. at 186.

they certainly will never attain to a faultless system of ethics."[43] Given the very different kinds of uncertainty that affect our grasp of both revealed and unrevealed divine law, it would seem to make sense on Austinian grounds to appeal to each as a check on the other. A true Austinian would seek a reflective equilibrium between the revealed and the unrevealed commands of God.

In his discussion of the duty to obey one's government, Austin at least implicitly illustrates how the revealed and the unrevealed divine law might illuminate each other in such reflective equilibrium. Austin argues that divine laws, both revealed and unrevealed, converge upon the general principle that every established government ought to be obeyed.

> If we take the principle of utility as our index to the [unrevealed] Divine commands, we must infer that obedience to established governments is enjoined generally by the Deity.[44]

But to justify this inference, Austin curiously quotes the revealed law of God (Romans 13: 1): "For, without obedience to 'the powers which be' there were little security and little enjoyment. The ground, however, of this inference, is the utility of government."[45] Austin would have strengthened his argument if he had followed Aquinas and Locke by explicitly arguing that both reason and revelation lead us to the same general principle. Of course, Austin here notoriously parts from his rule utilitarianism and concedes that the general principle of obedience might well admit of exceptions. "The members of political society who resolve this momentous question must, therefore, dismiss the rule, and calculate specific consequences."[46] Austin could, again, have strengthened his argument from utility if he had added that the revealed word of God also permits disobedience to evil regimes (Acts 5:29). In short, whether reasoning from utility or from Scripture, we converge on the same conclusion, namely, a presumptive duty to obey our governments unless those governments attempt to require us to do something gravely immoral. Of course, the fact that Austin never explicitly adopts this procedure raises doubts about the sincerity of his expressed respect for the revealed word of God.

9.4 All Obligation Rests on Divine Command

According to Austin, reason helps us to discover our duties but reason itself can create no duties. All duty or obligation stems from a command and a command stems from the will of a commander. Duty, command, and sanction are all strictly interdefinable terms: each one, says Austin, necessarily implies the others. Our duties may be ranked according to the expected disutility of their sanctions; where duties conflict, we are bound to perform the duty in which the expected disutility for non-performance is greatest.

---

[43] *Ibid.* at 80; *cf.* at 87.

[44] *Ibid.* at 53.

[45] *Ibid.*

[46] *Ibid.* at 54.

> The evils which we are exposed to suffer from the hands of God as a consequence of disobeying His commands are the greatest evils to which we are obnoxious; the obligations which they impose are consequently paramount to those imposed by any other laws, and if human commands conflict with the Divine law, we ought to disobey the command which is enforced by the less powerful sanction.[47]

Since God can inflict infinite suffering upon his creatures, no matter how infinitesimal is our prospect of incurring his terrible sanctions, it still follows by mathematical necessity that: "our motives to obey the laws which God has given us, are paramount to all others."[48] Nor can we discount God's sanctions by assuming them limited to a dubious hereafter: Austin is clear that God's sanctions "consist of the evils, or pains, which we may suffer here or hereafter (…)."[49] Because Austin grounds all moral and legal obligation in the prospect of incurring a sanction, the ultimate ground of all duties is God's command:

> In each of these cases [revealed and unrevealed divine law] the *source* of our duties is the same; though the *proofs* by which we know them are different. The principle of general utility is the *index* to many of these duties; but the principle of general utility is not their *fountain* or *source*. For duties or obligations arise from commands and sanctions. And commands, it is manifest, proceed not from abstractions, but from living and rational beings.[50]

For Austin, might creates duty and the Almighty creates all duty.

What is a sanction and how does it provide both a reason and a motive for obedience? Austin makes it clear that ordinary commands impose duties only insofar as those subject to them grasp both the content of the command and the relation of that content to the evil of a sanction:

> Being liable to evil from you if I comply not with a wish which you signify, I am *bound* or *obliged* by your command, or I lie under a *duty* to obey it. If, in spite of that evil in prospect, I comply not with the wish which you signify, I am said to disobey your command, or to violate the duty which it imposes.[51]

Austin often describes the duty imposed by a command in terms of a subject being "liable to" or "obnoxious to" its sanction,[52] but these expressions misleadingly create the impression that a duty arises merely because of the objective probability of a sanction when Austin's actual view is that the subjective prospect of a sanction is also necessary, as when he says above "in spite of that evil in prospect." In short, a duty arises, on his account, when someone is both objectively liable to a sanction and when he fears that sanction: "the party is *bound* or *obliged* to do or forbear, because he is obnoxious to the evil, and because he fears the evil."[53]

---

[47] *Ibid*. at 184.

[48] *Ibid*. at 42.

[49] *Ibid*. at 34.

[50] *Ibid*. at 43.

[51] *Ibid*. at 14.

[52] *Ibid*. at 160.

[53] *Ibid*. at 365; see also Austin, *Lectures*, *supra* note 2 at 444 and at 447 "The force of the obligation lies in our *desire* of avoiding the threatened evil" (emphasis his).

Austin's recognition of the subjective and psychological dimension of having a duty is important because many of his commentators are misled by his imprecise language into supposing that, for Austin, one incurs a duty simply by virtue of the objective liability to suffer a sanction. Herbert L. A. Hart, in particular, famously denies that Austin grasped the "internal aspect" of following commands or rules. Hart says that Austin "treats statements of obligation not as psychological statements but as predictions or assessments of changes of incurring punishments or 'evil'."[54] Since Austin does understand duty in psychological terms as the subjective "prospect" of incurring a sanction, Hart should not say that Austin disregards "a person's beliefs, fears, and motives," but that Austin focuses on the wrong beliefs, fears, and motives in his analysis of having an obligation.

Nonetheless, it is not clear how much of Austin's analysis of obligation and sanction in general applies to specifically legal obligations and sanctions, given that we often liable to legal sanctions whether or not we are subjectively aware of them, since, as Austin says, ignorance of the law is no excuse.[55] In the case of ordinary commands, ignorance of a command usually is an excuse, unless that ignorance is itself culpable. Negligence or recklessness aside, being unaware of a command normally excuses us from being liable to its sanction. But the situation is quite different in the case of legal commands. True, as Austin points out, non-culpable ignorance of fact can excuse us from specific kinds of criminal or civil liability. But ignorance of the law is never an excuse.[56] Hence, we are liable to legal sanctions whether or not we were aware of them: so in the case of law and of law alone, we are liable to a sanction without being under any obligation to obey the command annexed to that sanction. Law imposes a strict liability foreign to ordinary moral responsibility. So Austin's carefully constructed circle of interdefinability among duty, sanction, and command fails in the case of law, where we can be liable to a sanction without being under any duty. So the problem with Austin's account is not, as Hart says, that he defines obligation in purely objective terms but rather that we can be liable to legal sanctions which are not tethered to any legal obligations.

By erecting utility as a measure of the goodness of divine laws, Austin seems to deny those laws any independent moral content. This does not follow for two reasons. First, utility is an index only of the unrevealed divine law: our conduct ought to be guided by the unrevealed divine law only where we lack guidance from the revealed divine law. Even if the revealed divine law is evil, we must prefer it to the good unrevealed divine law because express language is a better index to the divine will

[54] "Some theorists, Austin among them, seeing perhaps the general irrelevance of the person's beliefs, fears, and motives to the question whether he had an obligation to do something, have defined this notion not in terms of these subjective facts, but in terms of the *chance* or *likelihood* that the person having the obligation will suffer a punishment or 'evil' at the hands of others in the event of disobedience." See Herbert L. A. Hart, *The Concept of Law* (Oxford: Clarendon Press, 1961) 83.

[55] Austin, *Lectures*, *supra* note 2 at 489.

[56] "In our law, *ignorantia juris non excusat* seems to obtain without exception." See Austin, *Lectures*, *supra* note 2 at 483.

than is tacit presumption. Our paramount reason and motive for all conduct must be conformity to God's will and "his express declarations are the clearest evidence of his will."[57] Second, even where the revealed law of God is consistent with the unrevealed law discovered by utility, the revealed divine laws might retain important independent moral content as specifications of the general principles of utility. If revealed divine law provided authoritative specifications of the principles of utility, they could provide moral guidance that is both consistent with utility but independent of it. So "keep holy the Sabbath" provides independent moral content to the principle of utility that we ought to honour God. In this way, utility remains the ultimate measure and test of divine law, while divine law remains the ultimate measure and test of human conduct. Utility is the ultimate test of the goodness of our duties, but divine law ultimately determines the content of those duties.[58] A rule of conduct is not good because God wills it, but it is obligatory because God wills it.

Austin's philosophy of positive law is motivated in part by an attempt to secure orderly compliance with law by showing that law has authority independent of moral truth. With respect to civil positive law, Austin followed Bentham's maxim of "obey punctually; censure freely." Yet because Austin claims that our duties to obey God are paramount to all others, he invites conscientious disobedience to the civil law. Following Austin, a rational judge will have a duty to refuse to enforce any civil law that directly violates either the express or the tacit will of God and a rational citizen will have a duty to refuse to obey any such law. Austin's own hierarchy of duties seems to undermine the independent authority of the civil law and to invite the anarchy that he frequently condemns. Here Austin's rhetoric is often at war with his own theory of obligation, for Austin frequently heaps abuse on conscientious resistance to civil law. He says that those who disobey civil law on the basis of religious or moral principles are usually just trying to hide naked self-interest: "and as for the moral sense, innate practical principles, conscience, they are merely convenient cloaks for ignorance or sinister interest."[59] Like Bentham, Austin scorns as "fanatics" those who disobey civil law by appeal to natural rights or divine law. In a famous passage, Austin considers a person who disobeys a very pernicious law on the grounds that it is "contrary to the law of God." According to Austin, if I make such a claim, the Court of Justice "will demonstrate the inconclusiveness of my reasoning by hanging me up, in pursuance of the law of which I have impugned the validity."[60] Here Austin attacks the reasoning of a conscientious objector by supposing that he disobeys on the false supposition that a pernicious law will not actually be enforced. But surely most conscientious objectors refuse to obey a pernicious law, not on the supposition that it will not be enforced, but on the supposition that there

[57] Austin, *The Province*, *supra* note 10 at 35.

[58] "In so far as the laws of God are clearly and indisputably revealed, we are bound to guide our conduct by the plain meaning of their terms." See Austin, *The Province*, *supra* note 10 at 42.

[59] Austin, *The Province*, *supra* note 10 at 186.

[60] *Ibid.* at 185.

are duties that trump the duty to obey civil law. On the basis of his own theory of obligation, Austin ought to have applauded the cogent reasoning of a resistor who rightly prefers the finite evil of a legal sanction to the infinite evil of a religious sanction.

On Austin's account, is it possible that we might have a duty to do what is morally wrong in order to obey God? Is it perverse to suppose that positive divine law might require a deed forbidden by the unrevealed divine law discovered by utility? In other words, is Abraham's dilemma possible for Austin? Austin seeks to avoid such quandaries by confidently asserting that God's revealed and his unrevealed law both aim at our happiness,[61] suggesting that even positive divine law is consistent with utility. But in several other places, Austin creates space for a positive divine law that might well conflict with utility, as when he says that utility determines only a part of our duties or that only a part of divine law can be styled natural. Certainly, our construal of positive divine law would include a presumption that it conform to the conclusions of utility, but any such presumption could be defeated by clear and express language. And where positive divine law is incompatible with utility, Austin is crystal clear that we must prefer God's express to his presumed will.

According to Austin, reasoning from utility normally yields general rules of conduct, not specific commands. So the unrevealed law of God will take the form of maxims governing whole classes of actions. This fact reduces the scope of possible conflict with positive divine law, which usually takes the form of commands targeted to specific groups (Jews or Jesus' Disciples) or even to individuals, such as Abraham. The ceremonial law imposed upon Jews or upon Christian clergy may well seem incompatible with basic aspects human happiness, but those divine commands would be even more incompatible with natural law were they framed as general rules for all human beings. God's specific command to Abraham certainly seems to violate the natural law norm against deliberate killing of the innocent, but is less of an outrage than a general command to sacrifice innocent children. In sum, despite Austin's ostensible reassurance that we need never fear a choice between our duty and what is good, at a deeper level his account of divine law opens the door to many such tragic dilemmas.

[61] *Ibid.* at 42–43.

Chapter 10
What Is in a Habit?

Michael Rodney

10.1 Introduction

Habitual obedience, that is to say behavioural compliance with the law, forms an important ingredient in Austin's definition of sovereignty. A sovereign body arises when the bulk of a "given society are in the habit of obedience or submission to the commands of a determinate and common superior" either of a certain individual or a determinate aggregate of individuals.[1] At the same time, reflecting the absence of habit, the entity to whom the status of sovereignty is attributed must not be in habitual compliance to any other determinate human superior.[2] The sense of repetitive conformity with the law suggested by habitual compliance implies the notion of a stable society with settled social practices and regularities of behaviour. Such circumstances are pre-supposed by Hart in his discussion of the necessities of a legal system.[3] They appear in Kelsen's writings with his assertion that the efficacy or effectiveness of a legal order "is a necessary condition for every single norm of the order."[4] More recently, Pettit refers to most accounts of norms concentrating on the regularities of non-linguistic behaviour and then seeks to argue that there is no

[1] John Austin, *The Province of Jurisprudence Determined* ed. by Wilfrid E. Rumble (Cambridge: Cambridge University Press, 1995) [first published, 1832] at 166.

[2] *Ibid.* at 166.

[3] Herbert L. A. Hart, *The Concept of Law* (Oxford: Oxford University Press, 1961).

[4] Hans Kelsen, *General theory of Law and State*, trans. by Anders Wedberg (first published by Cambridge, MA: Harvard University Press, 1945; Repr. Union, NJ: The Lawbook Exchange, 1999) at 119.

M. Rodney (✉)
Department of Law, London South Bank University,
103 Borough Road, SE1 OAA London, UK
e-mail: rodneyma@lsbu.au.uk

M. Freeman and P. Mindus (eds.), *The Legacy of John Austin's Jurisprudence*,
Law and Philosophy Library 103, DOI 10.1007/978-94-007-4830-9_10,

reason why they should not extend to regularities of a communicative kind.[5] Looking beyond jurisprudential writings, repetitive compliance with the law has been regarded as central to ensure the effective expression of legal authority. So for example, to be able to discharge such authority, "the lawgiver must be able to anticipate that the citizenry as a whole will (…) generally observe the body of rules he has promulgated."[6] In a similar manner, Easton considered that "effective leadership requires compliance with leaders' decisions form the bulk of the members [of society…] most of the time."[7]

Hart in his seminal work *The Concept of Law* proclaimed that the idea of habit was associated with a regularity of behaviour and predictability of conduct which was unreflective, effortless or engrained.[8] Hart considered that Austin's claim that habit was central to the operation of sovereignty and hence of a legal system was inadequate to satisfactorily identify the properties associated with the functioning of either. Looking generally at the operation of social rules and mere group habits before moving on to consider legal rules, he claimed that in both cases the behaviour in question must be general though not necessarily invariable and hence have a repetitive quality.[9] Differentiating the operation of mere group habits from that of social rules, Hart listed three distinctions.

Firstly, for a group to have a habit, it was enough that their behaviour converged and that deviation from the behaviour associated with the habit did not give rise to criticism.[10] Secondly, where such deviation occurred from behaviour considered to meet the requirement of a social rule, that was considered to constitute a good reason for criticising the departure.[11] Thirdly, adherence to social rules involved what Hart referred to as an internal aspect of rules.[12] Whereas the extent of adherence to conduct associated with the habit or considered to be proscribed by the social rule expressed itself through observable behaviour, the state of mind associated with the two was different. In the exercise of habitual behaviour, "no members of the group need think of the general behaviour, or even know that the behaviour in question is general."[13] It was simply sufficient that each individual behaved in a manner that conformed with the actual behaviour of others.[14] On the other hand with regard to

[5] Philip Pettit, "How Norms Become Normative" in *The Hart-Fuller Debate in the Twenty-First Century* ed. by Peter Cane (Oxford: Hart Publishing, 2010) at 230.

[6] Lon L. Fuller, "Human Interaction and the Law" in *The Rule of Law* ed. by Robert Paul Wolff (New York: Simon and Schuster, 1971) at 201.

[7] David Easton, "A Re-Assessment of the Concept of Political Support" (1975) 5 *British Journal of Political Science* 185.

[8] Hart, *Concept of Law*, *supra* note 3 at 51.

[9] *Ibid.* at 54.

[10] *Ibid.* at 54.

[11] *Ibid.*

[12] *Ibid.* at 55.

[13] *Ibid.*

[14] *Ibid.*

social rules, their existence had to involve some individuals looking at the behaviour in question "as a general standard to be followed by the group as a whole."[15] What was necessary was "a critically reflective attitude to certain patterns of behaviour as a common standard, and that this should display itself in criticism (including self-criticism), demands for conformity and in acknowledgements that such criticisms were [justified], all of which [found] their characteristic expression in the normative terminology of *ought*, *must*, and *should*, *right* and *wrong*."[16] Hence, Austin's endeavour to portray the sovereign-subject relationship as characterised by obedience, generated by the exercise of habit with the unreflective connotations with which Hart believed the term to be associated, was inadequate to the task of explaining the basis of conformity to the law and the operation of advanced legal systems.

The centrality of "habit" in Austin's model of sovereignty and Hart's view of its inadequacy in explaining the operation of legal systems provides the opportunity to undertake a survey of ideas associated with the term "habit" and to explore the role that it plays in contributing towards behaviour that is compliant with the law, whether or not such behaviour is of ordinary citizens or officials associated with administering a given legal system. Firstly, I will explore the place of habit in the writings of philosophers, psychologists and sociologists in their explanations of the nature of human existence.[17] Secondly to suggest a central constitutive role that habit plays in the process of human existence, I will explore the dramatic consequences that are likely to follow where there is a severe absence of familiar repetitive practices. Thirdly, by way of appropriate examples, I will suggest that the relationship between habit and rule-following is a complex one and that the former is always present in the operation of the latter even where legal officials are concerned. I will then return to Hart's critique of Austin in relation to the role that habit plays in the operation of legal systems and will argue that Hart posed the separation between the exercise of habit and the adoption of the internal point of view in an over-simplistic way. Finally, I will conclude by arguing that legal theorists need to engage with habit more extensively in their quest to deepen their understanding of the operation of the law.

10.2 Habit in Other Disciplines

It is probably the case that for many people the term "habit" denotes compulsive repetitive action, undertaken without a conscious purpose, by an individual who acts without care and who might well be unaware of what she or he is doing, at least for some of the time. This is clearly captured in Freud's exploration of habit where

[15] *Ibid.*

[16] *Ibid.* at 56.

[17] This will include reference to associated terms in particular those of routine and *habitus*.

he cites as typical examples "the playing with one's watch-chain [and] the fingering of one's beard."[18] But the qualities evoked by the use of the term "habit" and associated terms cannot be reduced to those above. Hence it will be the purpose of this part of the chapter to provide examples of the way that habit has been depicted in philosophical, psychological and sociological writings and to draw some observations as to the qualities associated with the operation of habitual activity.

10.2.1 Philosophical Coverage

Numerous philosophers have referred to habit as being a significant ingredient of the human condition. What follows is only meant to provide illustrations of such references that are diverse and extensive in character.[19] In philosophical writings, Aristotle, for example, thought that habits were the foundation of moral virtue and that it was the business of the legislator to make citizens by forming good habits.[20] Aquinas explored the principles of human action, which he considered to include habit, and that ethical behaviour involved the pursuit of "cardinal virtues" which were manifestations of it. Ockham conceptualised habits as permanent dispositions which remained in the mind and which manifested themselves through repetitive action.[21] For Hume, "the far greatest part of our reasonings, with all our actions and passions can be deriv'd from nothing but custom and habit."[22] He also considered that custom was the great guide of human life and that its absence "would be an end at once of all action, as well as for the most part to speculation."[23] In contrast, Kant counter-posed the exercise of habitual behaviour to that of moral behaviour, characterising it as repetitive behaviour which he considered deprived "even good actions

[18] Sigmund Freud, *The Psychopathology of Everyday Life*, Vol. 6 in *The Standard Edition of the Complete Works of Sigmund Freud* ed. and trans by James Strachey (London: Vintage, 2001) at 194.

[19] Aspects of its coverage in philosophy and sociology have been usefully covered by Clare Carlisle and Charles Camic. See Clare Carlisle, "Creatures of Habit: The Problem and Practice of Liberation" (2006) 38 *Continental Philosophy Review* 19; Clare Carlisle, "Between Freedom and Necessity: Felix Ravaisson on Habit and the Moral Life" (2010) 53(2) *Inquiry,* at 123; Charles Camic, "The Matter of Habit" (1986) 91(5) *The American Journal of Sociology* 1039.

[20] Bertrand Russell, *History of Western Philosophy* (New York: Routledge, 1961) at 185, *cf.* at 193.

[21] Thomas Aquinas, *Summa Theologiæ*, trans. by Joseph Rickaby, (London: Burns and Oates, 1892), quest. 61 "Of The Cardinal Virtues"; Elizabeth Karger, "Ockham's Misunderstood Theory of Intuitive and Abstractive Cognition" in *The Cambridge Companion to Ockham* ed. by Paul Vincent Spade (Cambridge: Cambridge University Press, 1999) at 206.

[22] David Hume, *A Treaties of Human Nature* ed. by Lewis Amherst Selby-Bigge (Oxford: Clarendon, 1978) at 118.

[23] David Hume, *Enquiry Concerning Human Understanding* ed. by Lewis Amherst Selby-Bigge (Oxford: Clarendon, 1975) at 44.

of their moral value because it detracts from our freedom of mind."[24] Hegel who extensively explored the nature and role of habit commented, *inter alia*, on the important role of individual habit in the production of an ethical order and that of education in instilling into its recipients the habits whose characteristics contribute towards the construction of such an order.[25] He considered that habit was "indispensable for the existence of all intellectual life."[26] Habit for him occupied a space between reason and nature in which desire and will come together.[27] Nietzsche separated "enduring" from "brief" habits considering that the former were tyrannical in nature and were brought on by the possession of an "official position" or of "constant relations with the same people" or "uniquely good health" while a life without the latter would produce an "intolerable" and "truly terrible" situation, namely "a life that continually demanded improvisation."[28] Dewey wrote extensively on the nature and role of habit. He adopted a wide meaning of habit and so it was not limited to repetitive behaviour but also included the "ordering or systematization of [the more] minor elements of [human] action, which is projective, dynamic in quality, ready for overt manifestation, and [operative] even when not obviously dominating activity."[29] So habit for Dewey was not limited to the manifestation of certain activities but also to the disposition to act in such ways. For him, the character of an individual itself was an interpenetration of habits.[30] He considered that habitual behaviour underwent change to ensure survival and that "habit is formed in view of possible changes and does not harden so readily."[31] Habit formation was dynamic and social in character as it was the outcome of inter-subjective relationships.[32]

More recently, Merleau-Ponty, the phenomenologist, declared that his body was "his basic habit, the one which conditions all the others, and by means of which they are mutually comprehensible."[33] An individual's existence was the outcome of habituated behaviour.[34] Habitual behaviour, such as the acquiring of a dance routine, for him was not achieved by intellectual analysis but through the "motor grasping of

---

[24] Immanuel Kant, *Anthropology from a Pragmatic Point of View* trans. by Mary J. Gregor (The Hague: Martinus Nijhoff, 1974) at 148–149.

[25] Georg W. F. Hegel, *Philosophy of Right* trans. by Thomas Malcolm Knox (Oxford: Oxford University Press, 1967) at 108 *(151)*, *cf.* at 260 *(151)*.

[26] Georg W. F. Hegel, *Philosophy of Mind* trans. by William Wallace and Arnold V. Miller (Oxford: Clarendon, 1971) at 143.

[27] Simon Lumsden, "Habit, Reason and the Limits of Normativity" (2008) 37(3) *SubStance* at 188, *cf.* at 200.

[28] Friedrich Nietzsche, *The Gay Science* ed. by Bernard Williams (Cambridge: Cambridge University Press, 2001) at 168.

[29] John Dewey, *Human Nature and Conduct* (New York: Holt, 1945) at 40–41. He contrasted "habit" with physiological functions as the former was acquired: *cf.* at 15.

[30] *Ibid.* at 38.

[31] John Dewey, *Experience and Nature* (New York: Norton and Co, 1925) at 281.

[32] *Ibid.* at 281.

[33] Maurice Merleau-Ponty, *Phenomenology of Perception* (London: Routledge, 1962) at 91.

[34] Nick Crossley, *The Social Body* (London: Sage Publications, 2001) at 89.

a motor significance" that is to say through practice[35] so that one developed a feel for what was and was not correct without having to engage in conscious calculation.[36] In his exploration of this point, he referred to the case of the experienced driver who determined whether he could get through a narrow opening. This was not by conscious calculation involving the comparison of the width of the opening with that of the car, for the car was not experienced by the driver as an object "with size and volume," but one possessing a potentiality of volume, alongside the road. This was experienced as having a restrictive potential which immediately appears "passable or unpassable."[37] Deleuze also explored the relationship between selfhood and habit considering that the latter was constitutive of the former declaring that "we are habits and nothing but habits" that and "habit is the root of reason and indeed the principle from which reason stems as an effect."[38]

10.2.2 Psychological Coverage

Freud's use of the term "habit" to describing repetitive, unreflectively and perhaps unknowing activity without purpose, may well summarise the thoughts of many when they think about the term habit. Another comparatively common usage of the term is what psychologically is described as "an impulse-controlled disorder which involves habitual maladaptive behaviour," such as drug addiction, Internet addiction syndrome and pathological gambling.[39] Camic has claimed that particularly from the late nineteenth in century in America, psychologists in their bid to develop psychology in a way that met the requirements of the physical sciences, increasingly described habitual activity in a reductionist way, frequently reducing it to a process of neuronal stimulus and response where all "introspectively isolable elements [such as] sensation, perception, imagery etc." were to be purged as was reflection.[40] As a result, American sociologists substantially removed habit from their own discourse, leaving it in the hands of the psychologists and came to develop their own theories of action in terms other than habit. They concentrated on action, which was

---

[35] Merleau-Ponty, *Phenomenology of Perception*, *supra* note 33 at 143.

[36] This sense of possessing a "feel for the game" emerges clearly in the writings of the sociologist Pierre Bourdieu in his development of the idea of *habitus*: See *infra*.

[37] Merleau-Ponty, *Phenomenology of Perception*, *supra* note 33 at 143.

[38] Gilles Deleuze, *Empiricism and Subjectivity. An Essay on Hume's Theory of Human Nature* trans. by Constantin V. Boundas (New York: Columbia University Press, 1991), *cf.* at 66.

[39] Andrew M. Coleman, *Dictionary of Psychology* (3rd ed., Oxford: Oxford University Press, 2009) at 330.

[40] John B. Watson, "Psychology As the Behaviourist Views It" in *A History of Modern Psychology* ed. by Duane Schultz (2nd ed., New York: Academic Press, 1975) at 199–207, referred to in Camic, "The Matter of Habit" *supra* note 19 at 1068.

reflectively undertaken, as exemplified for example, in the works of Talcott Parsons so that there was an overlooking of the importance of habitual behaviour and of the role of *habitus* in the shaping of human conduct.[41] Later on in the twentieth century, Burrhus Frederic Skinner, the behavioural psychologist, claimed that cognition played no role in the stimulus control of behaviour so that the latter was completely determined by the environment.[42] More recently writings such as those of Bargh have suggested that much of our perceptual and evaluative processes take place largely in an automatic way without the involvement of critical reflection, as do our routinised motor activities and motivations once they have been mastered through conscious involvement and that our consciousness operates in parallel with such automatic processes, constantly adapting and modifying them in ways that are affected by situational and cognitive factors.[43]

10.2.3 Sociological Coverage

As shall be seen below in relation to sociological writings, the "uncovering" of references to habit and *habitus* by Durkheim and Weber points towards more recent European sociological writings including those of Berger and Luckmann, Giddens, Bourdieu and Crossley where the process of habitualisation does inform their writings.[44] Initially, in Durkheim and Weber, numerous references to habit can be noted. Durkheim, for example, maintained that a society based on a division of labour requires "more and more intensive and assiduous work and [such work becomes] habitual."[45] He considered that "the ideas and reasons which develop in our consciousness [arise *inter alia* from] ingrained habits of which we are unaware."[46] Human action, whether individual or collective was regarded by him as oscillating between poles namely that of reflection on the one hand and that of habit on the other, with the latter pole being the more powerful.[47] He considered that in the

[41] Camic, "The Matter of Habit" *supra* note 19 at 1076–1077.

[42] Burrhus Frederic Skinner, "Why I Am Not a Cognitive Psychologist" in *Reflections on Behaviourism and Society* ed. by Burrhus Frederic Skinner (Englewood Cliffs, NJ: Prentice-Hall, 1978) at 97–112, referred to in John A. Bargh, "The Automaticity of Everyday Life" in *Advances in Social Cognition* ed. by Robert S. Wyer (Hillsdale, NJ: Erlbaum, 1997) vol. X, at 12.

[43] *Ibid.* at 52.

[44] Such writings include Peter Berger and Thomas Luckmann, *The Social Construction of Reality* (London: Penguin Books, 1966); Anthony Giddens, *The Constitution of Society* (Cambridge: Polity Press, 1984) and Crossley, *The Social Body*, *supra* note 34.

[45] Emil Durkheim, *The Division of Labour in Society* trans. by George Simpson (New York: Free Press, 1964) at 242.

[46] Emil Durkheim, "Marxism and Sociology: The Materialist Conception of History" [first published 1897] now in *The Rules of Sociology of Method* ed. by Steven Lukes (New York: Free Press, 1982) at 167–174.

[47] Camic, "The Matter of Habit" *supra* note 19 at 1039 and 1052.

absence of unexpected circumstances habitual behaviour dominates and where "non-adaptation occurs" reflection which otherwise "slows down, overloads or paralyses action" comes to the fore only to disappear when it has determined how to respond to the novel situation.[48] Thereafter habit reasserts itself and it was this that was "the real force that governs us."[49] While moral behaviour required more than habit, the latter constituted an indispensable ingredient. So he was of the opinion that to become attached to collective morality, each individual must have developed the habits of "self-control and restraint" as well as those of lucid thought and cooperative behaviour.[50] Consistent with his view that children were creatures of habit, he considered that educational institutions could foster a number of desirable habits including that of "group life," "self-control" and "wholesome intellectual habits which would strengthen his moral conduct."[51] Again considering education, he considered that the above would be best achieved by forging in each individual "a general disposition of mind and will, that is to say a *habitus* of moral being."[52]

Weber considered that the qualities associated with habit comprised an "unreflective set disposition to engage in actions that have long been practiced."[53] They played an important role in the development of social organisation. He observed in relation to economic activity that "the patterns of use and of relationship among the various economic units are determined by habit."[54] He defined the discipline required for the effective operation of factories "as the probability that by virtue of habituation a command will receive prompt and automatic obedience in stereotyped forms, on the part of a given group of persons."[55] The advancement of the means of production involved the replacement of the habits of the old occupations with those that fitted the military-like disciplinary demands of modern factory methods.[56] The development of military conflict itself was characterised by a

[48] Emil Durkheim, *Pragmatism and Sociology* [first published 1913–14] ed. by John B. Allcock (Cambridge: Cambridge University Press, 1983) at 38, see also at 79 and 83.

[49] Emil Durkheim, "The Evolution and the Role of Secondary Education in France" [first published 1905–6] in *Education and Sociology*, trans. by Sherwood D. Fox (New York: Free Press, 1956) at 152.

[50] Emil Durkheim, *Moral Education* [first published 1902–3] trans. by Everett K. Wilson and Hermann Schurer (New York: Free Press, 1961) at 233.

[51] *Ibid.* at 135, 143, 149, 249 and 297.

[52] Emil Durkheim, *The Evolution of Educational Thought* [first published 1904–5] trans. by Peter Collins (London: Routledge, 1977) at 28–29; Durkheim, *Moral Education*, *supra* note 50 at 2.

[53] Max Weber, "Zur Psychophysik der industriellen Arbeit" [first published 1908–9] now in *Gesammelte Aufsatze zur Soziologie und Sozialpolitik* (Tübingen: Mohr/Siebeck, 1924) at 61, *cf.* at 93–94 cited in Camic, "The Matter of Habit" *supra* note 19 at 1057.

[54] Max Weber, *Economy and Society* ed. by Günther Roth and Claus Wittich (Berkeley: University of California Press, 1978) at 335; Max Weber, *The Protestant Ethic and the Spirit of Capitalism*, trans. by Talcott Parsons (London: Routledge, 1992) at 62.

[55] Weber, *Economy and Society*, *supra* note 54 at 335; Weber, *The Protestant Ethic*, *supra* note 54 at 53.

[56] Weber, *Economy and Society*, *supra* note 54 at 731, *cf.* at 1156.

growth in disciplinary habits.[57] In relation to behaviour that complied with legal norms, he considered that it was an essential element of any legal order that the conduct of some people was guided by such norms but it was not necessary that everyone who engaged in such conduct did so as a result of that motivation. He considered that, on the contrary:

> The broad mass of the participants act in a way corresponding to legal norms, not out of obedience regarded as a legal obligation, but either because the environment approves of the conduct and disapproves of its opposite, or merely as a result of unreflective habituation to a regularity of life that has engraved itself as a custom.[58]

In a similar manner to Durkheim, Weber considered that habit also had a part to play in the development of norms, so he was to say that habitual activity caused such conduct eventually to be experienced as binding having the quality of *oughtness*, which eventually became underpinned by appropriate enforcement mechanisms.[59]

More generally, Weber considered that the "great bulk of all everyday action" approaches an "almost automatic reaction to habitual stimuli which guided behaviour in a course which has been repeatedly followed."[60] The development and exercise of habits was therefore a continuing theme which embraced both stability and resistance to change as well as existing as a consequence of change itself.

The importance of the role of habit to the construction of meaningful human existence was also present in more recent sociological writings including those of Berger and Luckmann, as well as those of Giddens.[61] Regarding the former, Berger and Luckmann distinguished between animal and human existence, associating the latter with the quality of world openness.[62] Individuals were "world open" in the sense that, in contrast to animal responses, they could draw upon and react to what they perceived to be their environment in a variety of ways that were not simply determined by their biological propensities. World openness provided the capacity for man to begin to liberate himself from the constraints of nature but this was also a profound threat to his ontological security as he was no longer shielded from the

---

[57] *Ibid.* at 1152.

[58] *Ibid.* at 312. This analysis is not inconsistent with Hart's with regard to members of a population who are not engaged in activities associated with legal officials.

[59] *Ibid.* at 326, *cf.* at 754. Durkheim in similar terms considered that habitual practice was capable of being transformed into rules of conduct: Durkheim, *The Division of Labour in Society, supra* note 45; quote from Steven Lukes, *Emile Durkheim – His Life and Work* (London: Penguin Books, 1973) at 164.

[60] Weber, *Economy and Society, supra* note 54 at 25, *cf.* at 337.

[61] Berger and Luckmann, *The Social Construction of Reality, supra* note 44; Giddens, *The Constitution, supra* note 44.

[62] Berger and Luckmann, *The Social Construction of Reality, supra* note 44 at 65–66.

chaotic flux of life by innate instinctual qualities which were weak.[63] Metaphorically, this ever-present threat of chaos appears in foundation myths in which the sovereign creator forms the world and cosmos out of an "undifferentiated, formless and limitless chaos."[64] The chaotic state portrayed here is one characterised by utter randomness rather than simple unpredictability. It points to a multiplicity and diversity of unrepeatable momentary impressions that are structureless as formulated by the neo-Kantian philosopher Cassirer or to the infinite flux posed by Deleuze and Guattari manifested by "all possible forms which spring up only to disappear immediately and without consistency or references."[65]

The overcoming of ontological insecurity potentially provoked by the unmediated confrontation with such chaos involves a number of mechanisms including the mediation of subjective human experience of reality through a variety of comparatively stable symbolic forms. Through the use of such forms, the human mind can make meaningful contact with the environment it confronts in an indirect way leading to the management of the threat of such chaos.[66] The most pervasive of these symbolic forms is language, which allows us to make sense of the world by enabling us to subsume the uniqueness of each instance of experience within generalised

---

[63] The phrase "ontological security" can be traced to the writings of the psychoanalyst Ronald David Laing and it features in the writings of the sociologist Anthony Giddens. The latter defines it as the "confidence or trust that the natural and social worlds are as they appear to be, including the basic existential parameters of self and social identity" in Giddens, *The Constitution, supra* note 44 at 375.

[64] Peter Fitzpatrick, *Mythology of Law* (London: Routledge, 1992) at 19. For example, the Pelgasian Creation Myth whose first sentence reads, "in the beginning, Eurynome, the Goddess of All Things, rose naked from Chaos but found nothing substantial for her feet to rest upon, and therefore divided the seas from the sky." See Robert Graves, *the Greek Myths* (London: Penguin Books, 1960) vol. 1 at 27–35. Another example of this point is Nietzsche's claim that "behind his very ground, beneath his every grounding" upon which philosophers construct their philosophies lurks "an abyss." See Friedrich Nietzsche, *Beyond Good and Evil* trans. by Marion Faber (Oxford: Oxford University Press, 1988) at 289, *cf.* at 173.

[65] Ernst Cassirer, *Logic of the Humanities* trans. by Clarence S. Howe (New Haven, CN: Yale University Press, 1961) at 42; Gilles Deleuze and Félix Guattari, *What Is Philosophy?* (London: Verso, 1994) at 51.

[66] Jürgen Habermas, *The Liberating Power of Symbols* (Cambridge: Polity Press 2001) at 24. Habermas in this area recognised the important contribution of Ernst Cassirer who authored four published volumes on the nature, role and manifestations of symbolic forms the most pervasive of which was language. See Ernst Cassirer, *The Philosophy of Symbolic Forms* (New Haven, CN: Yale University Press) *Volume 1 Language* (1953); *Volume 2 Mythical Thought* (1955); *Volume 3 The Phenomenology of Knowledge* (1957) and *Volume 4 The Metaphysics of Symbolic Forms* (1996). Reflecting the crucial nature of these symbolic forms for the possibility of meaningful human experience in Cassirer's view, he proclaimed in the fourth volume that "the negation or annihilation of the symbolic form, in order to return to life as something immediate would be (…) simultaneously to kill the mind itself" (at 231). Nelson Goodman's notion of "world-making" has much in common with Cassirer's approach. See Nelson Goodman, *Ways of Worldmaking* (Indianapolis: Hackett Publishing Co., 1978).

categories of meaning.[67] Language can be regarded as a profound manifestation of what Berger and Luckmann characterised as the process of habitualisation. The latter was a prominent pervasive aspect of human interaction and the development of social practices with their suggestion of repetition and routinisation of activity.[68] Habitualisation has been taken to be necessary to counter our world openness and to constituting an adaptive process to compensate for our lack of instinct, so that action that is frequently carried out becomes part of a pattern of behaviour that can be undertaken with an economy of effort.[69] It also enabled choices to be narrowed so that individuals could avoid the psychological anxiety and time expended of having to continually choose from a large or even limitless number of alternatives that might be undertaken to complete a particular task.[70] As a result, it reduced the number of decisions to be made and the need for each circumstance to be reflected upon anew. Hence habitualisation of much activity provided a stable background for conscious deliberation to occur as and when it is needed.[71] However, it did not close off the possibility of innovative change and provided a stable platform upon which it could take place. The ontological security provided by habitualisation enabled the relative uncertainty associated with innovative change, sought in reaction to it, to be more easily contemplated and tolerated.

The production and prevalence of routines within daily human activities is highlighted by Giddens who described it as "the habitual taken-for-granted character of the vast bulk of activities of day to day social life; the prevalence of familiar styles and forms of conduct, both supporting and supported by a sense of ontological security."[72] Much individual behaviour within social settings "involved an ontological

[67] Difference is therefore overlooked in the act of making sense of the world. This is captured by Nietzsche who states that "[e]very word (…) becomes an idea when rather than serving as a kind of reminder of the unique, entirely individualized first experience to which it owes its origin, it simultaneously must fit innumerable, more or less similar (which really means never equal and therefore altogether unequal) cases." See Friedrich Nietzsche, "On Truth and Falsity in Their Extramoral Sense" in *Friedrich Nietzsche Philosophical Writings* ed. by Reinhold Gimm and Caroline Molina y Vedia (New York: Continuum, 1997) at 91.

[68] Berger and Luckmann, *The Social Construction of Reality*, *supra* note 44 at 70–71.

[69] *Ibid.* at 65–66, *cf.* at 70; Merleau-Ponty, *Phenomenology of Perception*, *supra* note 33 at 146.

[70] Berger and Luckmann refer to the example of building a canoe which might be achieved in a multitude of ways that through habitualisation is repeatedly undertaken in one way only. See Berger and Luckmann, *The Social Construction of Reality*, *supra* note 44 at 71. There is a similarity between these observations and those by Nietzsche and Durkheim. See *supra*.

[71] Berger and Luckmann, *The Social Construction of Reality*, *supra* note 44 at 71. The idea of background plays an important part in the conceptualisation of the embedded agent which will be briefly explored below in the section of the paper where observations are made about the qualities associated with habit.

[72] Giddens, *The Constitution*, *supra* note 44 at 376. By the term *activity* both mental and physical acts are included. Others, for example John Dewey, have also referred to the routinisation of much daily life. See also John Dewey, *Human Nature and Conduct* (New York: Cosimo Classics, 2007).

security founded on an autonomy of bodily control within predictable routines and encounters."[73] The idea of routinisation suggested a lack of reflection at the time of undertaking the activities constituting the routine, that is to say a lack of "articulateness" about what one was doing which might form the substance of an explanation used to describe one's activities to someone else. Giddens referred to it as discursive consciousness.[74] A lack of reflection did not mean that the individual became an unthinking automaton since he was engaged in what Giddens has referred to as practical consciousness, that is to say a form of consciousness which enabled the individual to be aware of what he was doing and enabled him to reflexively respond to the unfolding situation without "thinking" about it in a reflective way.[75] However, this did not mean that such thought was logically or empirically precluded. So an engagement with a routine did not prevent the individual concerned from undertaking reflective thought about the nature of his engagement either to alter it or to cease to participate in it.

10.2.4 A Dispositional Approach to Habit

The dispositional dimension of habitual activity is suggested by a number of those so far covered. These include Ockham, Dewey and Merleau-Ponty discussed above. To such philosophical writings might be added the works of Aristotle and Husserl. Husserl considered that an individual's important judgements and lived experiences became sedimented in latent form in his *habitus* to be activated at any time by relevant associations.[76] In relation to sociological writings, Durkheim as mentioned above, claimed that the upholding of an acceptable collective morality required individuals to develop an appropriate disposition of mind and will. Weber characterised habit as a disposition to engage in activity that had long been practised.[77] The dispositional dimension is also suggested in Berger and Luckmann's idea of habitualisation and appears in definitions of the term "habit." So it has been defined as "a disposition to behave in a particular way or an established practice or custom."[78] Here one can see that habit is considered to be both the source and the result

---

[73] Giddens, *The Constitution*, *supra* note 44 at 64.

[74] *Ibid.* at 44 and Stephen Toulmin, "The genealogy of 'consciousness'" in *Explaining Human Behaviour:* Consciousness, Human Action and Social Structure ed. by Paul F. Secord (Beverly Hills: Sage, 1982).

[75] *Ibid.* at 44.

[76] Edmund Husserl, *Cartesian Meditations* (Dordrecht: Kluwer, 1991) at 67; Edmund Husserl, *Cartesian Meditations* (Evanston: North Western University Press, 1973) at 122–123.

[77] Durkheim, *Moral Education*, *supra* note 50 and Weber, *Economy and Society*, *supra* note 54.

[78] Coleman, *Oxford Dictionary of Psychology*, *supra* note 34 at 330.

of action.[79] This sense of disposition particularly among European thinkers has been denoted by the use of the Latin term for habit, namely *habitus*.[80]

It has been explicitly developed and foregrounded by the sociologist Pierre Bourdieu for whom the *habitus* was:

> The outcome of history and produced both individual and collective practices [...defined as...] a system of durable transposable dispositions, structured structures predisposed to function as structuring structures, that is as principles which generate and organise practices and representations that can be objectively adapted to their outcomes, without presupposing a conscious aiming at or an express mastery of the operations necessary in order to attain them.[81]

The *habitus* was structured by one's past and present circumstances including one's family upbringing, past experiences, economic and cultural positions and education. The development of the idea hence reflected Bourdieu's view that inter-subjective relationships were deeply affected by their history and the circumstances in which they developed. The *habitus* was structuring in that it contributed towards one's present and future practices.[82] The term "disposition" was meant to denote "a way of being, a habitual state (especially of the body) and in particular, a predisposition, tendency, propensity or inclination."[83] Being the product of history, such dispositions were open in nature rather than closed and were affected by experiences in ways that either reinforced or modified them.[84] The *habitus* was therefore an active resource, the outcome of the sedimentation of one's past experiences, that operated in the present, in the context of one's current circumstances, below the level of consciousness, to shape one's thoughts, perceptions, and actions.[85] It pointed to the fact that the *habitus* of an individual "is a socialised subjectivity."[86] The familiarities of daily social action were therefore largely negotiated not through processes of rational reflection or conscious rule-following but through ones in which one had "a feel for the game"[87] – a "game" which was processional and unfolded in a continuous flow.

---

[79] Carlisle, "Creatures of Habit" *supra* note 19 at 21.

[80] Camic, "The Matter of Habit" *supra* note 19 at 1046. Other theorists who described something similar to *habitus* include Aristotle, Aquinas, Husserl and, Elias.

[81] Pierre Bourdieu, *The Logic of Practice* trans. by Richard Nice (Palo Alto, CA: Stanford University Press, 1990) at 53; See also Pierre Bourdieu, *Outline of a Theory of Practice* (Cambridge: Cambridge University Press, 1977) at 81–82.

[82] Bourdieu, *The Logic of Practice*, *supra* note 81 at 53.

[83] Bourdieu, *Outline of a Theory of Practice, supra* note 81 at 214.

[84] Pierre Bourdieu and Loïc J. D. Wacquant, *An Invitation to Reflexive Sociology* (Cambridge: Polity Press, 1992) at 133; Bourdieu, *Outline of a Theory of Practice, supra* note 81 at 82.

[85] Bourdieu and Wacquant, *An Invitation to Reflexive Sociology*, *supra* note 84 at 127; Pierre Bourdieu, *Distinctions* trans. by Richard Nice (London: Routledge, 2010) at 468.

[86] Bourdieu and Wacquant, *An Invitation to Reflexive Sociology*, *supra* note 84 at 126.

[87] Pierre Bourdieu, "The Genesis of the Concepts of Habitus and of Field" (1985) 2(2) *Sociocriticism* 11, at 14; Giddens, *The Constitution*, *supra* note 44 at 3; Steven Loyal, *The Sociology of Anthony Giddens* (London: Pluto Press, 2003) at 53.

The *habitus* was dynamic in character as it developed in response to the social engagement of the individual with the world within which he was embedded and the inter-subjective relationships which constituted that embeddedness. The development of the *habitus* in turn affected the way that the individual engaged with the world of which he was part and so contributed towards the social structuring of that world, hence, Bourdieu's reference in the above quote to *habitus* comprising both a "structured structure" and "structuring structure." For Bourdieu, an individual's engagement with social practice was the result of a relationship between his *habitus* and two other concerns prominent in his writings, namely the field (of structured activity) and the position which that person occupied within that field.[88] Practices therefore were not simply the result of one's *habitus* but of the relationship between one's *habitus* and the circumstances. The *habitus* can therefore be seen as central to the process of habitualisation determining the extent to which the individual can effectively and routinely engage in regularised social practices.

That process of habitualisation also embraces the social practice of language itself, the most fundamental of routines, by which communication is effected through what are experienced to be fixed meanings. In the employment of language as a central means of communication, cognitive stabilisation is contributed to. The reality, of course, is that there is ultimately no inevitably as to the sound of any particular word or its meaning as expounded by Wittgenstein.[89] Reflecting the aforementioned, any rule is capable of an endless number of meanings as is any action whose content is evaluated against the requirement of the rule. Ultimately, Wittgenstein suggested, "no course of action could be determined by a rule, because every course of action can be made to accord with the rule and so the grasping of a rule is exhibited in actual cases."[90] And what is considered to constitute compliance with a normative rule is a social practice and cannot be based on some ultimate foundation that lies outside social life itself. For Bourdieu, whose approach to the relationship between normative rules and social practice was similar to that of Wittgenstein, the generative source of social practice was the dispositional quality of the *habitus* itself that could embrace the requirements of social practice associated with such rules. Seen in this way, behaviour considered to accord with the requirements of such rules is then capable of being exhibited by an individual in the context of the social practice of which it is part in an automatic way, and in a way where what is at the foreground of that individual's thought might well not be the rules, assuming they are known at all, but other matters ranging from the goals

[88] The field may be conceptualised in a number of ways but, put simply, it denotes particular socially structured spaces such as that of law or that of the arts or of education or politics and so on, and each, to use the analogy of the magnet, exerts a force upon individuals within them as to the acceptable ways of operating of which such individuals are not likely to be conscious.

[89] Ludwig Wittgenstein, *Philosophical Investigations* trans. by Elizabeth Anscombe (3rd ed, Oxford: Blackwell, 1967).

[90] *Ibid*. at 201.

which led to the behaviour in the first place to "nothing in particular." Such behaviour will involve a process of reactive monitoring and adjustments in response to the practicalities of the unfolding situation confronting that individual, but reflective and strategically orientated thought might also be involved.

10.3 The Removal of Routine

If the undertaking of, and engagement with, routine is of fundamental importance to the maintenance of meaningful human existence and social activity, the complete or near-complete removal of them so that life becomes very unpredictable would suggest distress or even profound crisis. One such circumstance where the routines of normal daily life were shattered is to be found in the regime of the concentration camp. Bettelheim in his illuminating study based on his internment in the concentration camps of Dachau and Buchenwald[91] captures the consequence of such circumstances:

> It was the senseless tasks, the lack of almost any time to oneself, the inability to plan ahead because of sudden changes in camp policies that was so deeply destructive. By destroying man's ability to act on his own or to predict the outcome of his actions, they destroyed the feeling that his actions had any purpose, so many prisoners stopped acting. But when they stopped acting they soon stopped living.[92]

Routine in the sense experienced in everyday life was almost completely absent.[93] That is not to say that prisoners were not severely constrained in what they did. They were on the whole strictly regulated and could be supervised moment-by-moment but the character of the regulation could dramatically alter without warning.[94]

Additionally, such regulation involved the denial to the prisoners of any privacy or easily exercised autonomy of bodily control or ability to influence their environments. This took place against the context of extreme deprivation, brutality and the profound uncertainty of not knowing why they were imprisoned or for how long.[95] One consequence to the prisoners of this process of profound disempowerment was their "turning into" walking corpses who ceased to have any self generated motivation

[91] Bettelheim's account was based on his internment in 1938–9, that is three years before the policy of mass extermination was instituted. See Bruno Bettelheim, *The Informed Heart* (New York: Free Press, 1960) at 109.

[92] *Ibid.* at 148.

[93] It was known for the prisoners to be subjected to alternating regimes of comparatively privileged conditions comprising good quarters and easy work followed by harsh ones of hard labour and reductions in food rations leading to appalling mortality rates. *Ibid.* at 150–151.

[94] *Ibid.* at 108.

[95] *Ibid.* at 108, *cf.* at 149.

to act, giving up all such action as being pointless and in the process they appeared to become emotionally deadened.[96] In essence therefore, such individuals ceased to respond to their environments and frequently death rapidly followed.[97] Prisoners could increase the chances of survival by ensuring their control of some significant, albeit small, aspect of their circumstances by the continuation of familiar routines in the face of daily encountered brutality.[98]

Such maintenance was much more likely to happen within the context of support provided by social bonding and interchange between prisoners which itself would generate routines of social exchange.[99] In establishing such practices, prisoners to a greater degree maintained familiar social continuities, despite the hostile environment of the camp and so functioned more effectively. What is suggested here is that there was a profound mismatch between the concentration camp environment and the dispositional qualities associated with the victim's *habitus*. Returning to the idea that the *habitus* is expressed through "a feel for the game," that in turn suggests that behaviour is the outcome of responses shaped "in relation to objective potentialities immediately prescribed in the present, things to do or not to do, things to say or not to say in relation to a probable 'upcoming' future."[100] But if an individual has never encountered such conditions before, then there will be a profound mismatch between his history and the circumstances that he now faces, so that his *habitus*, a product of such history and forged in very different conditions, will not give to him a "feel for the game" or an adequate range of effective responses to what he now faces. He will be "lost."[101] To increase his chances of survival, although certainly by no means to guarantee them given the brutal conditions he experiences, he will need to impose on the hostile environment, preferably together with others, as best that he can, a set of familiar routinised practices which do more clearly accord with those that were historically generated by his *habitus*.

---

[96] Bettelheim, *The Informed Heart*, *supra* note 91 at 151. These were known in camp slang as "musellmanner" or "musellman" in the singular. See http://www.holocaustcenterbuff.com/vocabulary.htm#m (last accessed on 10 August 2011).

[97] Bettelheim, *The Informed Heart*, *supra* note 91 at 151–152. Prisoners could significantly increase their likelihood of survival by ensuing control of some significant aspect of their lives through the continuation of routines in the face of daily encountered brutality. This is also brought out by other concentration camp survivors such as Primo Levi.

[98] *Ibid.* at 142. Primo Levi, for example in his autobiographical account of concentration camp life referred to the importance of maintaining the routine of daily washing to maximising one's chances of survival in an environment where there were no predictable social routines of a tolerable nature. See Primo Levi, *If This Is a Man* (London: Abacus, 1987) at 45–47.

[99] Shamai Davidson, "Human Reciprocity Among Jewish Prisoners in the Nazi Concentration Camps" in *The Nazi Concentration Camps – Structure and Aims, the Image of the Prisoner, the Jews in the Camps: Proceedings of the Fourth Yad Vashem International Historical Conference* ed. by Yisrael Gutman and Avital Saf (Jerusalem: Yad Vashem, 1984) at 555.

[100] Bourdieu, *The Logic of Practice*, *supra* note 81 at 53.

[101] Bourdieu referred to the *habitus* of an individual being out of touch with the social environment it found itself in as the *hysteresis* of the *habitus*: Bourdieu, *Outline of a Theory of Practice, supra* note 81 at 83.

10.4 Observations

Considering the survey above, while not claiming to present an exhaustive categorisation of different conceptualisations of habit, one can identify four basic levels with some individual writers ranging over more than one. At its most basic level, habit has been considered to be constitutive of selfhood itself as exemplified by Merleau-Ponty and Deleuze. Secondly, expressive of that selfhood is the general tendency or pre-disposition to develop habits in general as expounded by the aforementioned. Thirdly, there is also the pre-disposition to think and behave in particular ways in response to one's environment as implied by Berger and Luckmann via the process of habitualisation and through the agency of the *habitus* as most explicitly expounded by Bourdieu. For Bourdieu, this tendency generally operates at a pre-reflective level and can give to the individual "a feel for the game," that is to say an intuitive connection with the environment in which he is embedded, so that participation is experienced as natural and inevitable.[102] The actuation of the behaviour to which the individual is disposed is circumstantially dependent and is consistent with identifiable purposes but means-ends relationship are not normally considered from the individual's point of view. The behaviour exhibited can be subject to variation given the improvisational capacities of the *habitus* which itself continues to develop in the light of the experiences of the individual concerned so that it has been described as a moving equilibrium.[103] It is possible however for the individual engaged in the practice, through reasoned consideration, which might well include an assessment of the means-ends relationship posed by it, to consider and adjust his responses or even more radically to adopt responses that do not accord with behaviour he is pre-disposed to exhibit. Fourthly, as claimed for example by Giddens, concentrates upon much of the behaviour, undertaken by individuals, that is taken-for-granted and is described as routine. The range of routinised behaviour is enormous, varying widely as to its complexity and importance. The use of language, for example, as suggested above, is fundamental to social interaction and is a deeply sedimented element of social conduct that is an inescapable ingredient of human existence. It is involved in the constitution of and engagement with other routines. Many others are geared towards certain specific purposes which for Giddens involve practical consciousness that has a degree of similarity with Bourdieu's feel for the game and allows for a degree of improvisation. Means-ends relations again are not normally, from the individual's standpoint, subject to consideration. However, it is always possible for an individual, while engaging in a given routine and possibly in

[102] Bourdieu and Wacquant, *An Invitation to Reflexive Sociology*, *supra* note 84 at 127. Bourdieu describes this state as being like "a fish in water."

[103] Crossley, *The Social Body*, *supra* note 34 at 129.

reaction to it or to a behaviour that is underpinned by it, to have such thoughts that might result in that individual modifying his behaviour or abandoning it.[104]

From a review of habit, one begins to get a sense that human existence does not take place in isolation but that it is deeply embedded rather than detached from the world within which it operates. This is apparent in the approaches of Merleau-Ponty, Berger and Luckmann, Giddens and Bourdieu with the latter's idea of *habitus*. Capturing this idea, Merleau-Ponty was to claim that the "world and I are within one another."[105] In a similar vein, Bourdieu was to say in relation to the *habitus*, referring to Pascal, "that the world encompasses me but I comprehend it precisely *because* it comprises me."[106] In developing their ideas of the human agent as embedded within the world, they also, albeit in different ways, together with others, reacted to the ontologising of the disengaged perspective whereby the processes associated with it, namely the rational procedure of investigative thought and objectivity are read into the constitution of the mind itself suggesting that the intelligibility of our actual diachronic experience of the world can be fully explained and captured by them.[107] The idea of the embedded agent, on the other hand, suggests finitude, that is to say, as embedded agent, we occupy a world whose existence transcends our attempts as human beings to reduce it to the categories of our own thought so that we cannot command a God's-eye view of ourselves in the world.[108] It suggests that things in the world are disclosed as part of the world with which the agent has concerned involvement "within a totality of such involvements."[109] It also suggests that the intelligibility of our experiences of the world are made possible by an unarticulated background based on a prior understanding of which Bourdieu's *habitus*, for example, is suggestive.

The process of diachronic existence inevitably means that what one is focally aware of at any given moment is constantly shifting and that it is possible that what in one moment is located as part of one's background comes into the foreground as other considerations come to form part of the background. The important point to note is that intelligible experience will always involve a background and foreground whose relationship to each other is dynamic with the former contributing towards

[104] I have not included within this categorisation of habit, repetitive activities that are repetitive in quality where there is little if any variation or discernible purpose to the individual involved, that may not be triggered by specific circumstances and in respect of which he may not beware of undertaking it. See Freud, *The Psychopathology of Everyday*, *supra* note 18 at 194.

[105] Maurice Merleau-Ponty, *The Visible and the Invisible* (Evanston: Northwestern University Press, 1968) at 123.

[106] Bourdieu and Wacquant, *An Invitation to Reflexive Sociology*, *supra* note 84 at 127–8.

[107] Charles Taylor, *Philosophical Arguments* (Cambridge, MA: Harvard University Press, 1997) at 64–66. Others include Husserl, Heidegger and Wittgenstein in his later writings,

[108] Martin C. Dillon, *Merleau-Ponty's Ontology* (2nd ed., Evanston: Northwestern University Press, 1997) at 90; See *Concise Routledge Encyclopaedia of Philosophy* (London: Routledge, 2000) at 922.

[109] Taylor, *Philosophical Arguments*, *supra* note 107 at 73.

the sense of the latter. This clearly has consequences regarding the states of mind experienced when an individual acts compliantly with the law and more will be said about it below.

The concept of the individual as an embedded agent, and more particularly one whose condition embraces the property of embodiment, as developed in particular by Merleau-Ponty, is capable of casting a useful light upon the relationship between habitual and rational thought and in so doing revealing a limitation to Bourdieu's approach to the two. Bourdieu accepted that individuals were capable of engaging in reflective and strategically orientated thought, although it did not inevitably operate outside the *habitus* and that practical interaction with the environment generated by one's *habitus* was only one mode of action.[110] Yet at the same time, Bourdieu described the dispositions that constituted the *habitus* at one point as "categories of perception and assessment or as classificatory principles as well as being the organising principles" that determine the agents activities.[111] While he claimed that such acquired dispositions functioned simply at the practical level, it is difficult to see how they will not be engaged when deliberative thought is undertaken. Indeed Bourdieu, if anything, pointed to this possibility with his acceptance that such thought was bounded as a result of the thinker being trapped by the limits of his brain, that is within "the limits of the system of categories he owes to his upbringing and training."[112] This description embraces important aspects of the *habitus* but the connection between deliberative thought and the *habitus* was not explicitly drawn. The proposition therefore is that, even in relation to such thought, and the choices it considers, one's habitual propensities are engaged and one can derive a pathway between *habitus*, skill and know-how derived from it and deliberative thought. Making choices through deliberative thought presupposes a number of conditions including an already existing engagement with the world, a form of belonging to it and a meaningful view of it. It also assumes a set of competencies including reasoning and linguistic skills. These conditions and competencies possess habitual qualities.[113] Habit therefore acts as a grounding for such thought enabling it to occur in a meaningful and effective way. So one can see that such thought has an interactive relationship with the routinised behaviour that constitutes much of human behaviour which is expressive of the habitualisation process. That process enables change to be contemplated, meaningful deliberative thought to occur and adaptation to be achieved expressed by evolving routines.

---

[110] Bourdieu and Wacquant, *An Invitation to Reflexive Sociology*, *supra* note 84 at 131.

[111] Pierre Bourdieu, *In Other Words: Essays Towards Reflexive Sociology* trans. by Matthew Adamson (Cambridge: Polity Press, 1990) at 13.

[112] Bourdieu and Wacquant, *An Invitation to Reflexive Sociology*, *supra* note 84 at 126.

[113] Crossley, *The Social Body*, *supra* note 34 at 134.

10.5 A Consideration of the Positions of "Ordinary Citizens" and "Legal Officials"

The anxiety provoked by confronting an unfamiliar social practice which one wants to master is "part of life" and an occurrence that most people have probably experienced. Learning to drive, for example, can be a complex, bewildering and anxiety-provoking experience. What may motivate the individual to learn to drive is the promise of access to a more flexible mode of travel and greater independence from public transport and its inflexibilities. If one were to read a manual on how to drive that would only get one so far. It might well explain how one holds and uses the steering wheel gear stick, clutch and brake pedals, for example, but one's understanding would be limited because one would not at that stage have developed the skills needed to effectively and safely engage with the car. To do that requires supervised practice, which enables one to master the skill of driving a car so that it becomes a routinised activity. In so doing, one moves from having to consciously consider more or less continuously the procedures one adopts to drive, carefully monitoring one's adjustments to the conditions of the road and consciously considering when to change gear to a situation where driving becomes an "automatic" activity where reactive monitoring and adjustment become predominant with a reduction but not the elimination of the need for critical reflection.

But in the process of learning to drive the instruction one receives as to how to drive and manoeuvre the car on the roads will be inextricably linked to the legal requirements that regulate the activity. What is possible in terms of speed, location, relationship to other vehicles, manoeuvrings to change lane and turn from one road into another are all affected by such regulation and will in turn affect how the novice driver is instructed. Mindful of Wittgenstein's observation about obeying rules considered above and that such obedience is the result of social practice, the challenge for a novice is to master the practices that are considered to conform with them.[114] Engaging in activity which is considered to comply with a given social rule must involve a learning process which has been described as involving a number of stages ranging from that of the novice to that of demonstrating competence and even, in the case of some, to that of demonstrating expertise.[115] But to limit the process of familiarisation with the rules to that of simply learning them so that they could be recited word-for-word would be inadequate because it would not on its own ensure successful compliance with them, even if the individual had already achieved technical mastery of the skills necessary to drive a car.

---

[114] Wittgenstein, *Philosophical Investigations*, *supra* note 89 at 202. Reflecting this, it is possible to have someone who thinks they are complying with a rule when they are not in fact doing so in that their behaviour is not considered to amount to compliance with it and conceivably someone who is doubtful that they are in fact doing so is in fact complying with it.

[115] Hubert L. Dreyfus and Stuart E. Dreyfus, "The Challenge of Merleau-Ponty's Phenomenology of Embodiment for Cognitive Science" in *Perspectives on Embodiment* ed. by Gam Weiss and Honi Fern Haber (London: Routledge, 1999) at 105–110.

To reach the point where an individual can engage successfully with the social activity of driving requires practice under supervision and the meeting of standards of competence that are institutionally formulated, measured and enforced. The emphasis in learning to drive is upon "doing it" and the conscious learning of the driving code is ancillary to that. A "learner" will be expected to demonstrate knowledge of the code but an assessment of the extent to which he complies with them requires him to demonstrate in practice such compliance and not simply to describe how such compliance might be achieved. Driving might well initially involve the individual in consciously and critically reflecting on whether his driving practice complies with the driving code. An experienced driver, on the other hand, does not usually consciously "follow the rules" even though driving remains a rule governed activity to which on the whole he spontaneously and unreflectively conforms.[116] Whereas the code might well frequently form part of learner's mental foreground, it usually remains in the background for the experienced driver. So the driver through supervised practice develops driving know-how and competences through which he develops a feel for the driving game and which results in the driver engaging effectively in regularised driving practices in a routinised way.

Nevertheless, such routinisation does not completely dispense with the need for critical reflection about his driving practice or that of others. If he sees another driver failing to stop at a red light he may well criticise him for having driven badly without any conscious reflection on the details of the applicable part of the driving code or its underlying law in so far as he is aware of the latter. But if forced to justify to such a driver why he criticised him, the experienced driver might refer to the law in its generality or even to specific parts of it although the latter is less likely. The routine of driving is constituted by a practice where the relationship between the physical activity, the mental states associated with it and the extent to which the law is foregrounded in the mind of drivers is dynamic, shifting and complex. The maintenance of the social practice of driving involves its routinisation, from the perspective of engaged individuals, which, for its diachronic maintenance, involves critical reflection by such participants from time to time. Routinisation does not negate the need for critical reflection but simply the extent to which it is resorted. Routinisation and critical reflection associated with the activities constituted by it are interdependent.

However, there may be other practices to which the individual may not have easy access or sufficient motivation to master. It might be that the benefits of mastering them are outweighed by the burdens of doing so perhaps because of their complexity and because of the improbability of them being used sufficiently frequently to justify the effort necessary to achieve competence. In any event, the individual might not have the necessary academic qualifications or the funds to enable her to enter a training programme that might lead to such mastery. Let us consider the individual who has sustained an injury as a result of a defective footpath and wishes

[116] Mark A. Wrathall, "The Phenomenology of Rules" in *Reading Merleau-Ponty* ed. by Thomas Baldwin (London: Routledge, 2007) at 78.

to take legal proceedings against the public authority responsible for its maintenance on the ground of breach of duty. Let us call her Jill. The likely way that Jill will seek to pursue her claim will be to hand the matter over to a lawyer assuming that she can afford to do so. If asked for the reason for the hand-over, Jill's response might well be that "the lawyer is legally qualified and should know what he is doing while I do not." To not hand over the matter to a lawyer to save fees for example, would expose her to the complexities associated with litigation, the uncertainties and stresses associated with the exercise and its outcome and the potential of consequential financial loss caused, or contributed to, by incompetent engagement. If she were to personally conduct her own litigation, she might find that each stage of the procedure required considerable time and effort involving research into law and procedure. She might not consider herself to be equipped to undertake such research and might well be concerned not only with the "known unknowns" but more disturbingly with the possible existence of "unknown unknowns" and the consequences of errors being committed in relation to both which might give rise to criticism, financial loss and sanctions.[117] In endeavouring to undertake the procedure, it is possible that she might find that every step taken was accompanied by critical reflection, as she sought to determine what was legally required and whether what had already been done had been so correctly. One way of Jill improving upon her effectiveness as a litigator, might be for her to be guided by a do-it-yourself manual. However, even here, uncertainty and the anxiety associated with engaging with an unfamiliar practice might still arise as the contents of the manual might not be clear to Jill or she might doubt whether such contents are entirely accurate or sufficiently comprehensive or appropriate given the type of litigation she was undertaking. Even if she understood the contents of the manual in the sense of understanding its words, she might not be clear about what it all meant in practice. Added to all this might be a general uneasiness born out of an awareness that she has little or no knowledge or understanding of relevant underlying legal principles. She might also lack the language games and skills associated with litigation and the bargaining that frequently accompanies it to reach "out of court" settlements and to gain tactical advantages within the litigation process itself. So all in all, a person in these circumstances might well recognise that successful litigation will require her to hand over the matter to an experienced lawyer. If she were to conduct her own litigation, her difficulties would substantially be caused by it not being a routinised activity for her. She would have difficulty in ensuring that the critical reflection that she undertook was sufficiently focused in the way that it would be for an experienced lawyer. One danger for her would be that she might engage in too much critical reflection that

---

[117] The phrases "known unknowns" and "unknown unknowns" are commonly associated with Donald Rumsfeld, former US Secretary of Defence and were expressed by him at a press briefing on 12th of February 2002. The term "unknown unknowns" suggests circumstances of which an individual is unaware and is not aware that he is unaware of them. However that does not prevent him from experience the anxiety provoking situation of being aware in general terms that there may be circumstances of which he will be unaware and that he will not be aware of being unaware of them.

was insufficiently focused and too little that was sufficiently so. It might be very time-consuming and anxiety-provoking as well as not being very productive, perhaps accompanied by a deeper anxiety because it was not clear to her when and how such reflection should be applied. She would not have, echoing Bourdieu's point, a *habitus* that equipped her to have a "feel for the game" of litigation.[118]

What is suggested is that the expert, that is to say, in our case, the lawyer who is a "repeat player" in litigation, will not just understand from the client what he is required to undertake, namely the litigation or that he understands the procedural stages that will have to be undertaken.[119] It will not be simply that he has familiarity with relevant substantive law.[120] What is also likely to demarcate such a lawyer from a novice and a litigant-in-person is that he will "see" what needs to be done, will decide how to do and also will have the capacity to effectively and rapidly adjust his approach to the circumstances as they unfold.[121] Critical reflection, however, will not be removed from what for the experienced lawyer will be a substantially routinised activity. Limited choices will still have to be made at each stage of the litigation process and for the more important (or unusual) ones, such as those concerning assessments of liability and *quantum* or whether offers of settlement are acceptable, critical reflection is likely to be significantly engaged in. Generally, it will be more selectively used, more focused in its application and more productive in its outcomes against a backdrop of the lawyer having an intuitive sense of when it should be engaged and how it should be so.

When considering the position of an experienced judge, it is worthwhile initially considering Cardozo's insights into the nature of the judicial process. Referring to the writings of William James, he noted that the human condition involves "a stream of tendency" which directs and gives coherence to thoughts and actions from which judges cannot escape and which comprises "forces which they do not recognise and cannot name."[122] These were identified as "inherited instincts, traditional beliefs and acquired convictions" that influence their outlooks on life and conceptions of social need; these, when "reasons are nicely balanced must determine where choice shall fall."[123] This reference by Cardozo to "a stream of tendency" goes some way towards describing the character of the dispositions that constitute Bourdieu's *habitus* and also points to the kind of contextual factors that, for Bourdieu, would have been

---

[118] Bourdieu and Wacquant, *An Invitation to Reflexive Sociology*, *supra* note 84 at 128.

[119] Marc Galanter, "Why the 'haves' come out ahead: speculations on the limits of legal change" (1974) 9 *Law and Society Review* 95–160.

[120] The application of relevant law by experienced personal injury litigators is surprisingly limited. See James Marshall, "Are Small-Town Lawyers Positivists About the Law?" in *Law and Sociology* ed. by Michael Freeman (Oxford: Oxford University Press, 2006) at 290.

[121] Hubert L. Dreyfus and Stuart E. Dreyfus, "The Challenge of Merleau-Ponty's Phenomenology" *supra* note 115 at 109.

[122] Benjamin N. Cardozo, *The Nature of the Judicial Process* (New Haven, CN: Yale University Press, 1921) at 2.

[123] *Ibid.*

influential in determining the nature of such dispositions. Again, just as Bourdieu considered that the *habitus* operated below the level of consciousness, so did Cardozo think that his "tendencies" would operate.[124] His claim that judicial attitudes to life and social needs played a determinative role in a finely balanced case evokes the question as to whether they operate in any other circumstances and, later on, Cardozo claims that judicial objectivity was circumscribed by the judge's biographical circumstances whenever it is applied. This again has a similarity with the idea that the pre-dispositions possessed by individuals to behave and respond in particular ways are the outcome of the sedimentation of that individual's past experiences. Cardozo went on further to say that, "in the life of the mind as in life elsewhere there is a tendency to reproduction of kind" so that "every judgment has generative power" and the underlying basis for this tendency is "habit."[125]

Aspects of judicial practice that are likely to be engaged in without critical reflection are considerable and a limited number of examples are now provided. They range from the forms of dress and address adopted in court to the language games adopted in verbal and written exchange and procedures. There are also usually a large range of assumptions repeatedly made including the location of legal sources and the relationship between them, approaches as to how they are to be interpreted, legal and constitutional principles underpinning the operation of the law and the role of the judiciary and approaches to the framing of disputes within accepted legal categories. It is unlikely, particularly in the run-of-the-mill case, that an experienced judge, as embedded agent, will ponder upon many of the matters indicated above. Critical thought in relation to law and fact is likely again as with the experienced lawyer to be applied selectively in a focused manner and to a depth finely attuned to the complexity and importance of the issue that has to be determined. From the judge's perspective the assumed matters including those relating to the internal aspect are likely to remain as part of her background as embedded agent, capable of moving towards the forefront of her mind in the event they do have to be critically reflected upon.

To highlight the multilayered existence of habitualised behaviour in the courtroom, it is worthwhile briefly considering the position of Jill if she conducts her own litigation and represents herself in court. She will face the possibility of exclusion from the judicial process unfolding before her on a number of levels. It is not simply that she may well not know or understand the substantive or procedural law that is relevant to her case. She will be faced by professionals in their roles as judge and advocates who are united by a mastery of legal technique which is demanded by effective engagement within the legal field. The application of such technique may well result in responses to Jill's case by the presiding judge and defendant's lawyer that for her have little in common with "common sense" or her sense of fairness or

[124] Bourdieu, *Distinctions*, *supra* note 85 at 468.

[125] Cardozo, *The Nature of the Judicial Process*, *supra* note 122 at 5.

what for her is relevant.[126] It will be presented in a language whose effect contributes towards the construction of what for the litigant-in-person may well be experienced as an alien space in which the stakes of the conflict are recast by legal practitioners who achieve this without consciously willing or realising it.[127] Jill's alienation might well emerge in the context of judicial practice which, for its practitioners, is routine but which for her is anything but so. In contrast to them, she might feel like "a fish out of water." There might well be a profound mismatch between her *habitus* and the practices she encounters within the judicial field which in contrast accord closely to the *habitus* of the lawyers. In contrast to them, she might well feel like "a fish out of water" and experience a sense of confusion and disempowerment.[128]

10.6 A Return to the Austin/Hart Debate

The above explorations of the likely circumstances of what in Hartian terms are referred to as those of ordinary citizens and legal officials suggest, as do the theoretical writings so far covered, that the exercise of critically reflective thought is deeply influenced and affected by habitualisation in association with which it takes place. And that its focus, probity and utility is enabled by that process. It is now worthwhile returning to the approach to habit developed by Austin and Hart's critique thereon, bearing in mind the embedded nature of human existence, the various levels at which habit is posed and the relationship between habitual behaviour and reflection. There are a number of difficulties associated with Hart's claim that compliance with the law through the operation of habit cannot be accompanied by the exercise of critical reflection.

Firstly, it is worthwhile considering the nature of the requirement that concerns us, namely that Austin considered, *inter alia*, that for the sovereign to arise, "the bulk of society must be in the habit of obedience or submission to a determinate or common superior."[129] The frame of reference for this claim is at a high level of abstraction as it includes all human activity in respect of which the commands of the superior are engaged within a given society. If one were to endeavour to measure the extent of such obedience one would have to monitor all such activity which would span a wide range of behaviours. The extent of compliance with the superior's commands would have to be inferred from such observations. The wide range of individual behaviours monitored would probably involve individuals in diverse and

[126] Pierre Bourdieu, "The Force of Law: Toward a Sociology of the Juridical Field" (1986–1987) 38 *The Hastings Law Journal* 814, *cf.* at 820.

[127] *Ibid.* at 830.

[128] This would amount in the language of Bourdieu as an expression of "hysteresis" See *supra* note 101.

[129] Austin, *Province*, *supra* note 1 at 166.

shifting circumstance with an extensive array of mental states accompanying their compliance with the superior's commands over time. Looked at it like this, it is very difficult to see how Austin in his use of the term "habit" was concerned with anything other than the frequency of repeated compliance with a superior's commands irrespective of the nature of individual activities which gave rise to such compliance or mental states possessed by such individuals at the time of such compliance.

Secondly, consistent with this proposition, Austin himself in referring to habit did not discount the possibility of reflection by those who were subject to the superior's commands but was endeavouring by the use of the term to simply denote its repetitive nature. So for example, Austin considered that there were a number of reasons as to why a given community obeyed the commands emanating from a sovereign. These ranged from a commitment founded in "custom" and "prejudice" to ones founded in an adherence to monarchical government or democracy or most profoundly and pervasively to a general preference present in all or nearly all political societies to the "utility of political government." Austin's concern with the frequency of obedience is further suggested where he counter-posed circumstances where obedience to a "determinate superior" was "rare or transient" to those where it was "habitual or permanent."[130]

Thirdly, Hart himself, when describing the minimum conditions necessary for the existence of a legal system within a modern state, divided its population into two. The officials of the legal system that had to accept the rules of recognition, change and adjudication constituting the common public standards of official behaviour.[131] For ordinary citizens, conversely, there was no such requirement. All they and legal officials in their private capacities were required to do was to generally obey the "primary rules" of the system, that is to say those rules that were commonly called the legal rules of the system, valid according to the legal system's "ultimate criteria of validity."[132] As Hart put it:

> [Obeying a rule (or order) by an ordinary citizen] need involve no thought on the part of the person obeying that what he does is the right thing both for himself and for others to do: he need have no view of what he does as a fulfilment of a standard of behaviour for others of the social group, He need not think of his conforming behaviour as "right" or "correct" or "obligatory." His attitude, in other words, need not have any of that critical character which is involved whenever social rules are accepted and types of conduct are treated as general standards. He need not, though he may, share the internal point of view accepting the rules as standards for all to whom they apply. Instead, he may think of the rule only as something demanding action from *him* under threat of penalty; he may obey it out of fear of the consequences, or from inertia, without thinking of himself or others as having an obligation to do so and without being disposed to criticize either himself or others for deviations.[133]

As far as ordinary citizens were concerned there was an overlap between Hart and Austin in that both accepted that obedience to the law may be accompanied by

---

[130] *Ibid.* at 167.

[131] Hart, *Concept of Law*, *supra* note 3 at 113.

[132] *Ibid.* at 113.

[133] *Ibid.* at 112.

a number of reasons or no particular reason. But obedience to the law by such citizens must be seen in the context of their embedded circumstances as must the circumstances of legal officials, if the relationship between habit and critical reflection associated with the internal point of view is to be fully appreciated. What pervades the circumstances of both is that they are embedded agents engaged in largely regularised practices which are considered to constitute conformity to the law in the case of ordinary citizens, including legal officials in their private capacities, and in relation to the latter in their official positions, correct engagement with regularised practices associated with the administration of the law.

Returning to our driver who is committed to the normativity of the internal point of view, bearing in mind his diachronic existence, the likelihood is that for much of the time he may well not think of his general commitment to the law. As previously suggested, for the most part he may not consciously "follow" the relevant law in so far as he is aware of it and yet still drive in conformity with it.[134] Mindful of the insights of Bourdieu and Merleau-Ponty, his "feel for the driving game" might well embrace a sense of the potentialities attached to the car and roads in terms of how they can be used, in ways which already coincide with the legal requirements as he engages in the regularised practice of driving. His commitment to the internal point of view as well as his specific commitment to complying with laws related to driving might generally come to the fore of his mind together or separately at various times. This may occur, for example, when he considers that other drivers have misbehaved on the roads, so suggesting habits of thought and attitudes in relation to such commitments and to the exercise of critical reflection accompanying an assessment of such behaviour. That is not to deny that critical reflection is circumstantially dependent, but the individual's general approach to the circumstances in which he engages in critical reflection and the general way that he undertakes it, is likely to repeatedly express itself. It will do so in the context of, and possibly in reaction to, the routinised behaviour which it accompanies. One also has to stress what underlies the internal point of view. What leads our driver to adopt the position according to which the standards of conduct set by the law ought to be obeyed by himself and others? It might well be as a result of habitually adopted and unquestioned assumptions about the centrality of law to ensure the avoidance of chaos, or other factors, some of which were alluded to by Austin and mentioned above.

The operation of habit is also fundamental to the position of individuals operating as legal officials as suggested above in the comments of Justice Cardozo. Again, one can use the same approach to their adoption of, and commitment to, the normativity of the internal point of view as has been done in relation to ordinary citizens. His commitment expressed through his adoption of the rules of recognition, change and adjudication, to have any sustained effect, must be constituted by a regularised practice in which such rules are complied with, and in connection with which critical reflection to ensure adherence will be undertaken, possibly repeatedly, thus

[134] See *supra* 10.5.

constituting part of the judge's routine of engagement with such rules. It may well also be that the judge does not critically reflect upon his commitment to the rules but simply accepts it, this itself constituting part of the background to the routine of upholding them.

10.7 Conclusion

It has been shown in this chapter that the process of habitualisation is fundamental to human existence. Consistent with this, writings on the nature and operation of habit are rich and diverse and deserve in the context of the development of legal theory to be given greater prominence. This review has revealed the operation of habitual processes on a number of levels, ranging from the most profound to the comparatively trivial. What is also clear from these writings is that the relationship between reason and habit is a deeply interdependent one, and the latter cannot be separated from the operation of the former. Reason is predicated upon habit, which accompanies and is involved in the exercise of reason and the process of critical reflection that accompanies it.

It is true that Austin did not specifically point to the importance of critical reflection in relation to the standards that the law was designed to uphold in order to ensure the continued existence of a legal system. His model, nonetheless, did not positively discount that possibility by his reference to habitual obedience as being constitutive of the sovereign-subject relationship. His reference to habit was made to denote the necessity of repeated obedience to the law and so his usage of the term was different from Hart's since he was not primarily concerned with the states of mind of those involved in obeying the law.

For Hart, conversely, the operation of habit involved what he characterised as unreflective, effortless and engrained behaviour that he counter-posed to that of critical reflection which he considered would be needed to ensure the operation of the internal point of view. What can be seen from the above survey about habit is that such a counter-position is problematic. Habitual obedience to the law does not negate the possibility that the individual concerned will be committed to the internal point of view and engage in critical reflection associated with it. Looked at from the individual's point of view, it is quite possible that he will routinely adopt the relevant attitudes and acceptances that are necessary to satisfy it. As such therefore, the routine of obedience to the law can be linked to an engagement with critical reflection. Indeed, for some individuals, it might be that the routine incorporates that of the required critically reflective stance. If the individual concerned is a legal official, one also cannot expunge the operation of habit from his ongoing commitment to, and practice of, adopting the internal point of view and the critically reflective attitude associated with it. The disassociation of the critically reflective stance in the context of the operation of the internal point of view from habit as posed by Hart breaks down and is not credibly sustainable.

The weakness of Hart's approach however points to a wider problem which manifests itself in his notion of habit being rather underdeveloped and disconnected from the embedded diachronic nature of human existence and the activity of critical reflection that forms part of that reality. This chapter has endeavoured to show that there are a wide range of routinised activities which vary greatly in complexity and are normally characterised by narrowing but not eliminating the choices that can be made in connection with them. In this way limited improvisation is possible within a routine. This, in turn, points to the contribution that habitualisation makes towards the capacity of human beings to adapt to their unfolding circumstances. Adaptation occurs in limited ways within routines in reaction to the range of circumstances for which the routine was designed or in response to which it developed. However, in response to greater changes in circumstances, the routine may well undergo modification or new routines may emerge. Central to this adaptive process is the capacity of individuals involved in routines to engage in critical reflection to assess the extent to which change is required. While the operation of routine lessens the need for critical reflection, it does not dispense with it but in fact enables it. Such thought might well be employed when determining the limited choices that have to be negotiated within a routine. It is likely to be undertaken in reaction to the failure of a routine to meet certain circumstances and might well provoke an individual to change or abandon a routine he has hitherto adopted. Where the routine is associated with law with which it is considered to comply, such thought might well involve a consideration of whether an alteration or abandonment of it is compatible with such normative requirements. Such thought is likely to be bounded in ways influenced by, although not necessarily completely determined by, the individual's *habitus* and the circumstances in which it is being undertaken and so the operation of habit in its widest sense continues to be felt. What might be regarded as an innovation as a result of such an exercise today may well become part of routinised activity tomorrow, so that the development of regularised social practices involves a process of reactions to routine-triggering innovation, which then might become routinised. The departure by the judiciary from a routinised approach to a particular problem through an innovative judgement today might become part of a routinised approach tomorrow. A legal theory today exhorting the judiciary to approach their work in a certain manner, if successful in its influence, might give rise to changed and improved judicial habits tomorrow.[135] To omit the link between habitual behaviour and critical reflection as Hart has done, is to ignore the centrality of both in an interdependent relationship to the capacity of human beings to improve upon their circumstances and to consolidate those improvements in a process that involves both continuity and change.

Austin's reference to habit captures the obvious yet profound point that the diachronic existence of any social structure including a legal system requires regularised social practices which are constituted by the repeated activities of those that go

[135] As for example Ronald Dworkin, *Law's Empire* (Cambridge, MA: Belknap Press, 1986).

to make up such structures. In hindsight, on the one hand, it might have been better had he explained more clearly what he had meant by the term, given the way that it has been subsequently interpreted most obviously by Hart. On the other hand, Hart's underdeveloped notion of habit is consistent with and has perhaps contributed to habit's marginalisation, which afflicts some legal and associated theories. In them, consistent with Kant's legacy, reason is in effect sealed off or largely separated from habit, which remains absent in any significant sense. The task now, to which this chapter has hopefully contributed, is to develop a greater appreciation of the range and depth of writings that concern the nature and operation of habit and to bring such insights to bear more extensively upon the development of legal theory. This is an undertaking that John Austin might well have approved.

Chapter 11
Austin, Hobbes, and Dicey*

David Dyzenhaus

11.1 Introduction

In 1958 H. L. A. Hart set out in the pages of the Harvard Law Review a new manifesto for legal positivism.[1] There he sketched an understanding of the past of philosophy of law that still dominates much current thinking. For many philosophers of law today, serious thought about philosophy of law began with that manifesto and its elaboration in 1961 in Hart's *The Concept of Law*, a book that he said might be regarded as an "essay in descriptive sociology."[2] They thought that since Hart had taken all that what was useful from the history of legal philosophy, one could get on with the task of working out the conceptual structure of law, without distraction from natural law endeavours to show that law is in some way necessarily moral or from the manifestly wrong attempts within the positivist tradition to explain law as the commands of an uncommanded commander.

This state of affairs reflects a more general split within philosophy between a social or natural scientific approach and a humanistic one. Humanists see the problems of philosophy as age-old, incapable of being addressed without attention to the history of the discipline. For the scientists, the past is for the most part a dustbin of failed arguments that often addressed irrelevant questions. Hence, the philosophical

*I thank Michael Freeman for organizing the symposium on John Austin at University College London at which a draft of this paper was presented and the participants in that symposium for discussion.

[1] Herbert L. A. Hart, "Positivism and the Separation of Law and Morals" reprinted in Hart, *Essays in Jurisprudence and Philosophy* (Oxford: Clarendon Press, 1983) at 49.

[2] Herbert L. A. Hart, *The Concept of Law* (Oxford: Clarendon Press, 1961) at vii.

D. Dyzenhaus (✉)
University of Toronto, Faculty of Law, 78 Queen's Park, M5S 2C5 Toronto, Canada
e-mail: david.dyzenhaus@utoronto.ca

M. Freeman and P. Mindus (eds.), *The Legacy of John Austin's Jurisprudence*, Law and Philosophy Library 103, DOI 10.1007/978-94-007-4830-9_11,

task is to confront the questions of the day using whatever analytical methods seem best from the philosophical toolkit; and Hart, or so it is thought, made philosophers of law understand that that is their task.

While Hart did much to make a social scientific approach to law his legacy, he was not the most consistent practitioner of that approach. Throughout his career, he remained preoccupied with Bentham. Moreover, a social scientific approach is in some tension with the way Hart announced the manifesto for legal positivism in 1958; for he said that he would present his subject – his argument for legal positivism – "as part of the history of an idea" – "the need to distinguish, firmly and with the maximum of clarity, law as it is from law as it ought to be."[3] That idea became known as the Separation Thesis, and it was one of the ideas that Hart thought he took over from Bentham and Austin despite his rejection of much else in their versions of legal positivism.

Hart expressed the idea as "the contention that there is no necessary connection between law and morality or law as it is and ought to be,"[4] his summary of the lengthy passage he quoted from a long note in Austin that begins with the memorable sentence: "the existence of law is one thing; its merit or demerit another."[5] This idea and its defence were the central theme of Hart's 1958 essay, because he clearly shared with Bentham and Austin the claim that the Separation Thesis enabled "men to see steadily the precise issues posed by the existence of morally bad laws, and to understand the specific character of the authority of a legal order."[6]

Hart's understanding of his positivist tradition has Bentham as the founder and he did not in 1958 mention the other earlier figure in the history of English political thought who is usually considered to have put forward a positivist philosophy of law – Thomas Hobbes. In later work, Hart took Joseph Raz's work on authority and the kinds of reasons that law gives us as an elaboration of Hobbes's contribution to the understanding of law, since, Hart said, Hobbes had illuminated the idea of command as well as the "similarities and differences between commands and covenants as sources of obligation and as obligation-creating acts."[7]

However, as Hart made clear, Hobbes had to be excluded from his positivist pantheon for the following reasons. First, Bentham's innovation in legal philosophy is to insist on "a morally neutral vocabulary for use in the discussion of law and politics." In this Bentham distinguishes himself from Hobbes and indeed "all previous social theorists" in avoiding "persuasive definitions" that make our favoured

---

[3] Hart, "Positivism and the Separation of Law and Morals" *supra* note 1 at 50.

[4] *Ibid.* at 57, fn 25.

[5] *Ibid.* at 52. John Austin, *Lectures on Jurisprudence or The Philosophy of Positive Law* (5th ed., London: John Murray, 1885, reproduced by Verlag Detlev Auvermann KG: Glashütten in Taunus, 1972) volume I, note at 214–15.

[6] Hart, "Positivism and the Separation of Law and Morals" *supra* note 1 at 53.

[7] Herbert L. A. Hart, *Essays on Bentham: Jurisprudence and Political Philosophy* (Oxford: Clarendon Press, 1982) at 244.

practical conclusions follow from the definitions.[8] Put differently, Hart finds in Bentham the beginning of the endeavour to put philosophy of law onto a scientific footing. Second, while Bentham shared with Hobbes the idea that both legislative power and political society have to be seen as a human artefact, and indeed took over in many respects Hobbes's theory of law as the command of the sovereign, he rejected, rightly in Hart's view, Hobbes's claim that the command of the sovereign was law "because it was given to subjects already under a prior obligation arising from their contract with each other to obey him."[9]

Now Hart sees these two points as connected. Bentham in making the insistence on moral neutrality the "sane and healthy centre" of the legal positivism of which he was the founder, ensured that nothing in his definition of sovereignty was "owed to morality," and thus also ensured that "nothing follows from the statement that laws so defined exist as to any moral reason for obedience." That "vital issue, Bentham thought, must await the judgment of utility on the content of the laws."[10] Indeed, Hart worried that Raz's own work on authority strayed too far in a Hobbesian direction because Raz argues that the officials of a legal order must accept or at least pretend that they accept the claim of their legal order not only to have authority but also to have legitimate authority.[11] Hart's view is that it is only a contingent truth that many officials will have such an attitude, and thus that legal theory need not occupy itself with the actual reasons legal officials including judges might have for adopting what he called the "internal point of view" towards the law of their legal order. This is the view that they are under a duty to implement the law not because they will be punished if they do not, but because that is the correct thing to do in terms of the established or settled practice of their order.[12]

I wish to explore Hart's idea that with Bentham we should insist that legal theory be morally neutral in part for the reason that such insistence avoids the Hobbesian mistake of supposing that law makes any necessary or inherent moral claim on its officials or its subjects. Austin's legal theory is fertile ground for such exploration since, in his view, expressed in another long note, Hobbes was along with Bentham the most important figure in legal theory. Austin said of Hobbes that he knew of no other writer (excepting our great contemporary Jeremy Bentham) who has uttered so many truths at once new and important, concerning the necessary structure of supreme political government and the larger of the necessary distinctions implied by positive law. And he is signally gifted with the talent, peculiar to writers of genius, of inciting the mind of the student to active and original thought.[13]

---

[8] *Ibid.* at 28.

[9] *Ibid* at 221.

[10] *Ibid.* at 28.

[11] *Ibid.* at 153–61, 263–68, referring to Joseph Raz, *The Authority of Law: Essays on Law and Morality* (Oxford: Clarendon Press, 1979) at 155.

[12] Hart, *Essays on Bentham, supra* note 7 at 160–61. For the "internal point of view, see Hart, *Concept of Law, supra* note 2 at 87.

[13] Austin, *Lectures, supra* note 5 at 281.

Hart was well aware of this passage, but thought that Austin had taken over Hobbes's mistake in supposing that sovereignty is both legally illimitable and indivisible.[14] As Hart points out, if sovereignty is defined in this way, then legal positivism cannot give an "undistorted account of those legal systems where a rigid constitution imposes restrictions on the legislative power of its supreme legislature, or divides legislative power between a central federal legislature and a legislature of constituent states or provinces."[15] Bentham, in contrast, saw that sovereignty had to be understood in a way that could account for such systems. Hart sets out in detail the difficulties which Bentham encountered in applying to such systems his conception of law as the command of the uncommanded or legally unlimited sovereign whom subjects habitually obey. But he regards it as significant that Bentham *qua* social scientist saw the need to account for the features of the phenomenon he was trying to understand, instead of attempting, as Hart supposed Austin did, to define them away.[16]

I will show that a detailed analysis of these two long notes – the one on the Separation Thesis and the one on Hobbes – reveals not only much about Austin's thought, but also sheds light on the current predicament of contemporary legal positivism. Part of this endeavour involves bringing a third figure into the discussion of the relationship between Hobbes and Austin, A. V. Dicey, who despite his prominence in constitutional theory receives very little attention from the scientifically-minded philosophers of law.

As we will see, the orthodox view is that Austin took from Hobbes the idea that the sovereign is subject to no legal limits, and Dicey in turn took over that idea from Austin. Dicey's neglect is then easily explained, since Hart showed that any scientific theory of law has to account for the fact that every legal system contains fundamental rules that have to be followed by those with legal authority if they wish to have their acts recognized as law. Hence, those who follow Hart need not trouble themselves with theories that begin with the fundamentally mistaken assumption that sovereignty is legally unlimited.

I will show, however, that there is more continuity between Hobbes and Dicey then there is between either of them and Austin. Hobbes and Dicey share Hart's view that legal authority is legally constituted in that even those at the apex of the legal hierarchy, for example, the parliamentarians in a system of parliamentary supremacy, have to follow legal rules if they wish their laws to be recognized as such. In other words, Hobbes and Dicey are as committed as Hart to the thought that there is something like a "rule of recognition" in any legal order.[17] Their thesis that there is a legally unlimited sovereign is, they think, consistent with the basic idea of

[14] Hart, *Essays on Bentham*, *supra* note 7 at 225–27.

[15] *Ibid.* at 226.

[16] *Ibid.* at 227–42.

[17] Hart, *Concept of Law*, *supra* note 2, chapter VI.

a rule of recognition since all that thesis states is that those at the apex of the legal hierarchy are able to change the law of their legal order by issuing a law in proper form.

Hart, of course, does not deny this proposition at least when it is advanced as a truth about a parliamentary order, that is, a system of parliamentary supremacy. But the reason that I said that Hobbes and Dicey are committed to the existence of "something like" a rule of recognition in any legal order is that their sense of what is fundamental to legal order, the "key to the science of jurisprudence,"[18] is not a rule but the idea of legality. So while parliament is free of legal limits in that it can change any legal limit by enacting a law in proper form, it is always as a legal authority subject to the principles of legality: moral principles inherent in any legal order.[19]

The quality of being legal is not, however, among the necessary conditions for law to be such in Austin's theory. Hart likely did consider that law had to be legal,[20] but there cannot be any certainty since his position, developed mainly in response to Lon L. Fuller, was deeply ambiguous.[21] I will argue that an analysis of the relationship between the legal theories of Hobbes, Austin, and Dicey shows that Hart in the end did not break with Austin and that legal positivism today remains plagued by the problems Hart himself detected in Austin, in part because of its attempt to think about law free of what it perceives as the encumbrances of the past.

11.2 The Sovereign: Legal or Political?

Austin's main discussion of Hobbes occurs in *Lecture VI*, which immediately follows the long note on law and morality.[22] It in this lecture that Austin sets out his theory of sovereignty, whose marks he identifies as follows:

> 1. The *bulk* of the given society are in a *habit* of obedience to a *determinate* and *common* superior: let that common superior be a certain individual person, or a certain body or aggregate of individual persons. 2. That certain individual, or that certain body of individuals, is *not* in a habit of obedience to a determinate human superior.[23]

---

[18] Hart, "Positivism and the Separation of Law and Morals" *supra* note 1 at 59.

[19] See Stuart Lakin, "Debunking the Idea of Parliamentary Sovereignty: The Controlling Factor of Legality in the British Constitution" (2008) 28 *Oxford Journal of Legal Studies* 709.

[20] See John Gardner, "The Legality of Law" (2004) 17 *Ratio Juris* 168.

[21] See Jeremy Waldron, "Positivism and Legality: Hart's Equivocal Response to Fuller" (2008) 83 *New York University Law Review* 1135 and David Dyzenhaus, *Hard Cases in Wicked Legal Systems: Pathologies of Legality* (2nd ed., Oxford: Oxford University Press, 2010) chapters 7–10.

[22] Though he did not choose to place the note there. It was inserted by Robert Campbell, the editor, from John Stuart Mill's notes of the lectures as originally delivered: see Austin, *Lectures*, *supra* note 5 at 200, note 16.

[23] *Ibid.* at 220, his emphasis.

Austin considered that one component part of the English sovereign is the "numerous body of the *commons* (…) as share the sovereignty with the king and the peers, and elect the members of the commons' house."[24] This complex sovereign delegated to parliament the powers that it had and it delegated them not absolutely but in terms of an implicit trust that the parliament would not use the powers in violation of the trust, for example, it would not attempt "to annihilate the actual constitution of the supreme government." This trust was enforced by constitutional law, which is to say enforced by mere "moral sanctions"; though Austin hastens to add that all "constitutional law, in every country whatever, is, as against the sovereign, in that predicament."[25]

Thus Austin seems to suppose that sovereignty is a pre-legal political entity, a supposition reinforced by the fact that his main invocation of Hobbes in this lecture is in support of the claim that the "power of the sovereign is incapable of legal limitation."[26] It is not, Austin says, that the "foremost individual member of a so-called limited monarchy" is incapable of legal limitation. The problem lies in confusing that individual with the sovereign properly so called. And he quotes at length two famous passages from *Leviathan* to support his claim. The first is an argument for subjecting oneself to such an unlimited power: that such subjection is the only way to escape the evils of the state of nature where one is subject to the power of all other individuals in the "warre of every man against his neighbour." The second sets out the argument that is known today as the regress argument—that the sovereign cannot be subject to the "civill lawes" since if he were so subject there would have to be a judge "above him, and a power to punish him" which would be to make that judge the sovereign.[27]

That Austin's sovereign seems to be outside of the law leads Pavlos Eleftheriadis to suggest that the only true analogue to Austin's theory of sovereignty is to be found in Carl Schmitt's claim that the sovereign is both "*anterior* to and *above* the constitution,"[28] which means that in a democracy it is the people who are the sovereign, legally unlimited and illimitable. Eleftheriadis notes that Schmitt is not making just a sociological claim – he means the claim to be one "internal to constitutional law and to its theory of democratic legitimacy,"[29] one which has the intent of undermining the very idea of the rule of law.[30]

---

[24] *Ibid.* at 245, his emphasis.

[25] *Ibid.* at 246–47.

[26] *Ibid.* at 278.

[27] *Ibid.* at 278–79. The passages are to be found in Thomas Hobbes, *Leviathan* ed. by Richard Tuck (Cambridge: Cambridge University Press, 1997) at 144–45, 224.

[28] Pavlos Eleftheriadis, "Law and Sovereignty", University of Oxford Legal Research Paper Series, Paper No 42/2009, available at http:/ssrn.com/abstract=1486084 (last accessed 13 April 2012), his emphasis. See Carl Schmitt, *Constitutional Theory*, trans. and ed. by Jeffrey Seitzer (Durham: Duke University Press, 2008) at 64; Schmitt's emphasis.

[29] Eleftheriadis, "Law and Sovereignty" *supra* note 28 at 27.

[30] *Ibid.* at 29.

Eleftheriadis then tries to show how Schmitt must succumb to a kind of logic that drives his position to accepting implicitly a Hartian rule of recognition. The sovereign cannot be a person in a democracy – it is the people. But there must be some way of individuating the German people from the British, and so on, which entails that there is some rule that is constitutive of the people, so the people are not legally unlimited. To act as a people, they have to act in accordance with that rule – for Schmitt, the rule of "public opinion."[31]

Eleftheriadis's comparison between Austin and Schmitt is apt, though not quite in the way he describes. Schmitt in fact is clear that "the people" is not an individuated entity. Rather, it is called into being out of an amorphous mass of individuals by another individual who is able to attract acclamation from a group within the mass who recognize themselves as a group in the distinction that the individual draws between the friend and the enemy. To use the most obvious example, Hitler's call to the German people in the 1930s was to the group that recognized themselves as such – as the *Volk* – in large part by defining themselves in the terms of his call against the internal enemy – Jews and communists with German citizenship.

The German people, in other words, was not those individuals who happened to hold German citizenship. Rather, it was the substantively homogeneous group among those individuals who recognized themselves in the image of a united *Volk,* propagated by the Nazis. Moreover, the sovereign figure remains, according to Schmitt, unbound by law even when he chooses to rule by law. At any moment, the sovereign can break free of the torpor of legal life and assert his pre-legal authority, an assertion whose success will not depend not on its compliance with a fundamental rule, but on whether it works. As Hart was to put it, in dealing with a completely analogous situation, "here all that succeeds is success."[32]

Schmitt's account of sovereignty is thus what we might term anti-legal and anti-constitutionalist, and as such is not subject to the logic of subjection to ultimate constitutive rules. Of course, Schmitt's account is both implausible and repugnant. But that is a different matter from appreciating that it cannot fail as an account of law, an account that attempts to explain law's authority or other normative notions intrinsic to an account of law from the inside, from the internal point of view. It cannot so fail since its aim is precisely to debunk that kind of account.

The comparison between Austin and Schmitt is thus helpful with one qualification. Austin wants to explode what he regards as certain myths about law: natural law claims about a necessary connection between law and morality and Kantian and Hobbesian claims about the origins of obligation in a contract. Indeed, he explicitly rejects social contract theories because he finds the idea of original covenant incoherent. Such theories, he argues, take the basis of political obedience in calculations of utility and turn it into a doctrine "darkly conceived and expressed"[33] that seeks

[31] *Ibid.* at 29–30.

[32] Hart, *Concept of Law*, *supra* note 2 at 149.

[33] Austin, *Lectures*, *supra* note 5 at 302.

the "extension of the empire of right and justice" – a justice that is "absolute, eternal, and immutable" not a "creature of law," but "anterior to every law; exists independently of every law; and is the measure of or test of all law or morality."[34] But since Austin is steadfast in his determination to account in a non-mysterious way for law and its authority, he also would have rejected as darkly German a Schmittian account of sovereignty.[35]

Indeed, a careful look at Austin's account of sovereignty reveals that he no less than Bentham struggled with the idea that sovereignty is both legally constituted and yet legally unlimited. And he did so because he wished to combine in the same theory an account of law in which law is clearly recognizable as such, that is, recognizable in accordance with a rule of recognition, with the grant of an unfettered discretion to the supreme political authority to make judgements about the general welfare. Thus Austin does, in line with the standard view of his thought, claim that constitutional law cannot be enforced "against a sovereign body in its collegiate and sovereign capacity," since as against that capacity "constitutional law is positive morality merely, or is enforced merely by moral sanctions."[36] But he also countenances that the moral sanctions of constitutional law may be made into positive law and enforced, "against the members of the [sovereign] body considered severally."[37]

Moreover, in England during the period for which the members of parliament are elected he recognizes that "sovereignty is possessed by the king and the peers, with the members of the common's house, and not by the king and peers, with the delegating body of the commons." It follows, he says, that "if the commons were sovereign without the king and the peers, their present representatives in parliament would be the sovereign in effect, or would possess the sovereignty free from trust or obligation." Thus they could extend the life of the parliament or "annihilate completely the actual constitution of the government, by transferring the sovereignty to the king or the peers from the tripartite body wherein it resides at present."[38] It also follows, as he later makes clear, that since the electoral body cannot itself, or indeed, with the king and the peers, make any law,[39] since only parliament can enact a law, parliament as presently constituted can enact a law vesting sovereignty in the king. It would then be "absurd" to say the law was illegal, for if the parliament is the sovereign, "it is the author (…) of all of our positive law, and exclusively sets us the

[34] *Ibid.* at 301.

[35] However, he has no problem with the idea that consent is the basis of government, since consent can be inferred from obedience; *ibid.* at 298.

[36] *Ibid.* at 267.

[37] *Ibid.* at 267, 269.

[38] *Ibid.* at 245–6.

[39] He says that if the electorate were sovereign without the king and the peers, "not a single sovereign power" except the power of election of representatives would be exercised "by the sovereign directly"; *ibid.* at 245. But it also then follows that the electorate cannot make a law with the king and the peers.

measure of legal justice and injustice."[40] Such a law could properly be termed "unconstitutional," since it changes the constitution, or "irreligious" or "immoral," but it is perfectly valid. Thus he invokes Hobbes's claim that "no law can be unjust" since law is the measure of justice.[41]

Austin also supposes that parliament could enact a law that would permit enforcement of the terms of the trust against parliament, that is, by judicial remedies. But then parliament could abrogate the law "without the direct consent of the electoral body" and the electoral body could not "escape from that inconvenience, so long as its direct exercise of its sovereign or supreme powers was limited to the election of its representatives." In this regard he says that it is "possible" for there to be an "extraordinary and ulterior legislature," for example, if sovereignty resided in the commons without the king and the peers, the commons could make a judicially enforceable law that bound the ordinary legislature.[42]

A law of the parliament, or a law of the commons' house, which affected to abrogate a law of the extraordinary and ulterior legislature, would not be obeyed by the courts of justice. The tribunals would enforce the latter in the teeth of the former. They would examine the competence of the ordinary legislature to make the abrogating law, as they now examine the competence of any subordinate corporation to establish a by-law or other statute or ordinance.

As we can see, Austin never faces up clearly to the question of how the electorate together with the king and the peers could "make a law," that is, enact a statute that had this effect. And he does not do so since he has no answer to this question. Hence, he has to hypothesize parliament as the "extraordinary and ulterior legislature." That move permits him to engage in the thought experiment of a sovereign parliament enacting a law to limit itself, which in turns permits him to claim that he has demonstrated that there can be no legal limitation on sovereignty since parliament could at any time free itself of that limit by simply enacting another law. However, that makes much of his account of sovereignty irrelevant to legal theory, since it also turns out that sovereignty in the legally relevant sense is possessed by parliament.

Dicey highlighted this fact. Austin, he said, seems to offer two different definitions of sovereignty: the political definition – sovereignty resides in the electorate, the king and the peers; and the legal definition – parliament effectively wields sovereignty because during its lifetime it can make any law that it likes, including one that annihilates the constitution.[43] From the legal perspective, Dicey suggested, it would be more accurate to use "sovereignty" in the Austinian sense as "simply the power of law-making unrestricted by any legal limit."[44] The political sovereign is, as Austin saw, the body the "will of which is ultimately obeyed by the citizens of the

---

[40] *Ibid.* at 268 and the note at that page.

[41] *Ibid.*

[42] *Ibid.* at 247–48.

[43] Albert V. Dicey, *An Introduction to the Study of the Law of the Constitution* (8th ed., London: MacMillan, 1924) at 68–72.

[44] *Ibid.* at 70.

state," though Dicey suggested that, from the political perspective, the will of the electorate was more important than that of the electorate combined with the Lords and the Crown:

> We may assert that the arrangements of the constitution are now such as to ensure that the will of the electors shall by regular and constitutional means always in the end assert itself as the predominant interest in the country. But this is a political not a legal fact. The electors can in the long run always enforce their will. But the Courts will take no notice of the will of the electors. The judges know nothing about any will of the people except in so far as that will is expressed by an Act of Parliament, and would never suffer the validity of a statute to be questioned on the ground of its having been passed or being kept alive in opposition to the wishes of the electors. The political sense of the word "sovereignty" is, it is true, fully as important as the legal or more so. But the two significations, though intimately connected together, are essentially different, and in some part of his work Austin has apparently confused one sense with another.[45]

In other words, there are two understandings of sovereignty. From the legal perspective, one understands sovereignty from the inside, which involves adopting the perspective of a judge – of the public official who makes final determinations on what counts as a legal act. From the political perspective, one will be concerned with the preconditions of legal order, and thus with such issues as identifying the people who ultimately decide on whether to support the legal order. Such support is necessary for any legal order to exist, so that we might say that any legal order has to be considered legitimate, or at least not worth rebelling against, by at least some significant segment of the population subject to it. But why that segment has that view, or the precise content of the view, is not a matter for legal science; it is the proper study of social or political science. Hence, questions about the legitimacy of legal authority can safely be expelled from legal theory to be considered by other branches of academic inquiry.

The need to expel morality from legal science underpins Austin's principal objection to Hobbes. Hobbes goes wrong, according to Austin, in deriving the origin of political society and sovereignty from an "imaginary covenant" instead of "from a perception by the bulk of the governed of its great and obvious expediency." Austin regards the duty of obedience to law which Hobbes claims to have discovered as "religious" in nature because he detects in Hobbes a "divine right" of the sovereign "to exact and receive such submission." Indeed, Austin detects a contradiction in Hobbes since he supposes that the subjects were "induced to promise obedience, by their perception of the utility of government." They cannot therefore be logically held to abide by that promise "in those anomalous cases wherein the evils of anarchy are surpassed by the evils of submission," even if they promised to obey in such cases. This problem only becomes worse when one seeks to impose that obligation on those who succeed the original parties to the covenant.[46]

---

[45] *Ibid.* at 71–2.

[46] Austin, *Lectures*, *supra* note 5 at 280–81.

It is not that Austin is an enthusiastic supporter of the right of legal subjects to resist their sovereign on the basis of their disagreement with the sovereign's judgements about general utility, and he is very wary of any argument that seeks to strip law of its status by appeal to morality, from whatever source. In a passage from which Hart quoted with manifest approval in 1958, Austin says:

> Now, to say that human laws which conflict with the Divine law are not binding, that is to say, are not laws, is to talk stark nonsense. The most pernicious laws, and therefore those which are most opposed to the will of God, have been and are continually enforced as laws by judicial tribunals. Suppose an act innocuous, or positively beneficial, be prohibited by the sovereign under the penalty of death; if I commit this act, I shall be tried and condemned, and if I object to the sentence, that it is contrary to the law of God, who has commanded that human lawgivers shall not prohibit acts which have no evil consequences, the Court of Justice will demonstrate the inconclusiveness of my reasoning by hanging me up, in pursuance of the law of which I have impugned the validity. An exception, demurrer, or plea, founded on the law of God was never heard in a Court of Justice, from the creation of the world down to the present moment.[47]

For Austin, the stark nonsense talker is Sir William Blackstone in his claim that no human laws can contradict the superior divine laws. For Hart the stark nonsense talker is Gustav Radbruch, who claimed that German post-war courts should deal with cases in which pernicious Nazi statutes played a role by treating them as invalid despite their conformity to the "formal criteria of validity" because they "contravened basic principles of morality."[48] And Hart thought that his argument against Radbruch led inexorably to the conclusion that the "truly liberal answer" to the problem of morally bad laws is that "we should speak plainly" and say that "laws may be laws but too evil to be obeyed."[49]

Austin's argument is different. He said that the "abuse of language" in Blackstone's claim is "not merely puerile, it is mischievous." When we say that a law "ought to be disobeyed" we mean that that "we are urged to disobey it by motives more cogent and compulsory than those by which it is itself sanctioned." Now if the laws of God were certain, it would be incumbent on us to disobey any "human command at variance with them." But they are not certain and utility is an "insufficient guide" to their content. What appears "pernicious" to one person will appear "beneficial" to another. Further, any claims about "moral sense" or "innate practical principles" are "merely convenient cloaks for ignorance or sinister interest." People use such talk to dress up in more plausible clothes what is really their "hatred" for a law. In times of "civil discord the mischief of this detestable use of language is apparent."[50]

---

[47] *Ibid.* note at 214–15. For Hart's quotation of much of this passage, see Hart, "Positivism and the Separation of Law and Morals" *supra* note 1 at 73.

[48] *Ibid.* at 74.

[49] *Ibid.* at 75.

[50] Austin, *Lectures*, *supra* note 5 note at 215–16.

In "quiet times," in contrast, "the dictates of utility are fortunately so obvious that the anarchical doctrine sleeps, and men habitually admit the validity of laws which they dislike." In such times, it might be "highly useful" to provoke law reform by proving by "pertinent reasons that a law is pernicious." It "may" even be useful to incite the "public to resistance by determinate views of *utility*" since resistance, "grounded on clear and definite prospects of good, is sometimes beneficial." But "to proclaim generally that all laws which are pernicious or contrary to the will of God are void and not to be tolerated, is to preach anarchy, hostile and perilous as much to wise and benign rule as to stupid and galling tyranny."[51] And earlier in his *Lectures* Austin emphasizes the dangers in the calculation of the benefits of disobedience to particular laws to the extent that disobedience seems hardly ever appropriate.[52]

In sum, Austin, quite unlike Hart, is deeply concerned about the bad consequences of making the individual's moral conscience – the individual sense of justice – the ultimate tribunal for deciding question about obedience to law. Nor could it be otherwise, since, again following Hobbes, he supposed that justice is simply the standard set by the law. All that the term justice otherwise signifies is "mere dislike," which it would be "far better to signify by a grunt or a groan that by a mischievous and detestable abuse of articulate language."[53]

Thus, Austin was also anxious to defend Hobbes against the charge of being an apologist for tyranny. Austin points out that while Hobbes preferred monarchy to popular government, defence of monarchy was not Hobbes's main concern. Rather, Hobbes's "main design is the establishment" of two propositions: first, that sovereign power cannot be limited by positive law; second, that a government of whatever character "cannot be disobeyed by its subjects consistently with the common weal, or consistently with the law of God as known through utility or the scriptures."[54] As we have just seen, Austin disagrees with the second proposition since he thinks that it is logically possible that utility may on occasion justify disobedience, and he regards Hobbes's insistence on the contrary as caused by the fact that he was writing at a time of civil war and was of extremely timid character.[55] Hobbes's bad reputation is principally due, Austin says, to the alarm of the clergy at his argument that no religion could claim a political authority alongside or superior to secular government, and to the claim of republicans that Hobbes was an apologist for tyranny. Thus Austin allies himself with Hobbes's argument that one should not equate tyranny – or bad government – with monarchy but with misrule, whether democratic or monarchical. What matters much more than the form of government is the principal cause of misrule, which is ignorance among the multitude of sound "political science." It follows, as Hobbes insists, that the principal preventive of the evil must lie in the

[51] *Ibid.* at 216, his emphasis.

[52] *Ibid.* at 118–20.

[53] *Ibid.* at 218.

[54] *Ibid.* at 279–280.

[55] *Ibid.*

diffusion of such knowledge throughout the mass of the political community. "Compared with this, the best political constitution that the wit of man could devise, were surely a poor security for good or beneficent rule."[56]

Austin is an astute interpreter and user of Hobbes. Moreover, since Hobbes can be interpreted as a kind of proto-utilitarian and since Austin thinks that justified disobedience to law is very rare, the differences between them might seem to approach vanishing point.[57] However, there is one salient difference. When Austin relies on Hobbes for the claim that justice always refers to a standard and that the standard is a legal one, he does not take into account that for Hobbes the content of the standard is not altogether determined by facts about what the sovereign intended. Rather, the content has also to be determined in accordance with the laws of nature.

The reason for Austin's silence on this topic is simple. Hobbes says in Chap. 15 of *Leviathan* of the laws of nature that they are "Immutable and Eternall; for Injustice, Ingratitude, arrogance, Pride, Iniquity, Acception of persons, and the rest can never be made lawfull."[58] And he says in Chap. 26 that because the laws are immutable no judge, including the ultimate sovereign judge, can make a law contrary to the laws of nature.[59] Since Austin supposes, as we have seen, that all talk of justice as "absolute, eternal, immutable"[60] is dark nonsense, he would have not thought it worth his while to take trouble to understand the place of the laws of nature in Hobbes's legal theory. But, as I will argue in the next section, the issue is not simply one about getting Hobbes right; rather, it pertains to the nature of philosophy of law.

11.3 Hobbes and Dicey on the Rule of Law

I will reverse the chronology here and start with Dicey. According to Dicey, the sovereignty of parliament is but one of the two features of English political institutions, the other being the rule of law.[61] Dicey took the rule of law to include three "distinct though kindred conceptions."[62] First, the rule of law means that:

> No man is punishable or can be lawfully made to suffer in body or goods except for a distinct breach of law established in the ordinary legal manner before the ordinary Courts of the land. In this sense the rule of law is contrasted with every system of government based on the exercise by persons in authority of wide, arbitrary, or discretionary powers of constraint.[63]

---

[56] *Ibid.* at 281–82.

[57] Indeed, one should take into account in regard to disobedience the remarks of Hobbes that get referred to as the "rebel's catechism," in which he suggests that subjects may disobey when the sovereign's commands frustrate the ends of sovereignty; Hobbes, *Leviathan*, *supra* note 27 at 151.

[58] *Ibid.* at 110.

[59] *Ibid.* at 192.

[60] Austin, *Lectures*, *supra* note 5 at 301–2.

[61] Dicey, *An Introduction to the Study of the Law*, *supra* note 43 at 179.

[62] *Ibid.* at 183.

[63] *Ibid.* at 183–84.

Secondly, the rule of law means not only that "no man is above the law" but also "a different thing" that "every man, whatever be his rank or condition, is subject to the ordinary law of the realm and amenable to the jurisdiction of the ordinary tribunals."[64] This Dicey termed the "idea of legal equality, or of the universal subjection of all classes to one law administered by the ordinary Courts."[65]

The third meaning is rather more ephemeral, the rule of law understood as "the predominance of the *legal spirit* [that] may be described as a special attribute of English legal institutions":

> We may say that the constitution is pervaded by the rule of law on the ground that the general principles of the constitution (as for example the right to personal liberty, or the right of a public meeting) are with us the result of judicial decisions determining the rights of private persons in particular cases brought before the Courts; (…) whereas under many foreign constitutions the security (such as it is) given to the rights of individuals results, or appears to result, from the general principles of the constitution.[66]

The immediate consequence of Parliament's victory was the other main feature Dicey identified of English political institutions, the "undisputed supremacy throughout the whole country of the central government," an authority which had once belonged to the King as "the source of law," but which had passed into the "supremacy of Parliament."[67]

However, it is important to see that the rule of law is a necessary condition of parliamentary supremacy. In order for Parliament to be supreme, one has to establish the supremacy of law over the executive, which involves creating a centralized body for adjudication of disputes about law's limits, a body that is independent of the officials who claim to act in the name of the law. Hence, Dicey's genius lies in the insight that the rule of law makes parliamentary supremacy possible, since it provides the basis for accountability of the executive to law.

As Dicey noted, this feature can and has been seen as threatening the rule of law, since parliament's supremacy also makes possible parliamentary abolition of the rule of law. Indeed, he argues that parliament can abdicate its sovereignty altogether, by employing either a statute that dissolves itself and leaves no means "whereby a subsequent Parliament could be legally summoned," or a statute that transfers sovereign authority to some other person or body of persons.[68] And he does not think that in England judges have the authority to withstand parliament, which is why, like Austin he talks of the limits on parliament's ability to commit suicide as limits set by "constitutional morality."[69]

---

[64] *Ibid.* at 189.

[65] *Ibid.*

[66] *Ibid.* at 191, footnote omitted; my emphasis.

[67] *Ibid.* at 179.

[68] *Ibid.* note at 65–66.

[69] *Ibid.* at 23.

That Dicey supposes that judges lack such authority is often regarded as the factor that puts him into a seamless lineage from Hobbes through to Austin at least with respect to this issue. But from the perspective of legal philosophy, debate over this issue is a red herring because the fundamental question is whether law is answerable to legality, not whether judges in a particular legal order have the authority to enforce such answerability.

Notice that while the rule of law is a necessary condition of parliamentary supremacy, the converse does not hold. Parliamentary supremacy is not a necessary condition of the rule of law because, as Dicey noted, one can have the rule of law in what I will call a "bill of rights legal order," one which has a constitution that entrenches rights and freedoms that limit parliament's supremacy. It would still, however, be true of a bill of rights order that there must be an ultimate if not supreme legislature to whose law the executive is accountable. So in such an order the rule of law is still a necessary condition of that legislature's place in the legal order.

A bill of rights legal order has one apparent advantage over a parliamentary order in that judges will in such an order have the formal authority to declare invalid statutes that seek to annihilate constitutional fundamentals, including the rule of law. Despite this obvious difference, Dicey argued that the rule of law and the protection of individual rights are better served by a parliamentary order. For in such an order, the right to individual freedom is "part of the constitution because it is inherent in the ordinary law of the land, the right is one which can hardly be destroyed without a thorough revolution in the institutions and manners of the nation," while in the bill of rights order, the general rights it guarantees are "something extraneous to and independent of the ordinary course of law," hence subject to suspension.[70]

I will not evaluate this argument here. Rather, I want to focus on the fact that Dicey, since he thought that the rule of law is better served in a parliamentary order, must also have thought that a statute that undermines or annihilates a constitutional fundamental is not simply wrong in that it should be condemned by standards of morality external to legal order. Rather, it has something legally wrong with it. As he said of the Statute of Proclamations enacted by Henry VIII in 1593, which empowered the Crown to legislate by proclamation, it marked the "highest point of legal authority ever reached by the Crown" and he thinks it was probably repealed "because of its inconsistency with the *whole tenor* of English law."[71]

The emphasized phrase, like "legal spirit" in the quotation above,[72] tells us that for Dicey something goes wrong from what we might call law's own perspective when such a statute is enacted. It is one thing whether or not the public will find that such a statute is morally problematic, whether it is in Austin's terms, inconsistent

[70] *Ibid.* at 196.

[71] *Ibid.* at 48–49, my emphasis.

[72] *Supra* note 66.

with standards of positive morality, or with general utility. But it is another that it is problematic from law's own perspective, from the perspective of legality or the rule of law.[73]

Now Hobbes differs from Dicey in that he is hostile to the common law tradition. But in other respects, he puts forward almost exactly the same view of law and what we can think of as law's answerability to legality. The sovereign is only legally unlimited in that he can free himself from the constraints of statute by enacting a statute. He is however not legally unlimited, if what we mean by "legally" is the requirement of legality set out in the laws of nature.

In any controversy with the sovereign or a public official, the subject's first port of call will be a subordinate judge. Hobbes is clear that such controversies arise not only because the law may seem indeterminate. They also arise when the law seems clear but its clarity produces an unreasonable result in light of the laws of nature. Indeed, judges insult the sovereign, Hobbes says, if they impute an intention to him that is at odds with the laws of nature, so that they are under an interpretive obligation to try in so far as possible to show that the intention of his commands complies with the laws of nature. And if they cannot so find, they are under a duty to point that fact out to the sovereign.[74] As I have argued elsewhere,[75] such answerability to legality is a kind of accountability. But it comes about not because the sovereign owes any duties to his judges, nor from the duty of judges to legal subjects, but because of the duty the judges owe their sovereign, a duty inherent in the judicial role since judges must uphold the laws of nature.

Austin makes many of the same moves. As we have seen, almost despite himself at times, he has to recognize that the sovereign is both legally constituted and thus is subject to law. Moreover, with Hobbes he recognizes both that subjects may assert their legal rights against the sovereign, sue the sovereign in accordance with the law and that the sovereign's subordinates are bound to stay within their legal mandates.[76]

---

[73] Notice that in a parliamentary order that the statute is in this way problematic has two immediate practical consequences even on the assumption that judges do not have the authority to strike down the statute as invalid. First, when judges are confronted by a problem that results from the fact that a statute is plausibly interpreted as undermining the rule of law, the judges have a legal duty to try to interpret the statute in a way that preserves rather than undermines the rule of law. Second, if they find that they have no option but to interpret the statute as one that manifests an intention to undermine the rule of law, they are under a legal duty to point this out. And that should be seen as a signal both to parliament and to the public that parliament has strayed from its part in upholding the rule of law.

[74] Hobbes, *Leviathan*, *supra* note 27 at 194.

[75] David Dyzenhaus, "Hobbes's Constitutional Theory" in Thomas Hobbes, *Leviathan* ed. by Ian Shapiro (New Haven, CT: Yale University Press, 2010) at 453.

[76] A sovereign government may appear before a tribunal of its own appointment, but "from such an appearance of a sovereign government, we cannot infer that the government lies under legal duties, or has legal rights against its own subjects"; Austin, *Lectures*, *supra* note 5 at 287–88. Further: "where the sovereign government appears in the character of defendant, it appears to a claim founded on a so called law which it has set to itself. It therefore may defeat the claim by abolishing the law entirely, or by abolishing the law in the particular or specific case." Rights pursued against the government are therefore merely "*analogous*" to legal rights since the government can "extinguish [them] by its own authority"; *ibid.* his emphasis.

He leaves out, however, the idea of legality and that is because he sees law's function not as preserving legality but as transmitting as efficiently as possible the commands of law-makers to legal subjects. For this reason, the term "transmission account of law" might capture the essence of his theory better than the standard "command theory" since the latter does not altogether accurately convey the marks or characteristics of Austin's legal theory. His legal theory is, that is, one in which the political sovereign is the one who has unlimited political discretion to use the law to implement his judgements, and transmits those judgements to his subjects in the form of commands, recognizable as such by publicly accepted criteria, and which the subjects obey on pain of disobedience and because of a general sense of the disutility of disobedience.

11.4 The Transmission Account of Law

A transmission account is very well suited to utilitarianism, since that political philosophy needs a legal order that is designed to fit snugly into the general apparatus of social and political institutions that will arrive at and implement correct judgements about general welfare. It follows that the legitimacy of law comes not from any characteristics of law itself, but from the quality of the judgements that law transmits. But it also follows that the transmission account of law is detachable from utilitarianism in that it fits just as snugly with any political philosophy that has this view of law's lack of intrinsic legitimacy.

Once we see this, we can understand better the kinds of problems with which Bentham and Austin, and indeed legal positivism in general, grapple. For example, on this account of law, if the law that applies to a dispute does not have determinate content, that is, a content that can be imputed as matter of fact to the legislature, the only way for a judge to resolve that dispute is to legislate. This is, as it were, a fact of the matter, given the transmission account of law. But how to cope with that fact will depend on political, not legal philosophy, on an account of legitimacy external to law.

For Bentham, at least in his mature thought, the way to cope is to increase to the extent possible the amount of determinate law by codifying it, since the institution best trusted with making legitimate judgements about general utility is the legislature, not an elite of judges who will stand in the way of utility-driven reform. Hence, he disparages judges not because he thinks that they are incapable of making law, but because he does not think they can be trusted to make good law.

Austin explicitly distances himself from Bentham on this point since he regards a judicial elite as more likely to make good judgements than a legislature, which is beholden to the ignorant multitude, whom he regards in much the same light as colonial officials regarded the native inhabitants of the territories they governed. He describes them as given to "coarse and sordid pleasures," people with a "stupid indifference about knowledge."[77] It is true that he holds out the hope of progressive

[77] *Ibid.* at 134.

enlightenment of the multitude – "their ignorance is not altogether invincible."[78] But he clearly thinks that there is a limit to the process of enlightenment. Only in respect of the "groundwork" of utilitarian science and the "more momentous" of "practical truths" can the multitude be "freed from the dominion of authority: from the necessity of blindly persisting in hereditary opinions and practices; or of blindly turning and veering, for want of directing principles, with every wind of doctrine."[79] To the extent that the multitude of his day is unenlightened, and to the extent that they are doomed to at least some measure of general ignorance, they can legitimately, Austin thinks, be subjected to the dominion of elite rule.

Hence, Austin says that unlike Bentham he does not wish to use the "disrespectful" term "judge-made law" to describe what judges do when they legislate, since the better part of the law of every country that "was made by judges has been far better made than that part which consists of statutes enacted by the legislature." And he concludes that:

> Notwithstanding my great admiration for Mr. Bentham, I cannot but think that, instead of blaming judges for having legislated, he should blame them for the timid, narrow, and piecemeal manner in which they have legislated, and for legislating under cover of vague and indeterminate phrases (…) which would be censurable in any legislator.[80]

But whatever the differences between Bentham and Austin on this point, what they share is the idea that considerations of morality or legitimacy are external to law, and thus to be dealt with by some other branch of inquiry than philosophy of law.

This same feature also attends the account Austin gives of the habit of obedience.[81] Since law's legitimacy depends entirely on whether its transmitted content is legitimate, those who obey it have to have sufficient motivation for obedience for reasons quite apart from their sense of the legitimacy or illegitimacy of the law. That motivation seems to come, for Austin, from the sanctions provided for disobedience plus a general sense of the utility of government, no matter how bad, over the uncertainty of the situation that follows disobedience.[82] But that issue is again not properly within philosophy of law.

---

[78] *Ibid.* at 133.

[79] *Ibid.*

[80] *Ibid.* at 218–19.

[81] For example: "The proper purpose or end of a sovereign political government, or the purpose or end for which it ought to exist, is the greatest possible advancement of human happiness" (*ibid.* at 290). See further 292–93: One can infer "the causes of that habitual obedience which would be paid to the sovereign by the bulk of an enlightened society" from that purpose. "Supposing that a given society were adequately instructed or enlightened, the habitual obedience to its government which was rendered by the bulk of the community, would exclusively arise from reasons bottomed in utility."

[82] *Ibid.* at 294–95.

Now I claimed above that this account of law is detachable from utilitarianism and so can fit snugly with any political philosophy that regards law's legitimacy as contingent on the content of particular laws. There is another importance consequence to the feature of detachability, for that account can be explored as an account of law without any attention to the details of any political philosophy. This is why Austin is not completely inconsistent when he claims that he has no concern in his philosophy of law with "the ends or final causes for which governments *ought* to exist, or with their different degrees of fitness to attain or approach those ends"[83] while at many times he seems to reflect precisely on such ends.[84]

Hart, Raz, and other twentieth century legal positivists writing in English undertook precisely this kind of inquiry, one unconcerned with the oughts of political and moral philosophy. If one situates their work in the history of philosophy of law in English, the differences between them and Austin thus seem much less significant than the similarities, other than the fact that Austin wanted to forge an explicit link between utilitarian political philosophy and philosophy of law. Indeed, once one sees that the claim about the legally unlimited sovereign is completely consistent with the idea that there is a rule of recognition, indeed that such an idea is required by a transmission account of law, the similarities far outweigh the differences. And even in regard to the issue of the link between political or moral philosophy and philosophy of law, Hart, Raz, and their followers like to insist that a transmission account of law assists a liberal stance on the rights of individual conscience. For if all law does is transmit content more or less effectively the individual citizen does not have to accord any moral weight to the law as such when deciding whether to obey a morally suspect law.

The most significant difference is in Hart's claim that to understand law one needs to take account of the fact that law is normative – that law creates obligations and moreover obligations whose normative force cannot be explained in terms of sanctions. However, as we saw, Hart rejected Raz's argument that legal officials must either accept or pretend to accept the law they enforce as legitimate. Hart's account of the internal point of view of one who treats the law as a system of norms thus tracks Austin's account of the habit of obedience in attempting to show that morality need play no role in such an account. The notorious difficulties positivists have experienced with this issue, which still bedevil attempts today to find at all costs a convention-based account of legal duty, can be readily explained in light of the story thus far. They result from the attempt since 1958 to account for a phenomenon – law's inherent normative qualities – by a theory that is constitutionally opposed to the idea that law has such qualities.

83 *Ibid.* at 220.

84 For example: "To the ignorant and bawling fanatics who stun you with their pother about liberty, political or civil liberty seems to be the principal end for which government ought to exists. But the final cause or purpose for which government ought to exist, is the furtherance of the common weal to the greatest possible extent"; *ibid.* at 274.

I am not the first person to point this out. Lon L. Fuller made this claim about the positivist tradition in his 1958 debate with Hart,[85] and he was responsible for the most sustained attempt to develop a theory of law's answerability to legality in the twentieth century, a theory which arguably has troubled legal positivists more than Ronald Dworkin's choice of adjudication as the terrain on which to contest legal positivism. As Jeremy Waldron has shown, a careful analysis of Hart's critiques of Fuller from 1961 on supports the view that Hart's attempt to refute Fuller consists of a strategy that divides Fuller's argument into two separate components: first, the argument that law to be such must be answerable to principles of legality, that is, the failure substantially so to comply will render a particular law or a whole legal order illegal or not law; secondly, the argument that compliance with legality makes a positive moral difference to legal subjects.[86]

Waldron traces how Hart, as seemed convenient, adopted two inconsistent responses. On the one hand, Hart conceded that law must be answerable to legality but affirmed that such answerability is not only compatible with great iniquity but can actually exacerbate iniquity. On the other hand, he conceded that answerability to legality makes a positive moral difference, but affirmed that law need not be so answerable. Fuller did not, of course, suppose that his argument could be broken into these separate components. But Waldron's analysis shows the kind of difficulties positivists encounter as soon as they try to find a place on the terrain of legality, difficulties which arguably multiply in Raz's main attempt to deal with Fuller's argument.[87]

Much the same phenomenon attends the positivist discussion of adjudication since 1958. On the one hand, allegiance to the transmission account of law led to the claim both that judges are acting in a quasi-legislative capacity when they decide what came to be called hard cases, and that the question of how much capacity judges should have and how they should use it are not for philosophy of law to comment on, other than through an insistence that one not disguise the legislative nature of the activity with the "childish fiction" that judges do not make law.[88] On the other hand, the rise of so-called inclusive legal positivism, which more or less accepts a Dworkinian account of adjudication, can be explained by what happens when one attempts to capture the moral phenomenology of adjudication from the internal point of view of a judge, something also reflected, albeit differently, in Raz's suggestion that judges must at least pretend that the law is legitimate.

---

[85] Lon L. Fuller, "Positivism and Fidelity to Law – A Reply to Professor Hart" (1958) 71 *Harvard Law Review* 630.

[86] Waldron, "Positivism and Legality" *supra* note 21.

[87] Joseph Raz, "The Rule of Law and its Virtue" in Raz, *The Authority of Law*, *supra* note 11 210. See Dyzenhaus, *Hard Cases in Wicked Legal Systems*, *supra* note 21, chapters 7, 8 and 9.

[88] Hart, "Positivism and the Separation of Law and Morals" *supra* note 1 at 66, a term he took with approval from Austin.

It is also worth noting that Waldron might be subject to a version of his own critique of Hart. On the one hand, he is the most prominent member of a neo-Benthamite school of political positivists who argue that the scope of judicial legislation should be greatly diminished because only democratic legislatures have the legitimacy to legislate. On the other hand, he is also engaged in a detailed and sensitive exploration of legality, one which assumes that law is answerable to legality, and that exploration moves him ever closer to Dworkinian and Fullerian accounts of law.

In sum, my argument is that all of the difficulties just sketched have a common root – the desire of a philosophy of law, hostile to the idea that law is answerable to a moral ideal of legality, to make sense of that ideal. If one takes an historical perspective on contemporary philosophy of law, one will appreciate that the basic divide in legal theory is between a tradition whose basic intuition is that law is answerable to a moral ideal of legality and a tradition that sees law as the transmitter of political judgement. For the former, the rule of law tradition, the basic problem for philosophy of law is to explain the distinction between the rule of law and the arbitrary rule of men. For the latter, what we might call the rule by law tradition, the basic problem is to explain how law can effectively transmit the judgements made by political elites. As I suggested above in the brief comparison between Schmitt and Austin, those in the rule by law tradition do not wish to debunk the idea of government according to law, only the claims about the necessary moral quality of government according to law made by figures in the rule of law tradition.

However, the rule by law tradition encounters severe difficulties in making sense of the idea of government according to law without accepting the claims of those within the rule of law tradition about the morality of legality just because they do not wish to debunk the idea of legal order. These difficulties reach their height when legal positivists accept, following Hart, that philosophy of law has to understand law as a normative phenomenon, which in turns requires taking seriously the internal point of view of legal officials. One could well conclude, given these difficulties, that legal positivism cannot account for the phenomenon of law, at least as it has developed in Western societies. They cannot in particular account for how law developed in a way that provides judges with the resources to develop a jurisprudence in which individuals have rights against the government, resources which enable judges, as Hart once put it, to "change the practices of government for human good."[89]

If we are to understand law in this way we have to make full sense of the attitude of those who take an internal point of view towards law, as indicated in Raz's claims about belief or feigned belief in legitimacy. For they do not and cannot understand

---

[89] *Ibid.* at 197.

law as an alien, top-down projection of power into their lives, which they will resist or not depending on a calculation of costs and benefits. Rather, they must have a basis for understanding that law not only claims authority over them, but also, necessarily and plausibly, legitimate authority.[90]

[90] Harold J. Berman, in the conclusion to his history of the Western legal tradition, argues that positivists fail to see that such resources have played a constitutive role both in that tradition and in the tradition of the civil law. He takes the central idea of legal positivism to be that law is an "instrument of domination, a means of effectuating the will of the law-maker," but finds that this idea only captures part of the historical story. He argues that an understanding of law also has to account for the way it has evolved in part by providing mechanisms to protect the powerless from the arbitrary power of the powerful; Berman, *Law and Revolution: The Formation of the Western Legal Tradition* (Cambridge, MA: Harvard University Press, 1983) at 556.

Chapter 12
John Stuart Mill on John Austin (and Jeremy Bentham)

Philip Schofield

12.1 Introduction

John Stuart Mill's reviews of John Austin's work on jurisprudence, published in 1832 and 1863, bestowed uncompromising praise on Austin's intellectual abilities and emphasized his originality and skill in classifying, defining, and distinguishing the fundamental ideas that were embedded in each and every civilized system of law. In the course of his reviews, Mill dealt with the question of the influence of the thought of Jeremy Bentham. Both Mill and Austin were in some senses "disciples" of Bentham; both remained throughout their lives committed to utilitarianism (though Austin's position in this respect was closer to that of William Paley than to that of Bentham), and both could not but acknowledge Bentham's immense importance as a proponent of law reform. In comparing Bentham with Austin, Mill assigned to the former an essentially destructive role, carrying out the necessary task of sweeping away the absurdities and irrationalities that characterized the study of the law, and thereby leaving to Austin the task of reconstruction by means of definition and classification. This is puzzling, since Mill must have been aware of Bentham's extensive work on definition and classification, and not only his vigorous criticism of existing institutions, but also his deep commitment to designing new and better ones to replace them. Why did Mill lavishly praise what, as I shall argue, even he saw as the inferior and derivative work of Austin, while presenting a less than generous account of Bentham's achievements?

Mill had come into contact with Austin in 1819, when the latter, with his new wife Sarah, had taken up residence near to the houses of Bentham and the Mill family in Westminster. In his *Autobiography*, Mill recounted that the two friends of Bentham from whom he had derived most, and with whom he had most associated,

P. Schofield (✉)
Faculty of Laws, University Collage of London, Bentham House,
Endsleigh Gardens, WC1H OEG, London, UK
e-mail: p.schofield@ucl.ac.uk

M. Freeman and P. Mindus (eds.), *The Legacy of John Austin's Jurisprudence*,
Law and Philosophy Library 103, DOI 10.1007/978-94-007-4830-9_12,

had been George Grote and Austin. "On me," wrote Mill, "[Austin's] influence was most salutary. It was moral in the best sense. He took a sincere and kind interest in me, far beyond what could have been expected towards a mere youth from a man of his age, standing, and what seemed austerity of character."[1] According to the editor of Mill's correspondence, the Austins "were almost second parents" to him.[2] The young Mill certainly spent a great deal of time with the Austins. In the winter of 1821/2, Austin and Mill read Roman Law together.[3] In the autumn of 1822, Mill visited the Austins at Norwich, spending several hours each day with John reading Blackstone, and in the evening Bentham's *An Introduction to the Principles of Morals and Legislation*.[4] In the mid-1820s Mill and Austin were training together in the gymnasium which Bentham had established in his coach house.[5] In August 1830 Mill was in Paris with the Austins,[6] and in October 1832 he went on a walking tour of Cornwall with them.[7] Mill was, moreover, an assiduous attender at Austin's lectures at the University of London,[8] although on 7 August 1830 he complained to Sarah that the lectures were too repetitive, did not cover the whole of the subject, contained too much historical material, and recommended that, for the following year's course, Austin write an interesting introductory lecture.[9] Continuing to attend as and when the lectures took place, Mill reported to Thomas Carlyle that Austin was "lecturing to a very small but really select class, and getting daily a clearer insight into his subject, as well as into other subjects still more important."[10] The select class consisted, by February 1833, of six or seven.[11] Writing in relation to this period, Mill reminisced that he had been more in agreement with Austin than with any

[1] John Stuart Mill, *Autobiography and Literary Essays* ed. by John M. Robson and Jack Stillinger (Toronto: University of Toronto Press, 1981) in *Collected Works of John Stuart Mill* [hereafter *CWJSM*], I, at 75–9.

[2] *Additional Letters of John Stuart Mill* ed. by Marion Filipiuk, Michael Laine, and John M. Robson (Toronto: University of Toronto Press, 1991) in *CWJSM*, XXXII, at 3 fn.

[3] Mill, *Autobiography and Literary Essays* in *CWJSM*, I, at 67.

[4] *The Earlier Letters of John Stuart Mill: 1812–1848* ed. by Francis E. Mineka (Toronto: University of Toronto Press, 1963) in *CWJSM*, XII, 13.

[5] *The Correspondence of Jeremy Bentham: Volume 12: July 1824 to June 1828* ed. by Luke O'Sullivan and Catherine Fuller (Oxford: Clarendon Press, 2006) in *Collected Works of Jeremy Bentham* [hereafter *CWJB*]), at 146 and 368.

[6] *Earlier Letters of John Stuart Mill: 1812–1848* in *CWJSM*, XII, at 55.

[7] See "Walking Tour of Cornwall 3–9 October 1832", in John Stuart Mill, *Journals and Debating Speeches* ed. by John M. Robson (Toronto: University of Toronto Press, 1988) in *CWJSM*, XXVII, at 613–37.

[8] He later claimed that he had missed only one lecture: see *The Later Letters of John Stuart Mill: 1849–1873* ed. by Francis E. Mineka and Dwight N. Lindley (Toronto: Toronto University Press, 1972) in *CWJSM*, XVI, at 1143.

[9] *Earlier Letters of John Stuart Mill: 1812–1848* in *CWJSM*, XII, at 51–3. For the failure of Austin to attract students to his lectures see Wilfrid E. Rumble, "Austin in the Classroom: Why were his Courses on Jurisprudence Unpopular?" (1996) XVII *Journal of Legal History* 17–39.

[10] *Earlier Letters of John Stuart Mill: 1812–1848* in *CWJSM*, XII, at 134.

[11] *Ibid.* at 141.

other of the persons of intellect he had known, although they had later come to differ on political matters when Austin had adopted an anti-democratic stance.[12]

Mill repaid his debt by taking every opportunity to review Austin's work, and by praising fulsomely the mind that had produced it, while lamenting the paucity of his output.[13] He reviewed *Province of Jurisprudence Determined* for *Tait's Edinburgh Magazine* in December 1832, a review which is considered in more detail below. He wrote a leading article for the *Morning Chronicle*, 6 February 1847, on Austin on Centralization, describing the work as "the production of an eminently clear and precise thinker," and as "valuable not only as a contribution to its special subject, but as a model to the philosophical student."[14] In 1859 Mill reviewed Austin's "A Plea for the Constitution" in "Recent Writers on Reform". While almost totally rejecting the arguments put forward by Austin, who was "probably the most intellectual man who is an enemy to further reform," Mill noted that Austin's *Province of Jurisprudence Determined* had "stepped at once into the very highest authority on what may be termed the metaphysics of law," and that it was regrettable "that a mind so fitted by capacity and acquirements for untying the hard knots of which the philosophy of law is full of, and which are the great impediment to simplicity and intelligibility in its practice, should have accomplished only a small part of the work to which his peculiar combination of endowments especially called him."[15] Finally, he produced a review of Sarah Austin's edition of *Lectures on Jurisprudence*, together with "On the Uses of the Study of Jurisprudence", for the *Edinburgh Review* in October 1863, which is also considered in more detail below. In his *Autobiography*, Mill wrote: "The publication of Mr. Austin's *Lectures on Jurisprudence* after his decease, gave me an opportunity of paying a deserved tribute to his memory and at the same time expressing some thoughts on a subject on which, in my old days of Benthamism, I had bestowed much study."[16]

12.2 Mill on Austin's Science of Jurisprudence

In the review of *Province of Jurisprudence Determined* of 1832, having suggested that, because it was a difficult book, few people would bother to read it seriously, Mill explained that Austin distinguished "Jurisprudence" from the "philosophy of

---

[12] Mill, *Autobiography and Literary Essays* in *CWJSM*, I, at 185–7.

[13] In the mid-1840s Mill encouraged Austin to publish a reprint of *Province of Jurisprudence Determined*, together with its continuation, but to no avail. See *The Earlier Letters of John Stuart Mill: 1812–1848*, in *CWJSM*, XIII, at 655, and 711–12.

[14] John Stuart Mill, *Newspaper Writings: January 1835–June 1847* ed. by Ann P. Robson and John M. Robson (Toronto: University of Toronto Press, 1986) in *CWJSM*, XXIV, 1062–6, esp. at 1063, 1066.

[15] John Stuart Mill, *Essays on Politics and Society* ed. by John M. Robson (Toronto: University of Toronto Press, 1977) in *CWJSM*, XIX, at 341–70, esp. at 343–4.

[16] Mill, *Autobiography and Literary Essays* in *CWJSM*, I, at 268.

Legislation." Both sciences dealt with "laws in the strict sense," that is "laws set to man by man, in the character of a political superior," but while the philosophy of legislation dealt with the goodness or badness of laws, jurisprudence was akin to a natural science. It took "the existence of laws as a matter of fact," and by a process of "analytical exposition" aimed to identify those properties that were "common to all or most systems of law."

> Hence, if we were to strip off from the arrangement and technical language of each system of law, whatever is purely accidental, and (as it may be termed) historical, having a reference solely to the peculiar history of the institution of the particular people; if we were to take the remainder, and regularize and correct it according to its own general conception and spirit; we should bring the nomenclature and arrangement of all systems of law existing in any civilized society, to something very nearly identical.

According to Austin, noted Mill, the task of the science of jurisprudence was to form "a distinct conception" of the "natural groups" that were found in legal systems and to give them "compact and precise names."

> When this is done, a commanding view may be taken of the detailed provisions of any existing body of law, the rights and duties which it establishes: they may be rendered *cognoscible*, as Mr. Bentham would say; a common framework is obtained, into the compartments of which all bodies of law may be distributed; and a systematic exposition might be given with comparative ease, either of one or of any number of legal systems, in parallel columns.

With an "expository law book" produced according to Austin's method, the legislator who wished to codify or reform a system of law would gain a clear view of existing rights and duties, and "have an arrangement, and a technical language ready made, which would be an excellent basis for him to start from in framing his own. For though classification," continued Mill, "is not made by nature, but is wholly an affair of convenience, one most important part of the convenience of any classification is, that it shall coincide, as far as possible, with the mode in which the ideas have a natural tendency to arrange themselves." The science of jurisprudence still needed to be created, and there was no one more qualified to do it than Austin, drawing on the one hand "from the Roman lawyers and their German successors," and on the other hand "from our own immortal Bentham." Mill pointed out, however, that *Province of Jurisprudence Determined* was no more than an introduction, "and even in his oral lectures, the Professor had not space to complete more than a small part of his intended scheme."

Mill went on to suggest that the value of Austin's work was not only "in the intrinsic merits of its contents," but even more so "as a logical discipline to the mind," characterized as it was by "close and precise thinking."[17] This was a theme that Mill

[17] John Stuart Mill, *Essays on Equality, Law, and Education* ed. by John M. Robson (Toronto: University of Toronto Press, 1984) in *CWJSM*, XXI, 51–60, esp. at 53–7.

took up in the review of *Lectures on Jurisprudence* which appeared over 30 years later. It was in the course of this second review, moreover, that Mill compared most fully the contributions of Bentham and Austin. In developing his argument that Austin's significance lay in his provision of "a practical logic for some of the higher departments of thought," Mill contrasted Austin's achievement with that of Bentham. He admitted that "posterity" would not assign to Austin "a position in the philosophy of law either equal or similar to that [of] his great predecessor, Bentham. That illustrious thinker has done, for this important department of human affairs, what can only be done once." Bentham had used a "battering ram" to demolish the "castle of unreason" that represented the existing law,[18] and had attempted to lay a "foundation" for "a rational science of law by direct consideration of the facts of human life." It had been left to Austin to search among the "ruins" of the castle for "such valuable materials as had been built in among rubbish," and, using "the builder's trowel," fashion them into "the new and workmanlike shape which fitted them for a better edifice." Changing the metaphor, Mill noted that the "untying of intellectual knots" was Austin's peculiar strength, as he himself had confessed. This untying consisted in

> The clearing up of the puzzles arising from complex combinations of ideas confusedly apprehended, and not analyzed into their elements; the building up of definite conceptions where only indefinite ones existed, and where the current phrases disguised and perpetuated the indefiniteness; the disentangling of the classifications and distinctions grounded on differences in things themselves, from those arising out of the mere accidents of their history, and, when disentangled, applying the distinctions (often for the first time) clearly, consistently, and uniformly…

Bentham, in contrast, did not untie knots, but "cut them." He preferred to jettison the past, "and begin anew at the beginning." Though Bentham was often led into errors because of his neglect of untying, "success has justified his choice," in that his "effect on the world has been greater, and therefore more beneficial."[19]

The efforts of Bentham and Austin, in Mill's view, were complementary. First, Austin could not have achieved what he did "if Bentham had not given the impulse and pointed out the way." Austin's work, continued Mill, "was of a different character from Bentham's work, and not less indispensable."[20] Second, Bentham's subject was legislation, which was broader than Austin's subject of jurisprudence. The latter was one part of, and instrumental to, the former. Bentham was concerned with the morality of law, whereas Austin was concerned with the "clearing up and defining the notions which the human mind is compelled to form, and the distinctions which it is necessitated to make, by the mere existence of a body of law of any

[18] This imagery echoes Blackstone's famous description of the English constitution as a Gothic castle: see William Blackstone, *Commentaries on the Laws of England*, 4 vols. (Oxford: Clarendon Press, 1765–9), III, at 268.

[19] Mill, *Essays on Equality, Law, and Education* in *CWJSM*, XXI, at 167 and 168.

[20] *Ibid.* at 167–8.

kind, or of a body of law taking cognizance of the concerns of a civilized and complicated state of society." Returning to a point he had made in the earlier review, Mill argued that only by means of "[a] clear and firm possession of these notions and distinctions" could "the legislator know how to give effect to his own ideas and his own purposes. Without it, however capable the legislator might be of conceiving good laws in the abstract, he could not possibly so word them, and so combine and arrange them, that they should really do the work intended and expected."[21]

Austin's purpose had been to identify what Mill termed the "organic structure" of laws. Every body of law had certain points of agreement with every other. Just as there were resemblances in their substantive provisions (all bodies of law being designed for the same world and the same human nature), there was also a common groundwork of general conceptions. Mill emphasized that such a view did not commit Austin to a form of realism or idealism,[22] for such conceptions were not pre-existent, but the product of abstraction. There were certain combinations of facts and ideas which every system of law was forced to recognize, and certain "modes of regarding facts" which every such system required. There were special names, exclusive to law, that denoted these facts and combinations of thoughts. [A] "well-made lexicon of the legal terms of all systems would be a complete science of jurisprudence: for the objects, whether natural or artificial, with which law has to do, must be the same objects which it also has occasion to name."[23] Invoking Bentham in this context, as he had in the earlier review, Mill noted that the same terminology, nomenclature, and principle of arrangement that would render one system of law "definite, clear, and (in Bentham's language) cognoscible," would do so for any other.[24]

The practical result of Austin's science of jurisprudence was to devise a legal terminology in which any system of law might be expressed, and a general scheme of arrangement according to which any system of law might be distributed. Jurisprudence, as thus understood, noted Mill, was not so much a science of law, but the application of logic to law.[25] Mill explained that Austin had built chiefly on the foundation of Roman law, though, he added, "some earnest students" would have liked "something more decidedly original." Austin's approach made sense, however, because the conceptions and distinctions that belonged to law in general must exist in all bodies of law, and by stripping away the accidental or historical peculiarities of a given system, the universal elements would be arrived at with more certainty than through any process of construction *a priori*. Austin, believing that

---

[21] *Ibid*. at 168–9.

[22] Mill perhaps feared that Austin might be interpreted in this way, or indeed that he had been more influenced by German thought than he wished to admit.

[23] Mill, *Essays on Equality, Law, and Education* in *CWJSM*, XXI, at 169–70.

[24] *Ibid*. at 171.

[25] *Ibid*. at 172.

the Roman jurists selected those universal conceptions and distinctions of the law best fitted for the purpose, had based his own arrangement on theirs.[26]

Although Mill approved of much of Austin's jurisprudence – including his analyses of will, motive, intention, negligence, sanction, and the distinction between civil and criminal law,[27] and his arguments in favour of codification[28] – he went on to put forward two fundamental criticisms.[29] In the first place, having explained that Austin had followed the Roman jurists in taking the classification of rights as the basis of his system, Mill argued that Austin's definition of a right, whereby a person was invested with a right whenever a legal duty was to be performed towards or in respect of that person, was inadequate. According to Mill, it was necessary to add two further elements: the notion of the desirableness of the right, and the fact that the person possessing the right was specially interested in enforcing the corresponding duty.[30]

In the second place, Mill criticized Austin's analysis of the parts of a *corpus juris* and their mutual relations. Having adhered, for the most part, to the classification and arrangement of the modern expositors of Roman law, albeit having rejected the public v. private law distinction, Austin had taken as his leading division the law of persons v. the law of things. In sub-dividing the law of things, Austin had adopted the Roman lawyers' principle of grounding the general division of the *corpus juris* upon a classification of rights. However, he had selected as a primary division of rights (and corresponding duties) a distinction between primary and sanctioning rights that had not been specially recognized by the writers on Roman law. Primary rights and duties had a legal existence only by virtue of their sanctions, but in order to apply these sanctions, legal provisions were necessary by which other rights were created and duties imposed. These secondary rights and duties were the subject-matter of penal law and the law of procedure.[31]

Mill argued that the Roman jurists, by taking the classification of rights as the ground for their entire system, had adopted a principle suited only to what Bentham

---

[26] *Ibid.* at 173. It is unclear why any one system should be more suited to the task than any other, especially if all that remained, following Bentham's demolition of the existing structures, were ruins. It might have been more plausible to say that a particular student might find his task facilitated by dealing with a system with which he was more familiar, than with one with which he was less familiar. To be fair to Mill, he did note that the advantage with Roman Law lay in the superior quality of the commentaries.

[27] *Ibid.* at 181–2.

[28] *Ibid.* at 192–4.

[29] A third point of disagreement was in relation to Austin's view that the technical part of legislation was incomparably more difficult than the ethical – that it was far easier to conceive what would be useful law, than to construct that same law in such a way that it accomplished the will of the law-giver – though Mill admitted that the "qualifications" necessary to accomplish the two tasks were different. See *ibid.* at 191–2.

[30] *Ibid.* at 179–81.

[31] *Ibid.* at 194–7.

called the substantive law, and only to the civil branch of that law, and in so doing had reversed the order of filiation of juristical conceptions, and, therefore, missed the true aim of scientific classification. Austin had repeated their mistake. But, Mill added, this was secondary. To find the absolutely best systematic order for a body of law would be the ultimate result of the science of jurisprudence. The main problem was to give clearness, precision, and consistency to the juristical conceptions themselves, and in this consisted the great permanent worth of Austin's speculations.[32] Nevertheless, Austin's classification, based upon rights, although logically correct, was "not the best fitted for the purpose." A natural classification should not only be logical, but should turn upon the most important features of the things classified. In other words, there were two "different principles of division" that had to be considered: first, where division was based on those properties that were "most important practically, by their bearing on human interests;" and second, where it was based on those that were "most important scientifically, as rendering it easiest to understand the subject – which will generally be the most *elementary* properties." In the case of law, the two "principles of division" coincided. Hence, the best foundation for the division of law was the different purposes for which the different portions of law were designed.[33] The problem for Austin's classification was that the purpose of law was not always the rights that it had created. This was true in the case of primary rights, but in the law of civil injuries, crimes, and procedure, where there were rights (Austin's sanctioning rights), laws did not exist for the sake of these rights – on the contrary, the rights existed for the sake of the laws. The purpose of the law here was not the creation of rights, but the application of sanctions, and thus to give effect to rights created by other departments of law. The "filiation of ideas" (from simple to more complex) was: (1) primary rights, with correlative duties; (2) sanctions; (3) laws determining the mode of applying sanctions; (4) rights and duties established by these laws, for the sake of, and necessary to, the application of sanctions. The classification according to rights might be suitable to the civil code, but not to the penal code and the procedure code. The subject of the penal code and the procedure code should be sanctions. Hence, the primary division of law was into: (1) civil law, containing the definition and classification of rights and duties; (2) the law of wrongs and remedies, sub-divided into penal law (offences and punishments) and the law of procedure. This was not, added Mill, merely his own opinion, but that of Bentham, James Mill, and authors of all modern codes.[34] Furthermore, Austin's classification grounded wholly on rights failed to account for duties for which there were no corresponding rights, and, more importantly, it interpolated penal law and procedure

[32] *Ibid*. at 174.

[33] Mill here seems to be adopting the former division, despite his claim that the two divisions coincided.

[34] Mill, *Essays on Equality, Law, and Education* in *CWJSM*, XXI, at 198–200. The phrase "not best fitted for the purpose" appears at *ibid*. at 174.

between the civil law of things and the law of status, two subjects so allied that Austin himself could not find any scientific difference between them. The two portions of law dealt with the same general ideas, namely rights and their definitions, and yet one was put at the beginning of the *corpus juris* and the other at the end, and between them the law dealing with offences, punishments, judicature, and judicial procedure. Mill speculated that Austin would not have approved of this mode of arrangement had he managed to finish his course of lectures.[35]

12.3 Mill, Bentham, and Austin on the Logic of the Law

In both reviews, Mill suggested that Austin had made a startlingly original and important contribution to the science of jurisprudence. He had adopted Bentham's ideas as his starting-point, drawn on his study of Roman Law, and in consequence of his application of logic to the study of jurisprudence (a logic which bore striking similarities to that developed by Mill himself in *A System of Logic*) had gone on to make significant discoveries through his analysis and classification of legal concepts. As Mill later wrote in his *Autobiography*, Austin "had made Bentham's best ideas his own, and added much to them from other sources and from his own mind."[36] Yet in the later review, Mill put forward devastating criticisms of Austin's conclusions. Having explained that Austin had used the notion of a right as his central concept, he argued that Austin's definition of a right was inadequate. Having explained that Austin had built his structure of a body of law upon the Roman model, he argued that this scheme was flawed. In this latter case, and elsewhere as we shall see, Mill was, in effect, endorsing Bentham's views, rather than those of Austin. There is an apparent incongruity between Mill's statements concerning Austin's superiority to Bentham in terms of his analysis and classification of legal concepts, and the substance of his criticisms of Austin's conclusions where he allied himself with Bentham.

In the later review, having recognized that Bentham had established the parameters of legal study, Mill went on to suggest that Austin had invented, or at least developed, a new subject that he called "the logic of the law," involving the conceptual analysis of legal terms. Bentham had pointed out the ends to which the law should be directed, but had not provided the building materials out of which such a structure could be created. This latter had been Austin's achievement. It is surprising that Mill should ignore Bentham's lifelong concern with the application of logic to law, and in particular with the definition of key legal terms. Mill could not have been unaware of this concern, or indeed with any significant aspects of Bentham's

---

[35] *Ibid.* at 200–1.

[36] Mill, *Autobiography and Literary Essays* in *CWJSM*, I, at 67.

legal thought, given the nature of his upbringing and education, and his editing of Bentham's massive *Rationale of Judicial Evidence*.[37]

Bentham had set out an agenda for a work on what Austin came to term the science of jurisprudence in the "Preface" written for the delayed publication of *An Introduction to the Principles of Morals and Legislation* in 1789.[38] This was, of course, the text that Austin and Mill had studied together in 1822. In discussing what he confessed were "imperfections" in *An Introduction to the Principles of Morals and Legislation* (which had originally been conceived as an introduction to a penal code), Bentham explained that, "the analytical distinctions relative to the classification of offences would, according to his present views, be transferred to a separate treatise, in which the system of legislation is considered solely in respect of its form: in other words, in respect of its *method* and *terminology*."[39] This treatise would form the final one of the ten headings under which he intended to present the general principles on which a complete body of law would be based. It would be entitled:

> Plan of a body of law, complete in all its branches, in respect of its *form*; in other words, in respect of its method and terminology; including a view of the origination and connexion of the ideas expressed by the short list of terms, the exposition of which contains all that can be said with propriety to belong to the head of *universal jurisprudence*.

He then added the following note: "such as obligation, right, power, possession, title, exemption, immunity, franchise, privilege, nullity, validity, and the like." While the complete body of law itself would need to be adapted to the particular needs of the state in question, the general principles would be applicable to all.[40]

In the first two sections of *Of the Limits of the Penal Branch of Jurisprudence*, which was written as a continuation of *An Introduction to the Principles of Morals and Legislation*, but which was not published in any form until 1945, Bentham divided jurisprudence (or more strictly books of jurisprudence, since jurisprudence was a fictitious entity) into the study of what the law is, or expository jurisprudence, and the study of what the law ought to be, or censorial jurisprudence, or the art of legislation. Expository jurisprudence was either authoritative, where it was the product of the legislator himself, or unauthoritative, where it was the product of any person other than the legislator. There were then five further "modifications" of which jurisprudence was "susceptible," one of which was "the extent of the laws in question in point of dominion." This gave rise to the distinction between local and universal jurisprudence, depending upon whether the subject-matter was the laws of

[37] Jeremy Bentham, *Rationale of Judicial Evidence. Specially applied to English Practice* ed. by John Stuart Mill (London: Hunt & Clarke, 1827) 5 vols.

[38] The bulk of the text had been first printed in 1780.

[39] Jeremy Bentham, *An Introduction to the Principles of Morals and Legislation* ed. by J. H. Burns and H. L. A. Hart (London: Athlone Press, 1970) in *CWJB*, at 4.

[40] *Ibid.* at 6 and fn.

a particular nation or set of nations, or of all nations whatsoever. No two nations agreed exactly in their laws, either in substance or more especially in form, that is in the "strings of words" in which they were conceived. Universal jurisprudence, therefore, had "very narrow limits." It was in censorial jurisprudence that there was "the greatest room for disquisitions that apply to the circumstances of all nations alike," in that there were "some leading points … in respect of which the laws of all civilized nations might, without inconvenience, be the same." There could, however, be no such thing as authoritative expository universal jurisprudence (there was no universal legislator), nor any such thing as unauthoritative expository universal jurisprudence insofar as it dealt with the substance of the laws. "To be susceptible of an universal application, all that a book of the expository kind can have to treat of, is the import of words: to be, strictly speaking, universal, it must confine itself to terminology." "[A]mong the words that are appropriated to the subject of law," stated Bentham, "there are some that in all languages are pretty exactly correspondent to one another: which comes to the same thing nearly as if they were the same. Of this stamp, for example, are those which correspond to the words *power, right, obligation, liberty,* and many others." Hence, in the course of *Of the Limits of the Penal Branch of Jurisprudence*, Bentham, perhaps understating the point, noted that he had occasionally interspersed definitions which might "be considered as matter belonging to the head of universal jurisprudence."[41]

One key element in Bentham's universal expository jurisprudence (the "form" of law) – and indeed for Austin's command theory of law, though neither Austin nor Mill seem to have explicitly acknowledged it – was the logic of the will, which, he claimed in *An Introduction to the Principles of Morals and Legislation*, he had invented:

> Of this logic of the will, the science of *law*, considered in respect of its *form*, is the most considerable branch, – the most important application. It is, to the art of legislation, what the science of anatomy is to the art of medicine: with this difference, that the subject of it is what the artist has to work *with*, instead of being what he has to operate *upon*. Nor is the body politic less in danger from a want of acquaintance with the one science, than the body natural from ignorance in the other.[42]

While the logic of the understanding, associated with Aristotle, was concerned with argumentation, the logic of the will was concerned with imperation, or more broadly with "sentences expressive of volition." In relation to government, the branch of the language of volition that dealt with imperation was particularly applicable to legislation, while that which dealt with interrogation, being concerned with the collection of verbal information, was useful to both the legislative and executive departments.[43] In *Of the Limits of the Penal Branch of Jurisprudence* (there is no evidence that either Austin or Mill saw the work in manuscript), Bentham developed

---

[41] Jeremy Bentham, *Of the Limits of the Penal Branch of Jurisprudence* ed. by Philip Schofield (Oxford: Clarendon Press, 2010) in *CWJB*, at 16–18.

[42] Bentham, *Introduction to the Principles of Morals and Legislation* in *CWJB*, at 9.

[43] *Ibid.* at 299–300 fn.

in detail the relationships between the various aspects of the will – namely command, prohibition, permission, and non-permission – that could be adopted by the legislator, with the explicit purpose of bringing clarity, precision, and consistency to a body of law.[44]

As well as the logic of the will, Bentham had invented a series of logical techniques – archetypation, phraseoplerosis, and paraphrasis – in order to define, or more precisely provide expositions of, abstract names, which he termed names of "fictitious entities." In *A Fragment on Government*, published in 1776, Bentham had, for instance, presented an exposition of the terms duty and right, using his revolutionary method of paraphrasis, which he distinguished from the Aristotelian procedure of definition *per genus et differentiam*, and Blackstone's use of it, which, he argued, was inapplicable to such abstract terms. Hence, Bentham stated, "what you have a right to have me made to do (understand a political right) is that which I am liable, upon a requisition made on your behalf, to be *punished* for not doing."[45] Paraphrasis was the technique that he adopted for his exposition of law in *Of the Limits of the Penal Branch of Jurisprudence*,[46] and indeed for his exposition of the principle of utility, and terms such as sanction, intention, and motive, in *An Introduction to the Principles of Morals and Legislation*.[47] In *Of the Limits of the Penal Branch of Jurisprudence* he went on to provide expositions of the names of such fictitious entities as power, right, duty, conveyance, and contract. In view of Austin's definition of a right in terms of service, it is interesting to note that the link between rights and services was a feature of Bentham's thought. Where the law imposed a duty of the extra-regarding kind (as opposed to a duty of the self-regarding kind), stated Bentham, it conferred upon another person a right to services, in other words "a right to services to be render'd by the party on whom the duty is imposed: the doctrine of services, therefore, extends itself … over little less than the whole body of the law." The nature of the duty and service depended upon the nature of the act which the law commanded, or, what came to the same thing, on

[44] Bentham, *Of the Limits of the Penal Branch of Jurisprudence* in *CWJB*, at 115–41. Reading Mill's reviews, one would think that there had been no such attempt prior to Austin.

[45] See *A Comment on the Commentaries and A Fragment on Government* ed. by J. H. Burns and H. L. A. Hart (London: The Athlone Press, 1977) in *CWJB*, at 494–6 fn.

[46] Bentham, *Of the Limits of the Penal Branch of Jurisprudence* in *CWJB*, at 24–5: "A law may be defined an assemblage of sings *declarative* of a *volition* conceived or adopted by the *sovereign* in a state, concerning the conduct to be observed in a certain *case* by a certain person or class of persons, who in the case in question are, or are supposed to be, subject to his power: such volition trusting for its accomplishment to the expectation of certain events which it is intended such declaration should upon occasion be a means of bringing to pass, and the prospect of which it is intended should act as a motive upon those whose conduct is in question." The notion of a law is explained in terms of persons performing actions that result in changes to the physical world, whether internal or external to those same or other persons.

[47] Bentham, *Introduction to the Principles of Morals and Legislation* in *CWJB*, at 11, 34–7, 84–9, and 96–124.

the nature of the opposite act which, by prohibiting it, the law made into an offence. The party favoured might be an individual, a subordinate class, or the community, and hence the correspondent offence might be private, semi-public, or public.[48] This framework provided the basis for Bentham's division of offences which formed the organizing principle of his penal code.[49] In a related discussion on the nature of services, Bentham noted that services could be either positive or negative, that is either active services or services of forbearance. Again they could be classified according to the faculties by which they were performed (mind or body), and according to the object on which they were performed. In this latter case, the object must be either a person or a thing, hence services might be distinguished into services *in personam* and services *in rem*. "Each of these classes," continued Bentham, "again may be divided indefinitely according to the nature of the persons or things on which the acts in question are to be performed, according to the natures and tendencies of those acts which are to be performed, and according to the occasion or circumstances in which they are to be performed." He added that the division of services found in Roman law between personal and prædial was "ambiguous and unexhaustive," and did not "quadrate" with his own division.[50] It is worth noting that Austin not only followed Bentham in relating rights to services, but also in adopting the distinction between rights or services *in personam* as opposed to rights or services *in rem*.

It was in relation to the formulation of the structure of the *corpus juris* that Mill had invoked the notion of a natural classification of jurisprudence in order to criticize Austin's choice of a classification based upon rights. Mill was here echoing Bentham, who had, in *A Fragment on Government*, first distinguished between a technical and a natural classification of jurisprudence. A technical classification was based on "reasons peculiar to the *art*, peculiar to the profession." Technical reasons were the product of "Men of Law, corrupted by interests, or seduced by illusions."[51] In contrast, "that arrangement of the materials of any science may … be termed a *natural* one, which takes such properties to characterize them by, as men in general are, by the common constitution of man's *nature*, disposed to attend to: such, in other words, as *naturally*, that is readily, engage, and firmly fix the attention of any one to whom they are pointed out." Jurisprudence dealt with such actions as formed the subject-matter of law, and the property in actions which most readily engaged and fixed the attention of an observer was their tendency to promote happiness (utility) or mischief: "With respect then to such actions in particular as are among the objects

[48] Bentham, *Of the Limits of the Penal Branch of Jurisprudence* in *CWJB*, at 79–80.

[49] Bentham, *Introduction to the Principles of Morals and Legislation* in *CWJB*, at 187–280.

[50] Bentham, *Of the Limits of the Penal Branch of Jurisprudence* in *CWJB*, at 300–3. Bentham arguably went much farther than Austin in developing an exposition of legal concepts; there is no argument about the extent of their respective use of them in producing codes of law. To take just one example: Bentham had virtually completed his massive Constitutional Code by his death in 1832.

[51] Bentham, *Fragment on Government* in *CWJB*, at 417 and fn.

of the Law, to point out to a man the *utility* of them or the mischievousness, is the only way to make him see *clearly* that property of them which every man is in search of; the only way, in short, to give him *satisfaction*." The science of jurisprudence should, therefore, be arranged according to the principle of utility. "Governed in this manner by a principle that is recognized by all men, the same arrangement that would serve for the jurisprudence of any one country, would serve with little variation for that of any other."[52] It was, therefore, the recognition of the principle of utility that made possible a universal censorial jurisprudence. Under a natural arrangement, argued Bentham, laws would be characterized according to "the nature of the several *modes of conduct* which, by prohibiting, they constitute *offences*." The mischievousness of a bad law, that is a law that prohibited a mode of conduct (Bentham used the phrase "mode of conduct" in order to include omissions or forbearances as well as acts), would be detected by the difficulty of finding a place for it. "The *synopsis* of such an arrangement" – he continued – "would at once be a compendium of *expository* and of *censorial* jurisprudence …. Such a synopsis, in short, would be at once a map, and that an universal one, of Jurisprudence as it *is*, and a slight but comprehensive sketch of what it *ought to be*." In other words, such a map would combine universal expository jurisprudence with censorial jurisprudence. This was because the names of the classes into which the laws were arranged would indicate the reasons for their existence. Such reasons could consist only in either the good produced by the mode of conduct which the law enjoined, or the mischief produced by the mode of conduct which it prohibited. The only consequences of a law that men were interested in were pain and pleasure:

> In the synopsis then of that sort of arrangement which alone deserves the name of a natural one, terms such as these, terms which if they can be said to belong to any science, belong rather to Ethics than to Jurisprudence, even than to universal Jurisprudence, will engross the most commanding stations.[53]

The principle of utility, then, made possible not only censorial jurisprudence, but also universal expository jurisprudence.

The structure of the *corpus juris* which Mill went on to describe as superior to that put forward by Austin was, as he himself admitted, that advocated by Bentham, James Mill, and others. It would have been fairer to say that it had been invented by Bentham. Bentham's primary division of a body of law was into its substantive branch and its adjective branch or law of judicial procedure. The substantive law could itself be divided into a private branch and a public or constitutional branch, or alternatively divided into the civil and penal branches.[54] The civil branch of law was

[52] *Ibid*. at 415–16.

[53] *Ibid*. at 416–18.

[54] "First Lines of a proposed Code of Law for any Nation complete and rationalized", in Jeremy Bentham, "Legislator of the World: Writings on Codification, Law, and Education" ed. by Philip Schofield and Jonathan Harris (Oxford: Clarendon Press 1998) in *CWJB*, at 191–2. Bentham also referred to the remuneratory branch, which operated by assigning rewards.

concerned with the distribution of rights and duties (with the broader aim of promoting subsistence, abundance, security, and equality), while the purpose of the penal branch was "the giving execution and effect" to the civil branch, that is by assigning punishment (the purpose of which was compensation and prevention of future misdeeds) to those actions designated as offences.[55] The purpose of the law of judicial procedure, which constituted the adjective branch of law, was to give "execution and effect" to the substantive law, by means of "1. Right decision. 2. Execution conformable."[56] Finally, the purpose of the law concerning the judicial establishment was to give "execution and effect" to both the substantive and adjective branches, but "more particularly and immediately" to the law concerning judicial procedure "by making provision for the apt appointment and, in case of inaptitude, the eventual removal of those functionaries to whom the powers necessary for the giving execution and effect to the Law of Judicial Procedure are attributed."[57] Thus Bentham's division of the *corpus juris* (a term he used) into civil law, penal law, the law of judicial procedure, and the law of the judicial establishment, was precisely that fourfold division adopted by Mill when criticizing Austin's rights-based conception of the *corpus juris*.

Bentham had, therefore, not only conceived of the sort of treatise that Mill argued that Austin had attempted, but had in fact undertaken the task, and had invented a new branch of logic dealing with the will, and had developed original techniques of linguistic exposition in the logic of the understanding, with which to perform it. He had, moreover, produced a systematic arrangement of the *corpus juris* that was, in Mill's view, "the most fitted for the purpose."

12.4 On Logical Method and Legal Positivism

It is possible that personal gratitude and remembrance of an important friendship led Mill to bestow such unqualified praise on Austin's mental capacities, at the expense to some degree at least of Bentham's reputation. Mill's friendship with the Austins began to deteriorate from around 1848. Two factors are cited: first, diverging political views; and second, Harriet Taylor's dislike of Sarah, and Mill's impression that Sarah had gossiped about his relationship with Harriet.[58] In a passage written for, but not published in, his *Autobiography*, Mill gave a scathing account of Sarah, saying that she never cared for anyone beyond the surface, though she was quite ready to be friendly or helpful. She professed Benthamic opinions when Austin did, and German opinions when he did, but did not herself ever hold anything

[55] *Ibid.* at 208 and 209.

[56] *Ibid.* at 223–4.

[57] *Ibid.* at 229–30.

[58] *The Later Letters of John Stuart Mill: 1849–1873* in *CWJSM*, XIV, at 4 fn.

deserving the name of opinions. She slid into opinions agreeable to the well-to-do classes.[59] In the context of Mill's views on character, this was a damning indictment of a person who had once been like a second mother to him. Following Austin's death on 17 December 1859, Mill avoided as far as possible any contact with Sarah.[60] Nevertheless, this did not affect his regard for Austin. Shortly after Austin's death, Mill wrote to Janet Duff-Gordon, the Austins' granddaughter, that Austin was "one of the men whom I most valued, and to whom I have been morally and intellectually most indebted." He continued:

> I believe that few persons, so little known to the common world, have left so high a reputation with the instructed few; and though superficially he may seem to have accomplished little in comparison with his powers, few have contributed more by their individual influence and their conversation to the formation and growth of a number of the most active minds of this generation.
>
> For myself I have always regarded my early knowledge of him as one of the fortunate circumstances of my life.[61]

On first glance at least, in the important work of reconstruction through the development of a precise and clear universal legal vocabulary, according to Mill, the true master was Austin, and not Bentham. Yet while on the one hand praising Austin's abilities, on the other hand Mill in substance implicitly acknowledged the superiority of Bentham's conclusions. On a deeper reading, it seems that Mill was far more of a Benthamite than an Austinian.

Yet it may not simply have been gratitude and friendship that produced the apparent incongruity in these reviews. Mill's reviews may have reflected a tension between, on the one hand, the logical methods that he thought appropriate, and, on the other hand, the value of the practical conclusions drawn from those methods. Mill perhaps recognized a greater similarity between his own logical method and that of Austin than between his own and that of Bentham. Bentham did not think that "abstraction," based on conceptual analysis, was the proper logical operation in the exposition of key legal terms. For Bentham, it was by means of paraphrasis, by which propositions containing abstract names – or the names of fictitious entities – were replaced by propositions which contained concrete names – or the names of real entities – that terms such as right, duty, power, and law could be defined.[62] Mill was able to assimilate Austin's method of definition – based on a sophisticated application of the Aristotelian method of definition *per genus et differentiam* – but

---

[59] Mill, *Autobiography and Literary Essays* in *CWJSM*, I, at 186.

[60] Mill told Helen Taylor that a letter had arrived from Sarah "which seems to involve the unpleasant necessity of writing to her": *The Later Letters of John Stuart Mill* in *CWJSM*, XV, at 670–1. When supplying his lecture notes for Sarah's projected edition of *Lectures on Jurisprudence*, and which, following her death, finally appeared in 1869, he preferred to deal with Sarah's nephew Henry Reeve, rather than directly with Sarah herself: *ibid.* at 822 and fn.

[61] *Ibid.* at 658.

[62] See Philip Schofield, *Utility and Democracy: the Political Thought of Jeremy Bentham* (Oxford: Oxford University Press, 2006) at 1–27.

not Bentham's. Hence the ambivalence towards Bentham found in Mill's reviews of Austin perhaps reflects both his approval of Austin's method as being closer to his own than that of Bentham, and at the same time his acknowledgement of the superiority of Bentham's conclusions. Perhaps this was what Mill meant when he said that Bentham had cut knots – he had produced the right answers, but not by using the proper means.[63]

A final comment may be made in relation to legal positivism. When criticizing Austin's analysis of the notion of a right, Mill argued that Austin had overlooked the property of the "desirableness" of the right. When criticizing Austin's classification of a body of law, Mill argued that Austin had not produced the best possible classification in that he had overlooked those properties that affected "human interests." Both criticisms were concerned with the value or utility of Austin's analysis, and hence introduced ethical considerations. Using Bentham's terminology, Mill was drawing on censorial jurisprudence in order to criticize Austin's universal expository jurisprudence. If Austin was committed to a strict distinction between expository or descriptive jurisprudence (law as it is) as an ethically neutral activity, and censorial or prescriptive jurisprudence (law as it ought to be) as the application of ethics to law, then he might retort that Mill had confused the two branches of the subject, despite explicitly accepting the validity of the distinction. Moreover, it might be said that this was a distinction that characterized Bentham's approach to law. Hence Mill was, in fact, distancing himself from the legal positivism of both Bentham and Austin. Bentham, however, did not draw a strict line between jurisprudence as a descriptive and jurisprudence as a prescriptive activity. For Bentham, universal expository jurisprudence—the definition of legal terms—not only had its utility, but could be performed for better or for worse. H. L. A. Hart famously aligned himself with the utilitarian tradition of jurisprudence, which, he claimed, consisted in the command theory of law, the analysis of legal terms, and the distinction between law as it is and law as it ought to be. This latter distinction, in Hart's view, was equivalent to a conceptual separation between law and morality, which

[63] In his "Inaugural Address delivered to the University of St. Andrews" in 1867 (*Essays on Equality, Law, and Education*, now in *CWJSM*, XXI, at 245–6), Mill put forward a more complementary view of Bentham in comparison with Austin. Having defined the scope of jurisprudence according to Bentham's broader, as opposed to Austin's narrower, understanding of the subject, Mill argued that at the head of the "writers of our own or of a very recent time" who had provided "admirable helps" in the study of Jurisprudence stood Bentham, "undoubtedly the greatest master who ever devoted the labour of a life to let in light on the subject of law; and who is the more intelligible to non-professional persons, because, as his way, he builds up the subject from its foundation in the facts of human life, and shows by careful consideration of ends and means, what law might and ought to be, in deplorable contrast with what it is." Here, then, Mill praised Bentham for building up the subject from its foundation, rather than for merely demolishing existing legal systems. He went on to describe the work of two other "enlightened jurists," who had made "contributions of two kinds," the one being Maine in *Ancient Law*, and the other Austin. In *Lectures on Jurisprudence*. Austin had taken the Roman Law for his basis, identified "the principles and distinctions which are of general applicability, and employs the powers and resources of a most precise and analytic mind to give those principles and distinctions a philosophic basis, grounded in the universal reason of mankind, and not in mere technical convenience."

in turn is the defining feature of post-Hartian legal positivism. If there was a utilitarian tradition of jurisprudence which was committed to an insistence on the conceptual separation of law and morality, then whether Austin adhered to it I leave an open question, but Bentham, like Mill, did not.[64]

[64] See Philip Schofield, "Jeremy Bentham and H. L. A. Hart's 'Utilitarian Tradition in Jurisprudence'" (2010) I *Jurisprudence* 147–67.

Chapter 13
Austin and the Germans

Michael Lobban

13.1 Introduction

John Austin's work divides into two parts. The first part is made up of *The Province of Jurisprudence Determined*, the first six of his course of lectures at the University of London. These were published separately, first in 1832, and then again in 1861, 1954 edited by Herbert L. A. Hart, and 1995, edited by Wilfrid E. Rumble. The second part was made up of the rest of the course of lectures, and consisted in large part of fragments brought together by his long-suffering wife Sarah, with the help of John Stuart Mill, and ultimately under the editorship of Robert Campbell. These lectures have had a shorter publishing history, being published first in 1863, reaching a revised fifth edition in 1911, and a further abridged edition in 1920. The two parts enjoyed different fates: while the first part engaged generations of jurists with the problem of Austin's command theory, and provided the occasion for Hart to re-present English positivism in modern form, the second part found its heyday in the decades after their posthumous publication, as a dry-as-dust toolbox for a generation of law students seeking to put order to the chaos of the common law.[1] Yet they were part of a common project. John Austin set out this project in the *Outline* to his course of lectures, first published in 1831. The first part was to determine the province of jurisprudence. The second was to distinguish general jurisprudence, or the philosophy of positive law, from the particular jurisprudence, or system of positive law pertaining in any one place; and to explain "certain notions which

[1] On the reception of Austin, see Wilfrid E. Rumble, *Doing Austin Justice: the Reception of John Austin's Philosophy of Law in Nineteenth-Century England* (London: Continuum Press, 2005).

M. Lobban (✉)
Queen Mary School of Law, University of London, E14NS London, UK
e-mail: m.j.lobban@gmul.ac.uk

M. Freeman and P. Mindus (eds.), *The Legacy of John Austin's Jurisprudence*, Law and Philosophy Library 103, DOI 10.1007/978-94-007-4830-9_13,

meet us at every step."[2] This involved abstracting from particular contexts, to uncover what he called "principles notions and distinctions" which might be esteemed "necessary," insofar as "we cannot imagine coherently a system of law (or a system of law as evolved in a refined community), without conceiving them as constituent parts of it."[3]

Just as there were two aspects to Austin's work, so there were two different influences behind it. Two autobiographical quotations are telling. On the one hand the young Austin declared that he had "no violent desire for any other object than that of disseminating [Bentham's] doctrines."[4] On the other, he told his wife, "I ought to have been a schoolman of the twelfth century – or a German professor." Sarah added, "[t]he position of such illustrious and revered teachers as Hugo and Savigny seemed to him the most enviable in the world."[5] It was from Gustav Hugo's work, *Lehrbuch des Naturrechts, als einer Philosophie des positiven Rechts*, that Austin took the subtitle of his lectures, "the Philosophy of Positive Law." As is well known, he spent the winter of 1827–1828 in Bonn, where he prepared his lectures in the city of Ferdinand Mackeldey and August Wilhelm Hefter, and studied with a young German *Privatdozent*. When Sarah donated John's library to the Inner Temple, she donated textbooks by Mackeldey and Hefter, as well as Pandectist treatises by a number of other German authors, including Savigny, Thibaut and Hugo.

These rival influences took the two parts of Austin's work in different directions. Whereas the first six lectures were inspired by an English, positivist view of law, derived from his reading of Thomas Hobbes and Jeremy Bentham, the rest of the lectures were inspired by his reading of German Pandectism. If the English influences shaped Austin's theory of what law *was*, the German ones taught him how it *worked*. Yet the two parts did not sit easily together. When it came to exploring how law developed, in the second part of his work, Austin presented a view of law which was in many ways hard to reconcile with his command theory, for it seemed to suggest that the courts enforced a system of rights which did not directly owe their origin to the commands either of the sovereign or his judges. The contrasting directions taken in the different parts of the work may explain the differences in the later reception of Austin. Later nineteenth century English jurists who were sometimes uncomfortable with the command theory of the *Province* found much that was congenial in the analytical jurisprudence of the later lectures.[6] Austin's style of analysis also seemed to open the path to the formalist approaches of late nineteenth century American legal writers, for whom law was to be developed by scientific jurists rather than by

---

[2] John Austin, *Lectures on Jurisprudence, or The Philosophy of Positive Law* ed. by Robert Campbell (4th edition, rev., London: John Murray, 1873) at 32–4.

[3] *Ibid.* at 1108.

[4] Jeremy Bentham, *The Correspondence of Jeremy Bentham* ed. by Stephen Conway, vol. 7 (Oxford: Clarendon Press, 1989) at 336–7.

[5] Austin, *Lectures*, *supra* note 2 at 13.

[6] See Michael Lobban, "Legal Theory and Judge-Made Law in England, 1850–1920" (2011) 40 *Quaderni Fiorentini* 553–94.

legislators. By contrast, twentieth century philosophers of law, such as Hart, directed their attention to the *Province* and its command theory, finding little to comment on in the later lectures.

13.2 German Jurisprudence in the 1820s

If John Austin admired the Germans' learning of Roman law, he felt that they erred in mixing law and morality. While praising Hugo for speaking of natural law as a philosophy of positive law, he criticized the German for blending general jurisprudence with "the portion of deontology or ethics, which is styled the science of legislation."[7] The cardinal distinction which Austin sought to make in the first part of his work was that between law and morals, or rather, the distinction of that which *is* from that which *ought to be*.[8] For Austin, the jurist was only concerned with the law as it existed. This was essential information for both lawyer and citizen: for it was this which allowed law to be identified. Justice, at least in the legal sense, was determined solely by the sovereign's will. In making these points, Austin was aligning himself with the position taken by Thomas Hobbes and Jeremy Bentham, both of whom sought to establish that it was not legitimate to challenge the validity of a sovereign's law by reference to a distinct set of moral reasonings.

Bentham's position was first set out in the 1770s, in his attack on Blackstone's natural law arguments.[9] Yet by the time Austin had arrived in Bonn, the brand of natural law which Bentham saw in Blackstone's work – one which mixed up ethics and law – had also been discredited in Germany. The deductive natural law tradition which had dominated much eighteenth-century German legal thought – and which was associated most clearly with the work of Christian Wolff – had come under attack both from Kant and the historical school of jurists led by Hugo. Kant had shown that one had to distinguish between ethical standards, which were not enforced by any external authority but were "internal" matters of conscience, and legal standards which were enforced by external authority. Within the latter sphere, as Mathias Reimann has explained, Kant further distinguished between:

> Legal philosophy determining ideal standards (the province of the philosopher applying pure reason) and the science of positive law (the realm of the jurist drawing on experience).[10]

---

[7] Austin, *Lectures*, *supra* note 2 at 33 fn.

[8] *Ibid.* at 176–7.

[9] Bentham did this in his *Fragment on Government*, the 1776 Dublin edition of which was in Austin's library, as well as in his unpublished *Comment on the Commentaries*, which Austin may not have seen (*A Comment on the Commentaries and a Fragment on Government* ed. by James H. Burns and Herbert L. A. Hart (London: Athlone Press, 1977).

[10] For a useful summary of Kant's criticism of the old natural lawyers, see Mathias Reimann, "Nineteenth Century German Legal Science" (1989–90) 31 *Boston College Law Review* 837–97 at 842–6.

This science became a distinct one, to be taught in law schools rather than philosophy faculties.[11] It was to be empirical, focusing on the actual rules of law enforced, but also systematic, insofar as it sought to put them into a clear order.

Early nineteenth century German jurists agreed that the defining feature of law was that it was a coercive system enforced by the state. One such jurist was Niels Nikolaus Falck, an 1825 edition of whose *Juristische Encyclopädie* was in Austin's possession while he prepared his lectures. Falck was keen to separate juridical science from moral philosophy. As he explained, while reason could teach us to know the moral nature of man, and the duties which arose from this moral nature, it could not show us how to draw the line between moral rules and legal ones. When writers such as Grotius discussed "perfect" rights and obligations which could be protected by force, they failed (he argued) to look at the connection between natural law and positive law, and so left it unclear whether their discussions were a branch of practical philosophy, or moral theory, and whether their principles should be used by judges in developing the law.[12] Reason alone could not identify the distinguishing feature of legal rights and obligations. For Falck, the distinguishing feature of legal rules was that they were enforced through force by an exterior body – the state.[13] "By law," he stated at the outset of his work, "we understand a collection of principles, regulations and rules, by which men living in a state or in civic society are subjected, so that they can in case of need be constrained to obedience through the use of force."[14]

When Austin criticized jurists such as Hugo, it was not for mixing up law and private ethics or morality. It was because he mingled together the empirical study of positive law with the study of what that law should be – which for Austin was the

[11] See Paolo Becchi, "German Legal Science: the Crisis of Natural Law Theory, the Historicisms, and 'Conceptual Jurisprudence'" in *A History of the Philosophy of Law in the Civil Law World 1600–1900* ed. by Damiano Canale, Paolo Grossi and Hasso Hoffmann, vol. 9 of *A Treatise of Legal Philosophy and General Jurisprudence*, directed by Enrico Pattaro (Dordrecht: Springer, 2009) at 185–224.

[12] Niels Nikolaus Falck, *Juristische Encyclopädie* (2nd ed., Kiel: August Heffe, 1825) at 87 § 49: "Über das Verhältniß des Naturrechts zum positiven Rechte erklärten sich Mehrere gar nicht, und ließen es unentschieden, ob diese Wissenschaft bloß als ein Theil der praktischen Philosophie, als eine Art von Moral anzusehen sey, oder ob die aufgestellten Grundsätze von dem Richter zur Ergänzung des positiven Rechts anzuwerden wären."

[13] Falck, *Encyclopädie*, *supra* note 12 at 91 § 51: "Wenn also der gesuchte Unterschied der Pflichten nicht in den Geboten der Vernunft enthalten ist, so muß er nothwendig durch eine äußere Veranstaltung begründet seyn, welche dadurch daß für die Erfüllung einiger Pflichten eine Gewährleistung möglich gemacht wird, diesen Pflichten einen besondern Charakter ertheilt. Eine solche äußere Anstalt ist der Staat, und der Rechtsbegriff kann daher nur im Staate oder mit Rücksicht auf die Idee dieses Instituts entstehen."

[14] *Ibid.* at 4 § 1: "Unter Recht aber verstehen wir einen Inbegriff von Grundsätzen, Vorschriften und Regeln, denen die in einem Staate oder einer bürgerlichen Gesellschaft lebenden Menschen dergestalt unterworfen sind, daß sie nöthigenfalls durch Anwendung von Zwang zur Befolgung derselben angehalten werden können."

subject of the science of legislation. Austin was right to note that Hugo's approach to the philosophy of positive law entailed looking at more than just what the law was. As Hugo put it,

> While the immediately practical, trade-like, as it is correctly called, knowledge of law goes only to the question What is the law? the scientific knowledge of law asks also for the grounds, and since they are twofold, the grounds of reason and the historical ones, two questions follow: is something that is law reasonable? and how did it become law?[15]

However, not all Germans took Hugo's approach to the philosophy of positive law. Many jurists preferred to exclude speculations about justice from their analysis of positive law. Thus, Falck argued that the "philosophy of positive law" discussed by modern writers, who sought to use notions furnished by reason to uncover what could be just or lawful in the state, was simply not a part of the juridical sciences, but fell within the realm of the political sciences.[16] That part of Hugo's project which dealt with the reasonableness of law was thus seen to be part of a different science. Falck thus seemed to draw the same kind of line that Austin would draw between the province of jurisprudence and that of legislation. The towering figure of nineteenth century German jurisprudence, Savigny, also focused resolutely on the material of positive law, most importantly in his *System des heutigen römischen Rechts*, which was written too late to influence Austin's own lectures.[17]

Falck's notion that positive law was distinguished by the fact that it was enforced by the state and his point that juridical science was not concerned with the principles of legislation might well have been congenial to Austin. At the same time, there were significant differences in how Germans such as Falck thought about the state and legal development. For Austin, the "state" was an independent political society where the bulk of the people were in the habit of obedience to a sovereign, whose commands (and only whose commands) constituted law. By contrast, Falck (and other Germans) did not associate the state with such a sovereign, and so did not limit

---

[15] Gustav Hugo, *Lehrbuch der Juristischen Encyclopädie* (5th ed., Berlin: Mylius 1817) at 32–33, quoted in Reimann, "German Legal Science" *supra* note 10 at 848–9: "Statt daß die unmittelbar practische, wie man mit Recht sagt, handwerksmäßige Rechtserkenntnis nur auf die Frage geht: Was ist Rechtens? so fragt die wissenschaftliche auch nach den Gründen, und da diese doppelt sind: die Vernunftgründe und die geschichtlichen, so entstehen auch die beyden Fragen: Ist es vernünftig, dass Etwas Rechtens sey? und Wie ist es Rechtens geworden?" Kant had also argued that the jurist should study both "*Rechtsklugheit* (iurisprudentia)" and "*Rechtswissenschaft* (iurisscientia)": See *Einleitung in die Rechtslehre* (§ A) in *Die Metaphysik der Sitten* (Königsberg: F. Ricolovius, 1803) at *xxxi*.

[16] Falck, *Enclyclopädie*, *supra* note 12 at 94 § 53: "Es bleibt nur die Frage übrig, mit welchem Rechte die Philosophie des positiven Rechts zu den juristischen Disciplinen gezählt wird. Mit Rücksicht auf die Beschaffenheit der hier vorzutragenden Lehren und auf deren Verhältniß zum bestehenden Rechte, gehört die Philosophie des positiven Rechts zu den politischen Wissenschaften, und ist nichts anders als die Behandelung der juristischen Materien nach den Grundprinzipien der Politik. Diese Wissenschaft gehört daher nicht in den Kreis der juristischen Disciplinen."

[17] In Reimann's words, Savigny "unequivocally broke with the law of reason, firmly excluded all speculation about justice from the realm of legal science, and developed a jurisprudence strictly limited to positive law." Reimann, "Legal Science" *supra* note 10 at 851–2.

the sources of law to the commands of a sovereign lawgiver. In his view, the state originated in the people's need for self-preservation, and in their desire to secure their lives from arbitrary interference by the creation of rules backed by coercion. This required a sufficiently large number of people to associate on a mutual guarantee of public peace. The people thus generated both the state and the law, which consisted of "precepts whose observation is necessary to maintain peace among men living together and whose observation is assured by the common will of the members of the union."[18]

Falck identified three sources of law. Firstly, there were those norms which arose from "natural" relationships, which individuals wanted to have legally protected in society. Insofar as norms developed on considerations of the nature of human relationships and civic society did not rest on the evidence of custom or legislation, they could be called "natural."[19] Secondly, there were customary norms arising with the development of the community, or *Volk*. Thirdly, there were norms which came from voluntary activity in changing the law.[20] This last source consisted of legislation; while the first two made up unwritten law.[21] Falck defended the customary foundations of much law from a critique which had an Austinian flavour. He noted that since an increasing proportion of law had come to be fixed by legislation, it had become increasingly common to view customary law as imperfect, and to view all law in a state as derived from legislative power, with customary law being seen to obtain its power as law only from the implied consent of the lawgiver. Falck was unconvinced by this explanation of the binding nature of custom, arguing that one did not look for the original juridical principle of a custom in the legislator's will. He admitted that a custom once established only continued to have legal validity by virtue of the legislator's will, since the legislator could modify the custom at will;[22] but it did not owe its origin as a rule to that source. The legislative will was only known insofar as it was promulgated; whereas custom already obtained legal force

---

[18] Falck, *Encylopädie, supra* note 12 at 5–6 § 2: "Der Begriff des Rechts würde nun hiernach näher so zu bestimmen seyn, daß es aus denjenigen Vorschriften bestehe, deren Befolgung zur Erhaltung des Friedens unter zusammenlebenden Menschen nothwendig, und durch den gemeinsamen Willen der Vereinten gesichert ist."

[19] *Ibid.* at 15 § 8: "Insofern aber Rechtssätze nicht auf solchen Zeugnissen beruhen, sondern durch die Betrachtung der bürgerlichen Gesellschaft und der einzelnen darin vorkommenden Verhältnisse aufzufinden, und durch Folgerungen aus diesen Thatsachen abzuleiten sind, kann man den Inbegriff dieser Regeln, im Gegensatz des positiven, das natürliche Recht nennen."

[20] *Ibid.* at 14 § 7: "Es giebt demnach drei Rechtsquellen , nämlich die ursprüngliche Natur der menschlichen Verhältnisse, das Leben des Volks und die gesetzgebende Gewalt."

[21] Falck identified the "natural part" as part of customary law. He noted that customary law, as unwritten law, included the principles deduced from the nature of civic society and from the nature of those human relations protected by the state; but it also shared with legislation the feature that it had a positive origin: "Wie das Gewohnheitsrecht übrigens in der einen Beziehung zu dem ungeschriebenen Rechte gehört, welches außerdem die aus dem Wesen der bürgerlichen Gesellschaft und der unter den Staatsschutz gestellten menschlichen Verhältnisse abzuleitenden Grundsätze umfaßt, so hat es in anderer Beziehung mit den publicirten Gesetzen dieses gemein, daß es bezeugt seyn muß, und eben deswegen positiven Ursprung ist" (Falck, *Encyclopädie, supra* note 12 at 16 § 8).

[22] *Ibid.* at 16–18 § 9.

by virtue of the communal will, exhibited by its action. Custom did not need promulgation: the fact that it was custom showed that it was already known.

If legislation and custom were the two concepts being set against each other in much German jurisprudence – and if this clash lay at the heart of the dispute in 1814 between Thibaut and Savigny over codification – there was another source of law, which many Germans jurists regarded as the most important. As Falck put it, if all law only came from the positive will of the legislator, or from the articulated will of the people, both of which could be traced historically, there would be nothing more to say.[23] Yet it was undeniable that all positive laws and customs were incomplete, for they failed to furnish rules for all cases. This did not mean that law ran out in the new case. Rather, every state had a legal order – a *Rechtsordnung* – which made it possible to give a "lawful" – *rechtlich* – decision in every litigated case. One could not answer every new case either by simply applying past facts – brute precedent – or by using equity or discretion. Every law, precisely because it was incomplete, implied the tacit supposition that there existed principles of law (*Rechtsgrundsätze*) which could be seen and observed but which did not need special promulgation.[24]

The only way to discover the principles of law to apply in unforeseen cases was to demonstrate the general recognition of a rule as a juridical one. This involved two steps. Firstly, it had to be shown that the relationship in question between the parties was one which was placed under the guarantee of the state; or in other words that it was given legal protection. Secondly, the significance of the facts to be judged had to be shown in relation to the existing law. The key things for the jurist to do were to develop the legal consequences which came from the facts that a civil society and legal system existed, and to analyze the facts which constituted a legal relationship and understand their content. Falck therefore argued that there were universal juridical truths, which could be uncovered. Indeed, having dismissed the old idea of the law of nature as unsustainable, he argued said one that could speak of a "natural law" in the sense of a logical development of concepts, which could generate universal legal truths (*Rechtswahrheiten*).[25] The necessary existence of a rule could not, however, be founded on a moral theory, but had to build on deductions from established facts.

---

[23] *Ibid.* at 82 § 47: "Wäre das Recht lediglich aus einem positiven, historisch erkennbaren Willen des Gesetzgebers und aus dem in den Gewohnheiten enthaltenen des Volks abzuleiten, so könnte es natürlich keine andere Rechtsquellen geben, als jene Willenserklärungen selber. Es its aber (…) denkbar, daß Rechtsnormen da sind, die nicht auf geschichtlichen Zeugnissen beruhen."

[24] *Ibid.* at 95–6 § 54: "Soll aber jede Entscheidung den Character der Gerechtigkeit an sich tragen, so its es unmöglich, die Lücken des positiven Rechts durch bloße Billigkeitsgrundsätze oder auch durch neue Gesetze für vergangene Fälle zu ergänzen. Jedes Recht enthält also, eben weil es unvollständig ist, die stillschweigende Voraussetzung, daß für alle unbestimmte Fälle allgemein erkennbare und allgemein gültige Rechtsgrundsätze da sind, die als keiner Bekanntmachung bedürftig angesehen, und deswegen in den Gesetzen mit Stillschweigen übergangen werden."

[25] *Ibid.* at 95 § 54: "Obgleich die alte Idee vom Naturrecht als unausführbar aufgegeben werden muß, ohne daß die an die Stelle des Naturrechts gesetzte Wissenschaft die Bestimmung desselben erfüllt, so wird es doch möglich seyn, das Daseyn eines Naturrechts, in einem andern Sinne des Worts, eines natürlichen Rechts, oder allgemeiner Rechtswahrheiten nachzuweisen"; *cf. ibid.* at 97 § 55: "Der Name eines natürlichen Rechts ist ebenfalls passend, weil diese Grundsätze nicht auf besondern willkührlichen Bestimmungen beruhen."

Falck's discussion of the role of legal science was typical of Pandectists, and he has been selected for discussion here because his book was one which Austin read and drew on when writing his lectures. The idea that rational knowledge could be obtained through the development of concepts which were applied to empirical facts was not one peculiar to Falck. Savigny was (once again) the best known exponent of this method, and one who particularly championed the role of jurists in developing the law. Although he rooted all law ultimately in the *Volksgeist*, Savigny argued that as societies specialized over time, so law became part of the particular consciousness of a specific group of people, those skilled in law. Jurists – which included judges – had for Savigny a twofold task. The first was the "material" task of producing new law; for once law no longer developed spontaneously out of customs, it was developed by the judges as articulating the voice of the people. The second was the formal task, of giving unity and scientific form by the jurist.[26] The latter function was not merely descriptive, for in the process of giving a scientific form to the material which arose in practice, and by seeking to uncover the unity in the material, there arose "a new organic life which shapes and reacts upon the materials themselves, so that from science as such, a new sort of generation of law incessantly proceeds."[27] Jurisprudence was creative as well as cognitive.

13.3 Austin and the Lawyer's Craft

How did Austin's own version of jurisprudence fit with the German model? The Englishman's distinguishing feature was his insistence that all law was the command of a sovereign and his rejection that customs could be law before a judicial decision. His very invocation of law as a command owed a great deal to Hobbes's "masterly treatise,"[28] as well as Bentham's *Fragment on Government*. Austin's bifurcation of sovereign power into that exercised directly by the sovereign in the form of legislation, and that exercised indirectly through the judges was also very Hobbesian; for in his chapter on civil laws, Hobbes had said that "[i]n all courts of

[26] Friedrich Carl von Savigny, *System des heutigen römischen Rechts* vol. 1 (Berlin: Veit, 1840) at 45 § 14 (*Wissenschaftliches Recht*).

[27] *Ibid.* at 46–7 §14: "In dieser letzten Function erscheint die Wirksamkeit der Juristen zunächst als eine abhängige, ihren Stoff von außen empfangende. Indessen entsteht durch die dem Stoff gegebene wissenschaftliche Form, welche seine inwohnende Einheit zu enthüllen und zu vollenden strebt, ein neues organisches Leben, welches Bildend auf den Stoff selbst zurück wirkt, so daß auch aud der Wissenschaft als solcher eine neue Art der Rechtserzeugung unaufhaltsam hervorgeht."

[28] Austin, *Lectures*, *supra* note 2 at 275. When setting out his task (at 33), Austin quoted the comments of Hobbes (from the first paragraph of chapter 26 of *Leviathan*) that by civil law, he meant "laws that men are therefore bound to observe, because they are members, not of this or that commonwealth in particular but of a commonwealth."

justice, the sovereign, which is the person of the commonwealth, is he that judgeth."[29] Austin's concept of law was thus squarely an English one. Yet his notion of how judges developed the law was out of kilter with the view of his English masters. Austin did not share Bentham's abhorrence of "judicial legislation," nor did he share Hobbes's hostility to the development of law through judicial precedents. Unlike these predecessors, he was a strong defender of "judiciary law." Moreover, the "judiciary law" which he defended did not take the form of isolated commands, but developing judicial customs. Rather than consisting of commands, judiciary law consisted of norms which were enforced by the power of the state; and in developing the norms, judges were expected to use the juridical tools developed by analytical jurists such as himself. It may indeed be suggested that Austin's view of how the law should develop had more in common with the German writers he read in Bonn than it did with the English theorists who inspired his command theory.

Austin conceded that judges did not legislate, in the sense of articulating rules for the future. Although a judge might be aware that the grounds of his decision might govern future cases, his prime task was "the decision of the specific case to which the rule is applied, and not the establishment of the rule."[30] Before it could be a rule, the ground or principle of the decision had to be abstracted from the peculiarities of the case. This was not easy to do. The ground of the decision, or *ratio decidendi*, had to be extracted by jurists by a process of induction, in which the exact words used by the judge were not to be relied on: indeed, "the terms or expressions employed by the judicial legislator, are rather the faint traces from which the principle may be conjectured."[31] Though not a rule in form, the *ratio* was "tantamount to a general command" proceeding from the sovereign, since it was the known will of the sovereign that the general reason from one decision should govern future similar cases. This meant that the *ratio decidendi* "is itself a law, or performs the functions of a law."[32]

Although he suggested that the *ratio* might do the job of a law, he conceded that it was not in fact *law* at all, in the sense of his command theory. Answering Bentham's objection that judiciary law could not properly be called law, since it was not imperative, Austin countered that where it was perfectly well known that the legislator wanted the principles or grounds of legal judicial decisions to be observed as rules, and that violators would be punished, the intimation of the legislative will was complete. He added,

> The *ratio decidendi* of a decision may, perhaps, indeed be that properly called *not* a law, but a *norma* or model, which the law obliges you to observe, the law itself being properly the intimation of the legislator's will. But this would be equally a reason for excluding from the name *law* all the expository part; for instance, the description of the act which is to be done or forborne, previously to ordering that it be done or forborne.[33]

---

[29] Thomas Hobbes, *Leviathan* ed. by Richard Tuck (Cambridge: Cambridge University Press, 1991) at 187.

[30] Austin, *Lectures*, *supra* note 2 at 642.

[31] *Ibid.* at 651.

[32] *Ibid.* at 648–9.

[33] *Ibid.* at 663.

This was not a good answer to Bentham. As Bentham demonstrated at length in *Of the Limits of the Penal Branch of Jurisprudence*,[34] every "complete" law consisted of commanding matter (the penal part) and expository matter (the civil part). For the older jurist, the "expository" part of civil law was to be as much the product of legislation as the commanding part of penal law. By contrast, in Austin's characterization, the sovereign's command, and his enforcement via sanctions, stood behind the body of materials developed by judges. The sovereign was to be the enforcer of whatever rules were elaborated by judges in the courts, rather than the direct commander of any of them.

How did judges make the law? In explaining how law developed, Austin distinguished between the "sources" of law and the "causes" of law. All law derived its *validity* from the fact that it could be traced to the sovereign source – either directly, through legislation, or indirectly, through the decisions of judges. However, the *content* of law was itself shaped by a number of "causes." In particular, there were three ways judges could make a new rule. Firstly, rules could be established by judges at their own discretion (*ex proprio arbitrio*), "according to their own notions of what *ought* to be Law: whether the standard be utility or any other."[35] Secondly, rules which had grown up by custom (and were part of "positive morality") could become law by judicial adoption. Thirdly, much law was made "by judges adopting the views of authoritative expository writers, or the practice of conveyancers, and enforcing them as law, fashioning law on the opinions and practices of lawyers."[36] Although the first of these appears to suggest that Austin envisaged judicial legislators with great freedom to make law as they saw fit – exercising a strong discretion when law ran out – he was in fact quite keen to restrict the *arbitrium* of judges. Firstly, Austin work suggested judges would only rarely be confronted with an entirely new case, which would give them complete discretion. For the most part, the law developed as judges extended rules which were already part of the system by reasoning by analogy.[37] The system itself generated rules which judges had to work with. Judiciary law had to consist of rules if it was not to be "merely a heap of particular decisions inapplicable to the solution of future cases." He accordingly stressed that one should be careful not to confuse law – that body found in the *rationes decidendi* – with the *arbitrium* of the judge:

> Deciding arbitrarily, the judge no doubt may provide for all possible cases. But whether providing for them thus be providing for them by law, I leave it to the judicious to decide.[38]

[34] This work was not published in the nineteenth century, and Austin probably did not see it. However, Bentham's general views on the relationship between the civil and penal branches were to be found in works of his which were published in Austin's life time, notably the *Traités de Législation civile et pénale* ed. by Étienne Dumont (Paris: Bossange, Masson & Besson, 1802).

[35] Austin, *Lectures, supra* note 2 at 655.

[36] *Ibid.* at 656.

[37] *Ibid.* at 661: "The new rule is made what it is, *in consequence* of the existence of a similar rule applying to subjects which are *analogous* to (or of the same genus with) the subjects which itself particularly concerns."

[38] *Ibid.* at 686.

Secondly, Austin argued that judges were further controlled by public opinion, the legislature, appeal courts and the legal profession. The law they developed would therefore always keep in line with what the community needed. The influence of private lawyers was particularly important in securing the good development of the law. In a telling comment, Austin remarked, that the supervision of legal practitioners prevented judges from making deviations from the existing law, "unless they be consonant to the interests of the community, or, at least, to the interests of the craft." Although he added that the two interests generally chimed together,[39] it was clear that for Austin, as for the Pandectists, the influence of the profession was more important than the influence of the wider public. As he put it, "judiciary law made by the tribunals is, in effect, the joint product of the legal profession, or rather of the most experienced and most skillful part of it." It was – "[i]n the somewhat disrespectful language of Mr. Bentham" – the "joint product of Judge and Co.," with the profession imposing a rule on the judges "by a sort of moral necessity." In his discussion, Austin approvingly quoted Pomponius's comment that "the law cannot be coherent unless there is someone skilled in law by whom it may be clarified from day to day."[40] More significantly still, he closed his discussion of this point with the observation that

> Herr von Savigny describes the modern law as composed of two elements, the one element being a part of the national life itself, and the other element being the product of the lawyers' craft.[41]

If Austin's command theory rooted all law in the commands of the sovereign and his subordinate judges, his explanation of how judicial reasoning worked suggested that the body of law which was enforced by the sovereign was the product of a rather more complex combination of custom, opinion and decision, whose principal moderators were learned lawyers.

Austin admitted that there were flaws in uncodified systems. If there were in his view "groundless" objections to judicial legislation, there were also tenable objections. One of these was the fact that there was no test to establish the validity of a judicial rule. It was, he said, unclear whether it was the number of decisions in which a rule was followed, or whether it was the "elegentia" of the rule, or the reputation of the judge which mattered most. When making this point, he made reference to that part of Falck's treatise where the German observed that the question of when a rule of law emerged from a series of decisions was not an easy question to answer, for there had to be a sufficient number of precedents for an opinion to emerge on it.[42] For Austin, the resulting uncertainty was of the essence of judiciary law.

---

[39] *Ibid.* at 667.

[40] D.1.2.2.13, quoted in Austin, *Lectures*, *supra* note 2 at 667.

[41] Austin, *Lectures*, *supra* note 2 at 667–8: "The first he names the *political*, and the last the *technical* element."

[42] Falck, *Encyclopädie*, *supra* note 12 at 19 § 10 (cited in Austin, *Lectures*, *supra* note 2 at 677 fn). It was, he added, inappropriate to use a single precedent as such a source, save in particular cases of legal controversy when settled by high authority.

Yet he also argued that statute could also suffer from uncertainty. Although he did not think that uncertainty was of the *essence* of statute law in the same way, he did argue – anticipating Holmes – that where a statute was obscure or disliked, "it is evident that the statute law is not certainly law, unless it chime with the opinion of the judges and of the bar."[43]

The uncertainties of judge-made law inclined Austin to codification; but his view of codification was closer to Thibaut's proposal for Germany than to Bentham's *Pannomion*. Austin felt that a code could never be complete, but he argued that a code which digested and put in order the *rationes decidendi* of which judicial law was made up would be an advance on leaving it all embedded in cases. His view was that one should codify on the basis of induction from legal science. Austin addressed the concern that a code was incapable of being made, since it would be too great a work for one mind and since many minds would never agree. He answered this objection by noting that for 200 years, continental scholars had so mastered Roman law that they had produced successive works which had "the coherency commonly belonging to the productions of one master mind."[44] The history of Roman law scholarship showed that the project was possible. The code would not only have to be created by men who were expert in legal science, but they would also continue to develop the law thereafter:

> It is obvious that no instructed body of lawyers will ever confine themselves to the study of a code, however perfect soever it may be. Unless the history and philosophy of law were well understood, no good code could possibly be constructed; and unless those branches of knowledge continued to be studied, a good code, even when constructed, would infallibly deteriorate.[45]

Austin did not argue that the process of codification needed to be preceded by a thorough grounding in the science of legislation, which might have been expected of a pupil of Bentham's. Indeed, instead of admitting that Bentham's approach to codification was radically different, he went out of his way to attempt to reconcile Bentham's approach with that of the Germans. During his discussion of German objections to codification, Austin observed that "Bentham belongs strictly to the historical school of jurisprudence." Both Bentham and the Germans (he argued) agreed that "legislation ought to be governed by actual experience of the wants and exigencies of mankind" and that "a body of law cannot be spun out from a few general principles assumed *a priori*." In answering the worries of opponents of codification, Austin acknowledged that much law was inevitably "formed from customs which were rules of positive morality anterior to their adoption by the legislature" and he pointed out that Bentham himself had "again and again declared in his works that the reports of the decisions of the English Courts are an invaluable mine of experience for the legislator."[46] This was to overlook the rather more radical

[43] Austin, *Lectures*, *supra* note 2 at 678.

[44] *Ibid.* at 699.

[45] *Ibid.* at 695.

[46] *Ibid.* at 701–2.

nature of Bentham's *Pannomion* project, and the role of the principle of utility as underpinning his code. It was to make the code project more modest, and thereby more palatable. Hence, for Austin, "a code is merely an exposition sanctioned by the supreme legislator and by his will converted into law."[47]

13.4 The Problem of Rights and Commands

If Austin's approach to the lawyer's craft – elaborated in the broader body of lectures – owed a great deal to German influences, his concept of law as the command of the sovereign – elaborated in the *Province* – was resolutely English. Yet the two parts sat uncomfortably together. In particular, Austin's discussion of "Law considered with reference to its purposes and to the subjects with which it is conversant" (commencing at Lecture 40) was hard to square with his discussion of the nature of law in the first six lectures. In these chapters, Austin developed a model of arrangement which adapted those used by continental writers working in the civilian tradition, rather than following the model of arranging the body of law around interests protected by the penal law, as set out by Bentham in Chapter 16 of *Introduction to the Principles of Morals and Legislation*. Austin's choice shows that he was engaging in a similar enterprise as the German writers he was reading; but it left him with a model of rights which was hard to reconcile with his notion of law as commands.

In these later lectures, Austin did not abandon the concept of command. It continued to remain central. In part, this was because he felt that any notion of a legal right unrelated to a command would lead back to the very subjective moral reasoning he sought to avoid. In his view, German jurists fell into this trap in their discussions of objective and subjective rights. In using the words "objective" and "subjective," Austin argued, the German jurists silently assumed Kantian notions about subjective and objectives entities. Subjective entities, he noted, were in Kant's philosophy "either parcel of the understanding, or ideas which the understanding knows by itself alone;"[48] while objective ones lay outside the understanding. Austin derided the idea that rights were subjective in that sense:

> Though a right *resides* in the person, and so may be analogous to subjects of consciousness, most of that which a right necessarily implies, is, as to the person, *objective*. The law giving him the right (which according to themselves is objective), together with the relative duty which the law imposes upon others, is not *in* him, or *parcel* of him, but are as completely external to him, as an object of sensation is external to the percipient mind.[49]

Austin's aim in making this point was to reiterate his argument that all law came from the command of a sovereign authority, and not from any internal moral source.

---

[47] *Ibid.* at 703.

[48] *Ibid.* at 737.

[49] *Ibid.* at 737–8.

This was to champion the English positivism learned from Hobbes and Bentham against Kantian subjectivism. Yet Austin's criticism was misplaced. When German jurists spoke of "objective" rights, they referred to the general system of rules guaranteed by the state; when they spoke of "subjective" rights, they meant (in Mackeldey's words) "the legal authority to do or command something."[50] It was the right given to someone to invoke the law's power on his behalf.[51] Austin himself made a similar distinction between two senses of "right," the one connoting "law" in general, and the other connoting "faculty."[52]

Austin's jurisprudential point was that all law came from commands which imposed *duties*. "[P]arties invested with right *are* invested with rights," he wrote, "because other parties are bound by the command of the sovereign to do or perform acts, or to forbear or abstain from acts."[53] The very idea of law was centred on the notion of duty: "I *have* no right, independently of the injunction or prohibition which declares that some given act, forbearance or omission, would be a violation of my right." Rights were, in effect, the sphere of liberty left to the right holder, as the person not forbidden by law to act.[54] If this definition of right looked Hobbesian or Benthamic, it may also be noted that the German jurists agreed that every legal right depended on a correlative duty. The jurists whose works were in Austin's library argued that the very fact that law was a coercive system – the idea which underscored their analysis of positive law – meant that every right needed a correlative duty. Thibaut's *System des Pandektenrecht* (the 1828 seventh edition of which was in Austin's possession) began by noting that positive laws were laws which rested on duties enforced by compulsion.[55] Austin himself quoted Thibaut's comment that "every right carries with it the possibility of coercion, either to compel the obliged person to an act or to a forbearance."[56] Falck also accepted it as a truism that rights and duties were correlatives. He told his readers that one usually began one's exposition with the notion of the rights of the individual. He added that this was only for convenience's sake: one could as easily begin with duties as with rights;[57] though in his view rights came first, since the jurist should put the most elevated idea at the head of his science.

[50] Ferdinand Mackeldey, *Lehrbuch des heutigen römischen Rechts* (Giessen: G.F. Heyer, 1827) vol. 1, at 9 (First Division, § 10): "Ein Recht im subjectiven Sinne ist Befugniß etwas zu thun, oder von einem Andern zu fordern."

[51] As Austin put it, they used the word "subject" to refer to the right-bearer: it was "the party who has the right, or in whom it resides." (Austin, *Lectures, supra* note 2 at 737).

[52] *Ibid.* at 293 fn.

[53] *Ibid.* at 407.

[54] *Ibid.* at 816–17.

[55] See Anton Friedrich Justus Thibaut, *System des Pandekten-Rechts* (7th ed., Jena: Friedrich Mauke, 1828) §§ 3–6, esp. § 6: "Das Gebieten macht den Charakter eines Gesetzes, und ohne eine, ein Gebot vorasusetzende, Verbindlichkeit ist kein Rechts denkbar."

[56] Austin, *Lectures*, *supra* note 2 at 412. See Thibaut, *System*, *supra* note 55 at 44 (vol. 1 § 57): "Jedes Recht führt solches die Möglichkeit des Zwanges mit sich, entweder um den Verpflichten zu positiven Handlungen zu nöthingen, oder ihn davon abzuhalten." In practice, one might not need to invoke the coercive power exerted by the judge, but all rights rested on it.

[57] Falck, *Encyclopädie*, *supra* note 12 at 37, § 21.

Despite asserting the theoretical primacy of duties, Austin, like the Germans, organized his discussion of the "purposes and subjects" of law around rights, which were protected by the state's coercion. Analytically, all legal rights had to be seen as the product of duties imposed (in the form of commands) on others not to interfere with these rights. Any property right was hence the product of an infinity of duties imposed on others not to interfere with the item in question. However, in practice, it was unworkable to make every property right depend on an infinity of commands.[58] Instead, rights were conferred and extinguished, through titles to property, which acted as marks showing when one became a member of a class protected by the imposition of duties on others, and when one ceased to be so. To understand property rights, it was essential to know the titles through which they were conferred and extinguished. For Austin, as for the continental writers, it was the task of the jurist to explain what kinds of titles could exist, and how they came into being. The "penal" law which lay behind the protection of property – that part which stood out so prominently in Bentham's work – was relegated into the background here.

Austin's treatment of rights seemed to suggest that while the sovereign protected rights, it did not create them. In his view, the very end for which law existed was to protect certain "primary rights," such as the right to life, personal security, reputation and property. They were rights that existed "*in* and *per se*."[59] Austin did not clearly explain where these rights came from; but it may be inferred from his wider discussion of judicial reasoning that these rights predominantly came not from sovereign commands, but from norms originating in the community, which were recognized and developed by the judiciary and enforced by the state. He did not argue that rights were natural or inborn, however, for he held that they were all necessarily the creatures of law. He accordingly dismissed Blackstone's idea that rights such as the right to personal security could be "absolute," in the sense that it arose "without any title." But he did not argue that the rights arose from commands. Rather, following Thibaut here, he noted that all rights had to be annexed to some fact or investitive event.[60] In this case, the "fact" which invested the subject with the legal right was his birth; for the right "resides in a party, merely as living under the protection or within the jurisdiction of the state." In Austin's scheme, all rights came from titles, which were legally recognized facts marking the beginning of rights. The law could recognize any fact it chose, but its choice was usually condition by "utility, partial or general, well or ill understood."[61] Thus, the fact of birth alone was enough in the eyes of the law to confer the right to personal security; the fact of being born the child of the deceased was enough to confer the right to inherit his property.

Where did the legal recognition of these rights come from? Primary rights did not derive from commands, but from some form of power-conferring rule, the rule that courts would enforce rights obtained in a certain manner. Where did these

[58] Austin, *Lectures*, *supra* note 2 at 912.

[59] *Ibid.* at 789.

[60] *Ibid.* at 753. The latter phrase was probably borrowed from Bentham's analysis in the *Traités*.

[61] *Ibid.* at 913.

power-conferring rules come from? They were not generally set out in legislation (though particular statutes, such as the Statute of Frauds, might set out such rules). Nor, however, do they seem to have been created directly by judges. Austin's analysis of rights seemed to suggest that judges, rather than making commands creating rules, simply recognized and enforced rights which already existed. In his analysis, alongside "primary" rights stood "secondary" or sanctioning rights, which were rights arising from wrongs, from the violation of primary rights. The relationship between primary and secondary rights was complex, but both seemed to take for granted the existence of rights which did not depend on any command. On the one hand, Austin suggested that if obedience to law were perfect, only the primary rights and duties would exist, and there would be no need for the secondary rights. On the other hand, he argued that primary rights could be defined by the duties which protected them.[62] This meant that the only laws which were strictly speaking necessary in any legal system were the ones which gave remedies, since secondary rights "imply the existence of other rights and duties which they protected."[63] However, judges were only called upon to pronounce the law when a primary right had been violated and needed vindication:

> It is only by enforcing rights and duties which grow out of injuries, that [judges] enforce those rights and duties which arise from events or titles of other or different natures.[64]

This seemed to suggest that when judges gave remedies to parties asserting their "secondary" right to go to court and have a wrong redressed, they were not *creating* but *recognizing* a primary right.

This analysis was a long way from the Benthamic notion of law being made up of imperative commands giving clear guides to the citizen. In fact, none of the rights Austin discussed – neither the primary right protected nor the secondary right to have one's wrongs redressed by a court – derived from a command. Looking at the substance of Austin's discussion of how the law worked, one may well conclude that his view was not as far from the notion of legal development held by the Germans as his theoretical model seemed to suggest. For if the judges were not creating, but recognizing rights which originated in the community, this seemed to suggest that they were not transforming "positive morality" into law, but were enforcing rules derived from custom which were already regarded as binding. Although Austin himself resolutely held to his position that custom could not of itself be law, his nineteenth-century successors modified his position and did accept that there could be such a thing as customary law.

---

[62] Thus, in some cases, "the law which confers or imposes the primary right or duty, and which defines the nature of the injury, is contained by implication in the law which gives the remedy, or which determines the punishment." (See Austin, *Lectures*, *supra* note 2 at 794).

[63] *Ibid.* at 794: "For the remedy or punishment implies a foregone injury, and a foregone injury implies that a primary right or duty has been violated. And, further, the primary right or duty owes its existence as such to the injunction or prohibition of certain acts, and to the remedy or punishment to be applied in the event of disobedience."

[64] *Ibid.* at 791.

Chapter 14
Positivism Before Hart*

Frederick Schauer

14.1 Introduction

H. L. A. Hart did not invent legal positivism. Nor did his hugely influential version of legal positivism[1] render all earlier versions obsolete or irrelevant. And although the first of these statements is hardly controversial, the second is likely to be perceived in the precincts of modern English language analytic jurisprudence as somewhere between debatable and simply wrong. It is scarcely an exaggeration to observe that most of today's analytic jurisprudence starts with Hart,[2] treats his arguments against

* This paper was first prepared for the conference on *John Austin and His Legacy*, held at University College London on 16–17 December 2009. A slightly different version of what is contained here was published in the (2011) 24 *Canadian Journal of Law and Jurisprudence* 455–471. I am extremely grateful for the timely and challenging comments of Brian Bix and Brian Leiter, and to Scott Hershovitz, Don Herzog, and the students in the Law and Philosophy Workshop at the University of Michigan for their helpful questions and interventions.

[1] Herbert L. A. Hart, *The Concept of Law* (2nd ed.) ed. by Penelope A. Bulloch and Joseph Raz (Oxford: Oxford University Press, 1994).

[2] Consider the opening two sentences of Jules Coleman, "Incorporationism, Conventionality, and the Practical Difference Thesis" in *Hart's Postscript: Essays on the Postscript to the* Concept of Law ed. by Jules Coleman (Oxford: Oxford University Press, 2001) 99–147, at 99: "H. L. A. Hart's *The Concept of Law* is the most important and influential book in the legal positivist tradition. Though its importance is undisputed, there is a good deal less consensus regarding its core commitments, both methodological and substantive." (footnote omitted).

F. Schauer (✉)
School of Law, University of Virginia, 580 Massie Road, VA 22902
Charlottesville, VA, USA
e-mail: schauer@virginia.edu

M. Freeman and P. Mindus (eds.), *The Legacy of John Austin's Jurisprudence*, Law and Philosophy Library 103, DOI 10.1007/978-94-007-4830-9_14,

Austin[3] as conclusive,[4] and understands Bentham[5] as a founding father of legal positivism whose more particular insights, like Wittgenstein's ladder,[6] may have been necessary to get us where we are but retain little continuing importance.[7] Indeed, even when contemporary practitioners of analytic jurisprudence acknowledge modern legal positivism's roots in Hobbes, Bentham. and Austin, they tend to see at least the Benthamite and Austinian projects through a Hartian lens, attributing to Bentham and Austin an understanding of legal positivism that owes more to Hart and subsequent debates than to what Bentham and Austin actually wrote and likely believed.

My goal in this paper is to support the claims I have so far merely announced, and to show the continuing importance of two conceptions of legal positivism, and indeed of the jurisprudential enterprise, that are substantially at odds with much of the contemporary understanding. In contrast to the common view that legal positivism

---

[3] John Austin, *The Province of Jurisprudence Determined* ed. by Wilfrid E. Rumble (Cambridge: Cambridge University Press, 1995). Hart's critique is in Hart, *The Concept of Law*, *supra* note 1 at 18–78.

[4] See, for example, Leslie Green, "Positivism and the Inseparability of Law and Morals" (2008) 83 *New York University Law Review* 1035–1058, at 1049; Leslie Green, "Law and Obligations" in *Oxford Handbook of Jurisprudence and Philosophy of Law* ed. by Jules Coleman and Scott Shapiro (Oxford: Oxford University Press, 2002) 514–547, at 517; Neil MacCormick, "Legal Obligation and the Imperative Fallacy" in *Oxford Essays in Jurisprudence (Second Series)* ed. by Alfred William Brian Simpson (Oxford: Clarendon Press, 1973, 100–129. Recent attempts to defend Austin's focus on sanctions and coercion include Grant Lamond, "Coercion and the Nature of Law" (2001) 7 *Legal Theory* 35–57; Grant Lamond, "The Coerciveness of Law" (2000) 20 *Oxford Journal of Legal Studies* 39–62; Danny Priel, "Sanction and Obligation in Hart's Theory of Law" (2008) 21 *Ratio Juris* 404–411; Frederick Schauer, "The Best Laid Plans" (2010) 1220 *Yale Law* Journal 586–621; Frederick Schauer, "Was Austin Right After All?: On the Role of Sanctions in a Theory of Law" (2010) 23 *Ratio Juris* 1–21.

[5] Jeremy Bentham, *Of Laws in General* ed. by Herbert L. A. Hart (London: Athlone Press, 1970). Also relevant is Jeremy Bentham, *An Introduction to the Principles of Morals and Legislation* ed. by James H. Burns and Herbert L. A. Hart (London: Athlone Press, 1970).

[6] Ludwig Wittgenstein, *Tractatus Logico-Philosophicus* trans. by David F. Pears and Brian F. McGuinness (New York: Routledge, 1994) 6.54.

[7] I am describing the general tenor (with details to follow) of, for example, Jules Coleman, *The Practice of Principle: In Defense of a Pragmatist Approach to Legal Theory* (Oxford: Oxford University Press, 2001); Joseph Raz, *The Authority of Law: Essays in Law and Morality* (Oxford: Clarendon Press, 1979); Brian H. Bix, "Positively Positivism" (1999) 85 *Virginia Law Review* 889–923, at 903–17; Brian H. Bix, "Legal Positivism" in *The Blackwell Guide to the Philosophy of Law and Legal Theory* ed. by Martin P. Golding and William A. Edmundson (Oxford: Blackwell, 2005) 29–49; Jules Coleman, "Negative and Positive Positivism" in *Markets, Morals and the Law* (Cambridge: Cambridge University Press, 1988) 3–27; Jules L. Coleman and Brian Leiter, "Legal Positivism" in *A Companion to Philosophy of Law and Legal Theory* ed. by Dennis Patterson (Oxford: Blackwell, 1996) 241–260; Green, "Inseparability" *supra* note 4; Leslie Green, "General Jurisprudence: A 25th Anniversary Essay" (2005) 25 *Oxford Journal of Legal Studies* 565–580; Brian Leiter, "Positivism. Formalism, Realism" (1999) 99 *Columbia Law Review* 1138–1164, at 1150–1153; Andrei Marmor, "Legal Positivism: Still Descriptive and Morally Neutral" (2006) 26 *Oxford Journal of Legal Studies* 683–704; Scott J. Shapiro, "On Hart's Way Out" in *Hart's Postscript*, *supra* note 3 at 149–191.

says nothing about adjudication, one of the conceptions I explicate has closer connections to legal decision-making (which is not the same as adjudication, but encompasses it) than many contemporary positivists think possible, and in addition furnishes a useful metric for characterizing and evaluating different legal systems. This conception owes its roots to Bentham, although Austin is a more important figure in this account than is commonly supposed, and it is connected with, but not identical to the other conception I explain and analyze here, the normative version of positivism developed in the work of Tom Campbell,[8] Neil MacCormick,[9] Gerald Postema,[10] and Jeremy Waldron,[11] among others.[12] But although normative positivism will be the subject of some of what is to follow, my principal focus is on the relationship between legal positivism and legal decision-making. When Postema describes Bentham's promotion of "publicly accessible and empirically justifiable authoritative rules with fixed verbal formulations" as "strongly positivist,"[13] he therefore comes close to the understanding of positivism to which I am referring. This Benthamite conception of positivism as a characteristic of legal systems and not (only) of legal theories relates closely to the "limited domain" understanding of legal decision-making I have discussed elsewhere,[14] and it is a conception of positivism, intriguingly, that resembles the one employed by Ronald Dworkin in the process of alleging its descriptive inaccuracy and moral undesirability.[15] But my aim here is neither to show that this variety of positivism is represented in one or another actual legal system, nor that it should be understood as a normatively preferable model for any particular legal regime. Indeed, my goal is not even to show that positivism as a characterization of legal decision-making is superior to other forms of positivism.

[8] Tom Campbell, *The Legal Theory of Ethical Positivism* (Aldershot, UK: Dartmouth Publishing, 1996).

[9] Neil MacCormick, "A Moralistic Case for A-moralistic Law" (1985) 20 *Valparaiso Law Review* 20–47.

[10] Gerald J. Postema, *Bentham and the Common Law Tradition* (Oxford: Clarendon Press, 1986).

[11] Jeremy Waldron, "Normative (or Ethical) Positivism" in *Hart's Postscript*, *supra* note 3 at 411–433.

[12] For example, David Dyzenhaus, "The Genealogy of Legal Positivism" (2004) 24 *Oxford Journal of Legal Studies* 39–63; Liam Murphy, "The Political Question of the Concept of Law" in *Hart's Postscript*, *supra* note 3 at 371–409, Liam Murphy, "Better to See Law This Way" (2008) 83 *New York University Law Review* 1088–1107; W. Bradley Wendel, "Civil Obedience" (2004) 104 *Columbia Law Review* 363–426, at 383–385.

[13] Postema, *Bentham*, *supra* note 10, ix.

[14] Frederick Schauer, "The Limited Domain of the Law" (2004) 90 *Virginia Law Review* 1909–1956. See also Frederick Schauer, "Institutions and the Concept of Law: A Reply to Ronald Dworkin (with some help from Neil MacCormick)" in *Law as Institutional Normative Order* ed. by Maksymilian Del Mar and Zenon Bankowski (Farnham, UK: Aldershot, 2009) 35–44, at 41–43.

[15] Ronald Dworkin, *Law's Empire* (Cambridge, MA: Harvard University Press, 1986); Ronald Dworkin, *Taking Rights Seriously* (London: Duckworth, 1977). For the argument that supports characterizing Dworkin in these terms, see Schauer, "The Limited Domain of the Law" *supra* note 14; Frederick Schauer, "Constitutional Invocations" (1997) 47 *Fordham Law Review* 1295–1312.

It is only to show that this version of legal positivism, as well as normative positivism, have a distinguished historical provenance, considerable contemporary practical importance, and substantial analytical coherence.

The difference between these alternative positivisms and the contemporary mainstream understanding is not simply a matter of terminology. If all that were at stake were the application or non-application of the word "positivism," little would turn on the resolution of the issue. But the dispute is not entirely about words, although words, which function as labels and sorting devices, do make a difference. Rather, the issue is about the current embodiment of a venerable tradition. Those who claim that their Hartian or post-Hartian understanding of the core commitments of legal positivism is the exclusive (or demonstrably best, even if not exclusive) one, and they are legion,[16] may not only have misinterpreted the history of the tradition by viewing it too much through the lens of modern analytic philosophy of law, but may also, and more importantly, have assumed too easily that the pre-Hartian positivist tradition is irrelevant to contemporary legal theory. This is far from the truth, and the principal goal of this paper is to explain why this is so.

14.2 Some Words About a Word

It is curious that so much of the debate about the nature of legal positivism attaches to the word "positivism." Although Bentham and Austin, among others, talked about "positive law," and although the nineteenth century scientific positivism of Auguste Comte was explicitly described as such,[17] the use of the word "positivism" to describe a legal theory, regime, or attitude first surfaced in the early twentieth century[18] and was made substantially more visible by the anti-positivist Lon Fuller in 1940 in *Law in*

[16] See, for example, Bix, "Positively Positivism" *supra* note 7 at 903–015; Coleman in *Hart's Postscript*, *supra* note 3 ("instructing judges in their decision-making may have been what formalism (and realism) were about, but it was not the purpose of legal positivism, neither in the "classical" times of John Austin, nor in the modern times of Joseph Raz and Jules Coleman."); John Gardner, "Legal Positivism: 5 ½ Myths" (2001) 46 *American Journal of Jurisprudence* 199–227, at 211–218 ("The legal positivist tradition" [at 200] has no connection with adjudication and is "normatively inert" [at 213]); Kenneth Eimar Himma, "Judicial Discretion and the Concept of Law" (1999) 19 *Oxford Journal of Legal Studies* 71–94; Leiter, "Positivism. Formalism, Realism" *supra* note 7 at 1149–1153 ("positivism is not a theory about what judges do, but about the concept of law"); Marmor, "Legal Positivism" *supra* note 7 (legal positivism "is a whole tradition of thought" [at 685] that "has nothing to do with the question of what judges ought to do" [at 689]).

[17] Auguste Comte, *A General View of Positivism*, trans. by John Henry Bridges (Cambridge: Cambridge University Press, 2009).

[18] Anthony Sebok reports that "no such theory was discussed by name in legal literature before the late 1920s." See Anthony J. Sebok, *Legal Positivism in American Jurisprudence* (Cambridge: Cambridge University Press, 1998) at 2, but the term appears, with explicit reference to a legal theory, in Josef Kohler, *Philosophy of Law*, trans. by Adalbert Albrecht (Boston: Boston Book Co., 1914) at xliii. Interestingly, Kohler used the term in order to emphasize the dangers of focusing too much on existing law, dangers that were the ones emphasized (probably incorrectly) by Fuller and others in the years to follow.

Quest of Itself.[19] And though inaccuracies about positivism surface here and even more in Fuller's later work,[20] he does get one dimension of positivism more or less correctly when he defines "positivism" as a "direction of legal thought which insists on drawing a sharp distinction between the law that is and the law that ought to be."[21]

That few legal theorists, positivist or not, used the word "positivism" prior to Fuller is not merely an interesting historical tidbit. Rather, it is a signal, although no more than a signal, that we are dealing with contested terminological terrain. And by 1970, when Robert Summers urged that the word "positivism" be discarded from legal theory entirely because it had become "radically ambiguous and dominantly pejorative,"[22] the degree of contestation had become even greater. Forty years later, of course, the word is no longer a pejorative within serious analytic legal philosophy, although in the halls of some American law faculties it still retains much of the odour it had when Summers was writing and Fuller was thriving.[23] But the point of scanning the etymological landscape is only to emphasize that those who purport to have identified the "core" of legal positivism may have only identified the core of the conception that dominates the thinking and writing of Hart and those who have succeeded him. This may represent an important advance in thinking about the nature of law and the task of legal philosophy, but these gains have not come without costs. Whether Hart's conception is the only one, or even the correct one, or even the best modern version of ideas that started with Bentham and Austin and owe much to Hobbes as well, is sometimes exactly the matter at issue. On the question of how to understand the positivist tradition (as opposed to best understanding the nature of law), therefore, to start with Hart and presuppose his authoritativeness as the central figure in legal positivism is to assume the conclusion of exactly what we may sometimes valuably seek to determine.

14.3 Three Concepts of Positivism

For the sake of clarity, I want to distinguish among three positions, each of them (probably) held by both Bentham and Austin, among others. The first, which we can label, least controversially, as *conceptual positivism*, is very much the modern

[19] Lon L. Fuller, *The Law in Quest of Itself* (Boston: Beacon Press, 1940).

[20] See Lon L. Fuller, *The Morality of Law*, rev. ed. (New Haven, CN: Yale University Press, 1969) 110–112, 145–151; Lon L. Fuller, *The Anatomy of the Law* (New York: New American Library, 1968) 184–185.

[21] Fuller, *The Law in Quest of Itself*, *supra* note 19 at 8.

[22] Robert S. Summers, "Legal Philosophy Today – An Introduction" in *Essays in Legal Philosophy* ed. by Robert S. Summers (Oxford: Basil Blackwell, 1970) 1–21, at 15–16.

[23] See, for example, William Bradford, "'Another Such Victory and We Are Undone: A Call to an American Indian Declaration of Independence" (2004) 71 *Tulsa Law Review* 71–123, at 99–106; William N. Eskridge, Jr., "Metaprocedure" (1989) 98 *Yale Law Journal* 945–074, at 962–972; Pierre Schlag, "The Aesthetics of American Law" (2002) 115 *Harvard Law Review* 1047–1071; Jeffrey G. Sherman, "Law's Lunacy: W.S. Gilbert and the *Deus ex Lege*" (2004) 83 *Oregon Law Review* 1035–1096, at 1078; Robin West, "Three Positivisms" (1998) 78 *Boston University Law Review* 791–834.

understanding, although I bracket interesting variations and disagreements. Still, conceptual positivism focuses on a series of conceptual claims about the relationship between the domains of law and of morality. In its purest and most capacious form, a form coming closest to what in contemporary legal theory is called *incorporationism*,[24] *inclusive legal positivism*,[25] or *soft positivism*,[26] conceptual positivism holds that morality is not a necessary condition of legality in all possible legal systems in all possible worlds.[27] Put differently, the inclusive version of conceptual positivism maintains that morality, while often and sometimes even desirably part of law and part of the rule of recognition in this or that legal system, is not a component of the *concept* of law. And inclusive legal positivism's most significant opponent, *exclusive positivism*,[28] is also a conceptual thesis, insisting that legality necessarily does not implicate morality, in contrast to inclusive positivism's claim that legality does not necessarily implicate morality.[29]

Conceptual positivism is typically presented and supported as a descriptive thesis, assuming, for the sake of argument, that there are concepts, that their analysis can provide useful substantive information,[30] and that they can be described without taking on any moral or normative freight.[31] "Positivism" is thus an attribute of a concept, and the conceptual positivist is one who believes that it is in the nature of the concept of law that morality is either no part of it or is not necessarily a part of it.

---

[24] Coleman, in *Hart's Postscript*, *supra* note 3.

[25] Wilfrid J. Waluchow, *Inclusive Legal Positivism* (Oxford: Clarendon Press, 1994); Kenneth Einar Himma, "Inclusive Legal Positivism" in *The Oxford Handbook of Jurisprudence and Philosophy of Law, supra* note 4 at 125–165.

[26] Hart, *The Concept of Law, supra* note 1 at 238–276 and at 250–254.

[27] Jules Coleman, "Negative and Positive Positivism" *supra* note 7.

[28] See Andrei Marmor, "Exclusive Legal Positivism" in *The Oxford Handbook of Jurisprudence, supra* note 4, at 104–124; Joseph Raz, "Legal Positivism and the Sources of Law," in *The Authority of Law, supra* note 7; Joseph Raz, "Authority, Law and Morality" (1985) 68 *The Monist* 295–324.

[29] I borrow this way of expressing the difference between inclusive and exclusive positivism from Waldron, "Normative (or Ethical) Positivism" *supra* note 11 at 414.

[30] Doubts about the value of pure conceptual analysis in jurisprudence are prominently expressed in Brian Leiter, *Naturalizing Jurisprudence* (Oxford: Oxford University Press, 2007) at 121–202; Brian Leiter, "Legal Realism, Hard Positivism, and the Limits of Conceptual Analysis" in *Hart's Postscript*, *supra* note 3 at 355–70; Brian Leiter, "The Demarcation Problem in Jurisprudence: A New Case for Skepticism" (forthcoming 2012) 32 *Oxford Journal of Legal Studies*. See also Frederick Schauer, "On the Nature of the Nature of Law" (forthcoming 2012) 98 *Archiv für Rechts- und Sozialphilosophie*.

[31] The leading challenges to this last assumption are John Finnis, *Natural Law and Natural Rights* (Oxford: Clarendon Press, 1980) at 3–22; Stephen R. Perry, "Hart's Methodological Positivism" in *Hart's Postscript, supra* note 3 at 311–354; Stephen R. Perry, "Interpretation and Methodology in Legal Theory" in *Interpretation and Legal Theory: Essays in Legal Philosophy* ed. by Andrei Marmor (Oxford: Clarendon Press, 1997) 97–131.

Although recognizing the conceptual separation of law and morality may have advantages (apart from its descriptive accuracy) for a society and for the conceptual positivist herself, the conceptual positivist views these advantages, if indeed they exist, as no more than a fortunate side-effect. Law and morality would be conceptually distinct, the conceptual positivist believes, even if that were a sad fact about the world, and even if it led to injustice. But just as the pernicious effects of typhoid would not lead the rational observer to deny its existence, so too would any putative deleterious effects of the conceptual separation of law and morality be irrelevant to the question of its existence.

By contrast, *normative positivism*, the label chosen by Jeremy Waldron,[32] one of its proponents, is the view that the conceptual separation of law and morality is largely a function of *choosing* a concept of law that has this feature. The normative positivist views concepts – or understandings, if you will – as social artefacts, subject to creation and re-creation by the society within which they exist.[33] And thus the normative positivist believes that a positivist understanding of law should be chosen by a society (or, perhaps, by a theorist) because of the good that such an understanding will produce. Normative positivism promotes legal positivism possibly because a positivist outlook facilitates disobedience to iniquitous law (Hart[34]), possibly

---

[32] Waldron, "Normative (or Ethical) Positivism" *supra* note 11.

[33] See Frederick Schauer, "The Social Construction of the Concept of Law: A Reply to Julie Dickson" (2005) 25 *Oxford Journal of Legal Studies* 493–501. Waldron is unclear about the relationship between the normative part of normative positivism and the ontological status of the concept of law. When he describes normative positivism as viewing the separation of legal judgement as something "to be valued and encouraged," he does not directly address whether the something that is to be valued and encouraged has an existence antecedent to the valuing and encouraging. That we should value giant pandas and encourage those who would help them thrive does not suggest that giant pandas are socially constructed for normative reasons. Concepts, however, and certainly the concept of law, are social constructions, and to value and encourage the separation of legal and moral judgement might be to encourage the creation or re-creation of the concept of law so that legal and moral judgement will become or will remain separate. This is the position in Schauer, *ibid.*, but it is unclear whether it is Waldron's as well.

[34] Hart's writings do not resolve conclusively whether he should be understood as sympathetic to normative positivism. That positivism should be *chosen* for instrumental normative reasons is a plausible reading of H. L. A. Hart, "Positivism and the Separation of Law and Morals" (1958) 71 *Harvard Law Review* 593–629, and *The Concept of Law*, *supra* note 1 at 209, Hart described the "reasoned choice" between positivism and natural law as a matter of "comparative merit." Exercising this choice, says Hart, must involve determining which of them "will assist our theoretical inquiries, or advance our moral deliberations, or both." For Hart, positivism is preferable not because it is an accurate description, but because "nothing is to be gained in the theoretical or scientific study of law as a social phenomenon by *adopting* the narrower concept [of natural law]." (emphasis added). Moreover, he says (at 210), the view "that there is something outside the official system, by reference to which in the last resort the individual must solve his problems of obedience, is surely more likely to be kept alive among those who are accustomed to think that rules of law may be iniquitous, than among those who think that nothing iniquitous can anywhere have the status of law." Hart continues in this vein for two more pages, making clear that for him the moral virtues of a positivist "concept of law" (at 211) provide the best reason for a society to adopt such an understanding. Yet despite the foregoing, Hart elsewhere in *The Concept of Law*, and at times

because it facilitates law reform (Bentham), possibly because it fosters a valuable distance from or non-endorsement of law (Lyons[35]), possibly because it encourages greater appreciation of the functions of law (Waldron), or possibly for other reasons, but those who hold this position believe positivism is chosen by a society rather than just emerging, and offer reasons why it is better for some purpose other than descriptive accuracy for a theorist to choose positivism over its alternatives.

The normative positivism of Waldron and others is a program of legal understanding and not institutional design. At least for Waldron, although perhaps not for Postema, and certainly not for Campbell,[36] positivism is not about adjudication, nor about how non-adjudicative legal decisions should made, nor about how legal institutions should be designed in order to produce better decisions. And thus normative positivism should be distinguished from what we can call *decisional positivism*, recognizing that those who believe that conceptual positivism is the only genuine positivism will strongly resist applying the "positivism" label to any theory of adjudication or legal decision-making.[37] But let us temporarily bracket this objection, because confronting it will be the focus in the ensuing sections. For now, it is sufficient to say only that decisional positivism – some might call it formalism[38] – is a view about the design of legal institutions and legal decision-making procedures.[39]

---

even in the 1958 article, emphasizes that his primary goal is descriptive accuracy, see Green, "Inseparability" *supra* note 4 at 1039, a view explicitly and persistently reinforced throughout the "Postscript" (*e.g.* at 240). And thus because there are statements in Hart's work that would both support and rebut aligning him with normative positivism, it might be preferable to refrain from describing Hart's view of positivism as either descriptive or normative, in favour of relying on Julie Dickson's apt description of Hart's different views about the question as "awkward." Julie Dickson, "Is Bad Law Still Law? Is Bad Law Really Law?" in *Law as Institutional Normative Order*, *supra* note 14, 161–183, at 164. So even if the warrant for characterizing Hart as a normative positivist is questionable, the justification for claiming that his positivism was entirely descriptive is equally so.

[35] David B. Lyons, *Moral Aspects of Legal Theory: Essays on Law, Justice, and Political Responsibility* (Cambridge: Cambridge University Press, 1993) ix–x (where Lyons explains his earlier sympathy with positivism as based on his belief that positivism "embodied a fitting lack of reverence for the law," a position he then came to question). See also Frederick Schauer, "Positivism Through Thick and Thin" in *Analyzing Law: New Essays in Legal Theory* ed. by Brian H. Bix (Oxford: Oxford University Press, 1998) 65–78; Frederick Schauer, "Positivism as Pariah" in *The Autonomy of Law: Essays on Legal Positivism* ed. by Robert George (Oxford: Clarendon Press, 1996) at 31–56; Frederick Schauer, "Fuller's Internal Point of View" (1994) 12 *Law and Philosophy* 285–312.

[36] See Campbell, *The Legal Theory of Ethical Positivism*, *supra* note 8 at 41–68.

[37] See, for example, the theorists (and quotations) noted above, *supra* note 16. See also Green, "Inseparability" *supra* note 4 at 1036 ("legal positivists were not offering advice. They were trying to understand the nature of law.").

[38] See Sebok, *Legal Positivism in American Jurisprudence*, *supra* note 18. On form and formalism more generally, see Robert S. Summers, *Form and Function in a Legal System: A General Study* (Cambridge: Cambridge University Press, 2006).

[39] David Dyzenhaus, "The Genealogy of Legal Positivism" *supra* note 12, develops an account and defence of what he calls "judicial positivism," which is in the same neighbourhood as what I describe here. But there is no reason to believe that all or most important decisions of legal application, enforcement, and interpretation are made by judges, and the term I use is intended to emphasize that a positivist theory of how legal actors do or should behave need not be parochially focused on judges alone.

More particularly, it is a view that in its normative aspect seeks to create institutions relying on relatively precise rules, minimizing adjudicative discretion, limiting the law-making power of judges and other law-application officials, restricting legal decision-makers to a limited set of easily identifiable sources, and in general fostering predictability and limiting judicial authority.[40] Thus, it is a view about the role of posited law in legal decision-making, and it is precisely decisional positivism's view about the role of explicitly and clearly posited law that justifies giving it the positivist label. Bentham plainly held decisional positivist views, and Austin's favourable views about codification place him in much the same camp, albeit less obviously and less famously so.[41] Indeed, it is decisional positivism that best explains Postema's characterization quoted above.[42]

As exemplified most clearly by Bentham, decisional positivism has a normative agenda, but it is worthwhile emphasizing that the agenda need not have substantive moral or political goals. Bentham used the term "universal jurisprudence" to refer exclusively to questions of legal *form*,[43] and although Bentham's concerns with legal form were largely in the service of substantive reform, in theory it would be possible to prefer a decisional positivist view of codification, formalism, and judicial discretion for different substantive reasons at different times and in different places, or for no substantive reasons at all. Moreover, someone could prefer decisional positivism to its alternatives without believing that the legal system needed to be reformed at all, and could simply wish to endorse some legal system's existing approach to the application, enforcement, and interpretation of law.

The foregoing characterization of decisional positivism portrays it as normative, but it can have a descriptive aspect as well. As description, decisional positivism characterizes a legal system as positivist insofar as it relies on, for example, statutes rather than common law, insofar as those statutes are precise rather than vague, insofar as a formalist approach dictates questions of statutory interpretation,[44] insofar as it limits judicial discretion, and insofar as its domain of acceptable legal sources is a relatively small portion of the array of acceptable social sources. To use

[40] Note that, *pace* Marmor, "Legal Positivism" *supra* note 7, a decisional positivist need not have a view about a judge's *duties*, whether moral or otherwise. Decisional positivism is foremost a view about the design of legal decision-making institutions, and the positivist (or Benthamite, if you will) view of judicial decision-making might, through sanctions or otherwise, attempt to prevent a judge's reliance on her own moral judgements even if, from the judge's perspective, it would be right to rely on those moral judgements when they conflicted with the positive law.

[41] John Austin, *Lectures on Jurisprudence, or The Philosophy of Positive Law* ed. by Robert Campbell (4th edition, rev., London: John Murray, 1873), vol. II, at 108–35 (*Lecture XXXIX*, parts I and II). See also Eira Ruben, "John Austin's Political Pamphlets 1824–1859" in *Perspectives on Jurisprudence* ed. by Ellspeth Attwooll (London: Rowman & Littlefield, 1977) 20–41.

[42] See text accompanying note 13.

[43] See Postema, *Bentham*, *supra* note 10 at 304–308.

[44] See Frederick Schauer, *Thinking Like a Lawyer: A New Introduction to Legal Reasoning* (Cambridge, MA: Harvard University Press, 2009) 29–34, 148–170, 228–229; Frederick Schauer, "Formalism" (1987) 907 *Yale Law Journal* 509–541.

positivism as a description, or a scale along which to measure legal systems, is not necessarily to have a view about the desirability of a positivist approach to legal institutional design. A stringently code-based legal system, for example, could be described as positivist even by one who thought such a system a bad idea. Similarly, an approach in which legal decision-makers understood their task as making decisions based on a limited set of pedigreed legal materials rather than on larger conceptions of policy, morality, and pragmatism could be described as positivist even by someone who believed that the characterization was descriptively inaccurate when applied to a particular legal system. When Dworkin in *Taking Rights Seriously* describes his foil as "positivism," for example, it is decisional positivism he must have in mind, because it is only decisional positivism that would allow characterizing the dissenting opinion in *Riggs v. Palmer*[45] as positivist, and it is only decisional positivism that could explain Dworkin's view that positivism has little room for non-pedigreed principles of morality in judicial decision-making.

Thus, decisional positivism has both normative and descriptive dimensions. Normatively, it is the claim that legal systems should be designed to minimize the discretion of judges, police officers, and other legal officials, and descriptively it is the metric along which actual legal systems might be characterized. Descriptively, therefore, the extreme of the civil law ideal type (or, perhaps better, stereotype, or maybe even caricature), better exemplified by Bentham's aspirations than by the legal system in any real civil law country, might lie at the pole of extreme decisional positivism, and a legal system pervaded by common law methods, instrumentalism, and anti-formalism, arguably instantiated in the contemporary United States, might lie at the opposite pole of minimal decisional positivism.[46] Decisional positivism in its non-normative aspect is thus the scalar or non-binary measure of just how heavily legal decisions are constrained by the texts of formal legal sources and just how much the array of those sources is a limited subset of the full array of social sources, a subset identifiable by pedigree and not by content.

[45] 22 N.E. 188 (N.Y. 1889).

[46] See Patrick S. Atiyah and Robert S. Summers, *Form and Substance in Anglo-American Law: A Comparative Study in Legal Reasoning, Legal Theory and Legal Institutions* (Oxford: Clarendon Press, 1987); Richard A. Posner, *Law and Legal Theory in England and America* (Oxford: Clarendon, 1996); Robert S. Summers, *Instrumentalism and American Legal Theory* (Ithaca, New York: Cornell University Press, 1982). Among the iconic works of the American instrumentalist and anti-formalist tradition would be Guido Calabresi, *A Common Law for the Age of Statutes* (Cambridge, MA: Harvard University Press, 1982); Lon L. Fuller, *The Morality of Law* (New Haven: Yale University Press, rev. ed. 1969); Henry M. Hart, Jr. and Albert M. Sacks, *The Legal Process: Basic Problems in the Making and Application of Law* ed. by William N. Eskridge, Jr. and Philip P. Frickey (New York: Foundation Press, 1994); Oliver Wendell Holmes, Jr., "The Path of the Law" (1897) 10 *Harvard Law Review* 457–478; Karl N. Llewellyn, *The Common Law Tradition: Deciding Appeals* (Boston: Little Brown, 1960).

14.4 The Multiple Standpoints of Normative Positivism: A Brief Digression

Scholars have debated whether the purely descriptive pretensions of conceptual positivism are even possible,[47] but normative positivism does not require that descriptive conceptual positivism be impossible, and normative positivism's desirability does not presuppose its inevitability. Even if it were possible to discover and describe the concept of law in a value-neutral way, it could still be worthwhile to consider whether the concept so described should be endorsed or condemned, promoted or restricted, changed or perpetuated. As long as we acknowledge the socially constructed and thus non-eternal nature of the concept of law,[48] it is open to the theorist or citizen to consider what attitude to have – and what actions to take on the basis of that attitude – about the product of that social construction, even assuming the ability to describe what has been constructed at some moment in time.[49] Consequently, it is useful to reflect on the claims behind normative positivism, and, similarly, on the claims behind the normative version of decisional positivism. Partly by way of digression, therefore, a bit more can be said about normative positivism, with specific reference to the fact that it is not always clear from the relevant writings just what it is to be normative, who is to be normative, and what they are supposed to be normative about.[50]

Thus, although the normative is the domain of the "ought" rather than the "is," the question arises about who it is who ought to do what. Waldron, for example, is not entirely explicit about whether in urging normative positivism *he* is urging that law be understood in a positivist way, or urging other legal theorists to understand law in a positivist way, or describing the fact that legal theorists understanding law in a positivist way have good reasons for that understanding, or whether he is describing or joining those who believe that it would be better for society to understand law in a positivist way. Each of these positions is possible, but it is important to understand the nature of the normative claims that are being advanced.

---

[47] Compare, for example, Julie Dickson, *Evaluation and Legal Theory* (Oxford: Hart Publishing, 2001); Marmor, "Legal Positivism" *supra* note 7; Joseph Raz, "Can There Be a Theory of Law?" in *The Blackwell Guide to the Philosophy of Law*, *supra* note 7 324–42; Philip Soper, "Choosing a Legal Theory on Moral Grounds" (1986) 4 *Social Philosophy and Policy* 31–48; Wilfrid J. Waluchow, *Inclusive Legal Positivism*, *supra* note 26 at 86–98, with Ronald Dworkin, *Justice in Robes* (Cambridge, MA: Harvard University Press, 2006) at 140–240; Finnis, *Natural Law and Natural Rights*, *supra* note 31 at 3–22; See also texts by Perry, "Hart's Methodological Positivism" *supra* note 31.

[48] See Leslie Green, "The Concept of Law Revisited" (1996) 94 *Michigan Law Review* 1687–1717, at 1687–1692.

[49] The preceding sentences in the text summarize the argument in Schauer, "The Social Construction of the Concept of Law" *supra* note 33.

[50] A valuable discussion is in Stephen R. Perry, "The Varieties of Legal Positivism" (1996) 9 *Canadian Journal of Law and Jurisprudence* 361–388. See also Leslie Green's distinction between methodological and object-level claims in Green, "Inseparability" *supra* note 4 at 1038–1039.

Accordingly, if – and it is contested[51] – Hart is taking a normative stance in his debate with Fuller, the normative position he adopts is that it is better for society to understand law in a positivist way not because law and morality just are distinct, but because understanding them as distinct will foster the social good of disobedience to bad laws. Implicit in this view is the assumption that a concept of law is something that society constructs, and that can be constructed in one way or another. With the choice thus open, Hart's normative positivism can be seen as a plea to society to have a particular understanding about law,[52] and to frame its legal understanding such that law and morality are conceptualized as separate normative domains.

Alternatively, other normative positivists – Bentham is a good example – might be addressing their prescriptions about positivism to theorists and commentators, just as Bentham was, in part, addressing his prescriptions to Blackstone and those who might have been influenced by him. Such normative positivists would prefer that theorists and commentators be positivist for some instrumental reason, perhaps to motivate law reform efforts more effectively, or perhaps just to aid in clarifying their thought. Still, the normative posture is one of urging theorists and commentators to choose, promote, endorse, or encourage positivism for reasons other than descriptive accuracy.

Because normative positivism and one dimension of decisional positivism are normative postures, it is thus important to situate the normative voice in the various versions of these approaches. No particular voice, or standpoint, is necessarily superior to any other, but it is difficult to understand any normative position, including the normatively-focused positivisms I discuss here, without comprehending the source, the target, and the subject of the prescriptions being discussed.

14.5 Bentham's Agenda – And Austin's Too

Before delving into philosophical issues of conceptual priority and causation, it is worthwhile pursuing a largely historical inquiry. Thus, we know that Bentham subscribed to all three dimensions of positivism described above, although of course he never labelled any of them "positivist." Labels aside, however, there is little doubt that Bentham subscribed to the separation of law and morality, believing that the existence and identification of a norm as a legal one was to be distinguished from its

[51] See Hart, "Positivism and the Separation of Law and Morals" *supra* note 34.

[52] It would be extravagant to suppose that this plea would have any direct or immediate effect, but the same could be said about the normative voice in almost all of moral and political philosophy. The enterprises of normative moral, political, and legal philosophy are premised on the belief that philosophical progress might eventually and cumulatively translate into social change, but only the delusional participants in these enterprises believe that such change will take place in the short term or as the consequence of the efforts of any single theorist.

moral status or desirability. Moreover, Bentham was not only committed to the separability of law and morality, he believed that morality and positive law were in fact separate, even if, to his constant annoyance, people often failed to recognize it. What it means for law and morality to be separate is frequently contested and far from straightforward, but there is little doubt that Bentham believed law and morality to be distinct domains of thought. And thus if we seek to characterize Bentham in terms of the versions of positivism described above, the conclusion that Bentham was a conceptual positivist should attract little disagreement.[53]

But Bentham's conceptual positivism was not a function of disinterested observation, and nor, to a significant extent, was Austin's. Both were normative as well as[54] conceptual positivists by virtue of believing that there was a non-descriptive point in separating law from morality, and that point was to facilitate the reform of the law. Bentham was of course a vehement critic of existing law, both in detail and in the large. The common law was for him anathema, as was judicial legislation and the entirety of the law of evidence,[55] and these examples demonstrate the scale of Bentham's critique. His objections to English law went to large blocks of it – perhaps all of it – and separating what law is from what law ought to be, and thus separating law and morality, was essential to Bentham's aim of reforming the substance and structure of the English legal system. Moreover, and of particular relevance in the present context, Bentham's normative agenda was not subsidiary to his conceptual or descriptive program. On the contrary, it was his normative agenda that drove the importance of distinguishing law as it is from law as it ought to be. In terms of motivation – which is of course not the same as logical or conceptual priority – there is little doubt that Bentham's conceptual positivism was developed for normative reasons.

Things are not so clear with respect to Austin, who plainly had some goals that were purely descriptive. But Austin also pursued an extensive law reform agenda,[56] described the advantages of distinguishing the legal is from the legal ought for

[53] I bracket the interesting methodological question of whether conceptual and normative positivism are mutually exclusive. If the conceptual positivist believes that there is a pre-existing concept that can be described without having or presupposing normative commitments, and if the normative positivist believes that constructing a concept of law must be based on normative considerations, then the two are incompatible. But if one believes that concepts can be created for normative reasons without themselves being normative, or if one believes that people can have normative reasons for identifying and stressing non-normative concepts, then normative and conceptual positivism can co-exist, and that modest claim is all that I make about Bentham here.

[54] The "as well as" is important. Coleman warns against "confusing" legal positivism with "programmatic or normative interests certain positivists, especially Bentham, might have had," "Negative and Positive Positivism" in *Hart's Postscript*, *supra* note 3, but I do not deny that conceptual and normative positivism are different. I will presently challenge Coleman's claim that only the former is entitled to be called "positivism," and question his view that the latter (note the word "might") is contingent and secondary, but I freely acknowledge that the two are different.

[55] See William Twining, *Theories of Evidence: Bentham and Wigmore* (London: Weidenfeld & Nicolson, 1985).

[56] See Wilfrid E. Rumble, *The Thought of John Austin: Jurisprudence, Colonial Reform, and the British Constitution* (London: The Athlone Press, 1985).

reasons other than descriptive accuracy,[57] believed that his normative law reform positions were facilitated by his theory of law and that his theory of law flowed from his utilitarianism,[58] and in his later writings on codification showed an especially strong normative side.[59] Moreover, there is reason to believe that Austin's reputation as non-normative has been fuelled, in part, by the less normative goals of some of his successors – Thomas Erskine Holland, especially – whose expositions of Austinian ideas stripped away the normative aspects that for Austin co-existed with the descriptive.[60]

Turning from normative to decisional positivism, and returning to Bentham, we see that his proposals for reform reveal him also to be a decisional positivist. Embodying his well-known scorn for judges, Bentham became a champion of codes, of the civil law as he (perhaps mistakenly) understood it, and of a system of law in which judicial discretion was minimized. It was a feature of Bentham's legal codes, therefore, that they attempted to preclude judges and other legal decision-makers in individual cases from making political, policy, economic, or moral judgements. Judicial decision-making was limited, if it had to exist at all, to the application of linguistically clear codes to particular events, with legal outcomes to be reached almost entirely by applying the ordinary meaning of the terms in the legal codes to the facts of particular cases. Determining moral questions was simply not part of the process.[61]

Austin was more sympathetic to judicial legislation than Bentham, but not much more. They did differ sharply on whether judicial legislation existed and whether it was part of law properly so called, with Austin believing in the existence of judicial legislation and its status as law,[62] while Bentham denied that judicial legislation was entitled to be called law at all. With respect to the *desirability* of judicial legislation,

[57] *Ibid.*

[58] "Analytical positivism rests, first, on the command or imperative theory of law – that that is law which is laid down by duly constituted political authority – in the case of England, by the sovereign Parliament – and that only that is law. From the command theory of law is *derived* a normative proposition that judges have no business making law, for that is the business of the legislature and it would be usurping the legislator's functions for the judges to do so." Edward McWhinney, "English Legal Philosophy and Canadian Legal Philosophy" (1958) 4 *McGill Law Review* 213–241, at 226 (emphasis added). Although disagreeing with McWhinney that Austin denied the *existence* of judicial legislation, Austin's biographer William L. Morison does not take issue with the claim that the foregoing claim about the derivation of a view about adjudication from Austin's central descriptive and conceptual claims applies more to Austin than to other nineteenth century analytic philosophers of law. William L. Morison, "Some Myth About Positivism" (1958) 68 *Yale Law Journal* 212–233.

[59] Austin, *Lectures on Jurisprudence*, *supra* note 41.

[60] See Morison, *supra* note 58 at 152.

[61] This crude and simple characterization of Bentham's view about judging does not capture the far more sophisticated and nuanced position in Postema, *Bentham, supra* note 10, but it is sufficient here simply to stress Bentham's overall skepticism about the virtues of judicial power.

[62] By virtue of legislative authorization, Austin believed.

however, Austin's views shifted over time. In the *Province of Jurisprudence Determined,* he says very little about judging or judge-made law, but does describe it as "highly beneficial and even absolutely necessary,"[63] even while criticizing judges for legislating in a "timid, narrow, and piecemeal manner" and "legislating under cover of vague and indeterminate phrases." But by the time Austin turned his attention more directly to codification, he not only wrote extensively in support of legislative codification generally, but also described it as "expedient," especially in light of the "evils inherent in judiciary law," evils he discussed at some length.[64] The view that Austin was not critical of judicial legislation thus does not stand up to an examination of Austin's writings, nor to his active promotion of, and involvement in, the codification movement which flourished during his life. Austin supported codification, believed that judicial and parliamentary legislation should be specific and discretion-limiting, and, most importantly, believed that judicial legislation could and should be diminished were Parliament to legislate more clearly, precisely, and comprehensively. Unlike Bentham, Austin did not believe that judicial legislation was not really law or that it could be eliminated entirely. And, again unlike Bentham, Austin believed that codification should consolidate and clarify existing legal principles, rather than starting anew. But if normative decisional positivism is the view that the legal system should be structured so that both the subjects of the law and the legal decision-makers who apply, interpret, and enforce it need have little recourse to morality (or policy, for that matter), then Austin plainly qualifies as a decisional positivist, being far closer to Bentham than to the celebrants of the common law, whether in his time or now.

14.6 The Core Commitments of Legal Positivism

We are now in a position to identify and summarize the areas of common ground and those of disagreement. It is clear that Bentham and Austin, among others, subscribed to conceptual positivism, normative positivism, and decisional positivism. That this is so as historical fact is typically not denied by those who resist understanding both normative and decisional positivism as genuinely positivist. Rather, the critics insist that normative and decisional positivism (or any other view about adjudication) are simply contingent or accidental features of the thought and work of Bentham and Austin.[65] Only conceptual positivism, they insist, lies at the genuine

[63] Austin, *Province*, *supra* note 3 at 163.

[64] Austin, *Lectures on Jurisprudence, supra* note 41 at 108–135 (*Lecture XXXIX*, parts I and II).

[65] Coleman, *The Practice of Principle, supra* note 7 at 11: "Legal positivism makes a conceptual, or analytic claim about law, and that claim should not be confused with programmatic or normative interests certain positivists, especially Bentham, might have had."

core of legal positivism. For the critics, legal positivism is a descriptive claim about the concept of law – about the nature of law – often taking the form of some version of the Separation (or, better, Separability) Thesis[66] – the view that law and morality are conceptually separate (or, to some, separable).[67] The fact that Bentham, Austin, and Hart also believed that certain political, moral, and institutional design advantages flowed from understanding law in this way was little more than a fortunate side-effect of identifying the reality of the separability of legality and morality in the concept of law. And the fact that Bentham and Austin were supporters of codification and a limited domain conception of legal decision-making was again only a coincidence, or, more fairly, a feature of their thought not analytically connected with their positivism.

But exactly what kind of claim is the claim that conceptual positivism – or a claim about the nature of law – is the "core commitment"[68] of legal positivism? The claim is hazy, because there are different notions of what it is for something to be at the "core." The core, after all, is a spatial metaphor often ill-suited to capture notions of salience, importance, or theoretical centrality, which is why it is not self-evident that the core is the most important part of an apple or the most scientifically significant part of the planet Earth. To say that something is at the core in a non-physical way is thus to make an instrumental claim in need of further clarification. If the claim is historical, and if locating the historical core of positivism is largely an inquiry into motivation, or into the importance or salience of a particular question for particular people, then, as discussed above, it is difficult to deny that decisional or normative positivism and not conceptual positivism is the "core" commitment of legal positivism, at least as understood by Bentham, Austin, and most others of their generation.

Those who claim that conceptual positivism is the historically core commitment of positivism might derive some degree of support from Austin's occasionally more exclusively descriptive motivations, but their claim is typically a philosophical and

[66] And/or some variety of the Social Thesis (or, occasionally, the Sources Thesis), the view that what counts as law is a question of social fact. See Leiter, "Legal Positivism" *supra* note 7 at 1141; Raz, "Legal Positivism and the Sources of Law," in Raz, *The Authority of Law, supra* note 7 at 37–52.

[67] See, for example, Brian H. Bix, "Legal Positivism" in *The Blackwell Guide to the Philosophy of Law, supra* note 7 at 31: "Legal positivism is a theory about the nature of law, by its self-characterization a descriptive or conceptual theory. By its terms, legal positivism does not have consequences for how particular disputes are decided, how texts are interpreted, or how institutions are organized." Bix goes on to say that positivism does not have anything to say "about how certain ways of operating (…) should be evaluated or reformed" (*ibid.*). Also, "positivism is a theory of law, while formalism is a theory of adjudication. If positivism is one's theory of law, nothing substantial follows about one's theory of adjudication." See his "Legal Positivism" *supra* note 7 at 1149.

[68] Characterizing the issue in terms of the "core commitments" of legal positivism is ubiquitous. See, for example, Kenneth Einar Himma, "Substance and Method in Conceptual Jurisprudence" (2002) 88 *Virginia Law Review* 1119–1227, at 1152; Andrei Marmor, "Legal Positivism" *supra* note 7 at 685; Scott Shapiro, "Law, Morality, and the Guidance of Conduct" (2000) 6 *Legal Theory* 127–153, at 127 and 129.

not a historical one. More specifically, those subscribing to the view that the core commitment of legal positivism is a conceptual claim about separability make much of the fact that conceptual positivism is a necessary condition of both normative and decisional positivism, and is consequently logically and philosophically prior to them. Against this view, Waldron has insisted that the only conceptual positivism presupposed by normative positivism is a thin one accepted by Aquinas and Austin alike and well beyond controversy.[69] And Postema argues that treating conceptual positivism as the necessary condition of normative positivism rests on a view of concepts and language that fits poorly with the social nature of concepts in general and the concept of law in particular.[70] Waldron and Postema may well be correct, but to make things as difficult as possible for my own conclusion let us assume that their arguments are unsuccessful and that the possibility of a conceptual separation of law and morality is a logical prerequisite for normatively urging the conceptual separation of law and morality; and let us also assume that the (actual) conceptual separation of law and morality is a logical prerequisite for advancing the kind of adjudicative regime that Bentham, Austin, and others have urged. Thus I assume that the three varieties of positivism sketched above are in a logical and linear relationship to each other, with conceptual positivism being a prerequisite for both normative and descriptive positivism, and normative positivism being also a prerequisite for decisional positivism. The question then is whether, as a matter of philosophy and not of history, the first should be treated as the core of legal positivism and the second and third as mere contingent offshoots not entitled to the designation "positivist" at all. If the truth of conceptual positivism is a necessary condition for the truth – or falsity – of normative positivism, and so too, *mutatis mutandis*, for decisional positivism, then conceptual positivism is the core of positivism, with normative and decisional positivism being, at best, positivism by derivation, positivism by analogy, or simply perversions of positivism.

This argument assumes that when one thing is a necessary condition for another then the former is the core concept and the latter is merely contingent. But why should that be so? Consider the theory of natural selection. In order for natural selection to be correct, there must exist a mind-independent physical reality. That form of epistemic objectivism, controversial in some circles, is a necessary condition for the evolutionary theory of natural selection, but to describe the claim of a mind-independent physical reality as the core commitment of the theory of natural selection, rather than simply a precondition or presupposition of it, misses the point of the entire theory. Even though the theory of natural selection, like any other scientific theory, is a descriptive one, a descriptive theory – or account – has a point, and we lose the point of a descriptive theory if we treat it is subservient to the sometimes contested facts and theories that are preconditions of its plausibility. Conceptual analysis may well be logically prior to evaluation, as David Lyons argues in this

[69] Waldron, "Normative (or Ethical) Positivism" *supra* note 11.

[70] Postema, *Bentham*, *supra* note 10.

context,[71] but it is hardly clear that what is logically prior is more important or closer to some "core." For that we need further argument.

Not only is it not apparent that preconditions are more central than what they are preconditions of, but it is also not obvious that logical relationships are more important than other types of relationships. It is true that the relationship between conceptual and decisional positivism is neither logical nor conceptual. A conceptual positivist could well reject what I call decisional positivism and he calls formalism. More importantly, one could believe that law and morality are conceptually distinct and that legal decision-makers should make decisions on the basis only of the former, but one could also believe that law and morality are conceptually separate but that legal decision-makers should draw on both in making their decisions or should allow morality to trump positive law in cases of conflict. It is thus true that conceptual positivism as an account or theory of the nature of law in no way *entails* any view about what judges or other legal actors should do.

But why is logical entailment the correct kind of relationship to expect? It is true that *A* being a necessary condition of *B* does not mean that *A* logically entails *B*. And thus the fact that conceptual positivism is a necessary condition of decisional positivism does not deny that it could be a necessary condition of some alternative to decisional positivism as well. To say that conceptual positivism is the core commitment of positivism because it is a necessary condition of both decisional positivism and decisional non-positivism is to make the evaluative judgement that identifying the precondition is more important than the decision between the two consequences, but that determination is hardly logically compelled.

Moreover, there is no reason to believe that logical relationships are necessarily more important than empirical ones. Suppose, for example, that judges contingently internalized something we might call the legal point of view or legal consciousness. Were that the case, then as an empirical matter such judges might be more inclined to make decisions entirely on the basis of positive law in a society with a positivist concept of law than in one with a natural law concept. This relationship would be neither logical nor conceptual, but the contingent empirical connection between the two might explain associating the two in a relationship of probabilistic causality.

There are other types of relationships that might exist as well. John Gardner, for example, argues that the core commitments of positivism are those shared by Hobbes, Bentham, Austin, Kelsen, and Hart,[72] and secondarily by Coleman and Raz, but it is again curious as to why that which is shared by these admittedly major figures in the positivist tradition should be considered the core commitment positivism. If we can associate certain commitments with some but not all of those figures, are those commitments less important than the ones that all share? Moreover, other commitments – those of normative positivism, for example – are shared by Hobbes,

[71] David Lyons, "Founders and Foundations of Legal Positivism" (1984) 82 *Michigan Law Review* 722–739.

[72] Gardner, "Legal Positivism" *supra* note 16.

Bentham, Austin, MacCormick, Waldron, Postema, and conceivably (at least according to Waldron) Raz,[73] among others. So the question is then whether the commitments shared by some stalwarts of the positivist tradition but not others are the most important, and then we cannot avoid deciding why it is we want to know, as opposed to identifying by fiat the figures whose shared commitments are the most important. Indeed, if we put aside Kelsen and limit our inquiries to the English-language analytic tradition, the only figure on Gardner's primary list who is not associated with normative positivism is Hart, which is not only debatable, but brings us back to the beginning, and back to the question whether Hart's understanding of legal positivism should be considered uniquely authoritative as well as exclusive.

Moreover, perhaps the relationship between conceptual and decisional positivism is historical, psychological, or analogical. Or perhaps it is simply that the questions and issues posed by normative or decisional positivism are at some times and not others more important than those posed by conceptual positivism, although I emphasize the "perhaps," and make no actual claim about relative importance here. Rather, I seek only to show that even if conceptual positivism is a logical prerequisite for normative or decisional positivism, nothing about which lies at the core and which is at the fringe flows from that fact. And since the alleged priority of conceptual positivism follows even less historically than philosophically, there is no reason, at least on the basis of the existing arguments, for treating normative and decisional positivism as less entitled to the positivist mantle than conceptual positivism.

14.7 Conclusion: On the Diversity of Jurisprudential Inquiry

The question is not whether conceptual legal positivism is a true theory of the nature of law. Rather, it is whether the question to which conceptual legal positivism is the answer is the most important[74] question to be asked about law. It was not for Hobbes, it was not for Bentham, and it may not have been even for Austin. But that is not to say it is not important. Still, if we accept that there are other important questions, that those questions were central to many of the major figures in a positivist tradition that long predated Hart, and that some of those questions are important to us

[73] Or at least this is the interpretation of Raz offered by Waldron, "Normative (or Ethical) Positivism" *supra* note 11 at 412 fn 7.

[74] I emphasize that I do *not* take "important" to be synonymous with "practically important." There are philosophically important questions that have little or no practical or immediate importance, and there is no reason at all why philosophers of law should not treat such questions as worthy of their attention.

now,[75] we should worry about a definition of legal theory, or of the jurisprudential enterprise, that treats those other questions as less important, or even less important to those who have the philosophical skills to illuminate them.[76] Many of these questions have arisen in the positivist tradition, and if there is a definition of positivism that excludes from serious philosophical inquiry questions that were originally part of the tradition, and that were prominent in the thinking of many of the great historical figures of that tradition, then there are ample grounds to foster an understanding of the positivist tradition that does not cut off access to the questions that the tradition has thought important.

Thus, it is emphatically not my argument that either or both of normative and decisional positivism are preferable to conceptual positivism, or in any way more genuine, or somehow more entitled to be called "positivism." My claim is far more modest. It is only that both normative and decisional positivism have their roots well planted in the positivist tradition, no more but no less than conceptual positivism. Nor is there any reason to suppose that one more than the others lies at some supposed core of legal positivism. All are important for some purposes and less so for others, and little would be lost if we were to recognize that we have inherited from the positivist tradition a multiplicity of positivist views, each of which have their virtues, and each of which have their purposes.

[75] See Kent Greenawalt, "Too Thin and Too Rich: Distinguishing Features of Legal Positivism" in *The Autonomy of Law*, *supra* note 35, 1–30, observing (at 14) that the question of what is true about law in all possible legal systems "does not seem very important for understanding the legal systems under which we live."

[76] Leslie Green properly warns against taking current interest to legal practitioners as a necessary condition for fruitful jurisprudential inquiry. Leslie Green, "General Jurisprudence" *supra* note 7 at 580. But my claim here is different from the claim of Dworkin and others who appear to take the view to which Green properly objects. Unlike Dworkin, my plea with respect to a certain form of conceptual jurisprudence is not against its value, but only against its hegemony.

Chapter 15
Reconstructing Austin's Intuitions: Positive Morality and Law

Isabel Turégano Mansilla

15.1 Introduction

Austin's contribution to legal thought is still a controversial matter depending on how the role and nature of the theory of law and Austin's purposes are understood. Without denying the evident simplicity of Austin's theory and the limits of its actual development, it is only by elucidating his purposes that his achievements can be adequately evaluated. His interests were much wider than generally assumed and go from practical concerns to logical matters, as well as technical issues and descriptive undertakings.[1] First, Austin's broadest purpose was an ambitious project where the diverse natures of different types of laws were described as an organic whole that sought to provide certainty to individuals' action and restore the principle of authority. Second, his conception of jurisprudence, in general, was not yet reduced to general theory of law as in post-Austinian analytical jurisprudence. It included three kinds of legal studies: a systematic analysis of necessary principles, notions and distinctions, logically stemming from his definitions of the law and sovereignty; a dogmatic study of particular legal systems with theoretical and practical interest; and the impartial explanation of those principles, notions and distinctions that the great majority of legal systems have naturally adopted, because they rest upon generally accepted grounds of utility. So jurisprudence is oriented towards three types of inquiry: the logical analysis of law's structure, that is, of necessary notions and concepts; the analysis of legal systems' technicalities; and the description of both

[1] I developed this idea in my *Derecho y moral en John Austin* (Madrid: Centro de Estudios Políticos y Constitucionales, 2001) chapter 2.

I. Turégano Mansilla (✉)
Facultad de Ciencias Sociales, Universidad de Castilla-La Mancha,
Avda los Alfares, 44 16002 Cuenca, Spain
e-mail: Isabel.Turegano@vclm.es

M. Freeman and P. Mindus (eds.), *The Legacy of John Austin's Jurisprudence*,
Law and Philosophy Library 103, DOI 10.1007/978-94-007-4830-9_15,

the moral-political and the general principles shared by most legal systems. Third, conceptual analysis of the necessary features of the law was applied only to a part of jurisprudence, conceived in this broad fashion. The analysis of law's logically necessary elements is only a small part of the legal research program proposed by Austin. And legal theory is only one aspect of Austin's concern for norms to guide and provide certainty to human action. Fourth, a definition of law and sovereignty was needed in order to develop his general jurisprudence so as to delimit the boundaries of his legal theory. But much of what falls outside that definition is still significant to lawyers.

If Austin's thought consists, as Wilfrid Rumble has written, of "a diverse cluster of ideas," not all of them were equally accepted or commented upon.[2] Austin's work encompasses some intuitions of ideas of central importance in recent legal theory but that were not originally taken much into account. Raising awareness of these intuitions involves putting his legal thought into the broader context of his ethical, social and political concerns. Such a perspective shows how the traditional interpretation of his theory oversimplified his thought through selective choice among several ideas of his. The vulgarisation was in great measure the product of the haphazardous and incomplete state of composition and publication of his work. Austin's *The Province* received most of the attention, despite its narrow and preliminary character, together with the abridged editions of the *Lectures* that omitted important passages. Austin's purposes go way beyond the formal concern for clearing the law from any external elements while showing law's coercive face. Instead, as Sarah Austin claimed, her husband "had long meditated a book embracing a far wider field."[3]

The premises that can be evinced from an analysis of Austin's undeveloped purposes display a more complex theory in which all normative phenomena cannot be reduced to factual terms and the complexities of legal systems are reinterpreted or re-characterised to be accommodated in the design of his theory. The oversimplification distorts the nature and function of many relevant features of the law, such as the deformation operated by the notions of delegated legislature or tacit command to account for power-conferring rules;[4] the strained reading of the role of

---

[2] Wilfrid E. Rumble, *Doing Austin Justice. The Reception of John Austin's Philosophy of Law in Nineteenth-Century England* (New York: Continuum, 2005) at 4. As the author writes, the variety of Austin's ideas are anything but a model of uniformity (*Ibid.* at 8) and "[w]hat is clear is that Austin's conception of jurisprudence, or some elements of it, appear to have been more widely accepted than many of his other notions" (Ibid. at 5).

[3] John Austin, *Lectures on Jurisprudence, or the Philosophy of Positive Law*, rev. and ed. by Robert Campbell (5th ed., London: John Murray, 1885) *Preface* at 16.

[4] In Austin's theory, the use of powers by public bodies are not only assumed tacitly as sovereign commands but can derive from a written declaration. Austin talks of "the positive laws which determine the powers and duties of the ministers of justice, and of the other political and public persons subordinate to the sovereign government" (Austin, *Lectures, supra* note 3 at vol. II, 567–568). Nevertheless, these laws are interpreted as imperative and coercive (Austin, *Lectures, supra* note 3 at 567–568).

judges in the legal system; the inadequate explanation of legislature's subjection to the law in constitutional states; the different forms of state regulation; or the coordination or interrelation of the state's law with the law of other supranational entities. Possibly, if these, and various other features of contemporary legal phenomena, could be accommodated in Austin's theory only forcedly his whole arrangement should be rejected entirely. However, Austin's general jurisprudence was not intended to depict legal reality but to show its logical, consistent derivation from the definitional premises of imperativeness and coerciveness. According to his scientific tenets, it must necessarily be so. However these claims do not exhaust his wider practical concerns that contributed to a most intricate conception of law.

15.2 General Jurisprudence and System: A Compromise Between Empiricism and Idealism

From a historical and contextual perspective, Austin was interested in jurisprudence because he intended to subject the law to the prevailing scientific paradigm, raising the problem of a conceptual and systematic legal analysis from positivist foundations. The starting point of jurisprudence was a positive concept of law; that is, the law was conceived as an actual order of social coexistence at a certain time in history. Influenced by Hobbesian nominalism and the empiricism of the Utilitarian school, Austin defined law as an order, determined by empirical factors, originating in human will. At the same time, science was conceived as the search for universal laws, of what remains constant. The problem that legal positivism had to confront was the possibility of scientific knowledge in the variable field of law; that is, the universal validity of the investigations of a mutable and contingent object.

The empiricist model of science involves a concept of reality endowed with regularity and uniformity. Definitions and classifications of objects are not considered arbitrary human activities but a form of research that brings to light the regularity and common features of things. In this respect, we can talk of proper and improper definitions. According to John Stuart Mill, any fact that presents regularity in its occurrence is susceptible of scientific study, including human and social phenomena.[5] Accordingly he considered legal facts to be susceptible of scientific study, by holding Austin's analysis of these to be a kind of the moral sciences, the development of which he advocated. In his view, the purpose of Jurisprudence, as Austin conceived it, was to develop a clear legal terminology, attributing precise meanings to the words used in the law and apprehending the facts and combination of thoughts that these words denote. Defining and making practical provisions intelligible implies

[5] John Stuart Mill, "On the Logic of the Moral Sciences" in *A System of Logic, Ratiocinative and Inductive, Collected Works of John Stuart Mill* ed. by John M. Robson (Toronto: University of Toronto Press, 1974), vol. 8.

presenting these provisions on the backdrop of some principle of arrangement, grounded on their connection and association with one another.[6]

> The facts of which Law takes cognisance, though far from being identical in all civilized societies, are sufficiently analogous to enable them to be arranged in the same *cadres*.[7]

So jurisprudence assumes the existence of laws

> … as a fact, and treats of their nature and properties, as a naturalist treats of any natural phenomenon. It furnishes an analytical exposition, not indeed of any particular system of existing laws, but of what is common to all or most systems of Law.[8]

But Austin did not provide a justification for the basic premise allowing him to develop general jurisprudence from empirical foundations: the assumption that all systems of law shares certain facts and features. Such a premise is either a non-universal statement that needs testing in each application or an *a priori* claim that contradicts Austin's alleged empiricism. His disregard for comparative and extensive empirical analyses of the existing variety of legal systems shows that he assumed – without questioning the foundation of this assumption – the existence of certain principles, concepts and distinctions common to any legal system. This leads us to think that perhaps the recognition of a common legal structure responds to very different assumptions and purposes in which the notion of "system" and German idealism could have had a significant impact.

Despite his alleged empiricism, Austin did not abandon the idea that the law constitutes a logical order, capable of being represented in general and abstract terms. Nevertheless his philosophical reflections were not aimed at discovering standards of timeless validity, but to understand the law from a universal point of view. This meant transferring reason to positive legal systems. Although his manifest purpose was to develop the conceptual apparatus of a coherent legal system, he did not talk of this system as something beyond current legal orders. Rather he projected it onto them. The principles, notions and distinctions common to all legal systems are the rational element of every legal order. They are not the widest and simplest concepts in a process of abstraction, but the formal notions that are the foundation of every possible legal system, law's constant structure as an abstract normative system.[9] As a consequence, he applied a distinction coming from the rationalistic logic of natural law and transferred it to positive law: the distinction between formal and constant structure, on the one hand, and irrational and variable

---

[6] John Stuart Mill, "Austin on Jurisprudence" in *Collected Works of John Stuart Mill, supra* note 5, 1984, vol. XXI, 165–205.

[7] *Ibid.* at 171.

[8] John Stuart Mill, "Austin's Lectures on Jurisprudence" in *Collected Works of John Stuart Mill, supra* note 5 at 55.

[9] Felipe González Vicén, "El positivismo en la filosofía del derecho contemporánea" in *Estudios de Filosofía del Derecho* (Tenerife: Universidad de la Laguna, 1979) at 67.

content, on the other. He only considered the former to be susceptible of scientific knowledge.[10] The province of jurisprudence is not positive law, but its formal projection into the sphere of abstract thought.

Austin's adherence to this abstract gnoseology was a consequence of the great influence that the study of Roman law and conceptualist German literature[11] had exercised on him; and this implied continuation of natural law's epistemology. Legal positivism is not, in this respect, an heir of philosophical positivism but of abstract systematic thought. What characterises the philosophical change is not the methodology used but the historical concept of law. This continuity of the method and system of natural law within positivist legal science was evidenced by Gierke in his criticism of Laband's conceptual jurisprudence and, some years later, by Bekker.[12]

---

[10] Felipe González Vicén, [Preliminary Study to Spanish translation of] *On the Uses of the Study of Jurisprudence* (Madrid: Centro de Estudios Constitucionales, 1981) 5–22, at 20. In this sense, Mauro Barberis states that Austin's theory of law could be regarded "as a sort of conceptual natural law – a natural law providing not principles, but just concepts" (Mauro Barberis, "Universal Legal Concepts? A Criticism of 'General' Legal Theory" (1996) 9:1 *Ratio Juris* 1–14, at 10). Also Buckland comes to the same conclusion, asserting that Austin "takes on faith" the existence of general principles common to Western systems, "for he speaks of 'necessary notions, principles and distinctions', which language is so like that associated with the Law of Nature that some foreign writers treat Austin as a disguised supporter of the doctrine of *Naturrecht*." See William Warwick Buckland, *Some Reflections on Jurisprudence* (Cambridge: Cambridge University Press, 1949) at 69–70. Peter Stein suggests that natural lawyers influenced Austin indirectly through Pandectism. See Peter Stein, *Roman Law and English Jurisprudence Yesterday and Today* (Cambridge: Cambridge University Press, 1969) at 12.

[11] In this sense, William Archibald Dunning, *A History of Political Theories. From Rousseau to Spencer* (New York: Macmillan, 1930) at 224–225; Morris R. Cohen, "John Austin" in *The Encyclopaedia of Social Sciences* ed. by Edwin Seligman and Alvin Johnson (New York: Macmillan, 1931) vol. II, 317–318, at 318; Charles Anthony Woodward Manning, "Austin Today; or 'The Province of Jurisprudence' Re-examined" in *Modern Theories of Law* ed. by W. Ivor Jennings (Oxford: University Press, 1933) 180–226, at 185 and *cf.* at 220; Andreas B. Schwarz, "John Austin and the German Jurisprudence of His Time" (1934) August *Politica* 178–199, at 192–197; Gustav Radbruch, "Anglo-American Jurisprudence through Continental Eyes" (1936) 52 *The Law Quarterly Review* 530–545; Arduino Agnelli, *John Austin, alle origini del positivismo giuridico* (Torino: Giappichelli, 1959) at 21–34; Julius Stone, *Legal System and Lawyers' Reasonings* (Sydney: Maitland, 1964); Reginald Walter Michael Dias, *Jurisprudence*, (4th ed., London: Butterworths, 1976); González Vicén, "Preliminary Study" *supra* note 10 at 13–15; Michael H. Hoeflich, "John Austin and Joseph Story: Two Nineteenth Century Perspectives on the Utility of the Civil Law for the Common Lawyer" (1985) 29 *The American Journal of Legal History* 36–77; Josep Juan Moreso, "Cinco diferencias entre Bentham y Austin" (1989) 6 *Anuario de Filosofía del Derecho* 129–139; Michael Lobban, *The Common Law and English Jurisprudence. 1760–1850* (Oxford: Clarendon Press, 1991) at 223–224 and 227–234; Mauro Barberis, [Introduction to the Italian translation of *The Province*] John Austin, *Delimitazione del campo della giurisprudenza,* trans. by Giorgio Gjylapian (Bologna: Il Mulino, 1995) at 17 and 39 and Barberis, "Universal Legal Concepts?" *supra* note 10 at 4.

[12] Otto von Gierke, "Labands Staatrecht und die deutsche Rechtwissenschaft" in *Jahrbuch für Gesetzgebung, Verwaltung und Volkswirtschaft im deutschen Reich* ed. by Gustav von Schmoller (Berlin: Dunker & Humblot, 1883 – Jan) at 1191–1192; and Immanuel Bekker, *Über den Streit der historischen und philosophischen Rechtsschule* (Heidelberg: Akademische Rede, 1886) at 19–20.

Koschaker and Wieacker also showed how the restoration of Roman law that the Historical School carried out did not imply a break with the systematicity of natural law, from which it departed in its ethical apriorism.[13]

Therefore, legal formalism is not a method organically developed from the requirements of a given object; rather, it is a form of disintegration and re-interpretation of the object, that is, legal reality, to make it accessible from the premises of a method accepted as starting point.[14] In this sense, legal formalism implies a compromise between idealism and empiricism. Stemming from the concern to prove scientific the inquiry of positive law, the systematic approach of formalism ends up destroying the concept of law that it had given rise to. Legal positivism leaves out empirical considerations and conceives its work as logical and conceptual. But at the same time this rational task was intended to be an analytical reconstruction and an instrument of knowledge of legal reality.

Austin considered that the incompleteness, inconsistency and uncertainty of the laws of England allowed any judicial decision to meet legal justification. The task of legal science was to provide a conceptual apparatus that would present the law as a complete and coherent system. His concepts and classifications are analytic tools deduced from the notion of sovereignty to make the system coherent. The system is constituted by rules that define clusters of determined cases that, in turn, can be easily assimilated to the rule that governs them.

15.3 Austin's Project: The Relations Between Law, Positive Morality and Ethics

Today, concerns about the scientific character of jurisprudence are basically considered irrelevant. Furthermore, it has been stated that this concern did not have a purely cognitive nature but, primarily, a normative one. The analytic interest in turning legal into scientific propositions, cloaked in neutrality, served to justify the existing order, covering up the fact of bare power.

It is in this sense that Austin's jurisprudence has an ideological significance. The rigid separation between conceptual and normative inquiries into the law inspired an entire school of thought that justified existing laws and emphasised the value of certainty it guarantees. But the ideological consequences of scientific formalism do

---

[13] Paul Koschaker, *Europa und das römische Rechts* (München: Biederstein Verlag, 1947); Franz Wieacker, *A History of Private Law in Europe: with particular reference to Germany* (Oxford: Clarendon Press, 1995). The same idea is expressed in Mario G. Losano, *Sistema e struttura nel diritto*, vol. I, "Dalle origini alla scuola storica" (Torino: Giappichelli, 1968) and Enrique Gómez Arboleya, "Supuestos cardinales de la ciencia jurídica moderna" in *Estudios de teoría de la sociedad y del Estado* (Madrid: Instituto de Estudios Políticos, 1962).

[14] González Vicén, "Sobre los orígenes y supuestos del formalismo" *supra* note 9 at 167.

not imply that the Austinian concept of law, which was the starting point of general jurisprudence, had a political meaning. That is, it does not follow, on the one hand, that the imperative and coercive concept of a legal rule implies any strict legalistic conception of the law; and, on the other hand, that absolute and unlimited sovereignty meant an absolutist conception of politics. On the contrary, these well-known Austinian theses claimed to be the analytic devices needed to construct formal science.

Reconstructing Austin's legal thought requires a broader perspective that allows us to find a more complex concept of law than the one represented by the image of "commands backed by threats." The general purpose of Austin's intellectual endeavour was an ambitious project where "positive Law, positive morality, together with the principles which form the text of both, are the inseparably-connected parts of a vast organic whole."[15] His aim was to explain in a major work the diverse natures of each of these parts as well as their common relations. Such an essay would be divided into two parts, the first part would treat general jurisprudence and the second part ethics. Positive morality would not be treated in a third part because its principles "so far they are implicated with jurisprudence and ethics, they will be noticed in the departments allotted to those subjects."

It has been noted on many occasions ever since the publication of Austin's *Lectures* that his purpose was much broader than a treatise on jurisprudence. Most of the reviews to the first edition of *The Province of Jurisprudence Determined* tended to characterise it as a contribution to moral and political philosophy. This interpretation explains the emphasis of reviewers on the discussion on Austin's utilitarianism, which many considered the best and most original part of the book.[16] James Fitzjames Stephen observed that Austin sought to develop a vast scheme about human obligations in all its forms, legal and moral, of which only a small fragment was completed.[17] Radbruch conceived that Austin's strict separation between law and morals meant "above all the establishment of the methodical independence of the science of Law from Ethics and Politics." But it did not mean that

[15] Austin, *Lectures, supra* note 3 at 16. In this preface, Sarah Austin wrote that she well knew that "he had long meditated a book embracing a far wider field (…). His opinion of the necessity of an entire *refonte* of his book arose, in great measure, from the conviction, which had continually been gaining strength in his mind, that until the ethical notions of men were more clear and consistent, no considerable improvement could be hoped for in legal or political science, nor, consequently, in legal or political institutions" (*ibid.*). The outline attached, of which Austin's quotation is extracted, "sufficiently proves that he had seriously resolved to execute the great work he had planned."

[16] In this sense, Wilfrid E. Rumble, "Nineteenth-Century Perceptions of John Austin: Utilitarianism and the Reviews of *The Province of Jurisprudence Determined*" (1991) 3 *Utilitas* at 202. Rumble shares this view when considering the lessons on the principle of utility not only relevant for his contribution to moral philosophy, but also for their impact on Austin's legal theory: see Wilfrid E. Rumble, *The Thought of John Austin. Jurisprudence, Colonial Reform and the British Constitution* (London: The Athlone Press, 1985) chapter 3.

[17] James Fitzjames Stephen, "English Jurisprudence" (1861) 114 *The Edinburgh Review* 456–486, esp. at 462–463.

jurisprudence could be considered apart from the science of legislation, or that the separation could be pushed to the extent of complete severance.[18] As Julius Stone stated, "what Austin declared to be outside his analytical thinking still interested him greatly as a man."[19] Or, in the words of Raymond Cocks:

> The fact that Austin went to such extremes to show what was properly called law should not draw our attention away from his great concern with non-legal issues; the things that were *not* properly called Law always fascinated him. In brief he appeared to integrate the legal and the non-legal into a larger understanding of human existence.[20]

This being the general purpose of Austin, the published lectures are but a part of a wider treatise he never concluded. However, we find some evidence of it in the *Lectures on Jurisprudence*. Here Austin discussed moral and political topics, primarily in his disquisition on the theory of utility. Indeed, there are explicit references to the relationship between law and morality. Austin justifies his discourse on ethics, that "may seem somewhat impertinent," as a necessary link in a chain of systematic lectures concerned with the *rationale* of jurisprudence,[21] as:

> Many of the distinctions, which the science of jurisprudence presents, cannot be expounded, in a complete and satisfactory manner, without a previous exposition of those seemingly irrelative hypotheses.[22]

The science of legislation is not the science of jurisprudence; they are nonetheless connected by numerous and indissoluble ties.[23] Indeed:

> [The affinities of law with other rules] ought to be conceived as precisely and clearly as may be, inasmuch as there are numerous portions of the *rationale* of positive Law to which they are the only or principal key.[24]

Austin wrote that divine laws, positive morality and law are not separated in reality. On many occasions their content coincides. [25]

> [There are] numerous cases wherein Law and morality are so intimately and indissolubly allied, that, although they are of distinct natures and ought to be carefully distinguished, it is necessary nevertheless to consider them in conjunction.[26]

---

[18] Radbruch, "Anglo-American Jurisprudence" *supra* note 11 at 535–536.

[19] Stone, *Legal System and Lawyers' Reasonings*, *supra* note 11 at 80. Later on, the author states that "[the] 'law of God', 'the law of nature' and 'the law of reason' held interest for him only for the purpose of being distinguished and kept rigidly outside his scheme. He did not deny their importance, but he did deny that they had any special importance for a logical view of law. He did not deny that they might have binding force for men, but he denied that they could have *legal* binding force according to his logical system" (*Ibid.* at 86).

[20] Raymond Cocks, *Foundations of the Modern Bar* (London: Sweet & Maxwell, 1983) at 49. Also Arduino Agnelli places Austin's interests on the wider practical problem of individual action (Agnelli, *John Austin, supra* note 11 at *e.g.* 175, 258–259, 269).

[21] Austin, *Lectures*, *supra* note 3 at 82, vol. I.

[22] *Ibid.* at 155.

[23] *Ibid.* at 83.

[24] *Ibid.* at 81.

[25] *Ibid.* at 197.

[26] *Ibid.* at 746, vol. II. *Cf.* at 81, vol. I.

Specifically, "it is sometimes expedient to include in the *corpus juris* a part of what is really positive morality, because positive Law is not intelligible without it."[27]

Austin's separation of law and morals does not imply any denying of the circumstance that, as a matter of fact, the content of legal rules has largely been determined by morality or that there are important points of contact between them. This is the case, for example, of Austin's conception of interpretation and legal enforcement, which is not formal and mechanistic. Austin took into account that there are many interpretive problems that cause judicial discretion. His conception of interpretation was not objectivist. He acknowledged that many of the cases that arise in court require new and particular rules and he criticised what he called:

> The childish fiction employed by our judges, that judiciary or Common Law is not made by them, but is a miraculous something made by nobody, existing, I suppose, from eternity, and merely *declared* from time to time by the judges.[28]

So he considered the syllogism the least important part of judicial reasoning[29] and thought that it involved moral and political considerations that make the judicial task not merely deductive but also creative.

From this wider interpretation of Austin's interests, all rules shape an "organic whole" that is to provide certainty for individual action and restore the principle of authority.[30] Not in vain did Austin consider that moral standards are norms or rules because they are commands of a supreme being, reconciling the principle of utility with the necessary confidence in moral rules.[31] But, even though every rule that guides individual action is part of an organic whole, they are analytically distinguishable.[32] Austin's aim was to analyse each of the parts of this common normative

---

[27] *Ibid.* at 754.

[28] *Ibid.* at 634. See Lobban, *The Common Law and English Jurisprudence*, *supra* note 11 at 242.

[29] Austin, "Excursus on Analogy" in *Lectures*, *supra* note 3 at 1012, vol. II.

[30] See Agnelli, *John Austin*, *supra* note 11 at 175, 258–259, and 269; and Robert Moles, *Definition and Rule in Legal Theory: A Reassessment of H. L. A. Hart and the Positivist Tradition* (Oxford: Blackwell, 1987) at 15, 20, and 93. This is not an unanimous interpretation of Austin's thought. Many interpreters considered his disquisition on ethics irrelevant for his main purposes, see Albert V. Dicey, "The Study of Jurisprudence" (1880) 5 *The Law Magazine and Review* (4th series) 382–401, at 387; Henry S. Maine, *Lectures on the Early History of Institutions* (6th ed., London: John Murray, 1893) at 368–370; William Jethro Brown, *The Austinian Theory of Law* (London: John Murray, 1906); John Chipman Gray, *The Nature and Sources of the Law* (New York: Macmillan, 1909) at 144, and at 304–305; Frederic Harrison, *On Jurisprudence and the Conflict of Laws* (Oxford: Clarendon Press, 1919) at 20–21; Mario A. Cattaneo, *Il positivismo giuridico inglese. Hobbes, Bentham, Austin* (Milano: Giuffrè, 1962) at 236–237; Wolfgang Friedmann, *Legal Theory* (5th ed., London: Stevens and Sons, 1967) at 258; Lobban, *The Common Law and English Jurisprudence*, *supra* note 11 at 246, *cf.* at 254–256.

[31] Austin, *Lectures*, *supra* note 3 at 113–114.

[32] In this sense, Barberis, *Introduction*, *supra* note 11 at 22 fn 31.

structure separately and then display their mutual relations.[33] Connections between law and morality can confuse the student of law who has to restrict attention to legal aspects. So, the objective of *The Province* was to detach each normative field by means of defining the terminology associated to them.

> For the confusion of them under a common name, and the consequent tendency to confound Law and Morals, is one most prolific source of jargon darkness and perplexity. By a careful analysis of leading terms, Law is detached from morals, and the attention of the student of jurisprudence is confined to the distinctions and divisions which relate to Law exclusively.[34]

Accordingly, Austin's separation between law and morals has, primarily, an analytical sense. This well-known postulate, that influenced authors as diverse as Maine, Gray and Holmes, did not have an ideological meaning in Austin, as many critics of legal positivism have assumed.

Austin's broad interests were obscured by the process of "vulgarisation" by editors and interpreters that the transmission of his ideas was subjected to.[35] The body of Austin's work known to the public did not reflect in form or substance his claims, given its incomplete and fragmentary state. Moreover, his discussion of morality in law and the relationship between positive law, divine law, positive morality and utility were obliterated in the abridged editions which made Austinian jurisprudence popular. His thought was mainly taken to be a mere defence of the idea that the law is the measure of justice. This narrow vulgarised version, which discarded the inconsistencies and broader intentions, was the origin of a formal science of positive law dominated by systematisation, conceptualisation and exposition in a strict dogmatic manner.[36]

15.4 The Province of Jurisprudence Determined: Definitional Prolegomena to Jurisprudence

As opposed to empirical interpretations, the actual object of Austin's concept of law is not to *describe* the law of particular societies but to *define* the terms that delimit the province of jurisprudence. Austin considers that the conceptual analysis of law

---

[33] See Moles, *Definition and Rule in Legal Theory*, *supra* note 30 at 16–21. Moles is among those who mostly stressed the normative unity in Austin's work and the analytical purpose of the separation between each type of law. This reading allowed him to show that Hart's conclusions about Austin's position was "fundamentally flawed, because they are based on a complete misinterpretation of Austin's work" (*Ibid.* at 74).

[34] Austin, "On the Uses of the Study of Jurisprudence" in *Lectures*, *supra* note 3 at 1076, vol. II.

[35] David Sugarman, "Legal Theory, the Common Law Mind and the Making of Textbook Tradition" in *Legal Theory and Common Law* ed. by William L. Twining (Oxford: Basil Blackwell, 1986) 26–61, at 43.

[36] *Ibid.* at 44.

presupposes an accurate determination of the meaning of certain leading terms that will necessarily be employed;[37] primarily, including the very meaning of "law" since this is going to delimit the subject matter of the analysis. They are both quite different activities, since definition is an analytic device that aims to discriminate between when we are observing phenomena from a legal point of view and when we are not. Austin's definition does not claim to identify or describe the essence of law but to stipulate a meaning that allows him to set down the scope and purpose of the following lectures.[38] Definitions set the boundaries of jurisprudence: the necessary elements that will be analysed by general jurisprudence derive from the previous understanding of the concept of law. They are necessary in the sense of logically derived from, and coherent with, his conception of law.

The definitions of law and sovereignty are not the real subject of general jurisprudence. The aim of the latter is the analysis of concepts and classifications from a legal perspective. They allow lawyers to account for legal obligations and rights independently of their convenience or goodness. Law and sovereignty are "the prolegomena to jurisprudence," the presuppositions "about which we must clear our minds before embarking on jurisprudence itself."[39] In Manning's words, Austin's account of positive law "far from being the final fruit of Austin's labours as a jurist, was hardly more than the jumping-off point from which he started."[40] Austin takes the definition from the tradition of Bodin, Hobbes and Bentham but eliminates any ideological or political connotations and employs it as a criterion for identifying the legal sphere.[41]

Therefore, Austin's definitions of law and sovereignty do not aim to be valid for political and social philosophy. They are only of interest to the lawyer who can hereby analyse legal notions and distinctions coherently. Austin does not deny that law and power encompass more than his definitions state, but he denies that this "something more" is needed to identify the legal province. The definitions must be interpreted, in Harrison's terms, as if they stated the following:

> The business of the lawyer is to consider the force of all law as derived from that ultimate sovereign authority which exercises in all regular and normal communities obedient to magistrates, what for the purpose of Law we assume to be an unlimited power of command.[42]

---

[37] Austin, "On the Uses of the Study of Jurisprudence" in *Lectures*, *supra* note 3 at 1075.

[38] Moles, *Definition and Rule in Legal Theory*, *supra* note 30 at 26–30, and 61–62.

[39] Buckland, *Some Reflections on Jurisprudence*, *supra* note 10 at 3. In the same sense, Dias, *Jurisprudence*, *supra* note 11 at 469–470.

[40] Manning, "Austin Today: or 'The Province of Jurisprudence' Re-examined" *supra* note 11 at 182.

[41] Cattaneo thinks that therein lies the distinctive contribution of Austin: see his "John Austin" (1978) 8:1 *Materiali per una storia della cultura giuridica* at 49–50, *cf.* at 86–87, and *Il positivismo guiridico inglese*, *supra* note 30 at 223, *cf.* at 225–6.

[42] Harrison, *On Jurisprudence and the Conflict of Laws*, *supra* note 30 at 29. See also Fossey John Cobb Hearnshaw, *The Social and Political Ideas of Some Representative Thinkers of the Age of Reaction and Reconstruction. 1815–1865* (London: Barnes and Noble, 1932) at 178.

However it is an incomplete definition from other perspectives.

The Province does not aim to deal with every feature of a legal system in detail but only with the necessary features that separate law from morals. For this purpose, it was enough to refer to coercion and sovereignty as the ultimate source of power, because adding further elements to the definition would lead to a less adequate definition for the *general* theory of law.[43] Intending to be neutral with respect to the institutional peculiarities of different legal systems, the concept of law adopts a high level of abstraction that reduces it to sanctions and imperatives. His thesis was that law deals primarily with coercion and power relations, making other features contingent or secondary. In this sense, Austin does not deny that sovereignty has its foundation in practical reasons and not merely in obedience based on force or fear, nor that law is made up of different types of rules. But these considerations go beyond his purpose in writing *The Province*.

Coactivity and imperativeness are not negligible elements for such a definitional task.[44] As Morris wrote:

> Austin was not alone in feeling the grip of a certain idea, the idea that Law is simply the impressing of the will of the stronger upon the weaker. Austin's chief virtue was that he systematically developed, defended, and refined this idea, stripping it of excess philosophical baggage. In doing this he enabled us to focus with greater precision on those features of Law that connect it with coercion. More than this, his model presses us to remark upon its limitations, the respects in which viewing Law as coercion obscures its complicated role in our lives.[45]

Recently, Frederick Schauer stated that it is still an important question to deal with whether law can exist without sanctions. "[I]f the goal of the philosophy of Law," he argues, "is to offer a philosophically astute account of what makes Law different from other prescriptive enterprises, then the dominant place of coercion and sanctions in Law as it is experienced and as it exists in the world cannot so easily be ignored."[46]

---

[43] As Brian H. Bix writes, theories are efforts to "boil down" a complicated reality to find what is essential amid the differences. When they intend to be too inclusive they thwart their purpose. "They are like maps that are large and detailed, almost as big as the area they purport to describe, creating realistic portraits of the area, but doing so at such a large size that they are no longer functional, and can no longer serve their intended function of helping us to find quickly the best route from one place to another" (See *supra* chapter 1 by Brian Bix entitled *John Austin and Constructing Theories of Law*).

[44] Against the widespread thesis that a claim to correctness or to authority is a necessary element to define the law, some still deny the necessity of moral premises for definitional undertakings, such as Brian H. Bix, "Robert Alexy, Radbruch's Formula and the Nature of Legal Theory" (2006) 37 *Rechtstheorie* 139–149; Matthew Kramer, *In Defense of Legal Positivism. Law without Trimmings* (Oxford: Oxford University Press, 1999); Liam Murphy, "The Political Question of the Concept of Law" in *Hart's Postscript. Essays on the Postscript to "The Concept of Law"* ed. by Jules L. Coleman (Oxford: Oxford University Press, 2001) 371–409.

[45] Herbert Morris, "John Austin" in *Encyclopedia of Philosophy* ed. by Paul Edwards (New York: MacMillan, 1967) vol. I, 209–211, at 210.

[46] Frederick Schauer, "Was Austin Right After All? On the Role of Sanctions in a Theory of Law" (2010) 23:1 *Ratio Juris* 1–21, at 17.

In this sense, Hart's criticism concerning the variety of legal rules that cannot be accounted for in the coercive scheme and the internal point of view do not affect Austin's definitional enterprise since it can accommodate them into the model that only aims to underline the relevant features to define law. Hart himself authorises Austin's definition when he says that the secondary legal rules provide facilities to create structures of rights and duties "*within the coercive framework of the law*."[47] Although the relation between sanctions and the law is not predicable of every law taken separately, Hart still recognises that it is "at least plausible to argue that a legal system must, to be a legal system, provide sanctions for certain of its rules."[48] In fact, it has been argued that Hart too assumed that the "key" to jurisprudence lies not in the union of distinct kinds of rules or in the internal aspect of them, that can also be found in other institutional practices, but in the very nature of legal sanctions.[49] The internal attitude of acceptance could replace Austin's coercive definition only if it allows us to define law and distinguish it from any other normative systems, not merely being an additional and inessential feature of legal systems.[50]

Hart's normativism can therefore be called weak for a series of reasons: first, because the internal structure of actions is irrelevant for the majority of the population, which could be acting on quite different grounds, including fear of sanction; *i.e.* members of the community could identify law in purely coercive and imperative terms. The only condition for the existence of a legal system that ordinary citizens need satisfy is general obedience, no matter what motivations they may have for obeying. Their attitude need not have the critical character involved in the notion of acceptance of social rules.[51]

Moreover, the normative attitude required from officials is a weak acquiescence, not necessarily based on moral reasons. "For some rules may be accepted simply out of deference to tradition or the wish to identify with others or in the belief that society knows best what is to the advantage of individuals."[52] Normativity of law is not confined to prudential or moral reasons. Hart considered that, even though normative statements cannot be reduced to coercive empirical statements, they

[47] Herbert L. A. Hart, "Positivism and the Separation of Law and Morals" in *Essays in Jurisprudence and Philosophy* (Oxford: Clarendon Press, 1983) 49–87, at 60.

[48] *Ibid.* at 78.

[49] Anthony T. Kronman, "Hart, Austin and the Concept of a Legal System: The Primacy of Sanctions" (1974–1975) 84 *The Yale Law Journal* 584–607, at 606. Also Philip Soper, *A Theory of Law* (Cambridge, MA: Harvard University Press, 1984).

[50] I agree with Francisco Laporta that the conception of law as the union of primary and secondary rules or the normative point of view does not enable the conceptual distinction between law and morals (Francisco Laporta, "Sobre las relaciones entre derecho y moral: cuestiones básicas" in *Entre el derecho y la moral* (2nd ed., México DF: Fontamara, 1995) at 92.

[51] Herbert L. A. Hart, *Postscript* in *The Concept of Law* (2nd ed.) ed. by Penelope A. Bulloch and Joseph Raz (Oxford: Oxford University Press, 1994) at 110–117. See Moles, *Definition and Rule in Legal Theory*, *supra* note 30 at 97–99.

[52] *Ibid.* at 257.

nevertheless have a meaning in the legal field other than their moral significance. Allegiance to the system may be based on many different considerations, such as:

> Calculations of long-term interest; disinterested interest in others; an unreflecting or traditional attitude; or the mere wish to do as others do. There is indeed no reason why those who accept the authority of the system should not examine their conscience and decide that, morally, they ought not to accept it, yet for a variety of reasons continue to do so.[53]

In his Postscript, Hart insisted that the participants who appeal to rules as establishing duties or providing reasons for action must not believe that there is moral justification for conforming to them. Some rules may be accepted simply out of reasons such as the aforementioned.

> These attitudes may coexist with a more or less vivid realisation that the rules are morally objectionable. Of course a conventional rule may both be and be believed to be morally sound and justified. But when the question arises as to why those who have accepted conventional rules as a guide to their behaviour or as standards of criticism have done so I see no reason for selecting from the many answers to be given a belief in the moral justification of rules as the sole possible or adequate answer.[54]

So, Hart's theory of law accounts for the existence of legal duties even when there are no moral grounds. It is deemed to be a descriptive theory, with no justificatory aims. It does not seek to justify legal structures but conceive legal systems in neutral terms, a prerequisite of any moral criticism.[55] It adopts the point of view of the observer who describes how the existence of a legal system requires a weak common acceptance of its rules by officials. Both officials and citizens acquiesce with legal and other social rules for diverse reasons. If it is possible to distinguish between the law and other rules it is because of an additional condition: the existence of a complex practice expressed in terms of a rule of recognition.

The attitude of acceptance towards the law is not a mere concurrent practice based on individuals' independent reasons, but a consensus convention. According to Hart, the difference between a consensus of independent convictions and a consensus of convention is that in the second case general conformity of a group to a social practice is part of the reasons why individual members have to accept the practice as binding, while in the first case members of the group generally act in the same way for independent reasons:

> Certainly, the rule of recognition is treated in my book as resting on a conventional form of judicial consensus. Judges reasons for identification and application of Law include the fact that other judges "concur in this as their predecessors have done.[56]

Consequently, the normativity implied by Hart's internal point of view has a consensual or conventional character and thus differs both from prudential and moral duties. It is halfway between the *supposed* Austinian reductionism that

---

[53] *Ibid.* at 203.

[54] Hart, Postscript, *supra* note 51 at 257.

[55] *Ibid.* at 240.

[56] *Ibid.* at 266–267.

conceives legal duties in terms of factual probabilities, and moral normativity of theories that appeal to the belief in the legitimacy of the system, thus identifying legal duties with moral duties. To the question about why a judge must use the rule of recognition he does not merely give a conceptual answer for lawyers, lest not being able to identify valid rules. His answer is normative. However, he does not appeal to ultimate reasons but to conventional reasons that can be counterbalanced by others. The normative element lies in the acceptance of a practice based on the community's general accordance. Accordingly, the normative attitude is just a social convention, the purpose of which is not to justify legal systems morally, but to serve as an existential condition for social rules. And so, this is not too far from the Austinian prudential attitude and his conception of positive morality, which are, nevertheless, outside the scope of jurisprudence. Hart himself recognises that a possible device to preserve the terminology of obedience in the explanation of law is to overlook the whole official apparatus and forgo the description of the use of rules made in legislation and adjudication, and instead think of the whole official world as one person or body issuing orders which are habitually obeyed.[57]

Weak acceptance of rules by officials and acquiescence by ordinary citizens cannot serve as an absolute ground for the imposition of duties to citizens. For these legal obligations have no different meaning than that of the coercive and imperative model. According to Hart, saying that an individual has a legal obligation to act in a certain way means that such action may be demanded of him according to legal rules regulating such demands.[58] These rules may not be accepted by members of society, but only recognised as valid by courts using the rule of recognition. Rules imposing obligations need not be supported by any serious social pressure, but they are enforced by subsidiary rules that allow and require officials to respond to deviation with coercive measures. So obligation derives from the criteria of validity contained in a rule accepted by judges. The latter accept the rule of recognition for different reasons, not necessarily reflecting relevant social purposes. As Kramer states, Hart would have admitted the following:

> The requirements of moral norms are always prescriptions that constitute reasons-for-action for their addressees, whereas the requirements of legal norms can be stark imperatives that do not in themselves (*i.e.* in isolation from attached penalties) constitute such reasons-for-action.[59]

Hart's theory of law is, as a result, a descriptive theory that reduces law's normativity to statements about conventional practices. Therefore, if the Austinian "habit of obedience" is not interpreted as an irrational merely concurrent behaviour and his

[57] Hart, *The Concept of Law*, *supra* note 51 at 113. Although he recognises that this "is either no more than a convenient shorthand for complex facts which still await description, or a disastrously confusing piece of mythology" (*ibid*).

[58] Herbert L. A. Hart, *Essays on Bentham. Jurisprudence and Political Theory* (Oxford: Clarendon Press, 1982) at 160.

[59] Matthew Kramer, "Requirements, Reasons and Raz: Legal Positivism and Legal Duties" (1999) 109 *Ethics* 375–407.

theory is considered to take into account the conventional nature of the legal system, Austin's theory could be seen as a simple abbreviation of some Hart's complex elements intended to be left outside the scope of jurisprudence.

15.5 Institutional Positive Morality and the Rule of Recognition

The Austinian notion of sovereignty and the image of law it reflects as expression of the single governor's will assume that the structure and justification of this legislator is not relevant to jurisprudence. In this respect, it is neither a political, nor a legal, but a *pre-legal* question. At the beginning of his sixth lecture, Austin writes that:

> With the ends or final causes for which governments *ought* to exist, or with their different degrees of fitness to attain or approach those ends, I have no concern. I examine the notions of sovereignty and independent political society, in order that I may finish the purpose to which I have adverted above: in order that I may distinguish completely the appropriate province of jurisprudence from the regions which lie upon its confines, and by which it is encircled.[60]

According to him, societies where there is law are characterised by a certain prevalent attitude between its members: a habitual obedience or conformity to the system. What Austin calls "sovereign" is merely the correlation of that habitual obedience to the authority that makes the system subsist. The sovereign is the authority logically correlative to the prevailing attitude of obedience in political communities, independently of the reasons behind this obedience. All legal rules are supposed to derive their validity from the same ultimate will. The sovereign is not the supreme legal authority according to the constitution, but it is the authority that wills the change, or not, of the constitution.[61] It is not a plurality of individuals, but a collective body with its own personality. As such, it is an abstraction, not a real entity, which is part of a theoretical construction and supposed to be the nexus between the community's habitual obedience and the state organs' exercise of legal powers. The real causes and particular antecedents of historical governments are irrelevant for a formal representation of any given legal order. Therefore, the idea of sovereignty makes it possible to unify rules issued by different bodies. The ultimate act of the will which ensures the unity and consistency of the legal system emanates from the sovereign.[62] Leslie Stephen stated that if it does not exist it must be invented,

---

[60] Austin, *Lectures*, *supra* note 3 at 220, vol. I.

[61] Manning, "Austin Today" *supra* note 11 at 192. Cotterrell shares this interpretation of Austin's sovereign: See Roger Cotterrell, *The Politics of Jurisprudence. A Critical Introduction to Legal Philosophy* (London: Butterworths, 1989) at 70, 87.

[62] Ernesto Garzón Valdés, "Hermann Heller y John Austin. Un intento de comparación" (1983) 57 *Sistema* 31–50, esp. at 35–36, *cf.* at 47–48.

as Voltaire said of the Deity.[63] So, the ultimate source of validity is not a supreme norm or a constitutional structure but the collectivity that has the faculty to modify this structure or allow its subsistence.[64]

In the terminology used by Garzón Valdés, Austin's sovereign would not be the sovereign$_1$ but the sovereign$_0$. That is, it would not be the ultimate source of laws that regulate the conduct of the members of a State, but the creator of the State itself that has a pre-legal status. And it can be defined as follows: if the normative act of enacting a law is not in itself the content of any other higher law, then the agent that executes this act would be said to be acting as sovereign or supreme authority of the law in question.[65] In the cases of constitutional and federal states, Austin recognises that the sovereign is the constituent body and he speaks of a *latent* sovereign.[66]

We should not forget that Hart himself showed that the simple model of coercive commands differs from Austin's doctrine and that some ideas merely schetched out in his work serve to defend Austin from his critics. Among these, we recall the idea of an extraordinary sovereign legislature and the idea of unity and continuity of sovereignty based on some "generic mode" of acquiring it.[67] In a somehow obscure way, Austin talks of "title" and "claim" to occupy sovereignty legitimately,[68] expressions that require the existence of a rule. So Hart thinks that the necessity of the notion of rule flickers through his use of notions such as "a body of persons determined by a character generic," "a body capable of collective action" and "persons taking or acquiring sovereignty by a given generic mode."[69]

As a pre-legal concept, sovereignty is necessarily indivisible and legally unlimited. At the same time as it is considered an effective authority which depends on habitual obedience to its commands, it is defined as formally determinate. An indeterminate body of persons is not capable of corporate conduct and, therefore, cannot command or receive obedience or submission.[70] A person belongs to the sovereign

[63] Leslie Stephen, *The English Utilitarians* (London: Duckworth, 1900) vol. 3, at 329.

[64] This interpretation of Austin's sovereign as an abstraction that precedes his legal theory has been made on many occasions. See Barberis, *Introduction*, *supra* note 11 at 28; Mario A. Cattaneo, "John Austin" (1978) 8 *Materiali per una storia della cultura giuridica* 11–95, at 88; Dan Gerber, "A Note on Woody on Dewey on Austin" (1969) 79 *Ethics* 303–308, at 306; Lobban, *The Common Law and English Jurisprudence*, *supra* note 11 at 245–254; Moles, *Definition and Rule in Legal Theory*, *supra* note 30 at 71; Stone, *Legal System and Lawyers' Reasonings*, *supra* note 11 at 71–75. Austin himself acknowledged that his definition of independent political society and sovereignty did not describe reality adequately and were representative of specific or particular cases due to their imprecise import (Austin, *Lectures*, *supra* note 3 at 226–227, vol. I).

[65] Ernesto Garzón Valdés, "Acerca de las limitaciones legales al soberano legal" (1981) 43/44 *Sistema* 43–56, at 54–5.

[66] John Austin, "Centralization" (1847) 85 *The Edinburgh Review* 221–258, at 248 and 261.

[67] Hart, *The Concept of Law*, *supra* note 51 at 288.

[68] Austin, *Lectures*, *supra* note 3 at 191–3, vol. I.

[69] Herbert L. A. Hart, *Introduction* to John Austin, *The Province of Jurisprudence Determined* ed. by Herbert L. A. Hart (London: Weidenfeld, 1954) *vii-xviii*, at *xiii*.

[70] Austin, *Lectures*, *supra* note 3 at 224, vol. I.

body by being an individual who answers to a generic normative description. Both features concur in Austin's sovereign: the fact of obedience and the normative stipulation of its characters. This is so because the Austinian description of sovereignty is not a simple question of regularity of behaviour but a question of complex social practices for several reasons. Firstly, because the idea of habitual obedience is not a thoughtless pattern of conduct. It involves a rationality promoted, at the very least, by the reasonable interest in avoiding sanction. Nevertheless obedience to the law can also be the consequence of custom, prejudices, or perception of the expediency of political government.[71] The habit of obedience is not a merely convergent attitude but one upheld by common social interests.

Secondly, as Susan Woody states, one of the most interesting reaches of Austin is the question of the source of the characters that identify the sovereign person or body. "To provide for the identity of the sovereign by the selection of certain *generic* characters implies an on-going regularized and somewhat institutionalized situation."[72] Austin's discussion on the source and nature of the generic determinacy of the sovereign implies a tacit recognition of the role of rules in the analysis of political power, assuming that the norms that define the generic characters of the person or persons who constitute the sovereign have a crucial function. The characters of sovereignty are stated in rules. These, however, are not legal but moral, interpreted as social practices.[73] The sovereign habitually obeyed by subjects is not simply a determinate person who, in a concrete historical moment, wields factual power, but a definite person belonging to a general category established by positive morality.[74] This implies that the obedience necessary for the existence of the sovereign is not mere personal obedience, but conformity to mandates of the authority identified by constitutional order. In this regard, Austin considered necessary the use of extra-systemic elements to account for law. Against Kelsen's claim to explain the law out of itself, both Austinian positive morality and Hart's rule of recognition try to translate the logical problem of the validity of independent rules into a conventional problem. They thus avoid the vicious circle of the pure theory of law. As Juan Ramón de Páramo states, the criteria determining norms belonging to a determinate legal order could not be established by the same order, or otherwise we would end up in a vicious circle. The rule of recognition that determines such criteria should be readdressed in terms of facts determined by complex social practices.[75]

---

[71] *Ibid.* at 294, vol. I.

[72] Susan Minot Woody, "The Theory of Sovereignty: Dewey versus Austin" (1967–8) 78 *Ethics* 313–318, at 315.

[73] This moral nature of the rules that define the sovereign eludes the circularity criticised by Morison: See William L. Morison, *John Austin* (London: Edward Arnold, 1982) at 92 and 183. The author has to admit that, contrary to his assumed empiricism, Austin finally converts the question of legal validity in a question of rules (*Ibid.* at 74, *cf.* at 83 and 91).

[74] There are many occasions when Austin insists that he uses the notion of sovereign to refer not to particular individuals but to persons in his sovereign character or capacity. See Austin, *Lectures*, *supra* note 3 at *e.g.* 87, 97, 170, 178, 180, 187, 256, 269, 402, 404 (vol. I) and 540, 746 (vol. II).

[75] See Juan Ramón De Páramo, *H. L. A. Hart y la teoría analítica del derecho* (Madrid: Centro de Estudios Constitucionales, 1984) at 296.

The conception of the rule of recognition as a consensual convention with normative effects based on mutual expectations is not so different from the institutional interpretation that can be made of Austin's positive morality. They are both about describing the acceptance of the institutional existence of norms, that is, the recognition of the necessity of rules as a guide to behaviour. The proposed broader perspective of Austin's doctrine evidences that Austin considered that stability of social interaction does not depend exclusively on external regularities of behaviour but on the recognition and approval of a normative authority.

Austin employs a broad concept of positive morality that includes all human-made laws that "lack the essential difference of positive Law."[76] This concept allows him to account for the rules that have no place in his strict definition of law, such as customary rules before their reception by the courts, or constitutional laws referring to the sovereign. The centrality of positive morality in Austin's legal theory lies in the latter, since they are the ultimate foundation of legal order.

Since law is a set of commands given by a determinate person or body of persons, all its specificity lies in the characters of the person or persons that wield sovereignty. And the identification criteria of these characters are determined by constitutional law, that is, positive morality. This is, thus, central in explaining the validity of law yet external to it, since it identifies the source that qualifies a rule as legal. Certainly, as Marshall argued, the Austinian concept of constitutional law is highly restrictive, since it only determines who the sovereign is.[77] However, this constitutional law or positive morality understood as the opinions and sentiments experienced by an undetermined body of persons concerning who has the primary legal authority – serves to identify valid law. Without the notion of positive morality no complete explanation of legal systems would be possible.

The habitual obedience of most citizens is not addressed to the sovereign as a specific individual or set of individuals, but to persons who are part of the sovereign body and only in this character do they have the authority to create law. Austin's sovereign is not an individual or group of persons with factual power but an institutional authority. It is not a person or body who manages to impose its commands by force, but an authority that society recognises having faculty to create and impose a normative structure enabling coexistence. This implies a conventional concept of power: experiences of power take place within complex social practices of a normative nature. Power, at least in its most important forms of expression, is not an individual phenomenon that can be described in terms of facts, but a collective phenomenon that can only be accounted for by appealing to social norms. Power is embedded in the structure of societies. Without this social normative order power cannot be produced, nor understood.[78]

---

[76] Hart, *Introduction, supra* note 69, at *x*.

[77] Geoffrey Marshall, *Constitutional Theory* (Oxford: Clarendon Press, 1971).

[78] In this sense, Francisco Laporta, "Poder y derecho" in *El derecho y la justicia* ed. by Ernesto Garzón Valdés and Francisco Laporta (Madrid: Trotta, 1996) 441–453, at 446.

A kind of institutional morality is part of the Austinian positive morality: opinions and sentiments of the majority of the members of society who recognise and acquiesce the necessity of a normative authority and identify as such those individuals who have determinate characters. Citizens appeal to the sovereign in order to obtain a reliable guide of conduct so as to secure social order and they are prepared to obey the authority able to do this. So, practical reasons in favour of a stable structure of common coexistence are part of positive morality. If Austin excludes these norms from the legal field it is because the fact of habitual obedience to sovereign will suffice in order to explain the law.

Although the concept of constitution as the ultimate foundation of law is more evident in Austin's later writings. Yet it is already present in the *Lectures on Jurisprudence*. Here he argued that, even though constitutional laws are positive morality, knowledge of these is necessary to understand law. Austin said that:

> [A description] of the law which regards the constitution of the State, and which determines the ends or modes to and in which the Sovereign exercises the sovereign powers, is an essential part of a complete *corpus juris*, although, properly speaking, that so-called law is not positive Law.[79]

Austin's tendency towards a less formalist conception of law was developed in his last published work, *A Plea for the Constitution*, where he accentuates some of the ideas of a more traditionalist sense that were less emphasised in his earlier writings. I do not think, however, that Austin's evolution towards political conservatism implied such a profound rupture in his legal conceptions as Lotte and Joseph Hamburger claimed.[80] It is rather that Austin outlined in greater detail some of his earlier theses. So, the *sentiment of constitutionality*, that justifies compliance with the constitution, may have its precedent in the *moral sentiment* associated with Divine rules referred to in the second of his lectures.[81] And the historical conception of English Constitution as a product of centuries, and no spontaneous creation, can be found in the sixth lecture of *The Province*.[82]

In *A Plea for the Constitution* Austin argues that stability and efficiency of a legal order depends on a sentiment of attachment to the established form of government common to the great majority of the people and the recognition of its necessity to enjoy security and peace. The *sentiment of constitutionality* is a general opinion or feeling of attachment to the constitution of the sovereign government "in and for itself." Austin states that "[a]lthough it may involve a belief in the beneficent tendencies of the constitution, their attachment rests directly on authority and habit."[83] According to Austin, neither of the two branches in which British sovereignty

---

[79] Austin, *Lectures*, *supra* note 3 at 746, vol. I.

[80] Lotte and Joseph Hamburger, *Troubled Lives: John and Sarah Austin* (Toronto: University Press, 1985) at 189.

[81] Austin, *Lectures*, *supra* note 3 at 116–117, vol. I.

[82] *Ibid*. at 321.

[83] John Austin, *A Plea for the Constitution* (2nd ed., London: John Murray, 1859) at 37.

resides "would outweigh the others, if it met with persevering support from a decided majority of the nation."[84] Although the House of Commons exercises much of the supreme powers, the Crown and the Upper House are not supposed to be powerless because their power "rests on the attachment of the nation to those institutions."[85]

In Austin's thought, therefore, the idea of the necessity of a prior convention concerning the general criteria for identifying the source of law is not completely absent. His notion of sovereignty is situated at the intersection between the problem of the systematic structure of law and the issue of a common practical reason that justifies the need for political authority to organise society.[86] If it is true that his strict definition of law adopts an external perspective, the idea of positive morality is not far from Hart's rule of recognition, where it is understood as an opinion or sentiment held in common by a community favourable to the existing constitution in itself. As Moles stressed, Hart's failure to appreciate that the different aspects of Austin's work were all part of one enterprise undermines many of his criticisms.[87] The key to understanding Austinian theory in terms of rules for the identification of law lies in connecting law to positive morality.

[84] *Ibid.* at 4.

[85] *Ibid.* at 5.

[86] Juan Ramón De Páramo, Prologue to Isabel Turégano, *Derecho y* moral, *supra* note 1 at 19.

[87] Moles, *Definition and Rule in Legal Theory*, *supra* note 30 at 14.

About the Authors

Brian H. Bix is the Frederick W. Thomas Professor of Law and Philosophy at the University of Minnesota. He received a B.A. from Washington University in St. Louis, a J.D. from Harvard University, and a D. Phil. from Balliol College, Oxford University. He has published widely in Jurisprudence, Family Law, and Contract Law; his published books include *Jurisprudence: Theory and Context* (6th ed., London: Sweet & Maxwell, 2012), *Contract Law: Rules, Theory, and Context* (Cambridge: Cambridge University Press, 2012), *A Dictionary of Legal Theory* (Oxford: Oxford University Press, 2004), and *Law, Language, and Legal Determinacy* (Oxford: Oxford University Press, 1993).

Jes Bjarup is Prof. Em. in Jurisprudence from Stockholm University. Author of *Skandinavischer Realismus* (1978), he has written extensively on jurisprudential issues in Danish and English, *e.g. Social Interaction: The Foundation of Customary Law*, in *The Role of Customary Law in Sustainable Development* (Cambridge: Cambridge University Press, 2005), *Continental Perspectives on Natural Law Theory and Legal Positivism*, in eds. Martin P. Golding and William A. Edmundsson, *The Blackwell Guide to the Philosophy of Law and Legal Theory* (2005); *Scepticism and Scandinavian Legal Realists*, eds. Timothy Endicott, Joshua Getzler, and Edwin Peel in *Properties of Law, Essays in Honour of Jim Harris* (Oxford: Oxford University Press, 2006).

David Dyzenhaus is a professor of Law and Philosophy at the University of Toronto, and a Fellow of the Royal Society of Canada. He has taught in South Africa, England, Canada, Singapore, New Zealand, Hungary, and the USA. He holds a doctorate from Oxford University and law and undergraduate degrees from the University of the Witwatersrand, South Africa. In 2002, he was the Law Foundation Visiting Fellow in the Faculty of Law, University of Auckland. In 2005–06 he was Herbert Smith Visiting Professor in the Cambridge Law Faculty and a Senior Scholar of Pembroke College, Cambridge. In 2014–2015, he will be the Arthur Goodhart Visiting Professor in Legal Science in Cambridge.

M. Freeman and P. Mindus (eds.), *The Legacy of John Austin's Jurisprudence*, Law and Philosophy Library 103, DOI 10.1007/978-94-007-4830-9

Pavlos Eleftheriadis is a University Lecturer in the Faculty of Law and Fellow and Tutor in Law at Mansfield College. He is also a barrister in England and Wales. He teaches and publishes in the philosophy of law, European Union law and constitutional law. He is the author of *Legal Rights* (Oxford: Oxford University Press, 2008) and the co-editor of *Philosophical Foundations of European Union Law* (Oxford: Oxford University Press, forthcoming 2012).

Michael Freeman (F.B.A., LLM, Barrister) is Professor of English Law at University College London, after having lectured at the University of Leeds. He is the Founding Editor of the *International Journal of Children's Rights*; Editor of the *International Journal of Law in Context*, General Editor of *International Library of Medicine, Ethics and Law* and of the *International Library of Family, Society and Law* and former Editor of the *Annual Survey of Family Law*. He is the author of over 78 books in many areas of law and policy, including *The Moral Status of Children* (Dordrecht: Martinus Nijhoff, 1997) and *Introduction to Jurisprudence* (8th ed., London: Sweet & Maxwell, 2008). A world-leading researcher in the rights of children, he cultivates a broad interest for Ethics and the Law.

Andrew Halpin is a Professor of Law at the National University of Singapore. He previously held chairs in legal theory at the University of Southampton and Swansea University. He is the author of *Rights and Law – Analysis and Theory* (Oxford: Hart, 1997), *Reasoning with Law* (Oxford: Hart, 2001), and *Definition in the Criminal Law* (Oxford: Hart, 2004). A coedited collection *Theorising the Global Legal Order* was published in 2009 (Oxford: Hart).

Andrew Lewis is Emeritus Professor of Comparative Legal History at the Faculty of Laws, UCL, where he also acted as Vice-Dean. His main areas of interest include Roman Law, Legal History and Jurisprudence. He focuses on the history of legal institutions over the longterm. He is Area Editor for Roman Law for the *Oxford Encyclopaedia of Legal History* (Oxford: Oxford University Press, 2009).

Michael Lobban is Professor of Legal History at Queen Mary, University of London. He is the author of *A History of the Philosophy of Law in the Common Law World 1600–1900*, which is volume 8 of *A Treatise of Legal Philosophy and General Jurisprudence* (Dordrecht: Springer, 2007), and a co-author of *The Oxford History of the Laws of England*, vols. XI-XIII (Oxford: Oxford University Press, 2010). He has written widely on the history of English legal theory and legal practice.

Patricia Mindus is associate professor in Practical Philosophy at Uppsala University (Sweden), Ph.D. in EU Studies from the University of Turin (Italy) where she also is research affiliate at the Department of Political Studies. She teaches and publishes in ethics, political and legal theory, and EU law. With a specialization in philosophy of law, she is the author of *A Real Mind. The Life and Work of Axel Hägerström* (Dordrecht: Springer, 2009, awarded the *Guzzo Foundation Prize*).

James Bernard Murphy (Ph.D., Yale 1990) is Professor of Government at Dartmouth College. He has received grants and fellowships from the N.E.H., the A.C.L.S., the Earhart Foundation, The Manhattan Institute and the Pew Charitable Trusts. Author of *The Moral Economy of Labor: Aristotelian Themes in Economic Theory* and *The Philosophy of Positive Law*, both published by Yale University Press, he has published scholarly articles in *Political Theory*, *The Review of Politics*, *The Review of Metaphysics*, *Semiotica*, *The Thomist*, *The American Journal of Jurisprudence*, *The American Catholic Philosophical Quarterly*, and *Social Philosophy and Policy*; co-edited, with Richard O. Brooks, *Aristotle and Modern Law* (Dartmouth: Ashgate, 2003) and *Augustine and Modern Law* (Dartmouth: Ashgate, 2011); and, with Amanda Perreau-Saussine, *The Nature of Customary Law* (Cambridge: Cambridge University Press, 2007).

Michael Rodney is a solicitor and senior lecturer in law at the London South Bank University where he has over a number of years taught a range of legal subjects including most particularly public law and legal theory. His doctoral thesis was on the modelling of sovereignty and his current research interests are concerned with aspects of legal theory.

Wilfrid E. Rumble is professor emeritus of political science at Vassar College. He was born and raised in St. Paul, Minn., and received his B.A. and M.A. degrees from the University of Minnesota. He obtained his Ph.D. from the Johns Hopkins University in 1961, the same year that he began his long career of teaching at Vassar, where he held the Frederic Ferris Thompson Chair from 1972 until 1996. He is the author of three scholarly monographs, including two about John Austin's legal philosophy. Professor Rumble has also edited two other books, one of which is Austin's *The Province of Jurisprudence Determined* (5th ed., 1885). The new edition was published in 1995 as a Cambridge Text in the History of Political Thought.

Frederick Schauer is David and Mary Harrison Distinguished Professor of Law at the University of Virginia; previously Frank Stanton Professor of the First Amendment at the John F. Kennedy School of Government, Harvard University, and Professor of Law at the University of Michigan. A Fellow of the American Academy of Arts and Sciences, he has been vice-president of the American Society for Political and Legal Philosophy and chair of the Committee on Philosophy and Law of the American Philosophical Association. The author of numerous books and articles in legal and constitutional theory, his work is particularly prominent on rules, legal reasoning, constitutional theory and freedom of speech.

Philip Schofield is Professor of the History of Legal and Political Thought at the Faculty of Laws and Director of the Bentham Project, University College London. He is General Editor of the new authoritative edition of *The Collected Works of Jeremy Bentham*, and has edited or co-edited eight volumes in the series. He has published *Utility and Democracy: the Political Thought of Jeremy Bentham* (Oxford: Oxford University Press, 2006) and *Bentham: A Guide for the Perplexed* (London: Continuum, 2009).

Isabel Turégano Mansilla is Professor of Philosophy of Law at Universidad de Castilla-la Mancha (Spain). She is the author of an extensive monograph on Austin's legal and moral theory (Madrid: Centro de Estudios Políticos y Constitucionales, 2001), a study on English Analytical Jurisprudence (Madrid: Iustel, 2003) and a comparative survey of Austin's and John Stuart Mill's thought (Anuario de Filosofía del Derecho, 2006). She currently works on key issues in political theory, such as constitution and democracy, feminist political and moral theory, violence against women and problems of global justice.

Lars Vinx is assistant professor in the Department of Philosophy at Bilkent University in Turkey. He holds a Ph.D. in Philosophy from the University of Toronto (2006). He works in the fields of legal and political theory, and has a strong interest in the history of political thought. He is the author of *Hans Kelsen's Pure Theory of Law: Legality and Legitimacy* (Oxford: Oxford University Press, 2007).

Printed by Printforce, the Netherlands